Lecture Notes in Computer Science 8137

Commenced Publication in 1973
Founding and Former Series Editors:
Gerhard Goos, Juris Hartmanis, and Jan v

T0216596

Robert M. Hierons   Mercedes G. Merayo
Mario Bravetti (Eds.)

Software Engineering and Formal Methods

11th International Conference, SEFM 2013
Madrid, Spain, September 25-27, 2013
Proceedings

 Springer

Volume Editors

Robert M. Hierons
Brunel University
School of Information Systems, Computing and Mathematics
Uxbridge, Middlesex, UB8 3PH, UK
E-mail: rob.hierons@brunel.ac.uk

Mercedes G. Merayo
Universidad Complutense de Madrid
Departamento de Sistemas Informáticos y Computación
28040 Madrid, Spain
E-mail: mgmerayo@fdi.ucm.es

Mario Bravetti
Università di Bologna
Dipartimento di Scienze dell'Informazione
40127 Bologna, Italy
E-mail: bravetti@cs.unibo.it

ISSN 0302-9743   e-ISSN 1611-3349
ISBN 978-3-642-40560-0   e-ISBN 978-3-642-40561-7
DOI 10.1007/978-3-642-40561-7
Springer Heidelberg New York Dordrecht London

Library of Congress Control Number: 2013946018

CR Subject Classification (1998): D.2.4, D.2, F.3, D.3, D.2.4, D.1.5, C.2, C.2.4, F.4.1

LNCS Sublibrary: SL 2 – Programming and Software Engineering

Typesetting: Camera-ready by author, data conversion by Scientific Publishing Services, Chennai, India

Printed on acid-free paper

Springer is part of Springer Science+Business Media (www.springer.com)

Preface

This volume contains the proceedings of the 11th International Conference on Software Engineering and Formal Methods, SEFM 2013. The conference was held in Madrid, Spain, during September 25–27, 2013. The purpose of the SEFM conference is to bring together practitioners and researchers from academia, industry and government to advance the state of the art in formal methods, to facilitate their uptake in the software industry and to encourage their integration with practical engineering methods.

We received 58 submissions. After a careful reviewing process, the Program Committee accepted 21 regular papers. Therefore, the acceptance rate of the conference stayed close to 36%. The conference program was enriched by the keynotes of Thomas A. Henzinger, on *Behavioral Software Metrics*, and Wolfram Schulte, on *Building Billions of Software Artifacts*. In addition, Marius Bozga, one of the recipients of the 10 first editions of SEFM most influential paper award, gave an invited talk on *Modeling Heterogeneous Real-Time Components in BIP*.

Several people contributed to the success of SEFM 2013. We are grateful to the Steering Committee for its support. Its Chair, Prof. Antonio Cerone, deserves a special mention for his guidance and valuable advice. We would like to thank the general chair Manuel Núñez, the Program Committee, and the additional reviewers, for their work on selecting the papers. The process of reviewing and selecting papers was significantly simplified using EasyChair. We would like to thank the organisers of the collocated workshops for their commitment to SEFM 2013. Finally, the proceedings have been published through Springer-Verlag and we are grateful for the assistance provided by Alfred Hofmann and Anna Kramer.

On behalf of the SEFM organisers, we welcome all attendants to the conference and hope that you find the conference's program useful, interesting and challenging.

September 2013

Robert M. Hierons
Mercedes G. Merayo
Mario Bravetti

Organization

Program Committee

Wolfgang Ahrendt	Chalmers University of Technology, Sweden
Bernhard K. Aichernig	TU Graz, Austria
Jesús Almendros Jiménez	Universidad de Almería, Spain
Ade Azurat	Fasilkom UI, Indonesia
Luis Barbosa	Universidade do Minho, Potugal
Jonathan P. Bowen	Museophile Limited, UK
Mario Bravetti	Università di Bologna, Italy
Ana Cavalcanti	University of York, UK
Antonio Cerone	United Nations University, Macao
Benoît Combemale	Université de Rennes, France
Steve Counsell	Brunel University, UK
Hung Dang Van	UET, Vietnam National University, Vietnam
George Eleftherakis	CITY College of Thessaloniki, Greece
José Luiz Fiadeiro	University of London, UK
Martin Fränzle	Carl von Ossietzky Universität Oldenburg, Germany
Mercedes G. Merayo	Universidad Complutense de Madrid, Spain
Dimitra Giannakopoulou	NASA Ames, USA
Stefania Gnesi	ISTI-CNR, Italy
Klaus Havelund	Jet Propulsion Laboratory, California Institute of Technology, USA
Rob Hierons	Brunel University, UK
Mike Hinchey	Lero-the Irish Software Engineering Research Centre, Republic of Ireland
Florentin Ipate	University of Pitesti, Romania
Einar Broch Johnsen	University of Oslo, Norway
Panagiotis Katsaros	Aristotle University of Thessaloniki, Greece
Joseph Kiniry	Technical University of Denmark, Denmark
Martin Leucker	University of Lübeck, Germany
Peter Lindsay	The University of Queensland, Australia
Zhiming Liu	United Nations University, Macao
Antónia Lopes	University of Lisbon, Portugal
Tiziana Margaria	Universität Potsdam, Germany
Stephan Merz	INRIA Lorraine, France
Manuel Núñez	Universidad Complutense de Madrid, Spain
Mizuhito Ogawa	Japan Advanced Institute of Science and Technology, Japan

Fernando Orejas	Universitat Politècnica de Catalunya, Spain
Olaf Owe	Universitity of Oslo, Norway
Gordon Pace	University of Malta, Malta
Anna Philippou	University of Cyprus, Cyprus
Mario Piattini	University of Castilla-La Mancha, Spain
Sanjiva Prasad	Indian Institute of Technology Delhi, India
Anders Ravn	Aalborg University, Denmark
Jakob Rehof	Fraunhofer ISST and Technical University of Dortmund, Germany
Wolfgang Reisig	Humboldt-Universität zu Berlin, Germany
Leila Ribeiro	Universidade Federal do Rio Grande do Sul, Brazil
Bernhard Rumpe	RWTH Aachen University, Germany
Augusto Sampaio	Federal University of Pernambuco, Brazil
Ina Schaefer	Technische Universität Braunschweig, Germany
Gerardo Schneider	University of Gothenburg, Sweden
Steve Schneider	University of Surrey, UK
Massimo Tivoli	University of L'Aquila, Italy
Viktor Vafeiadis	MPI-SWS, Germany

Additional Reviewers

Arlt, Stephan
Bousse, Erwan
Breuer, Peter
Bøgholm, Thomas
Carvalho, Gustavo
Cavallaro, Luca
Clarisó, Robert
Colombo, Christian
Düdder, Boris
Ferrari, Alessio
Furia, Carlo A.
Gierds, Christian
Golas, Ulrike
Greifenberg, Timo
Habel, Annegret
Hildebrandt, Thomas
Hoelldobler, Katrin
Hu, Zhenjian

Jürjens, Jan
Keiren, Jeroen J.A.
Kolassa, Carsten
Korsholm, Stephan
Kühn, Franziska
Le Guilly, Thibaut
Legay, Axel
Li, Guoqiang
Mahdi, Ahmed
Markin, Grigory
Marques, Eduardo R.B.
Martens, Moritz
Massoni, Tiago
Mazzanti, Franco
Micallef, Mark
Mir Seyed Nazari, Pedram
Moelle, Andre

Müller, Richard
Oehlerking, Jens
Olsen, Petur
Petri, Gustavo
Petrocchi, Marinella
Qamar, Nafees
Schäf, Martin
Schönfelder, René
Sürmeli, Jan
Techaveerapong, Pakorn
Thoma, Daniel
To, Van Khanh
Trefler, Richard
Truong, Hoang
Yatapanage, Nisansala
Zavattaro, Gianluigi

Abstracts of Keynote Speeches

Behavioral Software Metrics

Thomas A. Henzinger

Institute of Science and Technology Austria

In this talk I show how the classical satisfaction relation between programs and requirements can be replaced by quantitative preference metrics that measure the *fit* between programs and requirements. Depending on the application, such fitness measures may include aspects of function, performance, reliability, and robustness.

Building Billions of Software Artifacts

Wolfram Schulte

Microsoft Corporation

Every day software developers all over the world build hundreds of thousands of software artifacts, ranging from executables, via libraries, to documentation, and websites. Build tools are thus one of the most important enablers for software developers. Consequentially, the last 30 years have seen a plethora of approaches to build languages and engines, ranging from dependency based builds using Make, via task based ones using Ant or MSBuild, to IDE integrated ones using Eclipse or Visual Studio, to embedded DSLs like SCons, Rake, Shake and others. But despite these efforts, many build systems still suffer from being unreliable, since dependencies are missing, not saleable, since they were designed for single machines only, ineffective, since builds are often unnecessarily sequentialized, and not multi tenancy capable, since many build systems and tools assume that they execute in particular locations.

During the past year my team has developed a new build system leveraging earlier work on dependency based builds, combining it with the benefits of DSLs, and hosting it in the Cloud. Conceptually, in our new system every software artifact is build from scratch. However by using proper design choices, we enable many optimizations to build things quickly or not at all, like parallel, cached, staged, incremental, distributed and multitenant builds. The system is meanwhile deployed for our first major customer.

In this talk I will present insights and highlight of our journey of creating a new build system for Microsoft, and I will give a glimpse of the results. I will describe the challenges we faced and the opportunities that lie ahead. And being at a formal methods conference, I will show that a little build theory can help in the design and for the promotion of a new technology, too!

Joint work with Adrian Bonar, Chandra Prasad, Danny van Velzen, Davide Massarenti, Dmitry Goncharenko, John Erickson and Seva Titov.

Modeling Heterogeneous Real-Time Components in BIP (Revisited)

Marius Bozga

UJF-Grenoble 1/CNRS VERIMAG

In this talk I will describe a methodology for modeling heterogeneous real-time components. I will present the BIP language for the description and composition of layered components as well as associated tools for executing and analyzing components on a dedicated platform. The language provides a powerful mechanism for structuring interactions involving rendezvous and broadcast. I will show that synchronous and timed systems are particular classes of components. Finally, I will provide examples, compare the BIP framework to existing ones for heterogeneous component-based modeling and review the impact in subsequent research lines of the original work.

Table of Contents

Static Analysis

Testing and Runtime Verification

Synthesis and Transformation

Verifying MARTE/CCSL Mode Behaviors Using UPPAAL

Jagadish Suryadevara[1], Cristina Seceleanu[1], Frédéric Mallet[2], and Paul Pettersson[1]

[1] Mälardalen Real-Time Research Centre, Mälardalen University, Västerås, Sweden
{jagadish.suryadevara,cristina.seceleanu,paul.pettersson}@mdh.se
[2] Aoste Team-project INRIA/I3S, Sophia-Antipolis, France
frederic.mallet@unice.fr

Abstract. In the development of safety-critical embedded systems, the ability to formally analyze system behavior models, based on timing and causality, helps the designer to get insight into the systems overall timing behavior. To support the design and analysis of real-time embedded systems, the UML modeling profile MARTE provides CCSL – a time model and a clock constraint specification language. CCSL is an expressive language that supports specification of both logical and chronometric constraints for MARTE models. On the other hand, semantic frameworks such as timed automata provide verification support for real-time systems. To address the challenge of verifying CCSL-based behavior models, in this paper, we propose a technique for transforming MARTE/CCSL mode behaviors into Timed Automata for model-checking using the UPPAAL tool. This enables verification of both logical and chronometric properties of the system, which has not been possible before. We demonstrate the proposed transformation and verification approach using two relevant examples of real-time embedded systems.

Keywords: MARTE, CCSL, Modes, Verification, Model-checking, UPPAAL.

1 Introduction

The increasing complexity and safety-criticality of real-time embedded systems in domains such as automotive and avionics, stresses the need for applying rigorous analysis techniques during system development in order to ensure predictability [8]. To meet this need, UML (The Unified Modeling Language) provides a domain-specific modeling profile called MARTE (Modeling and Analysis of Real-Time and Embedded systems) [14]. Besides modeling support for *performance* and *schedulability* analysis, MARTE includes CCSL – a time model and a clock constraint specification language, for describing both logical and physical (chronometric) clock constraints [3]. Also, CCSL can be used for specifying both synchronous and asynchronous constraints, based on the *coincidence* and *precedence* relationships between clock instances. On the other hand, semantic frameworks such as timed automata provide modeling and verification support for real-time systems [1,7,11,2], which CCSL-based models could benefit from. However, the expressiveness of CCSL poses challenges in providing rigorous analysis support, like exhaustive verification. The focus of our work, in this paper, is to address these challenges and provide a model-checking based verification support for

R.M. Hierons, M.G. Merayo, and M. Bravetti (Eds.): SEFM 2013, LNCS 8137, pp. 1–15, 2013.
© Springer-Verlag Berlin Heidelberg 2013

MARTE/CCSL behavior models. MARTE Statemachine models, called ModeBehaviors, can be used to specify the *mode*-based behavior of a system. In this view, a *mode* represents *an operational segment*, that is characterized by a *configuration* of system entities. For instance, during 'TakeOff', 'Flying' and 'Landing' modes of an aircraft, different parts of the control system may be active in different modes.

In this paper, we propose to constrain MARTE mode behaviors with CCSL specifications, taking advantage of the underlying MARTE time model. This facilitates precise specification of logical (of synchronous and asynchronous nature) as well as timing (chronometric) properties of a system in a mode. Next, as a main contribution, we present a technique to transform MARTE/CCSL mode behaviors into timed automata [1,7]. The transformation is based on the synchronized product of the state-based semantics of the CCSL constraints [4,12]. This proves to be non-trivial due to the expressiveness of CCSL constraints and the semantic domain of timed automata.

In brief, in this paper, we make the following contributions:

- We provide a mapping strategy to transform CCSL-extended MARTE mode behaviors into timed automata, and verify logical and chronometric properties using the UPPAAL model-checking tool [11].
- We propose novel techniques to address the limitations of mapping synchronous and chronometric semantics of CCSL into timed automata.
- We demonstrate the proposed modeling and verification approach using two representative examples of safety-critical embedded control systems, namely, a *temperature control system* and an *anti-lock braking system*.

The rest of the paper is organized as follows. In Section 2, we introduce example embedded systems and present the corresponding mode behavior specifications. In Section 3, we present an overview of CCSL, followed by the CCSL extended mode behaviors for the example systems. In Section 4, we present the proposed transformation technique for CCSL-extended mode behavior specifications, and in Section 5, we discuss verification results based on the transformed timed automata models of the example systems. The related work is discussed in Section 6. Finally, we conclude the paper in Section 7, with a discussion of the future work.

2   Example Systems and Mode-Behavior Specifications

In this section, we present the mode behavior specifications of the example embedded systems used in this paper. We have chosen two simple but representative systems, with functional and timing aspects commonly found in embedded systems.

MARTE Notation and Stereotypes. In MARTE, the stereotype *ModeBehavior* extends the UML Statemachine notation with stereotypes *Mode*, which extends State, and *ModeTransition*, which extends Transition (Fig. 1). A *ModeBehavior* specifies a set of mutually exclusive modes, that is, only one mode is active at a given instant. A *mode* represents an operational fragment of the system, called *configuration*, representing the set of system entities that are active during the mode instance. The dynamics of mode switching, either time or event triggered, is specified by means of *ModeTransitions*. Transitions are enabled in response to an event occurrence, that is, the activation condition triggering the mode switching.

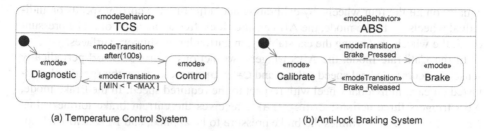

(a) Temperature Control System   (b) Anti-lock Braking System

Fig. 1. UML/MARTE mode behavior specifications

2.1   Example1: A Temperature Control System (TCS)

We consider a simplified version of a temperature control system that regulates the temperature inside a nuclear reactor core, using thermal-controlling rods. The rods are inserted into the core of the reactor when the temperature reaches a given upper limit, denoted by constant MAX, causing the temperature to gradually reduce (as neutrons in the reactor are absorbed by the control rods). Similarly, the control rods are removed when the temperature in the reactor falls below MIN. TCS operates in two *modes*.

In Diagnostic mode, the following *actions* are triggered that execute the corresponding *behaviors*[1]: Diagnostics examines the current status of the control rods, Reconfig replaces the ineffective control rods if any, and StatusUpdate updates the status of the rod configuration in the reactor. In Control mode, the system triggers three actions; PeriodicSense senses the temperature in the reactor, InsertRod inserts a control rod, and RemoveRod removes a rod from the reactor.

The TCS mode behavior is presented in Fig. 1. After 100 s in Diagnostic mode, the system changes to Control mode. However, the mode-change from Control to Diagnostic is triggered by an event occurrence, indicating the sensed temperature in the reactor is within the specified limits. The following specify the functional and timing properties of TCS:

TCS1 : Diagnostics is always followed by Reconfig.
TCS2 : The behavior of Reconfig is 'extended' by StatusUpdate, only when there is a change in the control rod configuration.
TCS3 : PeriodicSense executes periodically with a period of 10 s.
TCS4 : PeriodicSense is followed by InsertRod or RemoveRod but not both.
TCS5 : At most two rods can be used in sequence, for cooling the reactor core.

2.2   Example2: An Anti-lock Braking System (ABS)

ABS is a control unit in a car that ensures the stability of the vehicle during drive and extreme brake situations. It functions in two operational modes: Calibrate and Brake. The default mode is Calibrate. In this mode, the system maintains the required speed

---

[1] By *behavior*, we refer to primitive functionality often implemented as a single piece of code. We assume instantaneous execution of a behavior, if not specified otherwise.

equally on all the four wheels, by calibrating and adjusting the current speeds on individual wheels. In Brake mode, the ABS ensures lock-free application of brake pressure on all the wheels, enforcing the car stability, in particular on slippery surfaces.

In the Calibrate mode, the ABS triggers two actions: SenseSpeed periodically senses the current wheel speed values, and Calibrate estimates the speed to be adjusted on each individual wheel with respect to the required speed. In the Brake mode, ABS triggers three actions: SenseBrake receives the current brake torque value, BrakeControl determines the brake pressure to be applied, and BrakeWheel applies required brake pressure with anti-lock braking to individual wheels.

The ABS *mode*-behavior is shown in Fig. 1. The mode changes are caused by events *Brake_Pressed* and *Brake_Released*. The following properties specify the functional and timing constraints in ABS.

ABS1 : SenseSpeed is always followed by Calibrate.
ABS2 : SenseSpeed is periodic with a period of 100 ms.
ABS3 : Calibrate completes within 10 ms after SenseSpeed.
ABS4 : SenseBrake is always followed by BrakeControl.
ABS5 : BrakeControl is always followed by BrakeWheel.
ABS6 : SenseBrake is periodic with a period of 10 ms.
ABS7 : BrakeWheel completes within 1 ms after SenseBrake.

In the next section, we extend the mode behavior specifications of TCS and ABS, with CCSL constraints specifying the logical and chronometric properties.

3   CCSL

UML/MARTE provides modeling support for structural as well as functional and extra-functional aspects of a system. CCSL (The Clock Constraint Specification Language [4]), initially specified in an annex of MARTE, provides an expressive set of constructs to specify causality (both synchronous and asynchronous) as well as chronological and timing properties of the system models. The CCSL is formally defined making the specifications executable at the model level [9].

3.1   CCSL Constraints

CCSL is a declarative language that specifies constraints imposed on the logical *clocks* (representing activation conditions) of a model. CCSL clocks refer to any repetitive events of the system and should not be confused with system clocks. A CCSL clock is defined as a sequence of clock *instants* (event occurrences). If c is a CCSL clock, $c[k]$ denotes its kth instant, for any $k \in \mathbb{N}$. Below, we briefly describe the constraints used in this paper. A complete list of CCSL constructs can be found in André's work [4].

Synchronous Constraints. Rely on the notion of *coincidence* of clock instants. For example, the clock constraint "a isSubclockOf b", denoted by a $\boxed{\subset}$ b, specifies that each instant of the 'subclock' a must coincide with exactly one instant of the 'superclock' b. Other examples of synchronous constraints are discretizedBy or excludes (denoted $\boxed{\#}$). The latter prevents two clocks from ticking simultaneously. The former discretizes a dense clock to derive discrete chronometric clocks. *IdealClk*, a perfect dense chronometric clock, is predefined in MARTE Time Library, and assumed to follow the 'physical time' faithfully (with no jitter).

Asynchronous Constraints. Are based on instant *precedence*, a strict ($\prec$) or a non-strict ($\preccurlyeq$) form. The clock constraint "a isFasterThan b" (denoted by a $\boxed{\preccurlyeq}$ b) specifies that clock a is (non-strictly) faster than clock b, that is for all natural number k, the kth instant of a precedes or is coincident with the kth instant of b ($\forall k \in \mathbb{N}; a[k] \preccurlyeq b[k]$). *Alternation* is another example of an asynchronous constraint. It is a form of bounded precedence. The constraint "a alternatesWith b" (denoted by a $\boxed{\sim}$ b or a $\boxed{\prec_1}$ b) states that $\forall k \in \mathbb{N}; a[k] \prec b[k] \wedge b[k] \prec a[k+1]$, i.e., an instant of a precedes the corresponding instant of b which in turn precedes the next instant of a.

Mixed Constraints. Combine *coincidence* and *precedence*. The constraint "c = a delayedFor n on b" constrains c to tick synchronously with the nth tick of b following a tick of a. It is a mixed constraint since a and b are not assumed to be synchronous.

Table 1. CCSL constraints for logical and chronometric properties of TCS and ABS

Property	*CCSL Constraints*
TCS2	s $\boxed{\subset}$ c
TCS3	Clock p $\boxed{=}$ *IdealClk* discretizedBy 10 s
ABS2	Clock s $\boxed{=}$ *IdealClk* discretizedBy 0.1s
ABS6	Clock b $\boxed{=}$ *IdealClk* discretizedBy 0.01s
TCS1	d $\boxed{\sim}$ c
TCS4	p $\boxed{\sim}$ (i ∪ r)∧ i $\boxed{\#}$ r
TCS5	i $\boxed{\prec_2}$ r
ABS1	s $\boxed{\sim}$ l
ABS4	b $\boxed{\sim}$ r
ABS5	r $\boxed{\sim}$ w
ABS3	l $\boxed{\preccurlyeq}$ s delayedFor 1 on c_1
	where Clock c_1 = *IdealClk* discretizedBy 0.01s
ABS7	w $\boxed{\preccurlyeq}$ b delayedFor 1 on c_2
	where Clock c_2 = *IdealClk* discretizedBy 0.001s

3.2 CCSL Constraints for TCS and ABS

The functional and timing properties of the TCS and ABS, as CCSL constraints, are given in Table 1. These properties constrain the system behaviors with respect to causality and timing. The constraints are listed in three groups: *synchronous*, *asynchronous*, and *mixed*, in that order. The actions in TCS mode behavior are represented by the CCSL logical clocks as follows: Diagnostics: d, Reconfig: c, StatusUpdate: s, PeriodicSense: p, InsertRod: i, and RemoveRod: r. Similarly, for the ABS system, the correspondence between the primitive behaviors and the logical clocks is as follows: SenseSpeed: s, Calibrate: l, SenseBrake: b, BrakeControl: r, and BrakeWheel: w.

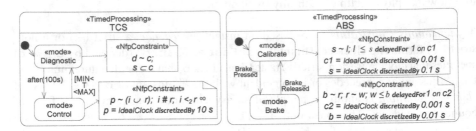

Fig. 2. MARTE/CCSL mode behavior specifications

In Fig. 2, we present the CCSL-extended mode behavior specifications of TCS and ABS. We use MARTE stereotype 'TimedProcessing' for mode behaviors. We also use stereotype 'NfpConstraint' to associate CCSL constraints to a mode. In this paper, we distinguish between the stateful CCSL-constraints that retain history during complete system 'runs' from those that retain history during a *mode* execution. History-enabled CCSL constraints are annotated with symbol ∞, for instance, the constraint i $\boxed{\prec_2}$ r for TCS Control mode.

3.3 Synchronized Product of CCSL Constraints: An Example

State-based semantics of CCSL operators has been defined, using Labelled Transition Systems (LTS) [12]. Thus, combined LTS of composed CCSL operators can be obtained using the synchronized product of the corresponding LTS [6]. As an example, we present the synchronized product for CCSL constraints of the TCS Diagnostic mode, as shown in Fig. 3. The LTS of the constraint d $\boxed{\sim}$ c is given in Fig. 3.(a). It specifies that only the clock d can tick in state 1, whereas in state 2 only the clock c. An empty transition, denoted by ϵ, represents that no clock ticks, and is useful for composing two LTSs. The LTS of s $\boxed{\subset}$ c, as shown in Fig 3.(b), specifies that, in state A, either only c ticks or both s and c tick synchronously (denoted by $<$ s, c $>$). The synchronized product of the above described LTS, as shown in Fig 3.(c), considers all possible states and transitions. For instance, in state 2A, the non-ϵ transition in state 2 of the first LTS, combines with either the ϵ, c, or $<$ s, c $>$ transition in state A of the second LTS, resulting in all possible transitions i.e. ϵ, c, or $<$ c, s $>$. For further details on the synchronization products of CCSL constraints, we refer to the work by Mallet [12].

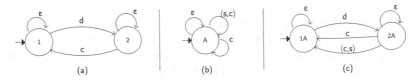

Fig. 3. Example LTS: a) d $\boxed{\sim}$ c   b) s $\boxed{\subset}$ c   c) Synchronized product of d $\boxed{\sim}$ c, s $\boxed{\subset}$ c

4 MARTE/CCSL Mode Behaviors to Timed Automata

In this section, we propose a mapping strategy to transform MARTE/CCSL mode behaviors, henceforth simply referred to as mode behaviors, into timed automata, to provide model-checking based verification support using UPPAAL, a model-checking tool. We first present a brief overview of timed automata modeling in UPPAAL.

4.1 Timed Automata and UPPAAL: An Overview

A timed automaton (TAn) is a tuple $< L, l_0, C, A, E, I >$, where L is a set of *locations*, $l_0 \in L$ is the initial location, C is the set of clocks, A is the set of actions, synchronization actions and the internal τ-action, $E \subseteq L \times A \times B(C) \times 2^C \times L$ is a set of edges between locations with an action, a guard, a set of clocks to be reset, and $I : L \to B(C)$ assigns clock *invariants* to locations. A location can be marked *urgent* (u) or *committed* (c) to indicate that the time is not allowed to progress in the specified location(s), the latter being a stricter form indicating further that the next transition can only be taken from the corresponding location(s) only. Also, synchronization between two automata is modeled by *channels* (e.g., **x**! and **x**?) with rendezvous or broadcast semantics.

UPPAAL extends the timed automata language, originally introduced by Alur and Dill [1], with a number of features such as global and local (bounded) integer variables, arithmetic operations, arrays, and a C-like programming language. The tool consists of three parts: a graphical editor for modeling timed automata, a simulator for trace generation, and a verifier for the verification of a system modeled as a network of timed automata. A subset of CTL (computation tree logic) is used as the input language for the verifier. For further details, we refer the reader to UPPAAL tutorial [11].

4.2 Transforming Mode Behaviors into Timed Automata

For the transformation of a MARTE/CCSL mode behavior into the corresponding timed automaton, several aspects need to be considered, such as, logical clocks, CCSL constraints, logical and chronometric time, modes and mode transitions. The transformation consists mainly of three steps: mapping composed LTS of CCSL constraints of modes into corresponding TA, referred to as LTS-TA, next modeling logical and chronometric timing aspects in the transformed TA, and finally associating mode-change behavior. The mapping strategy is described below and also summarized in Fig. 4.

Logical clocks and *CCSL Constraints*. For the logical constraints in modes, using the LTS-based semantics, we first construct the synchronized products. These LTS are then transformed into TA as follows: states are mapped to locations, transitions become edges in the corresponding TA. Further, the logical clocks are mapped to boolean variables, with 'ticking' configurations of the LTS transitions modeled as the update actions of the boolean variables for the corresponding TA action transitions.

Logical and Chronometric Time. The transformation correlates logical semantics of CCSL and chronometric time progress in TA. This is done by extending the LTS-TA of

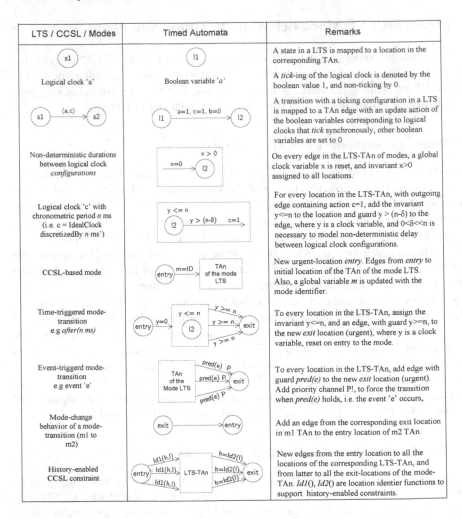

LTS / CCSL / Modes	Timed Automata	Remarks
s1	l1	A state in a LTS is mapped to a location in the corresponding TAn.
Logical clock 'a'	Boolean variable 'a'	A tick-ing of the logical clock is denoted by the boolean value 1, and non-ticking by 0.
s1 —⟨a,c⟩→ s2	l1 —a=1, c=1, b=0→ l2	A transition with a ticking configuration in a LTS is mapped to a TAn edge with an update action of the boolean variables corresponding to logical clocks that tick synchronously, other boolean variables are set to 0
Non-deterministic durations between logical clock configurations	x > 0 x=0 → l2	On every edge in the LTS-TAn of modes, a global clock variable x is reset, and invariant x>0 assigned to all locations.
Logical clock 'c' with chronometric period n ms (i.e. c = IdealClock discretizedBy n ms')	y <= n l2 —y > (n-δ) c=1→	For every location in the LTS-TAn, with outgoing edge containing action c=1, add the invariant y<=n to the location and guard y > (n-δ) to the edge, where y is a clock variable, and 0<δ<<n is necessary to model non-deterministic delay between logical clock configurations.
CCSL-based mode	(entry) —m=ID→ TAn of the mode LTS	New urgent-location entry. Edges from entry to initial location of the TAn of the mode LTS. Also, a global variable m is updated with the mode identifier.
Time-triggered mode-transition e.g after(n ms)	y <= n y >= n (entry) —y=0→ l2 —y >= n→ exit y >= n	To every location in the LTS-TAn, assign the invariant y<=n, and an edge, with guard y>=n, to the new exit location (urgent), where y is a clock variable, reset on entry to the mode.
Event-triggerd mode-transition e.g event 'e'	Pred(e) P TAn of the Mode LTS —pred(e) P→ exit pred(e) P	To every location in the LTS-TAn, add edge with guard pred(e) to the new exit location (urgent). Add priority channel P!, to force the transition when pred(e) holds, i.e. the event 'e' occurs,
Mode-change behavior of a mode-transition (m1 to m2)	exit ————→ entry	Add an edge from the corresponding exit location in m1 TAn to the entry location of m2 TAn.
History-enabled CCSL constraint	Id1(h,l) h=Id2(l) (entry) —Id1(h,l)→ LTS-TAn —h=Id2(l)→ exit Id1(h,l) h=Id2(l)	New edges from the entry location to all the locations of the corresponding LTS-TAn, and from latter to all the exit-locations of the mode-TAn. Id1(), Id2() are location identier functions to support history-enabled constraints.

Fig. 4. MARTE/CCSL mode behaviors to timed automata: A mapping strategy

the modes, described above, with timing mechanisms based on clock-variables, clock-guards, and invariants in TA. To begin with, every location in the LTS-TAn of a mode, is assigned the invariant $x > 0$, where x is a clock variable which is also reset on every edge in the TAn. This models the non-deterministic delay between two consecutive clock configurations. As the next step, we map the CCSL constraints that specify chronometric durations for the logical clocks (for some constraints, we need to separate logical and chronometric parts into separate constraints, as explained for ABS mode behavior transformation later in the section). For instance, a CCSL clock c with period 'n ms' is mapped using the invariant $y \leq n$ to all locations with an outgoing edge with action update $c = 1$. Also the edge is assigned the clock guard $y > (n - \delta)$. The value $\delta(<< n)$ is necessary to facilitate the non-deterministic delay described above.

Modes and Mode Transitions. We further extend the LTS-TA of modes, described above, to obtain the timed automata for modes, by adding an `entry`-location (urgent) and an edge from the new location to the initial location of the corresponding LTS-TAn. A global mode variable m may be updated with the mode identifier value. The mode TA are further extended to enable the mode transitions, as described below.

A mode transition, is either time- or event-triggered, and specifies the corresponding mode-change behavior. For each transition, an `exit`-location (urgent) in the corresponding source mode TAn, as well as new edges from every location of the TAn to the new location are added. For the time-triggered transition, that is, of the form '`after(n ms)`', we also add an invariant of the form $x \leq n$ to all the locations in the TAn, as well as, the guards $x \geq n$ for all the new edges. On the other hand, for an event-triggered transition, the event, say '`e`', is mapped by adding the event predicate, given by *pred*(e), as guard on all the new edges. To force the transition in case of event occurrence, we also use a priority synchronization channel '$P!$'. Finally, in both cases above, the actual mode-switch behavior of the transition is modeled by connecting the exit-location of the source mode TAn to the entry-location of the target mode TAn.

Mode History. The *Control* mode of the TCS (Fig. 2) contains a history-enabled constraint i $\boxed{\prec_2}$ r. This specifies that the clock i (for `InsertRod`) can tick faster than the clock r (for `RemoveRod`) but not by more than two instances. Clearly, the state of the constraint needs to be retained if the mode is exited and re-entered later. When a mode is transformed into a TAn, an history variable h is updated on all the edges leading to the exit-location. Moreover, additional edges are added from the entry-location of the mode TAn to all the locations (not just the initial location corresponding to the LTS-TAn), with guards based on the value of the variable h. However, to support the history mechanism, we assume functions 'Id1()' and 'Id2()' that return the location information with respect to the history-enabled constraint.

In this section, we have presented techniques to transform MARTE/CCSL mode behaviors into timed automata. We demonstrate the proposed mapping strategy using the mode behavior specifications of the example systems, presented earlier in this paper. We also discuss some additional issues in applying the techniques.

4.3   The Transformed Automaton for the TCS

In Fig. 5, we present the complete TAn model for the CCSL-based mode behavior (Fig. 2) of the TCS. The Diagnostic mode is transformed to the TAn using the synchronized product of constraints d $\boxed{\sim}$ c and s $\boxed{\subseteq}$ c. Similarly, the Control mode is transformed using the synchronized product of the constraints p $\boxed{\sim}$ (iUr), i $\boxed{\#}$ r, and i $\boxed{\prec_2}$ r. These mappings are shown in Fig. 5. For simplicity, the entry-locations of the mode TA are merged with the initial locations in the corresponding LTS-TA.

Next, we have mapped the mode-transitions that trigger the mode-change behavior, as follows: the time-triggered transition from Diagnostic to Control is mapped using the invariant $x \leq 100$ at all the locations of the Diagnostic TAn, and guards $x \geq 100$ for the edges to the exit-location. The mode-transition from Control to Diagnostic is event-triggered, by the predicate denoted by "t" (after the required temperature is

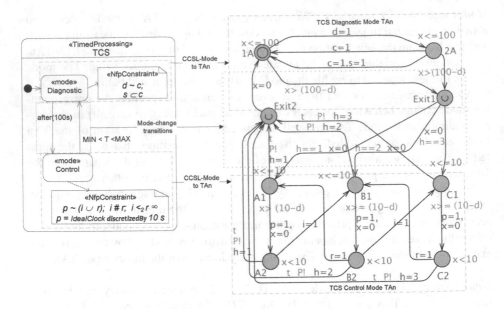

Fig. 5. TCS mode behavior to timed automaton

sensed). Finally, the mode-change for the above transitions are modeled by connecting the exit location of the source mode TAn to the initial location of the target mode TAn.

```
From CCSL 'alternatesWith' definition:

left [~] right : ∀ i ∈ N, left[i] < right[i] & right[i] < left[i+1] (where N,
    set of natural numbers).
And,  p [~] (i ∪ r) : ∀ i ∈ N*, p[i] < (i ∪ r)[i] & (i ∪ r)[i] < p[i+1]
Given 'p' periodic, i.e. n seconds : ∀ i ∈ N, p[i] = s[n*i − (n−1)] where 's'
    is a chronometric clock that counts the seconds.

For n=10, ∀ i ∈ N, s[10*i − 9] < (i ∪ r) [i] < s[10*i + 1]
```

Listing 1.1. Timing invariants derived from CCSL constraints.

The Control mode of the TCS contains a chronometric constraint for the logical clock p (for `PeriodicSense`). This is mapped to the location invariant $x \leq 10$, and guard $x \geq 10$ for the transitions causing the clock 'ticks' i.e. p=1. However, the other locations also need to be assigned the invariant, due to causality of the CCSL clocks. From the proof given in Listing 1.1, and under the assumption that the physical time (in TA) is s and s[1] is time 0, we infer s[10] is time 10. For i=1, s[1] < (i∪r)[i] < s[11], which gives the interval (0,10). This proves the invariants for the locations.

The Control mode contains a history-enabled CCSL constraint $i \boxed{\prec_2} r$. The state of the constraint, that is, the current location before exiting the TAn, is saved in a history variable 'h', when the mode is exited. Based on the variable value, the initial location is chosen, when the mode is re-entered.

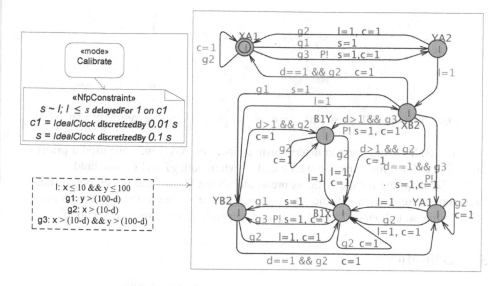

Fig. 6. Timed automaton for ABS Calibrate mode

4.4   The Transformed Automaton for the ABS

For the transformation of the ABS mode behavior, we chose to skip the complete automaton model, and focus only on the transformation of the Calibrate mode, given that the CCSL specification of the Brake mode is similar.

The synchronized product of CCSL constraints for the Calibrate mode can lead to a combinatory explosion, due to the mixed constraint `delayedFor`. However, we propose a novel technique to address this. We separate the causality and the chronometric aspects of the constraint, using an auxiliary logical clock c, such that the chronometric duration is specified as 'logical' ticks of c with additional constraint on c that specifies the actual chronometric duration. This facilitates the construction of the synchronized product and also provides an efficient mapping of the chronometric time to TA. Note that the invariant I (partly) and the guard $g2$ (in the mode automaton of Fig. 6) are due to the chronometric constraint on c (i.e. 10ms). Also, the invariant I at all locations is due to the chronometric time progress and the causality within the mode.

Another transformation issue arises when transforming the LTS of the CCSL constraint "$a \preccurlyeq b$ `delayedFor` 1 on c_1". This is obtained as the synchronized product of the two constraints $a \preccurlyeq x$ (precedes) and $x = b$ `delayedFor` 1 on c (coincidence), where x is an auxiliary logical clock introduced for the purpose. The LTS of both constraints are presented in Fig. 7. For the constraint $a \preccurlyeq x$, we have considered its unbounded semantics encoded by the variable d, which represents the number of instances of a that have preceded instances of x (Fig. 7.(a)). Ticks of x are not shown in the final automaton in Fig. 6, though 'ticks' of both x and a update d.

The transformed LTS-TAn for the ABS Calibrate mode is presented in Fig. 6. To make the model readable, we have not shown the update actions on d, logical clock resets on each edge (for the clocks that do not 'tick' in the configuration), as well as TA

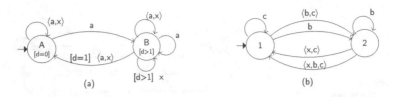

Fig. 7. LTS of CCSL constraints: a) a ⊴ x   b) x ⊟ b delayedFor 1 on c

clock resets. To avoid the non-determinism at location XA1, we have used a priority channel P, to force the transition with guard *g3* when both *g1* and *g2* also hold.

The TA mapping for the ABS, as presented above, shows that the proposed transformation addresses some of the critical issues that arise due to the expressiveness of CCSL, such as, unbounded operators, mixed constraints, and chronometric time.

5   Verification

In this section, we present a verification approach for MARTE/CCSL mode behaviors by model checking the corresponding TA, obtained using the transformation approach presented in the previous section. Verification is performed using the UPPAAL tool. A set of properties describing deadlock-freedom, liveness, causality, and chronometric time is specified and verified for the example systems. To support the verification, we use observer automata for specific kinds of properties, and extend the automata resulting from the transformation, to support synchronous (timewise) interactions with the observers. Such extensions can be easily automated during model transformation.

Deadlock-freedom. The property specified in Eqn.1, as a safety-property, describes the absence of deadlocks. A deadlock occurs when the system cannot progress further. For both TCS and ABS mode behaviors, the property is satisfied.

$$A\square \neg \textbf{deadlock} \tag{1}$$

Deadlock-Path identification problem for logical clocks. For CCSL specifications, one of very important verification problems is the identification of the execution paths, or sub-paths, for which a given set of clocks eventually do not 'tick'. In CCSL, such paths are referred to as deadlock-paths for a given set of logical clocks. For instance, for the TCS Diagnostic TAn, we have verified the presence of a deadlock-path, using property in Eqn. 2, for the logical clock s (StatusUpdate action). The equation models a liveness property, as a"leads to" property in UPPAAL (denoted by ⤳, implemented as --> in UPPAAL). The property (2) basically states that for all paths, it is always the case that the clock will eventually tick. In the TCS example, the property fails to hold and an execution path where s never ticks eventually is shown as a counter-example/diagnostic trace. The diagnostic traces show the execution path where s never ticks. The property can be extended to multiple clocks, as in Eqn. 3, where clocks c and s correspond to `Reconfig` and `StatusUpdate` respectively. The property is satisfied, indicating that the clocks together do not lead to any deadlock paths in Diagnostic mode.

$$s == 0 \leadsto s == 1 \tag{2}$$

$$(c == 0 \ \&\& \ s == 0) \leadsto (c == 1 \ || \ s == 1) \tag{3}$$

Chronometric durations of logical clocks and event chains. Another benefit provided by transforming mode behaviors into TA is the possibility of verifying chronometric aspects, such as, *minimum* and *maximum* inter-arrival times, (m, M), of a logical clock with no explicit chronometric constraints otherwise. For this, we use an observer automaton as shown in Fig. 8, and the corresponding property to be verified, given by (4). To enable (time-wise) synchronous interactions between the specification automaton and the observer, we introduce in the former, between the source and the target locations, a committed location that connects to the target location through an edge annotated with the synchronization channel 'sig!', as shown in Fig. 8. The observer computes the time between two 'ticks' of the logical clock r. By the timing property given by (4), one is able to verify that the (min, max) inter-arrival time of r is (0, 40) for the `RemoveRod` action.

$$A\Box \ (t == 1 \ imply \ (\ cx > m \ and \ cx < M)) \tag{4}$$

We can generalize the observer automaton for two events, to verify end-to-end timing of event chains that consist of a stimulus-response event pair. For instance, the ABS Calibrate mode has CCSL timing constraint '$1 \leq s$ delayedFor 10 ms', which specifies the end-to-end timing for s, 1 representing `SenseSpeed` and `Calibrate` respectively.

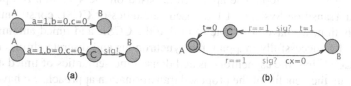

(a)   (b)

Fig. 8. a) Extending mode TA transitions b) Observer TAn for chronometric durations

6   Related Work

Wang et al. have recently proposed the MDM (Mode Diagram Modeling) framework for periodic control systems [15]. They have also provided a property specification language, based on the interval logic, to capture the temporal properties that can be verified against the MDM models, using statistical model checking. Unlike our approach, the complete verification is undecidable, as MDM may involve complex non-linear computations. Another comparable framework is that of *Modecharts* and RTL (real time logic) [10]. RTL assertions for events are comparable to CCSL constraints. Both approaches define a time structure to specify timed causality semantics of the system (CCSL is more expressive given its polychronous semantics), and provide structural organization of a system causality and timing behavior to efficiently reason about timing properties. In comparison, our approach provides the capability of verifying usual dense-time properties, but also combinations of logical and chronometric time properties, a feature not existing before. Transformation based approaches have been proposed for mapping the CCSL or a subset of it, into different semantic domains such as VHDL, Petri nets, and Promela. André et al. presented an automatic transformation of a CCSL specification into VHDL code [5]. The proposed transformation assembles instances of pre-built VHDL components while preserving the polychronous semantics of CCSL. The generated code can be integrated in the VHDL design and verification flow. Mallet and André have proposed a formal semantics to a kernel subset of MARTE, and presented an equivalent interpretation of the kernel in two different formal languages, namely Signal and Time Petri nets [13]. In their work, relevant examples have been used to show instances when Petri-nets are suitable to express CCSL constraints, as well as instances where synchronous languages are more appropriate. Ling et al. have proposed a transformation approach for logical CCSL constraints into Promela, using checkpoint-bisimulation approach, for verification with SPIN model-checker [16]. Also, some property specification patterns for expressing the properties of the model have been proposed. In comparison to above transformation based approaches, here we have proposed a model-checking based approach that addresses chronometric constraints of CCSL effectively, by overcoming the limitations in specifying synchronous behavior in otherwise asynchronous modeling framework of timed automata.

7   Conclusion and Future Work

In this paper, we have proposed a transformation approach for MARTE/CCSL mode behavior specifications into timed automata, to enable model-checking of the specifications using UPPAAL tool. The approach is based on the synchronized product of the Labelled Transition Systems (LTS) based semantics of CCSL constraints. As the main contribution, we have been able to bridge the CCSL and timed automata based frameworks, by successfully mapping the synchronous and discrete chronometric semantics of CCSL into the asynchronous and dense time semantics of timed automata. To demonstrate the benefits of the proposed transformation approach, we have verified both logical and chronometric properties using the mode behavior specification of the example systems in this paper. Since CCSL is an expressive language, we have considered a subset of CCSL constraints for the transformation, and plan to investigate other constraints as future work. To support the verification process, we will further investigate specific classes of logical and timing properties that can be verified, and model them as property patterns or timed automata observers. Currently, a prototype version of the tool for constructing synchronized products of CCSL constraints exists, so we intend to formalize the proposed model transformation technique to integrate the model-checking based verification within a MARTE/CCSL modeling framework.

Acknowledgment. This work has been partially funded by Swedish Research Council (VR) through ARROWS project, Mälardalen University (Sweden), Ericsson Research Foundation (Sweden) and ARTEMIS Grant N269362 – Project PRESTO - http://www.presto-embedded.eu.

References

1. Alur, R., Dill, D.: A theory of timed automata. Theoretical Computer Science 126(2), 183–235 (1994)
2. Amnell, T., Fersman, E., Mokrushin, L., Pettersson, P., Yi, W.: TIMES: a Tool for Schedulability Analysis and Code Generation of Real-Time Systems. In: Larsen, K.G., Niebert, P. (eds.) FORMATS 2003. LNCS, vol. 2791, Springer, Heidelberg (2004)
3. André, C., Mallet, F., de Simone, R.: Modeling Time(s). In: Engels, G., Opdyke, B., Schmidt, D.C., Weil, F. (eds.) MoDELS 2007. LNCS, vol. 4735, pp. 559–573. Springer, Heidelberg (2007)
4. André, C.: Syntax and Semantics of the Clock Constraint Specification Language (CCSL). Rapport de recherche RR-6925, INRIA (2009)
5. André, C., Mallet, F., DeAntoni, J.: VHDL observers for clock constraint checking. In: 2010 Int. Symp. on Industrial Embedded Systems (SIES), pp. 98–107 (July 2010)
6. Arnold, A.: Finite transition systems - semantics of communicating systems. Int. Series in Computer Science. Prentice Hall (1994)
7. Baier, C., Katoen, J.P.: Principles of Model Checking. Representation and Mind Series. The MIT Press (2008)
8. Bouyssounouse, B., Sifakis, J. (eds.): Embedded Systems Design: The ARTIST Roadmap for Research and Development. LNCS, vol. 3436. Springer, Heidelberg (2005)
9. DeAntoni, J., Mallet, F.: TimeSquare: Treat Your Models with Logical Time. In: Furia, C.A., Nanz, S. (eds.) TOOLS 2012. LNCS, vol. 7304, pp. 34–41. Springer, Heidelberg (2012)
10. Jahanian, F., Mok, A.: Modechart: a specification language for real-time systems. IEEE Transactions on Software Engineering 20(12), 933–947 (December)
11. Larsen, K.G., Pettersson, P., Yi, W.: UPPAAL in a Nutshell. Int. Journal on Software Tools for Technology Transfer 1(1-2), 134–152 (1997)
12. Mallet, F.: Automatic Generation of Observers from MARTE/CCSL. In: Int. Symp. on Rapid System Prototyping - RSP 2012. IEEE, Tampere (2012), http://hal.inria.fr/hal-00764066
13. Mallet, F., André, C.: On the semantics of UML/Marte Clock Constraints. In: Int. Symp. on Object/Component/Service-Oriented Real-Time Distributed Computing (ISORC 2009), pp. 301–312. IEEE, Tokyo (2009), http://hal.inria.fr/inria-00383279
14. OMG: UML Profile for MARTE, v1.0. Object Management Group (November 2009), formal/(2009-11-02)
15. Wang, Z., Pu, G., Li, J., He, J., Qin, S., Larsen, K.G., Madsen, J., Gu, B.: MDM: A Mode Diagram Modeling Framework. In: Proc. First International Workshop on Formal Techniques for Safety-Critical Systems, pp. 135–149. EPTCS (2012)
16. Yin, L., Mallet, F., Liu, J.: Verification of MARTE/CCSL time requirements in Promela/SPIN. In: 2011 16th IEEE Int. Conf. on Engineering of Complex Computer Systems (ICECCS), pp. 65–74 (April 2011)

A Transformation Approach
for Multiform Time Requirements

Nadia Menad[1] and Philippe Dhaussy[2]

[1] University of Science and Technology
of Oran Mohamed Boudiaf, Algeria
[2] UEB, LabSticc Laboratory UMR CNRS 6285
ENSTA Bretagne, France
firstname.name@ensta-bretagne.fr

Abstract. Many of the timing constraints expressed in physical pre-
scriptions of distributed systems and multi-clock electronic systems can
be expressed in logical concepts. A logical time model has been developed as a part of the official OMG UML profile MARTE, in order to
enrich the formalism of this profile and also to facilitate the description
and analysis of temporal constraints.

This time model is associated with CCSL (Clock Constraint Specification Language). Once the software is modeled, the difficulty lies in
both expressing the relevant properties and in verifying them formally.
We present an automatic transformation technique related to a method
for verifying properties by model checking, thus exploiting both the CDL
language (Context Description Language) and the OBP tool (Observer-
based Prover). The technique is based on a translation of MARTE models
and the CCSL constraints into Fiacre code. CDL can express predicates
and observers. These are verified during the exhaustive exploration of the
complete model by OBP. We illustrate our contribution by an illustrative
case.

Keywords: Formal verification, model-checking, CCSL time constraints,
observer automata.

1 Introduction

In the field of modeling software architectures of distributed systems, control-
command systems or multi-clock electronic systems, the specification of functional parts of systems is often associated with temporal constraint specifications.
These systems are often critical and the requirements to be respected during the
modeling step, concern not only the determinism but also temporal constraints
at a functional level. In the system development process, the designers look for
methods and languages that allow them to describe their architectures, throughout the cycle and at various levels of abstraction. At each level, the modeling of
such systems should allow the expression and the manipulation of time requirements, and the evaluation of the accuracy and efficiency of applications in terms
of temporal and measurable requirements.

R.M. Hierons, M.G. Merayo, and M. Bravetti (Eds.): SEFM 2013, LNCS 8137, pp. 16–30, 2013.
© Springer-Verlag Berlin Heidelberg 2013

For this purpose, the concept of abstract modeling of logical clocks has been introduced with the CCSL language (*Clock Constraint Specification Language*) [And09] within MARTE [MAS08] and adopted by the OMG [OMG10]. CCSL is a language to define causal, chronological and temporal relationships. It aims to complement the existing formalisms and to provide models which can be analysed so as to assess their accuracy with regard to requirements expressed by the designer. It is therefore essential to adopt temporal analysis approaches by integrating verification and validation processes based on robust formal notions, in order to meet current quality requirements of these systems.

To address this issue, several studies have proposed an engineering approach founded on models, and the use of semi-formal notations such as UML, enriched with formal notations. For example, UML-MARTE profile aims to express temporal constraints on UML models. The models that are built must not only be simulated but also interpreted during formal analysis so as to check the temporal requirements defined by the designer. In this study, we use *model-checking* verification techniques [QS82, CES86]. These techniques have become highly popular due to their ability to confirm software model properties automatically.

This paper describes exploratory work which studies the association of CCSL constraint specification and a formal property verification tool named OBP (Observer-Based Prover)[1] [DBRL12]. The verifications carried out by OBP are based on the exploration of Fiacre programs [FGP+08] as well as the exploitation of observers (Fig. 1). The OBP imports Fiacre models corresponding to a translation of UML-MARTE models including CCSL specifications. In addition, it imports CDL programs which describe the properties and context scenarios if required. OBP explores the model and evaluates, at each step of the running model, the value of predicates and the status of all involved observers. Through this approach, we endeavor to verify both functional and temporal properties of programs by combining CCSL constraints with the modeled software architecture.

Our contributions are as follow: (1) we generate Fiacre programs from UML-MARTE; (2) we exploit the CCSL specifications and enrich these programs by the addition of Fiacre constraint processes implementing CCSL, taking inspiration from the approach described in [YM11]. We describe, in this paper, the principles of the Fiacre code generation from CCSL constraints; (3) we show how to specify observer automata exploiting CDL and to use the OBP tool to verify them based on generated Fiacre code; (4) we illustrate our contribution with an example and describe the results of the proofs of the requirements conducted.

This paper is organized as follows: Section 2 presents related work in formal analysis and verification of CCSL constraints. We present the CCSL language in Sect. 3. An illustrative case study is presented in Sect. 4 and the principles of transformation of CCSL constraints into Fiacre are introduced in Sect. 5. Section 6 describes the verification technique based on observers and, in Sect. 7, we introduce and discuss some results of property proofs. We conclude in Sect. 8.

---

[1] http://www.obpcdl.org

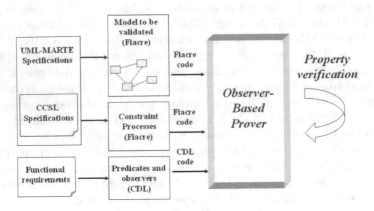

Fig. 1. OBP tool for verification

2 Related Work

Many studies have been conducted to formally verify CCSL constraints. For instance, the approach [YTB+11] presents an extension in response to CCSL specifications. The paper suggests a framework for translating CCSL specifications in dynamical systems, which are handled using the Sigali model-checker to apply the satisfaction of specified constraint relations. However, this approach is too restrictive because it only focuses on the implementation of CCSL constraints with Signal. [And10] proposed an approach for implementing observers [HLR93] for the formal verification of CCSL specifications. Observers, encoding CCSL constraints are translated into Esterel code. [Mal12] describes a technique to generate VHDL code from a CCSL specification. In these approach, a reachability analysis allows to determine whether an observer has reached an error state. The Times Square Environment [DMA08], dedicated to solving CCSL constraints and computing solutions, implements a code generator in Esterel. In contrast to these works, we propose a more general translation approach that verifies not only CCSL constraints implementation, but also properties on the complete model including all the functional components. Furthermore, in our approach these properties are separated from application model thanks to our CDL language, thus separating concerns.

[YM11] proposes a translation of CCSL specifications into a Promela model to formally verify the CCSL constraints by the SPIN model checker. We have been inspired by this work to design the automatic translation of CCSL constraints into Fiacre automata. Also, in this approach the properties to be checked are expressed in LTL logic. We propose to express properties with the CDL language with observer automata which allow a better expressiveness. For example, in our paper, we show a property (illustrated in Fig. 7) that would be tedious to express in LTL.

3   The CCSL Modeling

CCSL, introduced as an annex of MARTE, is a declarative language used to specify binary relations between events based on logical clock concepts. In a MARTE model, any event (for example a communication, transmission or reception action, as computing start) may be used to define a time base, considered to be a logical *clock*. A *clock* represents a set of occurrences of discrete events, called *instants*. These instants are strictly ordered and provide a temporal reference. We briefly recall below some examples of CCSL constraints.

3.1   Examples of CCSL Constraints

We present here some of the relations described in [And10, YM11], which are necessary for the model implementation of the illustrative case study described in this article, namely the relation of alternative, strict precedence and filtering.

An **alternative relation** (denoted *alternatesWith*) is a relation between two asynchronous clocks C_1 and C_2. It specifies that for any natural number k, the kth instant of C_1 occurs before the kth instant of C_2, and the kth instant of C_2 occurs before the $k + 1^{th}$ instant of C_1. For our case study, we illustrate the relation $write_i$ $alternatesWith$ $read_i$ by the chronogram in Fig. 2.a and the automaton in Fig. 2.b. Note that for the non-strict alternation in the expression (1) above, the symbol $\prec$ must be replaced by $\preceq$.

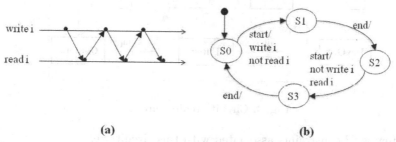

(a)   (b)

Fig. 2. Illustration of the alternation constraint : $write_i$ alternatesWith $read_i$

A **precedence relation** (denoted *strictPrec*) is an asynchronous relation between two clocks C_1 and C_2. C_1 is said to be strictly faster than C_2, where "C_1 strictly precedes C_2", noted C_1 $strictPrec$ C_2, specifies that for any natural number k, the kth instant of C_1 occurs before the kth instant of C_2, i.e $\forall k \in N^*$, $C_1[k] \prec C_2[k]$.

A **filter relation** (denoted *filteredBy*) is a relation which defines a sub-clock from a given discrete clock. The mapping between the two clocks is characterized by a *filtering pattern* (or simply filter) encoded by a finite or infinite binary word $w \in \{0,1\}^* \cup \{0,1\}^w$. C_1 $filteredBy$ w, defines the sub-clock C_2 of C_1 such as $\forall k \in N^*$, $C_2[k] \equiv C_1[w \uparrow k]$, where $w \uparrow k$ is the index of the kth 1 in the pattern w. The binary words are used to represent sequences of activations. When the latter are periodic, they can be represented by periodic binary words denoted by $w = u(v)^w$. u and v are finite binary words, called respectively prefix and period.

4 Illustration through a Simple Case Study

We consider a data acquisition circuit (C), with two channels, consisting of acquisition components ($Sensor_i$ and Acq_i) ($i \in \{1,2\}$), an acquired data processing component ($Comput$) and a filter ($Filter$) sampling the calculated values. Each acquisition channel i is associated with a pair of components $Sensor_i$ and Acq_i. We assume that, for each channel i, the component $Sensor_i$ receives data from the environment (from a device Dev_i outside the circuit) and transmits the value to Acq_i through a shared memory M_i. Each Dev_i sends N data $data_{ik}, k \in [0 \ldots N-1]$. Acq_i provides $Comput$ with each datum $data_{ik}$ via a synchronous communication port $portAcq_i$. $Comput$ applies the addition of $data_{1k}$ and $data_{2k}$ respectively received from Dev_1 and Dev_2 and provides the $Filter$ with the sum via a $fifo$. $Filter$ provides the sampled data (one in every three values) to Dev_{out}, external to the circuit.

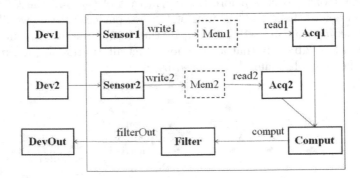

Fig. 3. Circuit architecture C

The temporal constraints associated with this circuit are:

- $Req1$: Each acquired datum $data_i$ is written in the memory M_i before being read by Acq_i (with $i \in \{1,2\}$).
- $Req2$: $Comput$ starts the calculation of a sum after two receptions of $data_ik$ from each Acq_i (with $i \in \{1,2\}$).
- $Req3$: $Filter$ provides the environment with a sampled value from a sequence of one in every three values calculated by $Comput$.

In summary, all the timing requirements for our case study, are specified with CCSL language as follows :

$$write_1 \; alternatesWith \; read_1 \qquad (Req1)$$
$$write_2 \; alternatesWith \; read_2 \qquad (Req1)$$
$$read_1 \; strictPrec \; comput \qquad (Req2)$$
$$read_2 \; strictPrec \; comput \qquad (Req2)$$
$$filterOut \; = \; comput \; filteredBy \; (001)^w \; (Req3)$$

In addition to the above time constraints, we express the requirements that are specifically associated with the expected behavior of the circuit. For example, we can express the following requirement:

- $Req4$: the data $result_j, j \in [0 \ldots (N-1)/3]$ provided to the environment after the sampling operation (one value in 3) must have the values $data_{1k} + data_{2k}$ with $k = (3 * j) + 2$.

5 Translation Principles of the CCSL Constraints into Fiacre Programs

This section presents the concepts of Fiacre programs and the translation principles of CCSL constraints into Fiacre programs. These principles have been implemented in our code generator.

5.1 The Fiacre Language

The Fiacre language (*Intermediate Format for the Architectures of Distributed Embedded Components*) has been developed within the TOPCASED project[2] as a key language linking high-level formalisms such as UML, AADL and SDL with formal analysis tools. Using an intermediary formal language has the advantage of reducing the semantic gap between the high-level formalisms and the descriptions internally manipulated by verification tools such as Petri nets, process algebras or timed automata. Fiacre is a language with a formal semantic that serves as input language for different checking tools. Fiacre allows the behavioral and timed aspects of real-time systems to be described. It integrates the notions of process and components as follows:

- the processes (*process*) describe automata with a set of states and a list of transitions between these states. These later reference classical operations (variable allocations, if-elsif-else, while, sequence compositions), non-deterministic constructions and communications done via ports and via shared variables;
- the components (*component*) describe compositions of processes. A system is built as a parallel composition (clause *par* with the || operator) of components and/or processes that can communicate via ports. The Fiacre processes can be synchronized with or without value passage via the ports. They can also exchange data via asynchronous communication queues using shared variables.

5.2 Translation Principles

The general idea of the translation is based on (1) the generation of a Fiacre *Scheduler* process, (2) the generation of Fiacre processes corresponding to the

---

[2] http://www.topcased.org

CCSL constraints and (3) the generation of Fiacre component. The principles of translating CCSL constraints into Fiacre programs and the generation of *Scheduler* code are inspired by the work described in [YM11]. We suppose here that the active objects of the UML model are generated into Fiacre processes with a translation which is not detailed in this paper.

The role of the *Scheduler* process is to determine the order of execution of functional processes based on the constraint process state. *Scheduler* is in charge of activating each functional process. To do so, *Scheduler*, the constraint processes and the functional processes are all synchronized through (synchronous) communication ports. Figure 4 illustrates partially the generation of code for *Sensor*1, *Acq*1 and the *alternatesWith* constraint. In this figure, we illustrate the synchronization links with dash lines. For example, *Sensor*1 is synchronized with *Scheduler* via the port *sync_pw*1 to execute a writing operation of a given datum *data* in memory $M1$ shared between *Sensor*1 and *Acq*1 processes. *AlternatesWith* process is synchronized with *Scheduler* via the ports *startA*1, *updateA*1 and *endA*1.

*Acq*1 and *Comput* communicate through port *portAcq*1 with a integer value. *Comput* and *Filter* communicate through a shared variable *fifoFromComput* of *fifo* type. *Filter* is synchronized with *Scheduler* via *sync_filter* for filtering operation. *sync_filter* carries a boolean value needed by the *Filter* behavior. The *Scheduler* process and constraint processes share logical clocks (table *tab_Clocks*) that correspond to events occurring in the circuit computation (*write*1, *write*2, *read*1, *read*2, *comput*, *filterOut*). The same translation process is applied to other functional processes *Sensor*2, *Acq*2, *Comput*, *Filter* and the other constraint processes *StricPrec* and *FilteredBy*.

For this case study, we implement the objects Dev_1, Dev_2 and Dev_{out} with the CDL language, because we consider that these objects run in the environment of the circuit[3].

Generation of a Fiacre Component: The Fiacre program includes a component called C (cf Listing 1) that contains the instances of the processes running at the same time (operator ||). As result of generation algorithm execution, the codes of functional processes, constraint processes and Scheduler are generated. The functional processes are generated from active objects of the UML model and correspond to the functional parts of the model.

For automatic code generation is possible, we must declare clock numbers and links between clocks and synchronization triggers generated by *Scheduler*. For example, the clock *read*1 is associated with *sync_pr*1 synchronization port to synchronize the first instance (*Acq:1*) of *Acq* process. The clock *filter* is associated with *sync_filter* synchronization port which carries a boolean value. For this last constraint, in our implementation, we need two indices in the table *tab_Clocks*. These attributes are specified as follows:

---

[3] The description of CDL language can be found at http://www.obpcdl.org

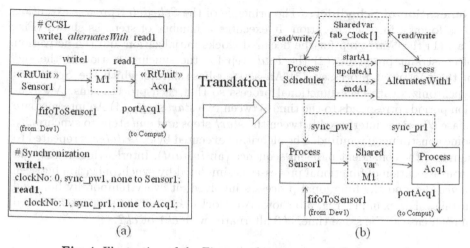

Fig. 4. Illustration of the Fiacre architecture partially generated

```
# Synchronization
write1: clockNo: 0, synchro: sync_pw1 none  to:  Sensor:1;
read1:  clockNo: 1, synchro: sync_pr1 none  to:  Acq:1;
write2: clockNo: 2, synchro: sync_pw2 none  to:  Sensor:2;
read2:  clockNo: 3, synchro: sync_pr2 none  to:  Acq:2;
comput: clockNo: 4, synchro: sync_comput none  to: Comput:1,
filterOut: clockNo: 5, synchro: sync_filter bool:true,
           clockNo: 6, synchro: sync_filter bool:false to: Filter:1;
```

In our case study, the code generator produces 12 processes: *Scheduler*, 5 constraint processes (2 for *alternatesWith*, 2 for *strictPrec*, 1 for *filterBy*) and 6 functional processes (*Sensor1, Sensor2, Acq1, Acq2, Comput* and *Filter*). The Fiacre code of the partial component part is generated as follows[4]:

```
component C is
var write1, read1, ..., M1 : int, tab_Clocks : T_ARRAY_CLOCK,
    fifoToSensor1, fifoFromComput : fifo, ...
port startA1, sync_pr1, sync_pw1, ... : none, portAcq1: int, ...
init write1 := 0; read1 := 1; ...        // clock numbers
par
//-------- Scheduler process ---------
 Scheduler [startA1, ... sync_pr1, sync_pw1, ...] (&tab_Clocks)
 //-------- constraint processes ---------
 || AlternatesWith [startA1, ...](&write1, &read1, &tab_Clocks)
 || ...
//-------- functional processes ---------
 || Sensor1 [sync_pw1] (&fifoToSensor1, &M1)
 || Acq1 [sync_pr1, portAcq1] (&M1)
 || ...
end C
```

Listing 1. Partial generated component program

---

[4] The complete code of the case study can be found on site http://www.obpcdl.org

Generation of Scheduler: The principle of the *Scheduler* process execution is as follows: for each iteration, It executes a number of steps as shown (Fig. 5.a): (1) the *Start* step for the declared clocks initialization and the activation of constraint processes. (2) the *End* step for the synchronization at the end of the constraint processes. (3) An active phase during which the *Scheduler* synchronizes with each functional process so that each process runs. A execution period corresponds to the time between two *start* steps. (4) An intermediate phase *Update* is interposed between the *start* steps and *end* steps to synchronize some constraints if required. The algorithm executed by *Scheduler* is repeated to simulate the coincident moment sequence (an *instant*). Interleaving or simultaneous execution of functional processes is simulated by synchronization between *Scheduler* and the functional processes involved, at every temporally bounded instants. For example, Fig. 5.b shows two clocks *ck*1 and *ck*2 that are activated in each case at the same time. *ck*3 alternates with *ck*1 or *ck*2.

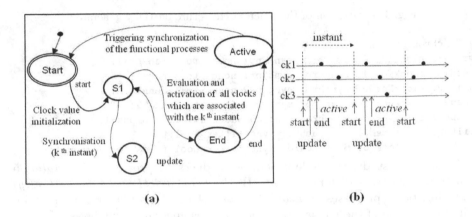

(a)   (b)

Fig. 5. Scheduler process automaton

From the point of view of the Fiacre implementation, and taking into account the Promela program implementation principle described in [YM11], each event in the model gives rise to a *clock* which is located by a Fiacre structure *tab_Clocks*. This structure is declared as follows:

```
type T_CLOCK is record clock_state:nat, enable_tick, dead: bool end
type T_ARRAY_CLOCK is array 7 of T_CLOCK
tab_Clocks: T_ARRAY_CLOCK
```

In each iteration of the *Scheduler*, each constraint process updates value *clock_state* which takes integer values 0, 1 or 2, in accordance with the execution of the automaton it encodes. Once the process has executed a loop constraint, *Scheduler* evaluates these values to set the value *enable_tic* to *true* or *false*. If *enable_tic* is evaluated as *true*, the functional process associated with the event is synchronized with *Scheduler*, which triggers an execution step in the functional process (for example with *sync_pw*1 for triggering *Sensor*1 as shown Fig. 4).

The assessment of the value *enable_tic* is set to *true* only if the *clock_state* value is equal to 2. In other cases, *enable_tic* are set to *false*. The value *dead* is set at *true* when the associated clock should not be active in the rest of the execution.

The generation automatically produces the *Scheduler* code including this part executed during the *Active* step:

```
... if (tab_Clocks [0].enable_tick) then sync_pw1
elsif (tab_Clocks [1].enable_tick) then sync_pr1
elsif (tab_Clocks [2].enable_tick) then sync_pw2
elsif (tab_Clocks [3].enable_tick) then sync_pr2
elsif (tab_Clocks [4].enable_tick) then sync_comput
elsif (tab_Clocks [5].enable_tick) then sync_filter (true)
elsif (tab_Clocks [6].enable_tick) then sync_filter (false)
end ...
```

Translation of Constraints: We implement each CCSL constraint by a Fiacre process that implements the automaton (cf Section 3.1) corresponding to the constraint (we called those processes *constraints processes*). These process are synchronized with *Scheduler* via the port *start*, *update* and *end* for the activation of automaton transitions. For example, we show the code for the *alternatesWith* constraint corresponding to the automaton shown in Fig. 2.b. The transitions of this automaton are triggered by signal ports *startA*, *updateA* and *endA* and update the value of *clock_state*. The encoding principle for the other two constraints, strict precedence and filtering is similar.

```
process AlternatesWith [startA, updateA, endA: in none] // ports
  (&c1: nat, &c2 : nat, &tab_Clocks: T_ARRAY_CLOCK)     // shared variables
is states s1, s2, s3, s4, s5
init to s0
from s0  startA;
  tab_Clocks [c1].clock_state := 2; tab_Clocks [c2].clock_state := 1; to s1
from s1  updateA;  to s2
from s2  endA; to s3
from s3  startA;
  tab_Clocks [c1].clock_state := 1; tab_Clocks [c2].clock_state := 2; to s4
from s4 updateA;  to s5
from s5 endA; to s0
```

6   Formal Verification of Properties

6.1   Verification Principles

To verify a set of requirements on a model, we must explore it exhaustively and have a formal expression of properties to be checked, for example in the form of logical formulas or observer automata. In our approach, we express the properties with CDL language.

Once the observers have been specified, the model is then explored and the exploration generates a labeled transition system (LTS). It represents all the behaviors of the model in its environment as a graph of configurations and transitions. On this LTS, the verification of the properties is carried out by applying a reachability analysis of observer error states.

6.2   Expressing Properties Using CDL

The CDL language allows the user to specify properties which are expressed as predicates or observer automata. Predicates in CDL reference variables values: for example, *predicate pred*1 *is* {{*Proc*}1 : *v* = *value*} means *pred*1 is true if the variable *v* of the first instance of the *Proc* process is equal to the value *value*. A predicate can also reference a process state: for example, *predicate pred*2 *is* {{*Proc*}1@*stateX*} means that *pred*2 is true if the first instance of the *Proc* process is in the state *stateX*. A predicate can also reference the amount of data contained in a *fifo* or a boolean expression combining the previous types of predicates.

This syntax provides a rich mode of expression that together with the observer, enables the expression of properties which would be difficult to express in linear logic (see the P2 observer Fig. 7). The predicates allow insights into the behavior of a model while providing expression which is easy to use and understand for the designer. In our work, we express properties in CDL following two complementary objectives: one to verify that the implementation of CCSL constraints is correct, the other to ensure that the functional parts of the circuit (*Sensor*1, *Sensor*2, *Acq*1, *Acq*2, *Comput*, *Filter*) are properly implemented.

Properties Associated with CCSL Constraints: Here we illustrate the specifications of some properties associated with CCSL constraints included in our system model. The goal is to prove the correct Fiacre implementation of Scheduler and constraint automata. To check a property *P*1 associated with the alternation requirement *Req*1, for example *write*1 *alternatesWith read*1, we declare the CDL events *evt_write*1 and *evt_read*1 (Fig. 6.a). With these events, we specify the observer, illustrated in Fig. 6.b), encoding the property *P*1 which satisfies the alternating synchronization *write*1 and *read*1. The initial state of the observer is the *Start* state and has an error state (*Reject*). Each transition of the observer is triggered by the occurrence of an event (*evt_write*1 or *evt_read*1).

In a similar way, we can specify observers to verify properties of the requirement *Req*2 by declaring the events *evt_read*$_2$ and *evt_comput*:

```
event evt_read2  is  {sync sync_pr1 from {Scheduler}1 to {Sensor}2}
event evt_comput is  {sync sync_comput from {Scheduler}1 to {Comput}1}
```

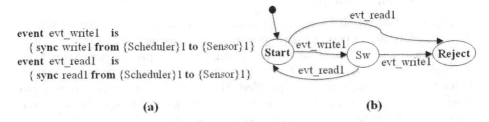

```
event evt_write1  is
  { sync write1 from {Scheduler}1 to {Sensor}1}
event evt_read1   is
  { sync read1 from {Scheduler}1 to {Sensor}1}
```

(a)   (b)

Fig. 6. Observer automaton corresponding to P1 property

The CDL language also allows to specify predicates that can be verified during the exploration of the model. For example, if we want to check that, in an instant, clocks *write*1 and *read*1 do not "tick" at the same instant, we can declare the following predicates:

```
predicate enable_tick_pw1_true is {{C}1:tab_Clocks [0].enable_tick = true}
predicate enable_tick_pr1_true is {{C}1:tab_Clocks [1].enable_tick = true}
predicate enable_tick_rw1_together is
                      {enable_tick_pw1_true and enable_tick_pr1_true}
```

We can now declare, with the operator *assert*[5], the following invariant: *not act_tick_rw1_together*. During the exploration of the model, the OBP tool checks that the invariant is not violated.

The CDL predicates can also facilitate the writing of more complex observers when they refer to a large number of events. For example, the requirement *Req*3 associated with the generation of *data* by *Comput* and the filtering constraint is expressed by the CCSL term: $filterOut = comput\ filteredBy\ (001)^w$. During the exploration, we need to verify that the sequence of data generated from *Filter* is the sequence generated by *Comput* with a sampling of one value in 3. In the current version of the model, the filter word (001) is stored in an array variable *tabFilter* of the constraint process *FilteredBy*. The $(i\ modulo\ 3)^{th}$ datum of the sequence generated by *Comput* will be copied in the sequence derived from *Filter* if the value *tabFilter*[*i modulo* 3] is equal to 1. Otherwise, it is not copied into the sequence of data supplied to the environment. To verify this constraint, we therefore declare the following predicates (for $x \in \{0, 1, 2\}$):

```
predicate bitx_true  is {{FilteredBy}1:tabFilter[x] = 1}
predicate bitx_false is {{FilteredBy}1:tabFilter[x] = 0}
```

Transitions of an observer can be decorated with one of the predicates together with the events *evt_comput*, *evt_filterTrue* and *evt_filterFalse* which trigger the transitions of the observer and they are declared as follows:

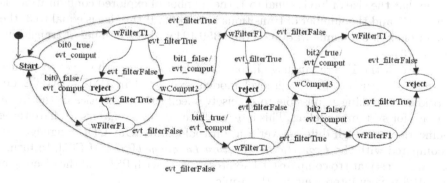

Fig. 7. Observer automaton corresponding to the P2 property

[5] See detailed syntax of the CDL language available at http://www.obpcdl.org

```
event evt_filterTrue  is {sync filter (true)  from {Scheduler}1 to {Filter}1}
event evt_filterFalse is {sync filter (false) from {Scheduler}1 to {Filter}1}
```

Figure 7 illustrates the observer encoding property $P2$ and referencing the above predicates and events.

If we want to verify other properties on the functional parts of our model, we specify these properties which characterize the behavior of the model. For example, the $Req4$ requirement, expressed in Section 4, can be expressed by an observer automaton using predicates and appropriate events.

7   Experimentation on the Case Study and Discussion

To conduct the experiments, we implemented the OBP tool (Fig. 1). OBP is structured in three modules. The *front end* OBP imports Fiacre models corresponding to a translation of UML-MARTE models including CCSL specifications. In addition, it imports CDL programs which describe the properties and context scenarios if required. *OBP Explorer* explores the model, and after each transition model run, it hands over to the *Observation Engine*. It captures the occurrences of events and evaluates, at each step of the running model, the value of predicates and the status of all involved observers. A verification of all invariants and reachability analysis of error state observers is thus conducted.

At the end of exploration, a report is generated by OBP, revealing the list of property evaluated to true or false. Also, OBP provides either counter examples on request on the *reject* or *success* observer state accessibility or invariant violations. These indications may refer the user to the scenario having the defeated properties. We are currently working to facilitate the interpretation of data provided by OBP and to display understandable data in the user's models, allowing ease of diagnosis.

With CDL, we specified observers to verify different properties concerning requirements ($Req1$ to $Req4$) expressed in Section 4. For this proposed case study, the complexity of exploration[6] is reasonable size. As an example, if we assume that the size of fifo is equal to 1, the number of explored configurations is then 45 040 and the number of transitions is 167 496. If the size is equal to 3, the number of explored configurations is then 359 104 and the number of transitions is 1 702 704.

The use of the Fiacre language in our translation approach serves to reduce the semantic gap between high-level models expressed in UML MARTE description, by making it possible to precisely specify the semantics of the input language for system modeling. This intermediate language enables to share these specifications through different verification tool-chains. Our CDL language can be compared with the *Property Specification Language* (PSL) [IEE05]. In future work, we investigate to compare CDL expressiveness with PSL and the discussion in [Mal12] is very interesting for this topic.

---

[6] The tests are run on a machine such as Windows 7, 64-bit - 4 GB RAM with OBP v.1.3.4.

8   Conclusion

In this work, we have presented an implementation of CCSL constraints in the Fiacre language and we expressed properties in the CDL language. The manipulation of CCSL expressions within the framework of modeling with UML-MARTE formalism can extend the expressiveness by integrating temporal constraints into the model. The logical time model proposed by the OMG to enrich the UML MARTE allows the description and analysis of temporal constraints. We have defined a automatic translation approach to generate Fiacre programs from UML-MARTE models enriched with CCSL constraints. This approach allows to verify formally the implementation of CCSL constraints and functional requirements.

We carried out a verification technique of properties by model-checking using the CDL language and the OBP tool. CDL can easily express predicates and observers which are checked during the exhaustive model exploration by OBP. We have shown that this language facilitates the expression of properties. They can be expressed with a very fine granularity, referencing variables and process states.

We can take benefits of the CCSL automata encoding. These automata are as reusable inputs to apply the verification. Our translation approach can be an important step toward the formal verification process of both MARTE models and CCSL specifications. Once the translation of CCSL constraints into Fiacre is complete, the operation requires only a single verification as it does not depend on the modeled application. Even though the model may change, the Fiacre code is reusable as this translation principle is independent of the application. We think that our approach contributes to clarify its role when addressing this domain by expressing temporal properties dedicated to CCSL relation constraints.

Acknowledgment. We wish to thank Dr Zoé Drey for her valuable and constructive suggestions related to this paper.

References

[And09]   André, C.: Syntax and semantics of the clock constraint specification language ccsl. Technical Report 6925, INRIA (2009)

[And10]   André, C.: Verification of clock constraints: Ccsl observers in esterel. Technical Report 7211, INRIA (2010)

[CES86]   Clarke, E.M., Emerson, E.A., Sistla, A.P.: Automatic verification of finite-state concurrent systems using temporal logic specifications. ACM Trans. Program. Lang. Syst. 8(2), 244–263 (1986)

[DBRL12]   Dhaussy, P., Boniol, F., Roger, J.-C., Leroux, L.: Improving model checking with context modelling. In: Advances in Software Engineering, ID 547157, 13 pages (2012)

[DMA08]   DeAntoni, J., Mallet, F., André, C.: Timesquare: on the formal execution of uml and dsl models. In: Tool Session of the 4th Model Driven Development for Distributed Real Time Systems (2008)

[FGP+08] Farail, P., Gaufillet, P., Peres, F., Bodeveix, J.-P., Filali, M., Berthomieu, B., Rodrigo, S., Vernadat, F., Garavel, H., Lang, F.: FIACRE: an intermediate language for model verification in the TOPCASED environment. In: European Congress on Embedded Real-Time Software (ERTS), Toulouse. SEE (January 2008)

[HLR93]   Halbwachs, N., Lagnier, F., Raymond, P.: Synchronous observers and the verification of reactive systems. In: Nivat, M., Rattray, C., Rus, T., Scollo, G. (eds.) Third Int. Conf. on Algebraic Methodology and Software Technology, AMAST 1993, Twente. Workshops in Computing, pp. 83–96. Springer Verlag (June 1993)

[IEE05]   IEEE. IEEE standard for property specification language (psl). Technical Report 1850 (2005)

[Mal12]   Mallet, F.: Automatic Generation of Observers from MARTE/CCSL. In: RSP 2012 - International Symposium on Rapid System Prototyping, Tampere, Finlande, pp. 86–92. IEEE (October 2012)

[MAS08]   Mallet, F., André, C., De Simone, R.: Ccsl: Specifying clock constraints with uml/marte. ISSE 4, 309–314 (2008)

[OMG10]   OMG. Uml profile for marte, v1.1. Object Managment Group, Document number: PTC/10-08-32 (August 2010)

[QS82]   Queille, J.-P., Sifakis, J.: Specification and verification of concurrent systems in CESAR. In: Dezani-Ciancaglini, M., Montanari, U. (eds.) Programming 1982. LNCS, vol. 137, pp. 337–351. Springer, Heidelberg (1982)

[YM11]   Yin, L., Mallet, F.: Correct transformation from ccsl to promela for verification. Technical Report 7491, INRIA (2011)

[YTB+11] Yu, H., Talpin, J.-P., Besnard, L., Gautier, T., Marchand, H., Le Guernic, P.: Polychronous controller synthesis from marte ccsl timing specifications. In: Memocode (2011)

Real-Time Migration Properties of rTiMo Verified in UPPAAL

Bogdan Aman and Gabriel Ciobanu

Romanian Academy, Institute of Computer Science
Blvd. Carol I no.11, 700506 Iaşi, Romania
baman@iit.tuiasi.ro, gabriel@info.uaic.ro

Abstract. This paper extends the TiMo family by introducing a real-time version named rTiMo. The rTiMo processes are able to move between different locations of a distributed environment, and communicate locally with other processes. Real-time constraints are used to control migration and communication in a real-time distributed system. In order to verify several properties of complex mobile systems described in rTiMo, we establish a relationship between rTiMo networks and a class of timed safety automata. The relationship allows the verification of temporal properties of real-time migrating processes using UPPAAL capabilities. In particular, we check whether certain configurations are reached, and that certain timing constraints hold for an entire complex evolution.

1 Introduction

A rather simple and expressive formalism called TiMo was previously introduced in [8] in order to describe complex distributed systems in which processes are able to migrate within an environment defined by a number of explicit locations. Processes are active entities that can move from location to location to meet and communicate with other processes rather than using the client/server method (various types of communication are presented in [4]). Each process has its own agenda and hence initiates and controls its interactions according to its needs and goals. Timing constraints are used to coordinate interactions in time and space by using migration and communication [9]. Timing constraints for migration allow one to specify a temporal interval after which a mobile process must move to another location. Two processes may communicate if they are present at the same location. Inspired by TiMo, a flexible software platform supporting the specification of agents and allowing timed migration in a distributed environment is presented in [7]. We have enriched this basic formalism with access permissions by using a type system [10]. More information on the TiMo family is available at iit.iit.tuiasi.ro/~fml/TiMo.

This paper is devoted to a real-time extension of TiMo named rTiMo, a calculus in which a global clock is used for the dynamic evolution of the whole system. In rTiMo, the discrete transitions caused by performing actions with timeouts are alternated with continuous transitions. Although the syntax of rTiMo is close to that of TiMo [10], their semantics are different. The number of semantic rules in rTiMo is higher than in TiMo. Other differences between rTiMo and TiMo are:

R.M. Hierons, M.G. Merayo, and M. Bravetti (Eds.): SEFM 2013, LNCS 8137, pp. 31–45, 2013.

- *action deadline* in rTIMO is a real positive number, while in TIMO it is a positive natural number;
- *clock* in rTIMO is a single global clock, while in TIMO there is a local clock for each location;
- *time step* in rTIMO can have any length, while in TIMO it has length 1 (at each location);
- *passage of time* in rTIMO is performed by delay rules, in contrast with TIMO where in each location l there is a local function ϕ_l that is used to decrement all timers by 1 at location l;
- *evolution step* in rTIMO is a sequence of individual actions followed by the passing of time, in contrast with TIMO where an evolution step is a sequence of individual actions happening at the same location l, followed by the passing of time and elimination of all special symbols ⑤ at location l (⑤ is a purely technical notation used in the formalisation of the structural operational semantics of TIMO; intuitively, ⑤P specifies a process P that is temporarily stalled and so cannot execute any action).

The semantics of rTIMO is provided by multiset labelled transitions in which multisets indicate the actions executed in parallel. In order to illustrate the coordination in time and space of a migrating process in rTIMO, we adapt the *TravelShop* example used in [9] where the clients buy tickets to predefined destinations from some travel agents. Since time is an important issue, it was studied in various papers [11,13]. Within rTIMO we investigate the possibility of verifying certain interesting real-time properties such as safety properties (a specified error cannot occur) and bounded liveness properties (configuration reachability within a certain amount of time). The development of effective techniques and tools is required by the automated analysis and verification of complex distributed systems. We establish a formal relationship between rTIMO and timed safety automata [15], allowing the use of the model checking capabilities of the software tool UPPAAL [17] to verify several temporal properties of distributed networks with migrating and communicating processes described in rTIMO.

2   Syntax and Semantics of rTIMO

The syntax of rTIMO is given in Table 1, where we assume:

- a set *Loc* of locations, a set *Chan* of communication channels, and a set *Id* of process identifiers (each $id \in Id$ has its arity m_{id});
- for each $id \in Id$ there is a unique process definition $id(u_1, \ldots, u_{m_{id}}) \overset{def}{=} P_{id}$, where the distinct variables u_i are parameters;
- $a \in Chan$ is a communication channel; l is a location or a location variable;
- $t \in \mathbb{R}_+$ is a *timeout* (deadline) of an action; u is a tuple of variables;
- v is a tuple of expressions built from values, variables and allowed operations.

Timing constraints applied to migrating processes allow one to specify how many time units are required by a process to move from one location to another.

A timer in rTiMo is denoted by $^{\Delta 3}$. When it is associated with a migration process $go^{\Delta 3}shop$ then P, it indicates that process P moves to location $shop$ after 3 time units. A timer $^{\Delta 5}$ associated with an output process $a^{\Delta 5}!\langle z \rangle$ then P else Q makes the channel a available for communication, namely it can send z for a period of 5 time units. It is also possible to restrict the waiting time for an input process $a^{\Delta 4}?(x)$ then P else Q along a channel a; if the communication does not happen before the deadline 4, the waiting process gives up and it switches to the alternative process Q.

Table 1. rTiMo Syntax

Processes	P, Q	$::= a^{\Delta t}!\langle v \rangle$ then P else Q |	(output)
		$a^{\Delta t}?(u)$ then P else Q |	(input)
		$go^{\Delta t}l$ then P |	(move)
		0 |	(termination)
		$id(v)$	(recursion)
		$P \mid Q$ |	(parallel)
Located processes	L	$::= l[[P]]$	
Networks	N	$::= L \mid L \mid N$	

The only variable binding constructor is $a^{\Delta t}?(u)$ then P else Q which binds the variable u within P (but *not* within Q). We use $fv(P)$ to denote the free variables of a process P (and similarly for networks); for a process definition, we assume that $fv(P_{id}) \subseteq \{u_1, \ldots, u_{m_{id}}\}$, where u_i are the process parameters. Processes are defined up-to an alpha-conversion, and $\{v/u, \ldots\}P$ denotes P in which all free occurrences of a variable u are replaced by v, possible after alpha-converting P in order to avoid clashes.

Mobility is provided by a process $go^{\Delta t}l$ then P that describes the migration from the current location to the location indicated by l within t time units. Since l can be a variable, and so its value is assigned dynamically through communication with other processes, this form of migration supports a flexible scheme for the movement of processes from one location to another. Thus, the behaviour can adapt to various changes of the distributed environment. Processes are further constructed from the (terminated) process 0, and parallel composition $P \mid Q$. A located process $l[[P]]$ specifies a process P running at location l, and a network is built from its components $N \mid N'$. A network N is well-formed if there are no free variables in N.

The first component of the operational semantics of rTiMo is the structural equivalence $\equiv$ on networks; it is the smallest congruence such that the equalities in Table 2 hold.

Table 2. rTiMo Structural Congruence

(NNULL)	$N \mid 0 \equiv N$
(NCOMM)	$N \mid N' \equiv N' \mid N$
(NASSOC)	$(N \mid N') \mid N'' \equiv N \mid (N' \mid N'')$
(NSPLIT)	$l[[P \mid Q]] \equiv l[[P]] \mid l[[Q]]$

The role of $\equiv$ is to rearrange a network in order to apply the rules of the operational semantics given in Table 3. Using the equalities of Table 2, a given network N can always be transformed into a finite parallel composition of located processes of the form $l_1[[P_1]] \mid \cdots \mid l_n[[P_n]]$ such that no process P_i has the parallel composition operator at its topmost level. Each located process $l_i[[P_i]]$ is called a component of N, and the whole expression $l_1[[P_1]] \mid \cdots \mid l_n[[P_n]]$ is called a *component decomposition* of the network N.

The semantics of rTiMo is presented in Table 3. The multiset labelled transitions of form $N \xrightarrow{\Lambda} N'$ use a multiset Λ to indicate the actions executed in parallel in one step. When the multiset Λ contains only one action λ, in order to simplify the syntax, we write $N \xrightarrow{\lambda} N'$. The transitions of form $N \overset{t}{\leadsto} N'$ represent a time step of length t.

In rule (Move0), the process $go^{\Delta t}l$ then P migrates from location l to l' and evolves as process P. In rule (Com), a process $a^{\Delta t}!\langle v \rangle$ then P else Q, from location l, succeeds in sending a tuple of values v over channel a to process $a^{\Delta t}?(u)$ then P' else Q' from location l. Both processes continue to execute at location l, the first one as P and the second one as $\{v/u\}P'$. If a communication action has a timer equal to 0, then by using the rule (Put0) for output action or the rule (Get0) for input action, the process $a^{\Delta 0} *$ then P else Q, for $* \in \{!\langle v \rangle, ?(x)\}$ continues as the alternative process Q. Rule (Call) simulates the evolution of a recursion process. The rules (Equiv) and (DEquiv) are used to rearrange a network in order to apply a rule. Rule (Par) is used to compose larger networks from smaller ones by putting them in parallel and considering the union of multisets of actions.

The rules devoted to the passing of time are starting with D. In rule (DPar), $N_1 \mid N_2 \not\xrightarrow{\lambda}$ means that no action λ (i.e, an action labelled by $l' \triangleright l$, $\{v/u\}@l$, $id@l$, $go^{\Delta 0}@l$, $a?^{\Delta 0}@l$ or $a!^{\Delta 0}@l$) can be applied to the network $N_1 \mid N_2$ (obtained using (Par) rules). We use negative premises: the passing to a new step is performed based on the absence of actions. According to [12], our semantics allows the use of negative premises without leading to an inconsistent set of rules.

A complete computational step is captured by a derivation of the form:

$$N \xrightarrow{\Lambda} N_1 \overset{t}{\leadsto} N'.$$

This means that a derivation is a sequence of individual actions followed by a time step. We say that N' is directly reachable from N. If there is no applicable action, we write $N \overset{t}{\leadsto} N'$ to indicate time progress.

The first item of the following proposition states that the passage of time does not introduce any nondeterminism into the execution of a process. Also, if a process is able to evolve to a certain time t, then it must evolve through every time moment before t; this means that the process evolves continuously.

Proposition 1. *For any networks N, N' and N'', the following sentences hold:*

1. *$N \overset{0}{\leadsto} N$;*
2. *If $N \overset{t}{\leadsto} N'$ and $N \overset{t}{\leadsto} N''$, then $N' \equiv N''$;*
3. *$N \overset{(t+t')}{\leadsto} N'$ if and only if there is a N'' such that $N \overset{t}{\leadsto} N''$ and $N'' \overset{t'}{\leadsto} N'$.*

Table 3. rTiMo Operational Semantics

(STOP) $\quad l[[0]] \not\xrightarrow{\;\;}$ $\qquad$ (DSTOP) $\quad l[[0]] \overset{t}{\rightsquigarrow} l[[0]]$

(DMOVE)
$$\frac{t \geq t' \geq 0}{l[[go^{\Delta t} l' \text{ then } P]] \overset{t'}{\rightsquigarrow} l[[go^{\Delta t - t'} l' \text{ then } P]]}$$

(MOVE0)
$$l[[go^{\Delta 0} l' \text{ then } P]] \xrightarrow{l \triangleright l'} l'[[P]]$$

(COM) $\quad l[[a^{\Delta t}!\langle v \rangle \text{ then } P \text{ else } Q \mid a^{\Delta t'}?(u) \text{ then } P' \text{ else } Q']] \xrightarrow{\{v/u\}@l} l[[P \mid \{v/u\}P']]$

(DPUT)
$$\frac{t \geq t' \geq 0}{l[[a^{\Delta t}!\langle v \rangle \text{ then } P \text{ else } Q]] \overset{t'}{\rightsquigarrow} l[[a^{\Delta t - t'}!\langle v \rangle \text{ then } P \text{ else } Q]]}$$

(PUT0)
$$l[[a^{\Delta 0}!\langle v \rangle \text{ then } P \text{ else } Q]] \xrightarrow{a!^{\Delta 0}@l} l[[Q]]$$

(DGET)
$$\frac{t \geq t' \geq 0}{l[[a^{\Delta t}?(u) \text{ then } P \text{ else } Q]] \overset{t'}{\rightsquigarrow} l[[a^{\wedge t - t'}?(u) \text{ then } P \text{ else } Q]]}$$

(GET0)
$$l[[a^{\Delta 0}?(u) \text{ then } P \text{ else } Q]] \xrightarrow{a?^{\Delta 0}@l} l[[Q]]$$

(DCALL)
$$\frac{l[[P_{id}\{v/x\}]] \overset{t}{\rightsquigarrow} l[[P'_{id}]]}{l[[id(v)]] \overset{t}{\rightsquigarrow} l[[P'_{id}]]} \text{ where } id(v) \overset{def}{=} P_{id}$$

(CALL)
$$\frac{l[[P_{id}\{v/x\}]] \overset{\Lambda}{\rightarrow} l[[P'_{id}]]}{l[[id(v)]] \overset{\Lambda}{\rightarrow} l[[P'_{id}]]} \text{ where } id(v) \overset{def}{=} P_{id}$$

(DPAR)
$$\frac{N_1 \overset{t}{\rightsquigarrow} N'_1 \qquad N_2 \overset{t}{\rightsquigarrow} N'_2 \qquad N_1 \mid N_2 \not\xrightarrow{\;\;}}{N_1 \mid N_2 \overset{t}{\rightsquigarrow} N'_1 \mid N'_2}$$

(PAR)
$$\frac{N_1 \xrightarrow{\Lambda_1} N'_1 \qquad N_2 \xrightarrow{\Lambda_2} N'_2}{N_1 \mid N_2 \xrightarrow{\Lambda_1 \cup \Lambda_2} N'_1 \mid N'_2}$$

(DEQUIV)
$$\frac{N \equiv N' \qquad N' \overset{t}{\rightsquigarrow} N'' \qquad N'' \equiv N'''}{N \overset{t}{\rightsquigarrow} N'''}$$

(EQUIV)
$$\frac{N \equiv N' \qquad N' \overset{\Lambda}{\rightarrow} N'' \qquad N'' \equiv N'''}{N \overset{\Lambda}{\rightarrow} N'''}$$

Example 1. We adapt the *TravelShop* example of [9] in which a client attempts to get a ticket to a predefined destination in a short time and at a good price. The scenario involves five locations and six processes.

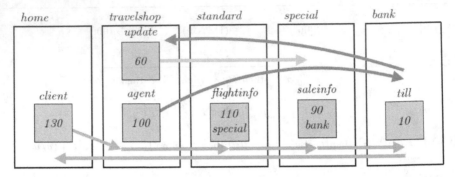

Fig. 1. The initial network indicates the migration paths of the processes [9]

The role of each process represented in Figure 1 is as follows:

- *client* is a process that initially resides in the *home* location, has an amount of 130 cash, and intends to pay for a flight after comparing two offers (standard and special) provided by the travel shop. After entering the *travelshop* location, the *client* receives the location of the standard offer where it should move to obtain this standard offer, and also the location where a special offer can be obtained. Then, it moves to the *special* location to receive the special offer. Finally, the *client* moves to the bank, pays for the special (cheaper) offer, and returns to the *home* location.
- *agent* is a process that initially resides in the *travelshop* location, has an amount of 100 cash, and informs the *client* where to look for the standard offer. It then moves to the *bank* in order to collect the money from the *till*. After that, the *agent* returns to the *travelshop*.
- *flightinfo* communicates the *standard* offer (110 cash) to clients as well as the location (*special*) of the *special* offer.
- *saleinfo* communicates the *special* offer (90 cash) to clients together with the location (*bank*) of the bank. It can also accept an update of the special offer coming from the *travelshop* location.
- *update* migrates from the *travelshop* to the *special* location in order to update the *special* offer to the amount of 60 cash.
- *till* resides at the *bank* location, has an initial amount of 10 cash, and can either receive e-money paid in by the clients, or transfer the accumulated e-money to the *agent*.

In what follows we use some shorthand notations:
$a!\langle v \rangle \to P$ stands for $a^{\triangle\infty}\langle v \rangle$ then P else 0;
$a?(u) \to P$ stands for $a^{\triangle\infty}(u)$ then P else 0.

The rTiMo syntax of these processes is as follows:

$client(init) = go^{\Delta 5}travelshop \rightarrow flight?(standardoffer) \rightarrow$
  go$^{\Delta 4}standardoffer \rightarrow finfo2?(p1, specialoffer) \rightarrow$
  go$^{\Delta 3}specialoffer \rightarrow sinfo2?(p2, paying) \rightarrow$ go$^{\Delta 6}paying \rightarrow$
  $payc!\langle min\{p1, p2\}\rangle \rightarrow$ go$^{\Delta 4}home \rightarrow client(init - min\{p1, p2\})$
$update(saleprice) = go^{\Delta 0}special \rightarrow info1!\langle saleprice\rangle$
$agent(balance) = flight!\langle standard\rangle \rightarrow$ go$^{\Delta 10}bank \rightarrow paya?(profit) \rightarrow$
  go$^{\Delta 12}travelshop \rightarrow agent(balance + profit)$
$flightinfo(price, next) = finfo2!\langle price, next\rangle \rightarrow flightinfo(price, next)$
$saleinfo(price, next) = info1^{\Delta 10}?(newprice)$
  then $saleinfo(newprice, next)$
  else $sinfo2!\langle price, next\rangle \rightarrow saleinfo(price, next)$
$till(cash) = payc^{\Delta 1}?(newpayment)$
  then $till(cash + newpayment)$
  else $paya!\langle cash\rangle!$ then $till(0)$ else $till(cash))$

A possible final network after 22 units of time is represented in Figure 2.

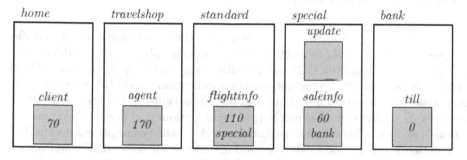

Fig. 2. A possible final network [9]

3   Timed Safety Automata

Due to their simplicity, timed safety automata have been used by several tools (e.g., Uppaal) for the simulation and verification of timed automata [1].

Syntax. Assume a finite set of real-valued variables $\mathcal{C}$ ranged over by x, y, $\dots$ standing for clocks, and a finite alphabet Σ ranged over by a, b, $\dots$ standing for actions. A clock constraint is a conjunctive formula of constraints of the form $x \sim m$ or $x - y \sim m$, for $x, y \in \mathcal{C}$, $\sim \in \{\leq, <, =, >, \geq\}$, and $m \in \mathbb{N}$. The set of clock constraints, ranged over by g, is denoted by $\mathcal{B}(\mathcal{C})$.

Definition 1. *A* **timed safety automaton** $\mathcal{A}$ *is a tuple* $\langle N, n_0, E, I\rangle$, *where*

- N *is a finite set of nodes;*
- n_0 *is the initial node;*
- $E \subseteq N \times \mathcal{B}(\mathcal{C}) \times \Sigma \times 2^{\mathcal{C}} \times N$ *is the set of edges;*
- $I : N \rightarrow \mathcal{B}(\mathcal{C})$ *assigns invariants to nodes.*

$n \xrightarrow{g,a,r} n'$ *is a shorthand notation for* $\langle n, g, a, r, n'\rangle \in E$. *Node invariants are restricted to constraints of the form:* $x \leq m$ *or* $x < m$ *where* $m \in \mathbb{N}$.

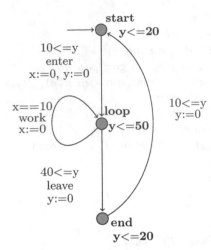

In other words, a timed safety automata is a graph having a finite set of nodes and a finite set of labelled edges (representing transitions), using real-timed variables (representing the clocks of the system). The clocks are initialised with zero when the system starts, and then increased synchronously with the same rate. The behaviour of the automaton is restricted by using clock constraints, i.e. guards on edges, and local timing constraints called *node invariants* (e.g., see Figure 3). An automaton is allowed to stay in a node as long as the timing conditions of that node are satisfied. A transition can be taken when the edge guards are satisfied by clocks values. When a transition is taken, clocks may be reset to zero.

Fig. 3. Timed Safety Automata

Networks of Timed Automata. A network of timed automata is the parallel composition $\mathcal{A}_1 \mid \ldots \mid \mathcal{A}_n$ of a set of timed automata $\mathcal{A}_1, \ldots, \mathcal{A}_n$ combined into a single system using the CCS-like parallel composition operator and with all internal actions hidden. Synchronous communication inside the network is by handshake synchronisation of input and output actions. In this case, the action alphabet Σ consists of $a?$ symbols (for input actions), $a!$ symbols (for output actions), and τ symbols (for internal actions). A detailed example is found in [15].

A network can perform delay transitions (delay for some time), and action transitions (follow an enabled edge). An action transition is enabled if the clock assignment also satisfies all integer guards on the corresponding edges. In synchronisation transitions, the resets on the edge with an output-label are performed before the resets on the edge with an input-label. To model urgent synchronisation transitions that should be taken as soon as they are enabled (the system may not delay), a notion of urgent channels is used. 1-to-many synchronisations are possible using broadcast channels: an edge with synchronisation label $a!$ emits a broadcast and any enabled edge with synchronisation label $a?$ synchronises with the emitting automata.

Let u, v, ... denote clock assignments mapping $\mathcal{C}$ to non-negative reals $\mathbb{R}_+$. Even though u and v and N are overloaded (we keep the initial notations in both formalisms), they are understood according to their context. $g \models u$ means that the clock values u satisfy the guard g. For $d \in \mathbb{R}_+$, the clock assignment mapping all $x \in \mathcal{C}$ to $u(x) + d$ is denoted by $u + d$. Also, for $r \subseteq \mathcal{C}$, the clock assignment mapping all clocks of r to 0 and agreeing with u for the other clocks in $\mathcal{C} \backslash r$ is denoted by $[r \mapsto 0]u$. Let n_i stand for the ith element of a node vector n, and $n[n'_i/n_i]$ for the vector n with n_i being substituted with n'_i.

A network state is a pair $\langle n, u \rangle$, where n denotes a vector of current nodes of the network (one for each automaton), and u is a clock assignment storing the current values of all network clocks and integer variables.

Definition 2. *The operational semantics of a timed automaton is a transition system where states are pairs $\langle n, u \rangle$ and transitions are defined by the rules:*

- $\langle n, u \rangle \xrightarrow{d} \langle n, u + d \rangle$ *if* $u \in I(n)$ *and* $(u + d) \in I(n)$, *where* $I(n) = \bigwedge I(n_i)$;
- $\langle n, u \rangle \xrightarrow{\tau} \langle n[n'_i/n_i], u' \rangle$ *if* $n_i \xrightarrow{g, \tau, r} n'_i$, $g \models u$, $u' = [r \mapsto 0]u$ *and* $u' \in I(n[n'_i/n_i])$;
- $\langle n, u \rangle \xrightarrow{\tau} \langle n[n'_i/n_i][n'_j/n_j], u' \rangle$ *if there exist* $i \neq j$ *such that*
  1. $n_i \xrightarrow{g_i, a?, r_i} n'_i$, $n_j \xrightarrow{g_j, a!, r_j} n'_j$, $g_i \wedge g_j \models u$,
  2. $u' = [r_i \mapsto 0]([r_j \mapsto 0]u)$ *and* $u' \in I(n[n'_i/n_i][n'_j/n_j])$.

4 Relating rTiMo to Timed Safety Automata

In order to use well-known tools such as Uppaal for the verification of distributed networks with migration and communication, we establish a relationship between rTiMo and timed safety automata.

Building a timed safety automaton for each located process: Given a component $l[[P]]$ of an rTiMo network, we associate to it a timed safety automaton $\mathcal{A} = \langle N, n_0, E, I \rangle$ with a local clock x, where $n_0 = l_0$, $N = \{l_0\}$, $E = \emptyset$, $I = \emptyset$. The nodes of the associated automata are labelled using the current location of the located process P (l in this case), and an index such that the nodes are uniquely labelled in this automaton (we start with the index 0, and increment it when necessary). Thus, l_0 means that we model a located process running at location l in rTiMo. The components N, E and I are updated depending on the structure of process P:

- for $P = a^{\Delta t}!\langle v \rangle$ then P_1 else P'_1 we have
  - $N = N \cup \{l_{i+1}, l_{i+2}\}$;
    * If P is running at location l, and N contains some indexed nodes l, namely $l_0, \ldots, l_i$ then add l_{i+1} and l_{i+2} to N. The two nodes indicate the two executions of the located process P, leading to either P_1 or P'_1.
  - $E = E \cup \{n, x < t, a!, x = 0, l_{i+1}\} \cup \{n, x == t, \tau, x = 0, l_{i+2}\}$;
    * If process P is running at location l, and $i > 0$ it means that the automaton already contains some edges, and a process P was launched from the then or else branch of a process P'. Since the translation is made depending on the structure of the processes, it means that the action leading to P is already modelled in the automaton. If $P' = b^{\Delta t'}!\langle w \rangle$ then P else P'' or $P' = b^{\Delta t'}!\langle w \rangle$ then P'' else P or $P' = b^{\Delta t'}?(x)$ then P else P'' or $P' = b^{\Delta t'}?(x)$ then P'' else P or $P' = go^{\Delta t'} l$ then P, then the action of P' is modelled by an edge with the last component l_k, and thus $n = l_k$.

      * Otherwise, $n = l_0$.

The edge $\{n, x < t, a!, x = 0, l'_{i+1}\}$ encodes the then branch leading to process P_1, while the edge $\{n, x == t, \tau, x = 0, l_{i+2}\}$ encodes the else branch leading to process P'_1. Channel a is an urgent channel (communication takes place as soon as possible).

- $I(n) = \{x <= t\}$.
  * The process should communicate before a maximum of t units of time have elapsed.
- for $P = a^{\Delta t}?(y)$ then P_1 else P'_1 we have
  - $N = N \cup \{l_{i+1}, l_{i+2}\}$;
    * If P is running at location l, and N contains some indexed nodes l (namely $l_0, \ldots, l_i$), then add l_{i+1} and l_{i+2} to N. The two nodes indicate the two executions of the located process P, leading either to P_1 or P'_1.
  - $E = E \cup \{n, x < t, a?, \{x = 0, y = v\}, l_{i+1}\} \cup \{n, x == t, \tau, x = 0, l_{i+2}\}$;
    * If process P is running at location l and $i > 0$, using a similar argument as for the output action, it holds that $n = l_k$.
    * Otherwise, $n = l_0$.

The edge $\{n, x < t, a?, \{x = 0, y = v\}, l'_{i+1}\}$ encodes the then branch leading to process P_1, while the edge $\{n, x == t, \tau, x = 0, l_{i+2}\}$ encodes the else branch leading to process P'_1. In order to use an assignment $y = v$ on the edge with $a?$, we impose the condition that channel a can be used at most once for output actions in the translated rTiMo network. This requirement reflects somehow the global asynchronicity of distributed systems (as it is described formally in process calculi).

- $I(n) = \{x <= t\}$.
  * The process should communicate before a maximum of t units of time have elapsed.
- for $P = go^{\Delta t}l'$ then P' we have
  - $N = N \cup \{l'_j\}$;
    * If N contains indexed nodes l' (namely $l'_0, \ldots, l'_{j-1}$), then add l'_j to N.
    * Otherwise, add l'_0 to N.

The new node indicates the execution of process P leading to P'.

  - $E = E \cup \{n, x == t, \tau, x = 0, l'_j\}$;
    * If process P is running at location l and $i > 0$, using a similar argument as for the communication actions, it holds that $n = l_k$.
    * Otherwise, $n = l_0$.
  - $I(n) = \{x <= t\}$.
    * The process should leave location n before a maximum of t units of time have elapsed.
- for $P = 0$ we have
  - N, E and I remain unchanged, and the construction of $\mathcal{A}$ stops.
- for $P = id(v)$ we have
  - N remains the same;

- $E = E \cup \{n, x == 0, \tau, \{x = 0, varid = v\}, l_0\}$;
  * If process P is running at location l and $i > 0$, using a similar argument as for the communication actions, it holds that $n = l_k$.
  * Otherwise, $n = l_0$.
- $I(n) = \{x <= 0\}$.
  * The process should leave location n in maximum of 0 units of time.
- for $P = P_1 | \ldots | P_k, k > 1$, and P_j does not contain operator $|$ at top level, then
  - $N = N \cup \{l_{i+1}\}$;
    * If P is running at location l, and N contains some indexed nodes l (namely $l_0, \ldots, l_i$), then add l_{i+1} to N.
  - $E = E \cup \{n, , a!, \{x = 0\}, l_{i+1}\}$;
    * If process P is running at location l and $i > 0$, using a similar argument as for the communication actions, it holds that $n = l_k$. We use a new channel labelled a as a broadcast channel, in order to start at the same time all the parallel processes from P.
    * Otherwise, $n = l_0$.
    The new edge leads to process P_1. For each of the other processes P_j, $j > 1$, a new automaton $\mathcal{A}_j = \langle N_j, n_{j0}, E_j, I_j \rangle$ is constructed, where:
    * $n_{j0} = l_0$; $N_j = \{l_0, l_1\}$; $E_j = \{l_0, , a?, \{x = 0\}, l_1\}$; $I_j(l_0) = \emptyset$.
    This automaton is constructed then recursively using the definition of P_j.
  - $I(n) = \{x <= 0\}$.
    * The process has to communicate in maximum of 0 units of time.

Building a timed automaton for each located process leads to the next result about the equivalence between an rTiMo network N and its corresponding timed safety automaton $\mathcal{A}_N$ in state $\langle n_N, u_N \rangle$ (i.e., $(\mathcal{A}_N, \langle n_N, u_N \rangle)$). Their transition systems differ not only in transitions, but also in states; thus, we adapt the notion of bisimilarity:

Definition 3. *A symmetric relation $\sim$ over TiMo networks and the timed safety automata, is a bisimulation if whenever $(N, (\mathcal{A}_N, \langle n_N, u_N \rangle)) \in \sim$:*

- *if $N \xrightarrow{\lambda} N'$, then $\langle n_N, u_N \rangle \xrightarrow{\tau} \langle n_{N'}, u_{N'} \rangle$ and $(N', (\mathcal{A}_{N'}, \langle n_{N'}, u_{N'} \rangle)) \in \sim$ for some N'.*
- *if $N \xrightarrow{t} N'$, then $\langle n_N, u_N \rangle \xrightarrow{d} \langle n_{N'}, u_{N'} \rangle$ and $(N', (\mathcal{A}_{N'}, \langle n_{N'}, u_{N'} \rangle)) \in \sim$ for some N', where $u_{N'} = u_N + d$.*

Having defined bisimulation, we can state our main theorem as follows.

Theorem 1. *Given an rTiMo network N with channels appearing only once in output actions, there exists a timed safety automaton $\mathcal{A}_N$ with a bisimilar behaviour. Formally, $N \sim \mathcal{A}_N$.*

Proof (Sketch). The construction of the timed safety automaton simulating a given rTiMo network is presented above. Due to the limitations of Uppaal, we imposed the requirement of using at most once an output actions in order to allow the assignment $y = v$ on edges with input labels (as used in the building of the automaton).

A bisimilar behaviour is given by:

- at the start of execution, all clock in rTiMo and their corresponding timed automata are set to 0;
- the consumption of a *go* action in a node l_i is matched by an τ edge obtained by translation;
- a communication rule is matched by a synchronisation between the edges obtained by translations;
- the passage of time is similar in both formalisms: in rTiMo the global clock is used to decrement by d all timers in the network when no action is possible, while in the timed automata all local clocks are decremented synchronously with the same value d when no edge can be taken.

Thus, the size of a timed safety automata $\mathcal{A}_N$ is polynomial with respect to the size of a TiMo network N, and the state spaces have the same number of states.

Reachability Analysis. One of the most useful question to ask about a timed automaton is the reachability of a given set of final states. Such final states may be used to characterise safety properties of a system.

Definition 4. *We write* $\langle n, u \rangle \to \langle n', u' \rangle$ *whenever* $\langle n, u \rangle \xrightarrow{\sigma} \langle n', u' \rangle$ *for* $\sigma \in \Sigma \cup \mathbb{R}_+$. *For an automaton with initial state* $\langle n_0, u_0 \rangle$, $\langle n, u \rangle$ *is reachable if and only if* $\langle n_0, u_0 \rangle \to^* \langle n, u \rangle$. *More generally, given a constraint* $\phi \in \mathcal{B}(\mathcal{C})$ *if* $\langle n, u \rangle$ *is reachable for some* u *satisfying* ϕ *then a state* $\langle n, \phi \rangle$ *is reachable.*

Invariant properties can be specified using clock constraints in combination with local properties on nodes. The reachability problem is decidable [5].

The reachability problem can be also defined for rTiMo networks.

Definition 5. *We write* $N \to N'$ *if* $N \xrightarrow{\lambda} N'$ *or* $N \xrightarrow{t'} N'$ *for actions* λ *of the form* $l' \triangleright l$, $\{v/u\}@l$, $id@l$, $go^{\Delta 0}@l$, $a?^{\Delta 0}@l$ *or* $a!^{\Delta 0}@l$. *Starting from an rTiMo network* N_0, *a configuration* N_1 *is reachable if and only if* $N_0 \to^* N_1$.

The following result is a consequence of Theorem 1.

Corollary 1. *For an rTiMo network with channels appearing only once in output actions, the reachability problem is decidable.*

Bisimulation. Two timed automata are defined to be timed bisimilar in [5] if and only if they perform the same action transitions and reach bisimilar states.

Definition 6. *A symmetric relation* $\mathcal{R}$ *over the timed automata and the alphabet* $\Sigma \cup \mathbb{R}_+$, *is a bisimulation if:*

- *for all* $(s_1, s_2) \in \mathcal{R}$, *if* $s_1 \xrightarrow{\sigma} s_1'$ *for* $\sigma \in \Sigma \cup \mathbb{R}_+$ *and* s_1', *then* $s_2 \xrightarrow{\sigma} s_2'$ *and* $(s_1', s_2') \in \mathcal{R}$ *for some* s_2'.

Proposition 2. *[6] Timed bisimulation is decidable.*

In a similar way to our previous approach in [2], we define the bisimulation over configurations of rTiMo networks.

Definition 7. *A symmetric relation* $\mathcal{R}$ *over the* rTiMo *networks and the set Act of actions, is a bisimulation if:*

- *for all* $(N_1, N_2) \in \mathcal{R}$*, if* $N_1 \xrightarrow{\lambda} N_1'$ *for* $\lambda \in Act$ *and* N_1'*, then* $N2 \xrightarrow{\lambda} N_2'$ *and* $(N_1', N_2') \in \mathcal{R}$ *for some* N_2'*.*
- *for all* $(N_1, N_2) \in \mathcal{R}$*, if* $N_1 \xrightarrow{t} N_1'$ *for* $t \in \mathbb{N}$ *and* N_1'*, then* $N_2 \xrightarrow{t} N_2'$ *and* $(N_1', N_2') \in \mathcal{R}$ *for some* N_2'*.*

The following result is a consequence of Theorem 1.

Corollary 2. *For two* rTiMo *networks with channels appearing only once in output actions, timed bisimulation is decidable.*

5   Verifying Properties of rTiMo by Using UPPAAL

By virtue of the results presented in the previous section, we can verify real-time systems corresponding to a subclass of rTiMo networks by using UPPAAL. In general, modelling and verification of real-time systems in UPPAAL were presented in [16]. UPPAAL can be used to check temporal properties of networks of timed safety automata, properties expressed in Computation Tree Logic (CTL). If ϕ and ψ are boolean expressions over predicates on nodes, integer variables and clock constraints, then the formulas have the following forms:

A [ ] ϕ - Invariantly ϕ;   A $\langle \, \rangle$ ϕ - Always Eventually ϕ;
E [ ] ϕ - Potentially Always ϕ;   E $\langle \, \rangle$ ϕ - Possibly ϕ;
$\phi \leadsto \psi$ - ϕ always leads to ψ. This is a shorthand for A [ ] $(\phi \Rightarrow$ A $\langle \, \rangle$ $\psi)$
The properties most commonly used in verification of timed systems are E $\langle \, \rangle$ ϕ and A [ ] ϕ. They represent safety properties (a specified error can not occur).

The properties A $\langle \, \rangle$ ϕ, E [ ] ϕ and $\phi \leadsto \psi$ represent unbounded liveness properties (used to express and check global progress), and are not commonly used in UPPAAL case studies. Bounded properties are important for timed systems.

Example 2. Using both types of properties, we performed some verifications in UPPAAL for the system presented in Example 1.

- E[ ]clientcash $<= 0$
  Checks if potentially always on some path *clientcash* $<= 0$ is not satisfied.
- A $<>$ till.bank1 imply till.x $>= 1$
  Checks if the *till* automaton is in the *bank* node, then the value of the local clock is $>= 1$.
- E $<>$ (clientcash $== 70$)&&(agentcash $== 170$)&&(bankcash $== 60$)
  Checks if there exists a state containing the configuration of Figure 2.
- A[ ] not deadlock
  Checks that there exists deadlocks. The error is due to state space explosion.

Several other properties of rTiMo systems can be verified by using UPPAAL.

```
Established direct connection to local server.
(Academic) UPPAAL version 4.0.13 (rev. 4577), September 2010 -- server.
E[] clientcash<=0
Property is not satisfied.
A<> till.bank1 imply till.x>=1
Property is satisfied.
E<> (clientcash==70) && (agentcash==170) && (bankcash==60)
Property is satisfied.
A[] not deadlock
The verification was aborted due to an error.
```

Fig. 4. Verification in UPPAAL

6 Conclusion

When modelling distributed systems it is useful to have explicit notions of locations, clocks, explicit migrations and resource management. Various process calculi derived from π-calculus [18] have been proposed to model some of these aspects. Various features were introduced over the basic π-calculus: e.g., explicit locations in distributed π-calculus [14], and explicit migration and timers in timed distributed π-calculus $(tD\pi)$ [11]. TIMO [8] is essentially a simplified version of $tD\pi$ designed to allow appropriate software architecture for implementation [7]. TIMO represents an attempt to bridge the gap between the existing (theoretical) process calculi and forthcoming realistic languages for multi-agent systems.

Several proposals for real-time modelling and verification are present in the literature: timed automata [1], timed CSP [20], timed ACP [3], and several timed extensions of CCS [19,21]. In this paper we defined a formalism called rTIMO that uses real-time and explicit timeouts, and so is useful for expressing certain temporal properties of multi-agent systems with migration and time constraints. In order to illustrate in rTIMO the coordination of migrating agents in time and space, we adapt the *TravelShop* example from [9] in which a client attempts to get a ticket to a predefined destination in a short time and/or at a good price. Although the syntax of rTIMO is quite close to that of TIMO, its semantics is different in many aspects: the number of semantic rules, number of clocks, time nature (continuous or discrete), systems evolution.

We established a formal relationship between rTIMO and timed safety automata allowing the use of model checking capabilities provided by UPPAAL to verify several temporal properties of distributed networks with migrating and communicating processes described in rTIMO. The verification performed on the *TravelShop* example also validates the rTIMO semantics.

As future work we intend to use this relationship for improvements in rTIMO (e.g., constraints on integers, lower and upper time bounds) in order to extend the classes of complex systems that can be modelled and analysed.

Acknowledgements. Many thanks to the reviewers for their useful comments. The work was supported by a grant of the Romanian National Authority for Scientific Research, project number PN-II-ID-PCE-2011-3-0919.

References

1. Alur, R., Dill, D.L.: A Theory of Timed Automata. Theoretical Computer Science 126, 183–235 (1994)
2. Aman, B., Ciobanu, G., Koutny, M.: Behavioural Equivalences over Migrating Processes with Timers. In: Giese, H., Rosu, G. (eds.) FMOODS/FORTE 2012. LNCS, vol. 7273, pp. 52–66. Springer, Heidelberg (2012)
3. Baeten, J.C.M., Bergstra, J.A.: Real Time Process Algebra. Journal of Formal Aspects of Computing Science 3(2), 142–188 (1991)
4. Baumann, J., Hohl, F., Radouniklis, N., Rothermel, K., Straßer, M.: Communication Concepts for Mobile Agent Systems. In: Rothermel, K., Popescu-Zeletin, R. (eds.) MA 1997. LNCS, vol. 1219, pp. 123–135. Springer, Heidelberg (1997)
5. Bengtsson, J., Yi, W.: Timed Automata: Semantics, Algorithms and Tools. In: Desel, J., Reisig, W., Rozenberg, G. (eds.) ACPN 2003. LNCS, vol. 3098, pp. 87–124. Springer, Heidelberg (2004)
6. Čerāns, K.: Decidability of Bisimulation Equivalences for Parallel Timer Processes. In: Probst, D.K., von Bochmann, G. (eds.) CAV 1992. LNCS, vol. 663, pp. 302–315. Springer, Heidelberg (1993)
7. Ciobanu, G., Juravle, C.: Flexible Software Architecture and Language for Mobile Agents. Concurrency and Computation: Practice and Experience 24, 559–571 (2012)
8. Ciobanu, G., Koutny, M.: Modelling and Verification of Timed Interaction and Migration. In: Fiadeiro, J.L., Inverardi, P. (eds.) FASE 2008. LNCS, vol. 4961, pp. 215–229. Springer, Heidelberg (2008)
9. Ciobanu, G., Koutny, M.: Timed Mobility in Process Algebra and Petri Nets. Journal of Logic and Algebraic Programming 80, 377–391 (2011)
10. Ciobanu, G., Koutny, M.: Timed Migration and Interaction With Access Permissions. In: Butler, M., Schulte, W. (eds.) FM 2011. LNCS, vol. 6664, pp. 293–307. Springer, Heidelberg (2011)
11. Ciobanu, G., Prisacariu, C.: Timers for Distributed Systems. Electronic Notes in Theoretic Computer Science 164(3), 81–99 (2006)
12. Groote, J.F.: Transition System Specifications with Negative Premises. In: Baeten, J.C.M., Klop, J.W. (eds.) CONCUR 1990. LNCS, vol. 458, pp. 332–341. Springer, Heidelberg (1990)
13. Hennessy, M., Regan, T.: A Process Algebra for Timed Systems. Information and Computation 117, 221–239 (1995)
14. Hennessy, M.: A Distributed π-calculus. Cambridge University Press (2007)
15. Henzinger, T.A., Nicollin, X., Sifakis, J., Yovine, S.: Symbolic Model Checking for Real-time Systems. Information and Computation 111, 192–224 (1994)
16. Hessel, A., Larsen, K.G., Mikucionis, M., Nielsen, B., Pettersson, P., Skou, A.: Testing Real-Time Systems Using UPPAAL. In: Hierons, R.M., Bowen, J.P., Harman, M. (eds.) FORTEST. LNCS, vol. 4949, pp. 77–117. Springer, Heidelberg (2008)
17. Larsen, K.G., Petterson, P., Yi, W.: UPPAAL in a Nutshell. International Journal on Software Tools for Technology Transfer 1(2), 134–152 (1997)
18. Milner, R.: Communicating and Mobile Systems: the π-calculus. Cambridge University Press (1999)
19. Moller, F., Tofts, C.: A Temporal Calculus of Communicating Systems. In: Baeten, J.C.M., Klop, J.W. (eds.) CONCUR 1990. LNCS, vol. 458, pp. 401–415. Springer, Heidelberg (1990)
20. Reed, G.M., Roscoe, A.W.: A Timed Model for Communicating Sequential Processes. Theoretical Computer Science 58(1-3), 249–261 (1988)
21. Yi, W., Pettersson, P., Daniels, M.: Automatic Verification of Real-time Communicating Systems by Constraint-solving. In: International Conference on Formal Description Techniques, pp. 223–238 (1994)

A Verified Protocol to Implement Multi-way Synchronisation and Interleaving in CSP

Marcel Vinicius Medeiros Oliveira[1,*], Ivan Soares De Medeiros Júnior[1], and Jim Woodcock[2]

[1] Departamento de Informática e Matemática Aplicada, UFRN, Brazil
[2] Department of Computer Science, University of York, England

Abstract. The complexity of concurrent systems can turn their development into a very complex and error-prone task. The use of formal methods like CSP considerably simplifies this task. Development, however, usually aims at reaching an executable program: a translation into a programming language is still needed and can be challenging. In previous work, we presented a tool, csp2hc, that translates a subset of CSP into Handel-C source code, which can itself be converted to produce files to program FPGAs. This subset restricts parallel composition: multi-synchronisation and interleaving on shared channels are not allowed. In this paper, we present an extension to csp2hc that removes these restrictions. We provide a performance analysis of our code.

Keywords: concurrency, multi-synchronisation, compilation, protocols.

1 Introduction

Concurrent applications are normally complicated since they consist of many components running in parallel. This usually yields to a complex and error-prone development [11]. In order to minimize these problems, formal methods like CSP [11] have been proposed. They are usually process algebras designed for describing and reasoning about synchronisation between processes. Furthermore, phenomena that are exclusive to the concurrent world, like deadlock and livelock, can be much more easily understood and controlled using such formalisms. The tools available for these languages increased their success. For CSP, the model-checker FDR2 [3] provides an automatic check of finite state specifications for correctness and properties like deadlock and divergence freedom. It accepts a machine-processable version of CSP, called CSP_M [11], which combines an ASCII representation with a functional language.

Using CSP, we can describe concurrent systems at various levels of abstraction: specifications, design, and implementation. This allows a stepwise development in a single framework. Nevertheless, a translation into a practical programming language is still needed. In order to minimize this gap, it is better to target languages that directly support the CSP style of concurrency through

---

* Partially supported by INES and CNPq: grants 573964/2008-4 and 560014/2010-4.

R.M. Hierons, M.G. Merayo, and M. Bravetti (Eds.): SEFM 2013, LNCS 8137, pp. 46–60, 2013.

channels, such as occam-2 [5] and Handel-C[1], or packages that add these features such as JCSP [13] for Java, CCSP [6] for C, and C++CSP [2] for C++.

This translation is usually non-trivial and rather problematic. In [9], we presented a methodology for developing verified concurrent applications in which developers: (i) specify the system's concurrent behaviour in CSP and *verify its correctness and further properties* using tools like FDR2; (ii) gradually refine it verifying the correctness of the transformation (again, using tools like FDR2); and finally, (iii) automatically translate the CSP_M implementation into Handel-C code, which can itself be compiled into a Hardware Description Language (HDL) to program Field-Programmable Gate Arrays (FPGAs).

The tool that supports the translation from CSP_M into Handel-C, csp2hc, accepts a subset of CSP_M that includes SKIP, STOP, sequential and parallel composition, recursion, prefixing, external and internal choice, alternation, guarded processes, datatypes, constants, functions, and some expressions. The translation of some of these constructs, however, was restricted. For instance, due to subtle differences in Handel-C's concurrency model, the translation of CSP_M parallel composition into Handel-C's par construct was only possible if: (i) all channels shared by the processes were in the synchronisation set (*e.g.* cs in the definition of sharing parallel composition at Page 48); and (ii) there was no multi-synchronisation (more than two processes synchronising on a given channel). In this paper, we present an approach to remove these restrictions.

Translations of process algebras into programming languages have already been presented. They target different programming languages like occam-2 [5], Ada [1], Java and C. Some of them have no tool support, whilst others have limited tool support. None of them, however, achieved a comprehensive support of CSP parallel composition as we do here. For instance, [4] proposes an automatic translation from CSP# [12] into code. They, however, only consider interleaving: parallel composition and multi-synchronisation are left aside. In [8], we presented a translation strategy from *Circus* [7] to Java. This strategy included the treatment of multi-synchronisation and its basic ideas are used here.

In Section 2, we introduce CSP_M, Handel-C, and the previous version of csp2hc. Section 3 describes the approach to implement CSP model of parallelism in Handel-C. In Section 4, we present a performance analysis of the translation and generated code. Finally, our conclusions and future work are in Section 5.

2   Background

In this section, we describe csp2hc's previous version and the languages involved in the translation focusing on the features used in the context of this paper.

2.1   CSP

CSP is a process algebra that can be used to describe systems composed by interacting components, which are independent self-contained processes with

---

[1] At http://www.mentor.com/products/fpga/handel-c/

```
--!!mainp SYSTEM
--!!int_bits 2
datatype ALPHA = a | b
datatype ID = Lt.ALPHA | unknown
channel enter, leave
channel cash, ticket, change : ID

--!!channel enter out within CAR
--!!channel leave out within CAR
CAR = enter -> leave -> CAR

--!!channel enter  in  within MACHINE
--!!channel cash   in  within MACHINE
--!!channel ticket out within MACHINE
--!!channel change out within MACHINE
MACHINE =
     enter -> cash?id -> ticket.id ->
          change.id -> MACHINE
```

```
--!!channel enter in within CUST
--!!channel leave in within CUST
--!!channel cash out within CUST
--!!channel ticket in within CUST
--!!channel change in within CUST
--!!arg id ID within CUST
CUST(id) =
  (enter -> cash!id ->
    (ticket.id -> change.id -> SKIP
    []change.id -> ticket.id -> SKIP));
  leave -> CUST(id)
CUSTOMERS =
   CUST(Lt.a) ||| CUST(Lt.b) ||| CUST(unknown)
PAID_PARKING = (CUSTOMERS
                   [| {|cash,ticket,change,enter|} |]
                   MACHINE) \ {|cash,ticket,change|}
SYSTEM = CAR [| {| enter,leave |} |] PAID_PARKING
```

Fig. 1. CSP$_M$ Example: a Paid Car Park

interfaces that are used to interact with the environment [11]. Most of the CSP tools, like FDR2 and ProBE, accept a machine-processable CSP, called CSP$_M$.

The two basic CSP$_M$ processes are STOP and SKIP; the former deadlocks, and the latter does nothing but terminate. The prefixing a -> P is initially able to perform only the event a; afterwards it behaves like process P. A boolean guard may be associated with a process: g & P behaves like P if the predicate g is true; it deadlocks otherwise. The operator P1;P2 combines P1 and P2 in sequence. The external choice P1[]P2 initially offers events of both processes. The performance of the first event or termination resolves the choice in favour of the process that performs either of them. The environment has no control over the internal choice P1|~|P2, in which the choice is resolved internally. The sharing parallel composition P1[|cs|]P2 synchronises P1 and P2 on the events in the synchronisation set cs; events that are not listed occur independently. The alphabetised parallel composition P1[|cs1|cs2|]P2 allows P1 and P2 to communicate in the sets cs1 and cs2, respectively; however, they must agree on events in cs1∩cs2. Processes composed in interleaving P1|||P2 run independently. The event hiding operator P\cs encapsulates the events that are in cs. Finally, P[[a<-b]] behaves like P except all occurrences of a in P are replaced by b. The CSP$_M$ interruption, untimed timeout, exceptions, linked parallel, and replicated operators are omitted here; they are not accepted by csp2hc.

By way of illustration, Figure 1 presents the specification of a parking spot. It contains special comments called directives (--!!), which give extra information to csp2hc, such as: information on whether simple synchronisation channels are input channels or output channels within a process; the types of processes arguments; the main behaviour of the system; the length of integers used in the system; and the moment in which internal choices should be resolved.

The process PAID_PARKING describes a parking spot with a pay and display machine that accepts cash, and issues tickets and change. First, we declare a datatype ALPHA: variables of type ALPHA can assume either value a or b. The next datatype, ID, represents identifications: the constructor Lt receives an ALPHA value and returns a value of ID (for example, Lt.a); another possibility is the unknown ID. After receiving the cash, the machine issues tickets and gives the change. The process CUST models a customer: after entering the parking spot, a customer must interact with the ticket machine: he inserts the cash into it, picks the ticket and the change in any order, and finally, leaves the parking spot. Customers have unique identification that guarantees that tickets and changes are only issued to the customer who inserted the cash. The identifications are used to instantiate each customer in process CUSTOMERS, which is defined as the interleaving of all customers. The paid parking spot is modelled by PAID_PARKING as a parallel composition of all customers and a machine; they synchronise on cash, ticket, change, and enter; all but enter are encapsulated. Finally, the main behaviour of the system, SYSTEM, is the parallel composition between the CAR and the parking. Using FDR2, we can verify that the SYSTEM is deadlock free and livelock free. Furthermore, using FDR2's refinement check, we can also verify that the SYSTEM satisfies the abstract specification that only requires that, after entering, a customer must leave before the next customer enters.

Despite being a simple example, this example was not accepted by the previous version of csp2hc. This is due to the existence of both (i) shared channels among the customers (*i.e* enter) that are not in the synchronisation channel set since customers are interleaved, and (ii) multi-synchronisation of a customer, the CAR and the MACHINE on channels enter and leave.

2.2   Handel-C

Handel-C is a procedural language, rather like occam, but with a C-like syntax. Its main purpose is the compilation into netlists to configure FPGAs or ASICs (Application-Specific Integrated Circuits). Although targeting hardware, it is a programming language with hardware output rather than a hardware description language. This makes Handel-C different from VHDL. A hardware design using Handel-C is more like programming than hardware engineering; this language is developed for programmers who have no hardware knowledge at all.

Handel-C offers a subset of C that includes common constructs like structures, functions, macros, arrays, pointers, logical operators (and their bitwise counterparts), and control flow constructs like while and for loops, if and switch. However, it does not include recursion and processor-oriented features like floating point arithmetic, which is supported through external libraries.

Handel-C extends C by providing constructs for describing parallel behaviour. The parallel construct par{P; Q;} executes instructions P and Q in parallel, which may communicate via channels. Its semantics corresponds to the CSP alphabetised parallel P $[|\alpha(P) || \alpha(Q)|]$ Q, where $\alpha(P)$ and $\alpha(Q)$ denotes all communications of P and Q, respectively. The prialt statement selects one of the channels that are ready to communicate, and communicates via this channel. The only data type allowed in Handel-C is int, which can be declared with a fixed size.

By way of illustration, we present a simple BUFFER that receives an integer value through a channel input and outputs it through channel output. This buffer can be decomposed into a process IN that receives an integer value and passes it through channel middle to another process OUT that finally outputs this value. A possible CLIENT can interact with the BUFFER by sending an integer value via channel input and receiving it back via channel output. The Handel-C code presented below implements this interaction.

```
set clock = external "clock1";
chan int 8 input, output, middle;
void IN(){ int 8 v; while(1) { input?v; middle!v; } }
void OUT(){ int 8 v; while(1) { middle?v; output!v; } }
void BUFFER(){ par{ IN(); OUT(); } }
void CLIENT(){ int 8 v; input!10; output?x; }
void main(){ par { BUFFER(); CLIENT(); } }
```

We define an external clock named clock1, and declare the channels used in the system. The Handel-C function IN implements the process of same name. It declares a local variable v and starts an infinite loop: in each iteration, it receives a value via channel input, assigns it to v, and writes its value on middle. The function OUT is very similar; however, it receives a value via middle and writes it on output. The BUFFER is defined as the parallel composition of IN and OUT. The main function is the parallel composition of the BUFFER with the CLIENT.

2.3   The Translator csp2hc

The automatic translation from CSP$_M$ to Handel-C is straightforward for some CSP$_M$ constructs because Handel-C provides constructs that facilitate the description of parallel behaviour based on CSP concepts. The version of csp2hc presented in [9] mechanised the translation of a subset of CSP$_M$ to Handel-C, which included SKIP, STOP, sequential and parallel composition, recursion, prefixing, external and internal choice, alternation, guarded processes, datatypes, constants, functions, and some expressions. It, however, restricted the use of some of these constructs like, for instance, parallel composition.

The implementation of concurrency in Handel-C differs from the CSP concepts. Handel-C has a degenerate kind of multi-way synchronisation, in which one writer and multiple readers can take part, but no participation control takes place: if just one reader and the writer are ready for communicating the synchronisation happens (the multi-synchronisation is not enforced like in CSP). For this reason, the translation of CSP$_M$ parallel composition into Handel-C's par construct was restricted to cases in which there were no multi-way synchronisation, and shared channels between two processes composed in parallel were in the synchronisation channel set of the composition. This guaranteed that processes only synchronised on multi-shared channels when all parts involved were willing to synchronise on that channel, and that processes did not synchronise on channels that were not in the synchronisation channel set.

The extension of csp2hc to accommodate multi-synchronisation and interleaving on shared channels is not trivial. The former requires the implementation of a centralised protocol in which a controller determines when the synchronisation is allowed to happen and the latter requires the translation of renaming. In the next section, we present the results that made it possible to deal with multi-synchronisation and interleaving on shared channels within csp2hc.

3 Parallelism in csp2hc

The CSP parallel composition cannot be directly translated into Handel-C's parallel constructor, par, for two reasons: (1) par does not enforce synchronisation between multiple parts (multi-synchronisation); and (2) par does not prevent the synchronisation on a channel if processes have access to the channel. In our example, such naïve translation would contain the following Handel-C code.

```
void PAID_PARKING(){ par{ CUSTOMERS(); MACHINE(); } }
void SYSTEM(){ par{ CAR(); PAID_PARKING(); } }
void main(){ SYSTEM(); }
```

This implementation, however, is wrong because it does not prevent customers synchronising on enter and does not enforce the multi-synchronisation on enter between the CAR, the MACHINE, and one of the customers. In this section, we describe the approach used in csp2hc to accomplish this behaviour.

Our approach has two restrictions that are automatically verified by csp2hc. The first restriction guarantees communications on synchronised channels by requiring the existence of exactly one writer for every channel that is being shared in parallel compositions. For example, c?x -> SKIP [|{|c|}|] c?y -> SKIP is not accepted by the approach. Its translation would result in a code in which both parallel branches are reading on a channel, hence, waiting to some other process to write on it. This would characterise a deadlock in the implementation that does not correspond to the specified behaviour in CSP_M, which does not deadlock and terminates. The second restriction guarantees that every parallel branch is either a reader or a writer to every channel, but not both. By way of illustration, c!0 -> c?x -> SKIP [| {| c |} |] c?x -> c?y -> SKIP is not accepted by the approach. This process satisfies the first restriction but not the second restriction because the left branch treats c as both an output and an input. In this example, a similar deadlock state is reached in the Handel-C code.

As we discuss in Section 4, the solution follows the expected performance results discussed in [14]. The computational arrangements for allowing any of the synchronising processes to back off (which CSP allows) is even more costly than allowing both parties to back off during channel synchronisation. For this reason, we only use the solutions presented here if there are multi-synchronised channels or if we need to enforce interleaving of channels. Otherwise, the parallel composition is directly translated as presented in [9].

The solution for multi-synchronisation is based on a protocol we presented in [15] that controls the accesses to the channels in a parallel composition and the solution to enforce the interleaving is based on CSP_M renaming. Both solutions use the concept of parallel branch that we describe in the sequel. Their application directly affects the translation of prefixing, external choice and the arguments of the processes within the system, which are slightly changed.

3.1 Analysis of Parallel Compositions

Our tool starts the branch identification from the main process given in the directive --!!mainp (in our example SYSTEM) and sets an identification to each

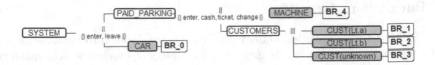

Fig. 2. Example Branches Identification

one of the running parallel branches. The result of this identification process in our example is presented in Figure 2.

The implementation of the concept of branch reuses the solution for datatypes presented in [9] by considering an implicit `datatype BRANCH = B_0 | ... | B_4`. As a result, we have the following extra lines of code.

```
#define BRANCH unsigned int 3
#define BR_0 0
...
#define BR_4 4
```

The translation of a parallel branch considers the current identification of the branch being translated: every process has an extra argument that identifies the branch from which it has been invoked. Our tool translates the left branch first and, before translating the right branch, it updates the current branch identification (BR_ID) by incrementing it with the number of sub-branches of the left branch. We have the following translation for the main process.

```
void main(){ BRANCH BR_ID; BR_ID = 0; SYSTEM(BR_ID+0); }
inline void SYSTEM(BRANCH BR_ID){ par{ {CAR(BR_ID+0); }; { PAID_PARKING(BR_ID+1); } } }
```

In the main process, we declare BR_ID and initialise it to zero. The SYSTEM behaves like a parallel composition between CAR and PAID_PARKING; they are parametrised by the branch identification. The translation of CAR is the first one, hence, the value BR_ID + 0 is used as argument. Nevertheless, this process itself is a branch; hence, the value BR_ID + 1 is used as argument to invoke PAID_PARKING. The translation of processes PAID_PARKING and CUSTOMERS though are slightly different as we can see in the code below.

```
inline void PAID_PARKING(BRANCH BR_ID) {
  par{ {CUSTOMERS(BR_ID+0);} ; {MACHINE(BR_ID+3);} } }
inline void CUSTOMERS(BRANCH BR_ID) {
  par{ {CUST(BR_ID+0,ID_Lt_LUT[a]);};
       {par{ {CUST(BR_ID+1,ID_Lt_LUT[b]);}; {CUST(BR_ID+2,unknown);} };} } }
```

In the translation of PAID_PARKING, the process MACHINE is given the local variable BR_ID incremented by three because the left branch, CUSTOMERS, has three branches. In the translation of CUSTOMERS, the first invocation to CUSTOMER does not increment the BR_ID; the following invocations, though, do increment it.

The branches identification is used in an analysis of the parallel structure of the system that results on a list of synchronisation for each channel. In our implementation, a synchronisation is a set that contains the identification of all branches that take part in the synchronisation. By way of illustration, in our example, there are three possibilities of synchronisation on enter: the CAR (BR_0) and the MACHINE (BR_4) take part in all of them; the third (and last) element is one of the clients. The list of synchronisations for the channel enter is $\langle\{\text{BR\_0}, \text{BR\_4}, \text{BR\_1}\}, \{\text{BR\_0}, \text{BR\_4}, \text{BR\_2}\}, \{\text{BR\_0}, \text{BR\_4}, \text{BR\_3}\}\rangle$. Similar mappings are created for each individual channel.

The branches identification and the synchronisation list play an important role in both solutions presented in this paper: the multi-synchronisation protocol and channel interleaving described in Sections 3.2 and 3.3 that follow. A synchronisation whose cardinality is greater than two characterises a multi-synchronised channel and a synchronisation list with more than one element indicates the need to enforce the interleaving on that channel.

csp2hc's analysis of the parallel structure is based on the channels rather than on the events. For this reason, the translation of some specifications might use the solutions presented in Sections 3.2 and 3.3 unnecessarily. For instance, the customers are composed in interleaving and our strategy uses the solution presented in Section 3.3 to enforce the interleaving on ticket because all customers use this channel. Nevertheless, this is not necessary because the synchronisation on ticket is parameterised by the customers identification. The translation of such channels uses an array of channels whose size is defined by the cardinality of the channel type. Each element of the array is a different channel that corresponds to a different value. Hence, despite using the same channel, different customers never synchronise (CUST(unknown) and CUST(Lt.a) work on ticket[unknown] and ticket[Lt_a]). Although being semantically correct, the use of the protocol adds performance costs (see Section 4) unnecessarily. An optimisation to remove this unneeded use of the protocol is in our research agenda. It requires a static analysis of CSP_M expressions that allows comparing events rather than only channels.

3.2   The Multi-synchronisation Protocol

In [15], we used the *Circus* refinement calculus to develop a protocol that implements an abstract multi-way synchronisation using only pairwise synchronisation: each multi-synchronised channel has a central controller and references to this channel are implemented as a client of this controller. In what follows, we extend the protocol from [15] by allowing both multi-synchronised channels and interruptions (possibly carrying values) to take part in external choices.

Controllers. The controllers are implemented as an infinite loop in which it iteratively runs a two-phase commitment protocol described later in this section. Hence, termination of the controller needs to be guaranteed by external managers. The first one, PManager, monitors the main behaviour of the system and communicates its termination to the controllers' manager using endManager.

```
inline void PManager() { BRANCH BR_ID; BR_ID = 0; SYSTEM(BR_ID+0); endManager!syncout;}
```

The controllers' manager (CManager) receives this communication and propagates it to each controller MSyncController_*i* using channel end_controller_*i*. Each client receives message from the controller on channel fromSync and sends

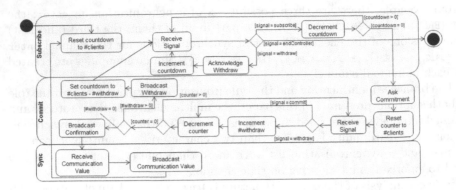

Fig. 3. Controller Activity Diagram

message to the controller on channel `toSync`. A controller has reference pointers to two arrays of channels `fromSync[]` and `toSync[]`. These arrays contain all controller-client communication channels. They are used as argument in each controller's instantiation. We present below the controllers' manager of a system with two multi-synchronised channels A and B.

```
inline void CManager (){
    chan SYNC end_controller_A; chan SYNC end_controller_B;
    par{ seq{ endSystem?syncin;
            par{ end_controller_A!syncout; end_controller_B!syncout; }; };
        MSyncController_A(&toSync_A[0], &fromSync_A[0] , &end_controller_A);
        MSyncController_B(&toSync_B[0], &fromSync_B[0] , &end_controller_B); }; }
```

The Handel-C `main` function is the parallel composition of both controllers.

```
void main(){ par{ {PManager();} ; {CManager();} } }
```

Handel-C's `prialt` construct is used in the implementation of the controller to offer a choice among various channels. This construct, however, cannot be changed dynamically because Handel-C requires all choices to be statically defined. For this reason, our Handel-C implementation of the protocol provides a different version of the controller for each possible number of multi-synchronisation parts. The behaviours of these versions are almost identical; they only differ in the number of elements in the arrays of channels that are offered in the choices. This is due to the complexity and length. We refrain from presenting the details of the resulting code, which can be found at the project webpage[2]. In what follows, we informally described the protocol workflow.

In Figure 3, we present the controllers' activity diagram. It can be divided into three phases whose composition is presented below: subscription, commitment and synchronisation. Only in some of these phases, the controller allows clients to withdraw from the synchronisation.

---

[2] Project webpage at http://www.dimap.ufrn.br/~marcel/research/csp2hc/

Subscribe The controller waits for the clients to indicate their intention to synchronise on the channel (subscribe). A local `countdown` controls the loop that implements the corresponding tail recursion in the original CSP implementation of the protocol. When all clients have subscribed, the controller moves to the commitment phase. While receiving subscriptions, if the controller receives an indication to terminate, it does so. The controller does not need to broadcast the withdraw because a termination signal will only arrive when the clients have terminated.

Commit The controller asks all clients to commit to the synchronisation and receives answers from all of them. If all clients answer positively, the controller broadcasts a confirmation to all clients and moves to the synchronisation phase.

Sync The controller receives the communication value from the writer and broadcasts this value to all other clients. The controller recurses and goes back to the initial state of the subscription phase.

Withdraw During the subscription phase, if a client withdraws, the controller acknowledges the signal, increments the `countdown` and keeps receiving signal from other clients. If, however, a client withdraws in the commitment phase, the controller broadcasts the withdraw and goes back to the subscription phase. Nevertheless, it expects new signals only from those clients that have withdrawn. Hence, the `countdown` is set to the difference between the total number of clients and the number of clients that have withdrawn.

Clients. At the other end of the protocol, we have the multi-synchronisation clients, which are used in the translation of the processes from the original CSP specification. In this translation, however, communications and choices that involve multi-synchronised channels are replaced by an invocation to a client's execution. The client offers all channels involved in the choice possibly interacting with different controllers. Its execution terminates only when a successful communication takes place. For simple communication, the termination of the client's execution indicates a successful multi-synchronisation. For external choices, however, the termination of the client returns an identification of the communication (either multi-synchronised or not) that happened. The behaviour of the process after this communication depends on this information.

In Figure 4, we present the client's activity diagram. Its behaviour can also be divided into the phases of subscription, commitment and synchronisation. The client's phases are composed as follows.

Subscribe The client sends a subscription to the multi-synchronisation controller. It is possible, though, that a client is involved in many multi-synchronisations. In such cases, this signal is sent to all the corresponding controllers. The client waits to receive a confirmation request from one of the controllers. When such a signal arrives, it moves to the next phase.

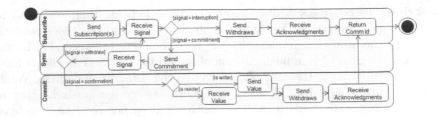

Fig. 4. Clients Activity Diagram

Commit The client commits to communicating with the controller and re-
frains from communicating on other channels. The client is not
allowed to withdraw. It receives from the controller either a confirmation or a withdraw. If the former is received, the client moves to
the synchronisation phase.

Sync If the client is the writer, it sends the communication value to the
corresponding controller. If, however, the client is a reader, it receives this value from the controller. Finally, it sends a withdraw signal to all other controllers, terminates and returns an indication of a
successful communication on the corresponding multi-synchronised
channel.

Withdraw During subscription, non-multi-synchronised channels (interruptions) may also happen. In such cases the client sends a withdraw to
all controllers that are interacting with it, terminates, and returns
a successful communication on the interruption. In the commitment
phase, if the controllers sends withdraws, the client returns to the subscription phase. It, however, does not send a new subscription because
the controller is already aware of its intention.

3.3   Forced Interleaving

As explained in Section 3, a naïve translation of our example would result in an
incorrect implementation because it would not prevent customers to synchronise
on enter. In this section we present a strategy that transforms the specification
in a correct manner to enforce the interleaving on enter between the customers.

The strategy is based on the synchronisation information described in Section 3.1 and makes use of CSP renaming. The main idea is to apply the transformation that follows at the source level before the actual compilation. The
transformation consists of the following phases: (1) Definition of each branch's
renaming for each channel; (2) Creation of renamed copies of the branches;
(3) Translation of the extended specification. In what follows, we present a detailed description of each of these phases.

In the **definition of each branch's renaming**, csp2hc defines what renaming must be applied to each individual branch. Formally, for every channel c

and branch b in the system, the renaming [[c <- c_i]] must be applied to
b if, and only if, the *i-th* element of the synchronisation list contains b. For
instance, processes CAR (BR_0) and MACHINE (BR_4) take part in all synchronisation
of channel enter; the renaming [[enter <- enter_0, enter <- enter_1, enter
<- enter_2]] needs to be applied to them. On the other hand, each client takes
part in only one synchronisation on enter. For example, CUST(Lt.a) (BR_1) needs
to be renamed using [[enter <- enter_0]]. The renaming definition of each
branch is done in an identical manner for all other channels in the system.

In the **creation of renamed copies of the branches**, the original specification is extended with the declaration of the new channels and the definition
of renamed copies of all processes. The copies are needed because a process may
be instantiated in different branches requiring different renamings. In our example, we have three renamed copies of CUST (one for each instantiation), and
one renamed copy of every other process in the system. The new channels are
also included in the synchronisation channel sets in which the original channel
is present. For conciseness, we present below only the changes related to enter.
Our example, however, also renames channels leave, cash, ticket, and change.

```
CAR_RNO     = CAR [[enter <- enter_0, enter <- enter_1, enter <- enter_2, ...]]
MACHINE_RNO = MACHINE [[enter <- enter_0, enter <- enter_1, enter <- enter_2, ...]]
CUST_RNO(id) = CUST(Lt.a)[[enter <- enter_0, ...]]
CUST_RN1(id) = CUST(Lt.b)[[enter <- enter_1, ...]]
CUST_RN2(id) = CUST(unknown)[[enter <- enter_2, ...]]
CUSTOMERS_RNO = CUST_RNO(Lt.a) ||| CUST_RN1(Lt.b) ||| CUST_RN2(unknown)
PAID_PARKING_RNO = (CUSTOMERS_RNO
                    [| {|enter,enter_0,enter_1,enter_2,cash,...,ticket,...,change,...|} |]
                    MACHINE_RNO) \ {|cash,...,ticket,...,change,...|}
SYSTEM_RNO = CAR_RNO [| {| enter,enter_0,enter_1,enter_2,leave,... |} |] PAID_PARKING_RNO
```

The extended specification is finally translated resulting in an implementation
that correctly implements multi-synchronisation and interleaving.

The **translation of the extended specification** follows the strategy from [9]
extended with multi-synchronisation as discussed in Section 3.2. Hence, this
translation naturally deals with multi-synchronised channels like enter_0. A further extension needed to the original strategy presented in [9] was the translation
of renaming explained below.

The translation of functional renaming (channels are renamed once) is rather
simple: the original channel is simply replaced by the new channel. For example,
CUST_RNO(id) is translated as CUST(id) but replaces enter to by enter_0.

The translation of non-functional renaming is slightly more elaborate. In these
cases, a channel is renamed to more than one new channel, like in CAR_RNO.
The result of such translations replaces references to the original channel to an
external choice between all new channels. By way of illustration, we present
below the specification that corresponds to the translation of CAR_RNO.

```
CAR_RNO = (enter_0 -> SKIP [] enter_1 -> SKIP [] enter_2 -> SKIP);
          (leave_0 -> SKIP [] leave_1 -> SKIP [] leave_2 -> SKIP); CAR_RNO
```

It is important to emphasize that, as expected, the external environment is
oblivious of the renaming used in our strategy. This is achieved by forbidding
channels that are used to communicate with the environment (marked as buses

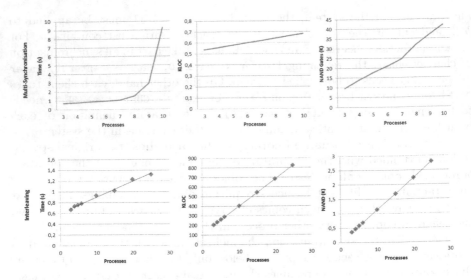

Fig. 5. Experiments Results

using directives) to be interleaved. Hence, the interleaved channels are not visible to the environment and their renaming does not affect the system's interface. The overall resulting code can be found at the project's webpage.

3.4 Formalisation

In [15], we presented a calculational approach to prove the correctness of a protocol for multi-synchronised channels that are not part of an external choice and do not communicate values. The protocol extension presented here accepts both multi-synchronised channels and interruptions (possibly carrying values) in external choices. A relatively simple adaptation of the proof from [15] guarantees the validity of our extension.

Using FDR2, we also verified that a specification with multi-synchronised channels and interruptions being offered in a choice is refined by its corresponding instance of the multi-synchronisation protocol. This verification ensures the correctness of the protocol for a comprehensive instance of the problem with bounded channel types. The same approach was used to ensure the correctness of the translation of interleaved channels.

4 Experiments

In our experiments, we translated simple CSP$_M$ specifications containing multi-synchronised and interleaved channels and compiled the resulting Handel-C code. The experiments were executed on an Intel i3, 2.53GHz, with 3GB RAM, running Windows 7 (64 bits). We considered the translation time and dimensions of the compiled code like number of lines of code (in thousands - KLOC) and the number of NAND gates (NANDs) and Flip Flops (FFs). The experiments were executed with an increasing number of processes taking part in the multi-synchronisation and interleaving, and we monitored the growth rate of the collected data. These rates were almost identical for the number of NANDs and FFs; hence, we omit below the results on the number of FFs.

Figure 5 presents the results of the experiment. For multi-synchronisation, they presented an exponential growth in the translation time, which enforces csp2hc users to make limited use of this feature. The growth rate of the generated code and its compilation, however, proved to be linear. This indicates the practical usefulness of the protocol on a large scale. Nevertheless, optimisation in the translation process is essential. The results for interleaving presented a linear growth rate and allowed us to consider a much larger number of processes. In these experiments, the growth rates of the generated code and its compilation were linear indicating the scalability of our solution.

5   Conclusions

In [9], we presented a translation from CSP$_M$ to Handel-C and a tool that automates this translation. They foster a methodology that starts from a CSP$_M$ specification, which is verified, gradually refined, and automatically translated into Handel-C code. The results presented here provide a further step towards providing a framework that fully supports the development of verified hardware.

Previous versions of csp2hc supported a useful subset of CSP, but imposed restrictions on parallel composition: its translation was allowed only if channels shared between the processes were in the synchronisation set and not multi-synchronised. In this paper, we present translation strategies to both limitations. Although some conditions are still required, we considerably extend the translation strategy of csp2hc by providing means to translate multi-synchronisation and interleaving as those of the example presented in Figure 1.

A relatively simple adaptation of the proof of the protocol we used as a basis presented in [15] guarantees the validity of our extensions. We have also verified that an abstract specification with various multi-synchronised channels and interruptions being offered in a choice is refined by its instance of the multi-synchronisation protocol. The same approach has been used to ensure the correctness of the translation strategy of interleaved channels.

Using csp2hc, we are able to translate some of the classical CSP$_M$ problems (e.g. the dining philosophers) including many of the examples provided with the FDR2 distribution and a complex specification provided by our industrial partner that involves multi-synchronisation and interleaving. There are, however, still optimisations and extensions to be done in csp2hc.

The experiments demonstrated the feasibility of the multi-synchronisation protocol for large networks. The translation, however, presented an exponential growth in time. For this reason, the current translation of multi-synchronisation is feasible only for small networks (up to 11 in our example). An optimisation in the translation process is essential and left as future work. The investigation of the performance of a purely distributed protocol [10] is in our research agenda. Furthermore, in a near future, we will also address an optimisation to remove the unneeded use of the extensions discussed in this paper.

Specifications not accepted by csp2hc need to be manually transformed. This transformation is often possible and can be verified using FDR2. A complete automatic translation from CSP_M to Handel-C requires the translation of further CSP_M constructs and expressions, which includes FDR2's functional language.

References

1. Burns, A., Wellings, A.: Concurrency in Ada, 2nd edn. Cambridge University Press (November 1997)
2. Brown, N., Welch, P.: An Introduction to the Kent C++CSP Library. In: Broenink, J.F., Hilderink, G.H. (eds.) Communicating Process Architectures 2003, pp. 139–156 (September 2003)
3. Formal Systems Ltd. FDR: User Manual and Tutorial, version 2.82 (2005)
4. Lin, S.-W., Liu, Y., Hsiung, P.-A., Sun, J., Dong, J.S.: Automatic generation of provably correct embedded systems. In: Aoki, T., Taguchi, K. (eds.) ICFEM 2012. LNCS, vol. 7635, pp. 214–229. Springer, Heidelberg (2012)
5. Hinchey, M.G., Jarvis, S.A.: Concurrent Systems: Formal Development in CSP. McGraw-Hill, Inc., New York (1995)
6. McMillin, B., Arrowsmith, E.: CCSP-A Formal System for Distributed Program Debugging. In: Proceedings of the Software for Multiprocessors and Supercomputers, Theory, Practice, Experience, Moscow, Russia (September 1994)
7. Oliveira, M.V.M.: Formal Derivation of State-Rich Reactive Programs using *Circus*. PhD thesis, Department of Computer Science, University of York (2006)
8. Oliveira, M., Cavalcanti, A.: From*Circus* to JCSP. In: Davies, J., Schulte, W., Barnett, M. (eds.) ICFEM 2004. LNCS, vol. 3308, pp. 320–340. Springer, Heidelberg (2004)
9. Oliveira, M., Woodcock, J.: Automatic Generation of Verified Concurrent Hardware. In: Butler, M., Hinchey, M., Larrondo-Petrie, M.M. (eds.) ICFEM 2007. LNCS, vol. 4789, pp. 286–306. Springer, Heidelberg (2007)
10. Parrow, J., Sjödin, P.: Designing a multiway synchronization protocol. Computer Communications 19(14), 1151–1160 (1996)
11. Roscoe, A.W.: The Theory and Practice of Concurrency. Prentice-Hall Series in Computer Science. Prentice-Hall (1998)
12. Sun, J., Liu, Y., Dong, J.S., Chen, C.: Integrating specification and programs for system modeling and verification. In: Proceedings of the Third IEEE International Symposium on Theoretical Aspects of Software Engineering, pp. 127–135. IEEE Computer Society, Washington, DC (2009)
13. Welch, P.H.: Process oriented design for Java: concurrency for all. In: Arabnia, H.R. (ed.) Proceedings of the International Conference on Parallel and Distributed Processing Techniques and Applications, pp. 51–57. CSREA Press (June 2000)
14. Welch, P.H., Wood, D.C.: Higher Levels of Process Synchronisation. In: Bakkers, A.W.P. (ed.) Proceedings of WoTUG-20: Parallel Programming and Java, pp. 104–129 (1997)
15. Woodcock, J.C.P.: Using *Circus* for Safety-Critical Applications. Electronic Notes Theoretical Computer Science 95, 3–22 (2004)

From Extraction of Logical Specifications to Deduction-Based Formal Verification of Requirements Models

Radosław Klimek

AGH University of Science and Technology,
al. A. Mickiewicza 30, 30-059 Krakow, Poland
rklimek@agh.edu.pl

Abstract. The work relates to formal verification of requirements models using deductive reasoning. Elicitation of requirements has significant impact on the entire software development process. Therefore, formal verification of requirements models may influence software cost and reliability in a positive way. However, logical specifications, considered as sets of temporal logic formulas, are difficult to specify manually by inexperienced users and this fact can be regarded as a significant obstacle to practical use of deduction-based verification tools. A method of building requirements models, including their logical specifications, is presented step by step. Requirements models are built using some UML diagrams, i.e. use case diagrams, use case scenarios, and activity diagrams. Organizing activity diagrams into predefined workflow patterns enables automated extraction of logical specifications. The crucial aspect of the presented approach is integrating the requirements engineering phase and the automatic generation of logical specifications. Formal verification of requirements models is based on the deductive approach using the semantic tableaux reasoning method. A simple yet illustrative example of development and verification of a requirements model is provided.

Keywords: requirements engineering, formal verification, deductive reasoning, use case diagrams, use case scenarios, activity diagrams, workflows patterns, temporal logic, logical specifications, semantic tableaux method.

1 Introduction

Software modeling enables better understanding of the domain problem and of the system under development. Requirements engineering is an important part of software modeling. Requirements elicitation should lead into a coherent structure of requirements and have significant impact on software quality and costs. Thinking of requirements must precede the analysis, design, and code generation acts. Requirements models are descriptions of delivered services in the context of operational constraints. Identifying software requirements of the system-as-is, gathering requirements and formulation of requirements by users allows defects to be identified earlier in a life cycle.

R.M. Hierons, M.G. Merayo, and M. Bravetti (Eds.): SEFM 2013, LNCS 8137, pp. 61–75, 2013.
© Springer-Verlag Berlin Heidelberg 2013

UML, i.e. the Unified Modeling Language [16], which is ubiquitous in the software industry can be a powerful tool for the requirements engineering process. Use cases are central to UML since they strongly affect other aspects of the modeled system and, after joining the activity diagrams, may constitute a good vehicle to discover and write down requirements. Temporal logic is a well established formalism which allows to describe properties of reactive systems, also visualized in UML. The semantic tableaux method, which is a proof formalization for assessing logical satisfiability, seems intuitive and may be regarded as goal-based formal reasoning.

Formal methods enable precise formulation of important artifacts arising during software development and help eliminate ambiguity. There are two well established approaches to formal reasoning and system verification [5]. The first is based on state exploration ("model checking") and the second is based on deductive reasoning. However, model checking is an operational rather than analytic approach.Deductive inference enables the analysis of infinite computation sequences. On the other hand, one important problem of the deductive approach is the lack of automatic methods for obtaining logical specifications considered as sets of temporal logic formulas. The need to build logical specifications manually can be recognized as a major obstacle to untrained users. Thus, the automation of this process seems particularly important. Moreover, application of the formal approach to the entire requirements engineering phase may increase the maturity of requirements models.

Motivation, Contributions and Related Works. The motivation for this work is the lack of tools and practical applications of deductive methods for formal verification of requirements models. Another motivation, which is associated with the previous one, is the lack of tools for automatic extraction of logical specifications from software models. However, requirements models built using use case and activity diagrams seem to be suitable for such an extraction process. All of the aforementioned aspects of the formal approach seem to be an intellectual challenge in software engineering.

The contribution of the work is a method for building formal requirements models, including their logical specification, based on some UML diagrams. A complete deduction-based system which enables the automated and formal verification of requirements models is proposed. Another contribution is a method for automating the generation of logical specifications. The generation algorithm for selected workflow patterns is presented. The reasoning process is performed using the semantic tableaux method for temporal logic. The proposed method is characterized by the following advantages: introducing workflow patterns as primitives to requirements engineering and logical modeling, scaling up to real-world problems, and logical patterns once they are defined and widely used. All these factors are discussed in the work and summarized in the last section.

There are some fundamental works on requirements engineering, c.f. the work by van Lamsweerde [15], which is a comprehensive study of many fundamentals of this area. The work by Chakraborty et al. [4] discusses some social processes associated with requirements engineering. In the work by Rauf et al. [17], a method for extracting logical structures from documents is presented. In the work by Kazhamiakin [11], a method based on formal verification of requirements using temporal logic and model checking approach is proposed, and a case study is discussed. Hurlbut [10] provides a very detailed survey of selected issues concerning use cases. The informal character of scenario documentation implies several difficulties in reasoning about the system behavior and validating the consistency between the diagrams and scenario descriptions. Barrett et al. [2] presents the transition of use cases to finite state machines. Zhao and Duan [20] shows formal analysis of use cases; however, the Petri Nets formalism is used. Eshuis and Wieringa [8] addresses the issues of activity diagram workflows but the goal is to translate diagrams into a format that allows model checking. There are some other works in the area of the formal approach and UML-based requirements engineering but there is a lack of works for deduction-based formal verification with temporal logic and the semantic tableaux method for UML-based requirements models. The work [12] is a (very) preliminary version of this one, and the differences include: a lower level of formalization, differences in predefined workflow patterns, more casual algorithm for generating logical specifications, and the lack of an accurate case study.

2   Methodology

The outline of the procedure and guidelines used for the construction of a requirements model, as it is understood in the work, is briefly discussed below. It constitutes a kind of methodology and its subsequent steps are presented in Fig. 1. The entire procedure can be summarized in the following items:

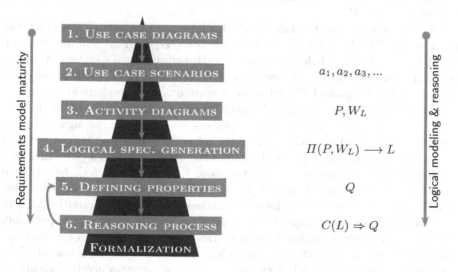

Fig. 1. Software requirements modeling and deduction-based verification

1. use case diagrams – use case modeling to understand functions and goals of a system;
2. use case scenarios – identifying and extracting atomic activities;
3. activity diagrams – modeling workflows using predefined patterns;
4. automatic generation of logical specifications from requirements models;
5. manual definition of the desired model properties;
6. formal verification of a desired property using the semantic tableaux method.

All steps are shown on the left side of Fig. 1. The first three steps involve the requirements modeling phase but the last three steps involve generation of logical specification and analysis of requirements model properties. The loop between the last two steps refers to a process of both identifying and verifying more and more new properties of the examined model. Some symbols and notation resulting from the introduced formalization are on the right side of Fig. 1 and they are discussed in further sections of the work. Generally, it leads, step by step, from an abstract view of a system to more and more detailed and reliable and, finally, verified requirements models.

3   Use Cases and Identification of Activities

Defining use cases and scenarios is important not only to understand the functionalities of a system but also to identify elementary activities. The activities play an important role when building logical specifications, i.e. the logical specification is modeled over atomic activities. The *use case diagram* consists of actors and use cases. *Actors* are objects which interact with a system and create the system's environment, thus providing interaction with the system. *Use cases* are services and functionalities which are used by actors. The use case diagrams are a rather descriptive technique and do not refer to any details of the system implementation [18].

Let us present it more formally. In the initial phase of a system modeling, use case diagrams $UCD_1, ..., UCD_n$ are built. Every UCD_i diagram contains some use cases $UC_1, ..., UC_m$ which describe the desired functionality of a system. A typical and sample use case diagram is shown in Fig. 2. It consists of three actors and three use cases, UC_1, UC_2 and UC_3, modeling a system of car insurance and damages liquidation. The diagram seems to be intuitive and is not discussed in detail.

Use cases are commonly used for capturing requirements through *scenarios* which are brief narratives that describe the expected use of a system. A scenario is a possible sequence of steps which enables the achievement of a particular goal resulting from the functionality of a use case. Every use case UC_i has its own scenario. From the point of view of the approach presented here, scenarios play an additional important role, which is identification of atomic activities used to build individual scenario steps. An *activity* is the smallest unit of computation. Thus, every scenario contains some activities $a_1, ..., a_n$. The set of *atomic activities AA* contains all activities identified and defined for all scenarios. The most valuable situation is when the entire use case scenario involves identified activities and the narrative does not dominate and is limited to model behavior, which is later formally shown in activity diagrams.

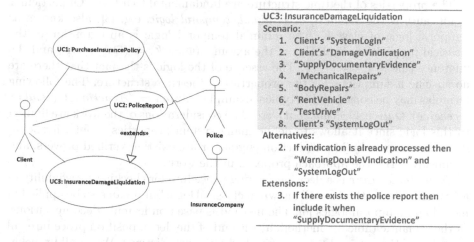

UC3: InsuranceDamageLiquidation
Scenario:
1. Client's "SystemLogIn"
2. Client's "DamageVindication"
3. "SupplyDocumentaryEvidence"
4. "MechanicalRepairs"
5. "BodyRepairs"
6. "RentVehicle"
7. "TestDrive"
8. Client's "SystemLogOut"
Alternatives:
2. If vindication is already processed then "WarningDoubleVindication" and "SystemLogOut"
Extensions:
3. If there exists the police report then include it when "SupplyDocumentaryEvidence"

Fig. 2. A sample use case diagram UCD "CarInsuranceLiquidatingDamages" (left) and a scenario for the use case UC_3 "InsuranceDamageLiquidation" (right)

A sample scenario for the use case UC_3, i.e. "InsuranceDamageLiquidation", is shown in Fig. 2. It contains some atomic activities which are identified when preparing the scenario. The alternative and extension points are defined. The "DamageVindication" activity represents the registration process in the insurer system and the start of the process of recovery damages. While the car repair process is carried out ("MechanicalRepairs" and "BodyRepairs"), the client can hire a replacement vehicle ("RentVehicle"). The level of formalization presented here, i.e. when discussing use cases and their scenarios, is intentionally not very high. This assumption seems realistic since this is an initial phase of requirements modeling. Dynamic aspects of activities are to be modeled strictly when developing activity diagrams, c.f. section 5.

4   Logical Background

Temporal logic TL introduces symbolism for reasoning about truth and falsity of formulas throughout the flow of time, taking the changes of their valuations into consideration. Two basic and unary operators are $\Diamond$ for "sometime (or eventually) in the future" and $\Box$ for "always in the future"; these are dual operators. Temporal logic exists in many varieties; however, these considerations are limited to the *linear-time temporal logic* or *linear temporal logic* LTL. Linear temporal logic refers to infinite sequences of computations and attention is focused on the *propositional linear time logic* PLTL. These sequences refer to the Kripke structure which defines the semantics of TL, i.e. a syntactically correct formula can be satisfied by an infinite sequence of truth evaluations over a set of *atomic propositions* AP. It should be pointed out that atomic propositions are identical to atomic activities defined in section 3, i.e. $AA = AP$. The basic issues related to the TL syntax and semantics are discussed in many works, e.g. [7,19].

The properties of the time structure are fundamental to a logic. Of particular significance is the *smallest*, or *minimal*, *temporal logic*, e.g. [3], also known as temporal logic of class K. The minimal temporal logic is an extension of the classical propositional calculus of the axiom $\Box(\Phi \Rightarrow \Psi) \Rightarrow (\Box\Phi \Rightarrow \Box\Psi)$ and the inference rule $\vdash \Phi \Longrightarrow \vdash \Box\Phi$. The essence of the logic is the fact that there are no specific assumptions for the properties of the time structure. The following formulas may be considered as typical examples: *action* $\Rightarrow \Diamond reaction$, $\Box(send \Rightarrow \Diamond receive)$, $\Diamond alive$, $\Box\neg(badevent)$, etc. The considerations of the work are limited to this logic since it allows to define many system properties (safety, liveness); it is also easier to build a deduction engine, or use existing verified provers, and to quickly verify the approach proposed in the work.

Semantic tableaux is a decision-making procedure for checking satisfiability of a formula. The method is well known in classical logic but it can also be applied in modal and temporal logics [6]. The method is based on formula decompositions. In the semantic tableaux method, at the end of the decomposition procedure, all branches of the received tree are searched for contradictions. When all branches of a tree have contradictions, it means that the inference tree is *closed*. If a negation of the initial formula is placed in the root, this leads to the statement that the initial formula is true. This method has some advantages over the traditional axiomatic approach. In the classical reasoning approach, starting from axioms, longer and more complicated formulas are generated and derived. Formulas become longer and longer step by step, and only one of them will lead to the verified formula. The method of semantic tableaux is characterized by a reverse strategy. The method provides, through so-called *open* branches of the semantic tree, information about the source of an error, if one is found, which is another and very important advantage of the method. Summing up, the tableaux are global, goal-oriented and "backward", while resolution is local and "forward".

A simple yet illustrative example of an inference tree is shown in the left side of Fig. 3. The relatively short formula gives a small inference tree, but shows how the method works. The label $[i, j]$ means that it is the i-th formula, i.e. the i-th decomposition step, received from the decomposition transformation of a formula stored in the j-th node. The label "1 :" represents the initial world in which a formula is true. The label "$1.(x)$", where x is a free variable, represents all possible worlds that are consequences of world 1. On the other hand, the label "$1.[p]$", where p is an atomic formula, represents one of the possible worlds, i.e. a successor of world 1, where formula p is true. The decomposition procedure adopted and presented here refers to the first-order predicate calculus and can be found, for example, in the work [9]. All branches of the analyzed trees are closed ($\times$). There is no valuation that satisfies the root formula. This, consequently, means that the formula before the negation is always satisfied.

An outline architecture of the proposed deduction-based verification system is presented in Fig. 3. A similar system is proposed in work [13]. The system works automatically and consists of some important elements. The $\boxed{\text{G}}$ component generates logical specifications which are sets of a usually large number of temporal logic formulas (of class K). Formula generation is performed automatically from

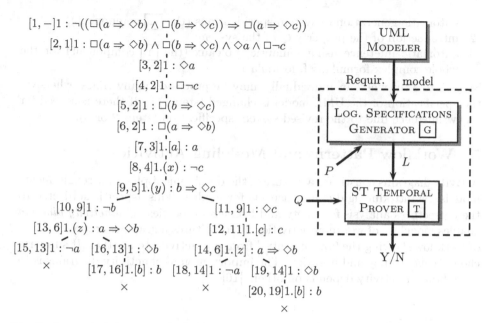

$[1, -]1 : \neg((\Box(a \Rightarrow \Diamond b) \land \Box(b \Rightarrow \Diamond c)) \Rightarrow \Box(a \Rightarrow \Diamond c))$

$[2, 1]1 : \Box(a \Rightarrow \Diamond b) \land \Box(b \Rightarrow \Diamond c) \land \Diamond a \land \Box \neg c$

$[3, 2]1 : \Diamond a$

$[4, 2]1 : \Box \neg c$

$[5, 2]1 : \Box(b \Rightarrow \Diamond c)$

$[6, 2]1 : \Box(a \Rightarrow \Diamond b)$

$[7, 3]1.[a] : a$

$[8, 4]1.(x) : \neg c$

$[9, 5]1.(y) : b \Rightarrow \Diamond c$

$[10, 9]1 : \neg b$ $\qquad$ $[11, 9]1 : \Diamond c$

$[13, 6]1.(z) : a \Rightarrow \Diamond b$ $\qquad$ $[12, 11]1.[c] : c$

$[15, 13]1 : \neg a$ $\quad$ $[16, 13]1 : \Diamond b$ $\qquad$ $[14, 6]1.[z] : a \Rightarrow \Diamond b$

$\times$ $\qquad$ $[17, 16]1.[b] : b$ $\quad$ $[18, 14]1 : \neg a$ $\quad$ $[19, 14]1 : \Diamond b$

$\qquad\qquad$ $\times$ $\qquad\qquad$ $\times$ $\qquad$ $[20, 19]1.[b] : b$

$\qquad\qquad\qquad\qquad\qquad\qquad$ $\times$

Fig. 3. A sample inference tree (left) and a deduction-based verification system (right)

workflow models, which are constructed from predefined patterns for activity diagrams. The extraction process is discussed in section 6. The whole specification L can be treated as a conjunction of formulas $f_1 \land \ldots \land f_n = C(L)$, where every f_i is a formula generated during the extraction process. The Q formula is a desired property for a requirements model. Both the system specification and the examined properties are input to the [T] component, i.e. *Semantic Tableaux Temporal Prover*, or shortly *ST Temporal Prover*, which enables the automated reasoning in temporal logic using semantic tableaux. The input for this component is the formula $C(L) \Rightarrow Q$, or, more precisely:

$$f_1 \land \ldots \land f_n \Rightarrow Q \qquad (1)$$

Due to the fact that the semantic tableaux method is an indirect proof, i.e. *reductio ad absurdum*, after the negation of the formula 1, it is placed at the root of the inference tree and decomposed using well-defined rules of the semantic tableaux method. If the inference tree is closed, it means that the initial formula 1 is true. The output of the [T] component, and therefore also the output of the entire deductive system, is the answer Yes/No. This output also realizes the final step of the procedure shown in Fig. 1. However, the verification procedure can be performed for the further properties, c.f. the loop in Fig. 1.

The verification procedure which results from the deduction system in Fig. 3 can be summarized as follows:

1. automatic generation of system specifications (the $\boxed{\text{G}}$ component);
2. introduction of the property Q of the system;
3. automatic inference using semantic tableaux (the $\boxed{\text{T}}$ component) for the whole complex formula, c.f. formula 1.

Steps 1 to 3, in whole or individually, may be processed many times, whenever the specification of the UML model is changed (step 1) or if there is a need for a new inference due to the revised system specification (steps 2 or 3).

5   Workflow Patterns and Modeling Activities

Activity diagrams constitute a closure of the development phase for requirements models, by introducing dynamic aspects for models. This aspect is subjected to the correctness analysis for safety and liveness properties. The *activity diagram* enables modeling of workflow activities. It constitutes a graphical representation of workflow showing the flow of control from one activity to another. It supports choice, concurrency and iteration. The important goal of activity diagrams is to show how an activity depends on others [16].

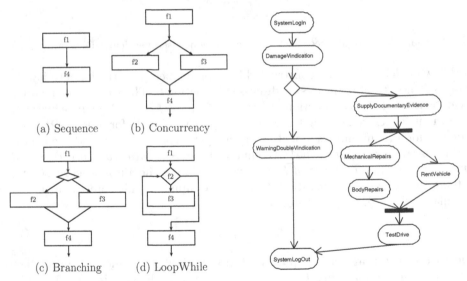

Fig. 4. Workflow patterns for activities (left) and a sample activity diagram AD_3 for use case UC_3 "InsuranceDamageLiquidation" (right)

From the viewpoint of the approach presented in the work, it is important to introduce a number of predefined workflow patterns for activities that provide all workflows in a structural form. A *pattern* is a generic description of the structure of some computations. Nesting of patterns is permitted. The following workflow patterns are predefined: *sequence, concurrent fork/join, branching* and *loop while* for iteration as they are shown in Fig. 4. It is assumed that only predefined patterns can be used for modeling of activity behavior. Such structuring is not a limitation when modeling arbitrarily complex sets of activities.

For every use case UC_i and its scenario, a activity diagram AD_i is developed/-modeled. The activity diagram workflow is modeled only using atomic activities which are identified when building a use case scenario. Furthermore, workflows are composed only using the predefined design patterns shown in Fig. 4. A sample activity diagram AD_3 is shown in Fig. 4. It models behavior of the UC_3 use case shown in Fig. 2, using activities from the scenario in Fig. 2. After the start of the vindication process, i.e. "DamageVindication", it is checked whether it is already being processed. If yes, the decision to register this fact is made, as it is likely another attempt at vindication of the same event, c.f. "Warning-DoubleVindication". The scenario analysis and the nature of other activities, i.e. "MechanicalRepairs", "BodyRepairs" and "RentVehicle", leads to the conclusion that they can and should be performed concurrently.

6   Generating Logical Specifications

The phase of modeling requirements is complete when all activity diagrams for all scenarios are built, c.f. Fig. 1 and section 5. Then, the phase of generating logical specifications and formal analysis of the desired properties begins. The logical specification generation process must be performed in an automatic way. Such logical specifications usually consist of a large number of temporal logic formulas and their manual development is practically impossible since this process can be monotonous, error-prone and the creation of such logical specifications is difficult for inexperienced analysts. On the other hand, the verified properties of the system constitute usually easier formulas, not to mention the fact that they are rather individual temporal logic formulas.

The proposed algorithm for automatic extraction of logical specifications is based on the assumption that all workflows for activity diagrams are built using only well-known workflow patterns, c.f. Fig. 4. The process of building a logical specification can be presented in the following steps:

1. analysis of activity diagrams to extract all predefined workflow patterns,
2. translation of the extracted patterns to a logical expression W_L,
3. generating a logical specification L from logical expressions, i.e. receiving a set of temporal logic formulas.

Predefined workflow patterns constitute a kind of primitives which are defined using temporal logic formulas. Therefore, an *elementary set* $pat()$ of formulas over atomic formulas a_i, where $i > 0$, which is also denoted $pat(a_i)$, is a set of temporal logic formulas $f_1, ..., f_m$ such that all formulas are syntactically correct (and restricted to the logic K). For example, an elementary set $pat(a, b, c, d) = \{a \Rightarrow \Diamond b, b \Rightarrow \Diamond(c \lor d), \Box \neg((a \lor b) \land \neg c)\}$ is a three-element set of PLTL formulas, created over four atomic formulas. Let Σ be a set of *predefined design patterns*, i.e. $\Sigma = \{Sequence, Concurrency, Branching, LoopWhile\}$. The proposed temporal logic formulas should describe both safety and liveness properties of each pattern. Let us introduce some aliases: *Seq* as *Sequence*, *Concur* as *Concurrency*, *Branch* as *Branching* and *Loop* as *LoopWhile*.

Every activity workflow is designed using only predefined design patterns. Every design pattern has a predefined and countable set of linear temporal logic formulas. The workflow model can be quite complex and it may contain nesting patterns. Let us define a logical expression, which is similar to well known regular expressions, to represent any potentially complex structure of the activity workflow but also to have a literal representation for these workflows. The *logical expression* W_L is a structure created using the following rules:

- every elementary set $pat(a_i)$, where $i > 0$ and every a_i is an atomic formula, is a logical expression,
- every $pat(A_i)$, where $i > 0$ and every A_i is either
  - an atomic formula, or
  - a logical expression $pat()$,
  is also a logical expression.

Examples of logical expressions are given in the section 7.

```
                                             /* ver. 6.04.2013 */
Sequence(f1,f4):
f1 => <>f4 / ~f1 => ~<>f4 / []~(f1 & f4)
Concurrency(f1,f2,f3,f4):
f1 => <>f2 & <>f3 / ~f1 => ~(<>f2 & <>f3)
f2 & f3 => <>f4 / ~(f2 & f3) => ~<>f4
[]~(f1 & (f2 | f3)) / []~((f2 | f3) & f4) / []~(f1 & f4)
Branching(f1,f2,f3,f4):
f1 => (<>f2 & ~<>f3) | (~<>f2 & <>f3)
~f1 => ~((<>f2 & ~<>f3) | (~<>f2 & <>f3))
f2 | f3 => <>f4 / ~(f2 | f3) => ~<>f4 / []~(f1 & f4)
[]~(f2 & f3) / []~(f1 & (f2 | f3)) / []~((f2 | f3) & f4)
LoopWhile(f1,f2,f3,f4):
f1 => <>f2 / ~f1 => ~<>f2
f2 & c(f2) => <>f3 & ~<>f4 / ~(f2 & c(f2)) => ~(<>f3 & ~<>f4)
f2 & ~c(f2) => ~<>f3 & <>f4 / ~(f2 & ~c(f2)) => ~(~<>f3 & <>f4)
f3 => <>f2 / ~f3 => ~<>f2
[]~(f1 & f2) / []~(f1 & f3) / []~(f1 & f4)
[]~(f2 & f3) / []~(f2 & f4) / []~(f3 & f4)
```

Fig. 5. A predefined set of patterns P and their temporal properties

The last step is to define a logical specification which is generated from logical expressions. The *logical specification* L consists of all formulas derived from a logical expression W_L using the algorithm Π, i.e. $L(W_L) = \{f_i : i \geq 0 \wedge f_i \in \Pi(W_L, P)\}$, where f_i is a TL formula. Generating logical specifications is not a simple summation of formula collections resulting from a logical expression. The generation algorithm has two inputs. The first one is a logical expression W_L which is a kind of variable, i.e. it varies for every (workflow) model, when the workflow is subjected to any modification. The second one is a predefined set P which is a kind of constant, i.e. once defined then widely used. The example of such a set is shown in Fig 5. However, the formulas are not discussed in the work because of its limited size. They might be a subject of consideration in a separate work. Moreover, the formulas can and should be prepared by an expert with skills and theoretical background. It guarantees that an inexperienced software analyst or engineer will be able to obtain correct logical models. Most elements of the predefined P set, i.e. comments, two temporal logic operators, classical logic operators, are not in doubt. The slash allows to place more formulas in a single line. f_1, f_2 etc. are atomic formulas for a pattern. They constitute a kind of formal arguments for a pattern. $\Diamond f$ means that sometime (or eventually in the future), activity f is satisfied, i.e. the token reaches the activity. $c(f)$ means that the logical condition associated with activity f has been evaluated and is satisfied. All formulas describe both safety and liveness properties for a pattern [1].

The output of the generation algorithm is a logical specification understood as a set of temporal logic formulas. The algorithm (Π) is as follows:

1. at the beginning, the logical specification is empty, i.e. $L = \emptyset$;
2. the most nested pattern or patterns are processed first, then, less nested patterns are processed one by one, i.e. patterns that are located more towards the outside;
3. if the currently analyzed pattern consists only of atomic formulas, the logical specification is extended, by summing sets, by formulas linked to the pattern currently being analyzed $pat()$, i.e. $L = L \cup pat()$;
4. if any argument is a pattern itself, then
   (a) firstly, the $f1$ formula, and next
   (b) the $f4$ formula
   of this pattern (if any), or otherwise considering only the most nested nesting far left, or right, respectively, are substituted separately in the place of the pattern as an argument.

Let us supplement the algorithm by some examples. The example for the step 3: $Concur(a, b, c, d)$ gives $L = \{a \Rightarrow \Diamond b \wedge \Diamond c, \neg a \Rightarrow \neg(\Diamond b \wedge \Diamond c), b \wedge c \Rightarrow \Diamond d, \neg(b \wedge c) \Rightarrow \neg\Diamond d, \Box\neg(a \wedge (b \vee c)), \Box\neg((b \vee c) \wedge d), \Box\neg(a \wedge d)\}$. The example for the step 4: $Branch(Seq(a,b), c, d, e)$ leads to $L = \{a \Rightarrow \Diamond b, \neg a \Rightarrow \neg\Diamond b, \Box\neg(a \wedge b)\} \cup \{a \Rightarrow (\Diamond c \wedge \neg\Diamond d) \vee (\neg\Diamond c \wedge \Diamond d), \neg a \Rightarrow \neg((\Diamond c \wedge \neg\Diamond d) \vee (\neg\Diamond c \wedge \Diamond d)), c \vee d \Rightarrow \Diamond e, \neg(c \vee d) \Rightarrow \neg\Diamond e, \Box\neg(c \wedge d), \Box\neg(a \wedge (c \vee d)), \Box\neg((c \vee d) \wedge e), \Box\neg(a \wedge e)\} \cup \{b \Rightarrow (\Diamond c \wedge \neg\Diamond d) \vee (\neg\Diamond c \wedge \Diamond d), \neg b \Rightarrow \neg((\Diamond c \wedge \neg\Diamond d) \vee (\neg\Diamond c \wedge \Diamond d)), c \vee d \Rightarrow \Diamond e, \neg(c \vee d) \Rightarrow \neg\Diamond e, \Box\neg(c \wedge d), \Box\neg(b \wedge (c \vee d)), \Box\neg((c \vee d) \wedge e), \Box\neg(b \wedge e)\} = \{a \Rightarrow (\Diamond c \wedge \neg\Diamond d) \vee (\neg\Diamond c \wedge \Diamond d), \neg a \Rightarrow \neg((\Diamond c \wedge \neg\Diamond d) \vee (\neg\Diamond c \wedge \Diamond d)), c \vee d \Rightarrow \Diamond e, \neg(c \vee d) \Rightarrow \neg\Diamond e, \Box\neg(c \wedge d), \Box\neg(a \wedge (c \vee d)), \Box\neg((c \vee d) \wedge e), \Box\neg(a \wedge e), b \Rightarrow (\Diamond c \wedge \neg\Diamond d) \vee (\neg\Diamond c \wedge \Diamond d), \neg b \Rightarrow \neg((\Diamond c \wedge \neg\Diamond d) \vee (\neg\Diamond c \wedge \Diamond d)), \Box\neg(b \wedge (c \vee d)), \Box\neg(b \wedge e)\}$. The first set follows from the ⎡nested⎤ pattern, the second set follows directly from the algorithm point ⎡4a⎤, and then the third set follows from the algorithm point ⎡4b⎤, while the ⎡final⎤ specification is the sum of all generated sets.

Remarks. Formulas $f1$ and $f4$ play an important role for every pattern, i.e. they are certainly the first and the last, respectively, active activity/task for a pattern. In the case of nested patterns, $f1$ and $f4$ enable considering the pattern as a whole, which is the goal of the last step of the algorithm. It is mandatory for every two patterns to have disjoint sets of atomic activities; moreover, every two patterns contained in a logical expression are either disjointed or completely contained in one another, c.f. formula 2, which, in conjunction with a particular role of $f1$ and $f4$, does not lead to potential contradictions. Formulas $f1$ and $f4$ must be considered separately, c.f. 4a and 4b of the algorithms, in order to guarantee access to a pattern both to/from the "front" and to/from the "back" of a pattern with respect to both the preceding and the following pattern. It may cause some redundancy of generated formulas, but on the other hand it covers all properties of combined patterns, i.e. it guarantees reachability (liveness), if necessary, of all (individual) activities.

7   Reasoning and Verification

Let us summarize the entire method proposed in the work. The first phase, let us call it the *modeling phase*, enables development of requirements models and includes the following steps:

- modeling of all use case diagrams $UCD_1, ..., UCD_m$, where $UC_1, ..., UC_n$ are all use cases contained in all use case diagrams;
- modeling of scenarios for all use cases $UC_1, ..., UC_n$ and identification of atomic activities $AA = \{a_1, ..., a_l\}$;
- modeling of activity diagrams $AD_1, ..., AD_n$ for all scenarios using predefined workflow patterns, c.f. Fig. 4, and using the identified atomic activities.

All the above steps require the assistance of an engineer and cannot be done automatically. The next phase, let us call it the *analytical phase*, introduces a certain degree of automation and includes the following steps:

- translation of all activity diagrams $AD_1, ..., AD_n$ (and their workflows) to logical expressions $W_{L,1}, ..., W_{L,n}$;
- generation of logical specifications $L_1, ..., L_n$ for all logical expressions using the Π algorithm, i.e. $\Pi(P, W_{L,i}) \longrightarrow L_i$ for every $i = 1, ..., n$;
- summing of specifications, i.e. $L = L_1 \cup ... \cup L_n$;
- (manual) definition of the desired property Q;
- start of the process of automatic reasoning using the semantic tableaux method for formula $f_1 \wedge ... \wedge f_k \Rightarrow Q$, where $f_1, ..., f_k$ are formulas which belong to the logical specification L.

The above steps illustrate the entire operation of the system shown in Fig. 3. The loop between the last two steps, c.f. Fig. 1, refers to a process of both introducing and verifying more and more new properties (formula Q) of the examined model.

Let us consider the activity diagram AD_3 shown in Fig. 4 for use case UC_3 "InsuranceDamageLiquidation". Activity diagrams constitute the input for the deduction system shown in Fig. 3. The logical expression $W_{L,3}$ for AD_3 is

$Seq(SystemLogIn, Branch(DamageVindication, Concur($
$SupplyDocumentaryEvidence, Seq(MechanicalRepairs, BodyRepairs),$
$RentVehicle, TestDrive), WarningDoubleVindication, SystemLogOut))$

Substituting letters of the Latin alphabet in places of propositions: a – SystemLogIn, b – DamageVindication, c – SupplyDocumentaryEvidence, d – MechanicalRepairs, e – BodyRepairs, f – RentVehicle, g – TestDrive, h – WarningDoubleVindication, and i – SystemLogOut, then the expression $W_{L,3}$ is

$$Seq(a, Branch(b, Concur(c, Seq(d, e), f, g), h, i)) \qquad (2)$$

Replacing propositions (atomic activities) by Latin letters is a technical matter. In the real world, original names of the activities would be used.

A logical specification L for the logical expression $W_{L,3}$ is built in the following steps. At the beginning, the specification of a model is $L = \emptyset$. Most nested pattern is Seq. The next considered pattern is $Concurrency$, and then $Branching$. The most outside situated pattern is once again Seq. The resulting logical specification contains the formulas

$$
\begin{aligned}
L = \{ &d \Rightarrow \Diamond e, \neg d \Rightarrow \neg \Diamond e, \Box\neg(d \wedge e), c \Rightarrow \Diamond d \wedge \Diamond f, \neg c \Rightarrow \neg(\Diamond d \wedge \Diamond f), \\
&d \wedge f \Rightarrow \Diamond g, \neg(d \wedge f) \Rightarrow \neg \Diamond g, \Box\neg(c \wedge (d \vee f)), \Box\neg((d \vee f) \wedge g), \\
&\Box\neg(c \wedge g), c \Rightarrow \Diamond e \wedge \Diamond f, \neg c \Rightarrow \neg(\Diamond e \wedge \Diamond f), e \wedge f \Rightarrow \Diamond g, \\
&\neg(c \wedge f) \Rightarrow \neg \Diamond g, \Box\neg(c \wedge (e \vee f)), \Box\neg((e \vee f) \wedge g), \\
&b \Rightarrow (\Diamond c \wedge \neg \Diamond h) \vee (\neg \Diamond c \wedge \Diamond h), \neg b \Rightarrow \neg((\Diamond c \wedge \neg \Diamond h) \vee (\neg \Diamond c \wedge \Diamond h)), \\
&c \vee h \Rightarrow \Diamond b, \neg(c \vee h) \Rightarrow \neg \Diamond b, \Box\neg(c \wedge h), \Box\neg(b \wedge (c \vee h)), \\
&\Box\neg((c \vee h) \wedge i), \Box\neg(b \wedge i), b \Rightarrow (\Diamond g \wedge \neg \Diamond h) \vee (\neg \Diamond g \wedge \Diamond h), \\
&\neg b \Rightarrow \neg((\Diamond g \wedge \neg \Diamond h) \vee (\neg \Diamond g \wedge \Diamond h)), g \vee h \Rightarrow \Diamond b, \neg(g \vee h) \Rightarrow \neg \Diamond b, \\
&\Box\neg(g \wedge h), \Box\neg(b \wedge (g \vee h)), \Box\neg((g \vee h) \wedge i), \\
&a \Rightarrow \Diamond b, \neg a \Rightarrow \neg \Diamond b, \Box\neg(a \wedge b), a \Rightarrow \Diamond i, \neg a \Rightarrow \neg \Diamond i, \Box\neg(a \wedge i)\} \quad (3)
\end{aligned}
$$

Formula 3 represents the output of the $\boxed{G}$ component in Fig. 3.

Formal *verification* is the act of proving the correctness of a system (liveness, safety). *Liveness* means that the computational process achieves its goals, i.e. something good eventually happens. *Safety* means that the computational process avoids undesirable situations, i.e. something bad never happens. The liveness property for the model can be

$$b \Rightarrow \Diamond f \qquad (4)$$

which means that **if the damage vindication is satisfied then sometime in the future the replacement car is reached**, formally $DamageVindication \Rightarrow \Diamond RentVehicle$. The safety property for the examined model can be

$$\Box\neg(h \wedge f) \qquad (5)$$

which means that **it never occurs that the rental of a vehicle and the double vindication are satisfied in the same time**, or more formally $\Box\neg(WarningDoubleVindication \wedge RentVehicle)$. When considering the property expressed by formula 4 then the whole formula to be analyzed using semantic tableaux, providing a combined input for the $\boxed{\text{T}}$ component in Fig. 3, is

$$((d \Rightarrow \Diamond e) \wedge (\neg d \Rightarrow \neg\Diamond e) \wedge \ldots \wedge (\neg a \Rightarrow \neg\Diamond i) \wedge (\Box\neg(a \wedge i))) \Rightarrow (b \Rightarrow \Diamond f) \quad (6)$$

When considering the property expressed by formula 5 then the whole formula is constructed in a similar way as

$$((d \Rightarrow \Diamond e) \wedge (\neg d \Rightarrow \neg\Diamond e) \wedge \ldots \wedge (\neg a \Rightarrow \neg\Diamond i) \wedge (\Box\neg(a \wedge i))) \Rightarrow (\Box\neg(h \wedge f)) \quad (7)$$

In both cases, i.e. formulas 6 and 7, after the negation of the input formula within the prover, the inference trees are built. Presentation of a full inference tree for both cases exceeds the size of the work. (The simple inference tree from Fig. 3 gives an idea how it works.) All branches of the semantic trees are closed, i.e. formulas 4 and 5 are satisfied in the considered requirements model. In the case of falsification of the semantic tree the open branches are obtained and provide information about the source of an error what is another advantage of the method.

Although the logical specification was generated for only one activity diagram AD_3, that is $L = L_3$, c.f. formula 3, the method is easy to scale up, i.e. extending and summing up logical specifications for other activity diagrams and their scenarios. Then, it will be possible to examine logical relationships (liveness, safety) for different activities coming from different activity diagrams.

8   Conclusion

The work proposes a two-phase strategy for formal analysis of requirements models. The first one is carried out by an engineer using a defined methodology and the second one can be (in most) automatic and enables formal verification of the desired properties (liveness, safety). Introducing logical patterns as logical primitives allows for breaking of some barriers and obstacles in receiving logical specifications as a set of a large number of temporal logic formulas in an automated way. Application of formal verification, which is based on deductive inference, helps to significantly increase the maturity of requirements models considering infinite computations and using a human-intuitive approach.

Future works may include the implementation of the logical specification generation module and the temporal logic prover. Considering graph transformations [14] is encouraging for requirements models involving distributed representation of knowledge and their efficient implementation. It should result in a CASE software which could be a first step involved in creating industrial-proof tools, i.e. implementing another part of formal methods, hope promising, in industrial practice.

Acknowledgement. The author would like to thank the anonymous Reviewers for their valuable comments that helped to improve the work. This work is co-financed by the EU, Human Capital Operational Programme, SPIN project no. 502.120.2066/C96 and co-financed by the AGH Research Fund no. 11.11 120.859.

References

1. Alpern, B., Schneider, F.B.: Defining liveness. Information Processing Letters 21(4), 181–185 (1985)
2. Barrett, S., Sinnig, D., Chalin, P., Butler, G.: Merging of use case models: Semantic foundations. In: 3rd IEEE International Symposium on Theoretical Aspects of Software Engineering (TASE 2009), pp. 182–189 (2009)
3. van Benthem, J.: Temporal Logic. In: Handbook of Logic in Artificial Intelligence and Logic Programming, vol. 4, pp. 241–350. Clarendon Press (1993–1995)
4. Chakraborty, S., Sarker, S., Sarker, S.: An exploration into the process of requirements elicitation: A grounded approach. Journal of the Association for Information Systems 11(4), 212–249 (2010)
5. Clarke, E., Wing, J., et al.: Formal methods: State of the art and future directions. ACM Computing Surveys 28(4), 626–643 (1996)
6. d'Agostino, M., Gabbay, D., Hähnle, R., Posegga, J.: Handbook of Tableau Methods. Kluwer Academic Publishers (1999)
7. Emerson, E.: Temporal and Modal Logic. In: Handbook of Theoretical Computer Science, vol. B, pp. 995–1072. Elsevier, MIT Press (1990)
8. Eshuis, R., Wieringa, R.: Tool support for verifying uml activity diagrams. IEEE Transactions on Software Engineering 30(7), 437–447 (2004)
9. Hähnle, R.: Tableau-based Theorem Proving. ESSLLI Course (1998)
10. Hurlbut, R.R.: A survey of approaches for describing and formalizing use cases. Tech. Rep. XPT-TR-97-03, Expertech, Ltd. (1997)
11. Kazhamiakin, R., Pistore, M., Roveri, M.: Formal verification of requirements using spin: A case study on web services. In: Proceedings of 2nd International Conference on Software Engineering and Formal Methods (SEFM 2004), Beijing, China, pp. 406–415 (September 28-30, 2004)
12. Klimek, R.: Proposal to improve the requirements process through formal verification using deductive approach. In: Filipe, J., Maciaszek, L. (eds.) Proceedings of 7th Int. Conf. on Evaluation of Novel Approaches to Software Engineering (ENASE 2012), Wrocław, Poland. pp. 105–114. SciTePress (June 29–30, 2012)
13. Klimek, R.: A Deduction-based System for Formal Verification of Agent-ready Web Services. In: Advanced Methods and Technologies for Agent and Multi-Agent Systems, Frontiers of Artificial Intelligence and Applications, vol. 252, pp. 203–212. IOS Press (2013), http://ebooks.iospress.nl/publication/32843
14. Kotulski, L.: Supporting software agents by the graph transformation systems. In: Alexandrov, V.N., van Albada, G.D., Sloot, P.M.A., Dongarra, J. (eds.) ICCS 2006. LNCS, vol. 3993, pp. 887–890. Springer, Heidelberg (2006)
15. van Lamsweerde, A.: Requirements Engineering - From System Goals to UML Models to Software Specifications. John Wiley & Sons (2009)
16. Pender, T.: UML Bible. John Wiley & Sons (2003)
17. Rauf, R., Antkiewicz, M., Czarnecki, K.: Logical structure extraction from software requirements documents. In: 19th IEEE International Requirements Engineering Conference (RE 2011), Trento, Italy, August 29-September 2, pp. 101–110. IEEE Computer Society (2011)
18. Schneider, G., Winters, J.: Applying use cases: a practical guide. Addison-Wesley (2001)
19. Wolter, F., Wooldridge, M.: Temporal and dynamic logic. Journal of Indian Council of Philosophical Research XXVII(1), 249–276 (2011)
20. Zhao, J., Duan, Z.: Verification of use case with petri nets in requirement analysis. In: Gervasi, O., Taniar, D., Murgante, B., Laganà, A., Mun, Y., Gavrilova, M.L. (eds.) ICCSA 2009, Part II. LNCS, vol. 5593, pp. 29–42. Springer, Heidelberg (2009)

Model Checking of Security-Critical Applications in a Model-Driven Approach

Marian Borek, Nina Moebius,
Kurt Stenzel, and Wolfgang Reif

Department of Software Engineering,
University of Augsburg, Germany
{borek,stenzel,moebius,reif}@informatik.uni-augsburg.de

Abstract. This paper illustrates the integration of model checking in SecureMDD, a model-driven approach for the development of security-critical applications. In addition to a formal model for interactive verification as well as executable code, a formal system specification for model checking is generated automatically from a UML model. Model checking is used to find attacks automatically and interactive verification is used by an expert to guarantee security properties. We use AVANTSSAR for model checking and KIV for interactive verification. The integration of AVANTSSAR in SecureMDD and the advantages and disadvantages over interactive verification with KIV are demonstrated with a smart card based electronic ticketing example.

1 Introduction

Security-critical system vulnerabilities are reported constantly. Such systems range from a desktop application (e.g., a browser) to security-critical systems like MasterCard and VISA [22] or the Google single sign-on password system [21]. To identify and eliminate protocol flaws during development model checking can be used. Therefore, an input model for the model checker has to be created which is then used to find attacks or automatically check security properties. There are several model checkers (e.g. NuSMV[8], SPIN[12], PRISM[11]) but only a few are tailored towards cryptographic protocols. AVANTSSAR[1] is a project for Automated Validation of Trust and Security of Service-oriented Architectures. It integrates three different model checkers (Cl-AtSe, SATMC, OFMC) by using a common input language called ASLan++[20]. It can be used to find flaws in cryptographic protocols [2] or to prove security properties under some assumptions (e.g. a fixed number of loop executions or a fixed trace length). Cryptographic protocols are based on message exchange over channels that are influenced by an attacker. Since the specification of a system using cryptographic protocols can quickly become too large and complex for a model checker due to computing resource constraints, it is necessary to abstract and simplify this specification. When security properties are to be checked for an application using cryptographic protocols (such as an electronic ticketing system) then usually the whole application has to be abstracted. This is time-consuming, error-prone and needs a lot of expertise.

R.M. Hierons, M.G. Merayo, and M. Bravetti (Eds.): SEFM 2013, LNCS 8137, pp. 76–90, 2013.
© Springer-Verlag Berlin Heidelberg 2013

SecureMDD is a model-driven approach for developing security-critical applications. From a platform independent model runnable code as well as a formal specification for interactive verification of application-specific security properties can be generated automatically. Interactive verification is time-consuming and requires expert know-how but it guarantees the properties for an arbitrary number of protocol runs and loop executions. On the other hand, classic model checking assures an automatic validation of properties, but only for fixed number of protocol runs. In our approach, model checking is meant to be an addition to interactive verification by an expert and can be used to find attacks. It is also useful to eliminate some security flaws before using interactive verification.

This paper focuses on the integration of AVANTSSAR into SecureMDD as well as on the question how far a model of an application which is used to generate runnable code can be abstracted automatically for validation of application-specific security properties with AVANTSSAR. As a result, a SecureMDD application can be model-checked automatically.

This paper is structured as follows. Section 2 gives an overview of the model-driven approach and Section 3 pictures an eTicket example. Section 4 describes the transformation from a SecureMDD model into an ASLan++ specification and section 5 shows some abstraction rules. Section 6 explains some security flaws using the eTicket example and section 7 compares model checking and interactive verification. Section 8 discusses related work and concludes this paper.

2   The SecureMDD Approach

SecureMDD is a model-driven approach to develop security-critical systems. From a model that represents a system, runnable code, a formal specification for interactive verification and an ASLan++ specification for model checking can be generated automatically. The formal specification is used to verify application-specific security properties for an infinite number of agents and protocol runs. The ASLan++ specification is only used to find security flaws due to the limitations like a finite number of agents and protocol runs. Examples for mentioned security-properties are that during a transfer in an online banking system no money is lost, that security-critical data remains secret or that a Dolev-Yao attacker [10] cannot harm the system.

The SecureMDD approach (see Fig. 1) uses a platform-independent UML model, a UML profile as well as a platform-independent and easy to use modeling language MEL [17] [6] to define security-critical applications. Based on the platform-independent application model a formal specification and three platform-specific models (one for each component type) are generated. The formal specification is the basis for the verification of application-specific security properties [18] using the theorem prover KIV[4]. The platform-specific models are tailored for their target platforms, e.g., Java Card for a smart card, Java for a terminal or a PC, and Java based Web services for a service. A smart card is a secure device that can be accessed only via a predefined interface and is tamper-proof: nobody has access to the operating system or the internal memory

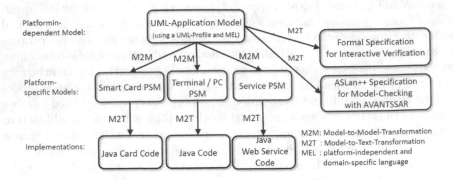

Fig. 1. SecureMDD Approach

directly. A terminal is also a secure device that receives instructions from a user and can have an interface for the communication with a smart card. A PC is a personal computer where the user has access to internal storage. A service will be deployed on servers that are assumed to be secure devices. Services can be connected by terminals or other services over a network. To perform tasks, a service can orchestrate other services, or several autonomous services can collaborate together. Services can only be accessed via their specified interfaces.

The approach illustrated in Fig. 1 is fully tool-supported and all model transformations are implemented. In this paper, we focus on the integration of AVANTSSAR in SecureMDD.

3   Electronic Ticket Example

By using the electronic ticketing system a user is able to buy train tickets online. The tickets are stored on his smart card and can be inspected multiple times. Only a genuine inspector device is able to validate and "punch" tickets. Additionally, only the card owner is able to buy tickets and to view or delete his purchased tickets.

Fig. 2 shows the deployment diagram of the application. It defines the components, the communication structure and the abilities of the attacker. There are two kinds of users involved in the system, the card owner (*User*) and the inspector (*Inspector*). The card owner can use his home PC (*UserDevice*) to buy, show or delete tickets on the card (*ETicketCard*). To buy a new ticket, the *UserDevice* connects to a server called *ETicketServer*. An *Inspector* is able to validate and "punch" tickets on a valid card with his inspector device (*InspectorDevice*) without access to the *ETicketServer*. The attacker has full Dolev-Yao abilities on the connections. That means an attacker can read, send and suppress messages that are exchanged over any connection. This is represented by the stereotype ≪Threat≫ with the properties {*read, send, suppress*}. *InspectorDevice*, *ETicketCard* and *ETicketServer* are secure devices. This means that neither the modeled participants nor the attacker have access to their internal storage.

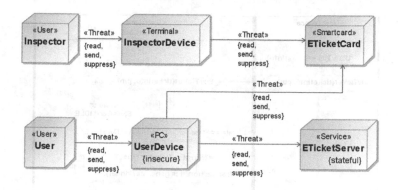

Fig. 2. Deployment diagram of the application

The assumptions are that a terminal is a closed and sealed device (e.g., an ATM or cash card reader) and that the attacker has no physical access to the servers running the services. *UserDevice* represents a personal computer, with its user being able to access its internal storage. Additionally, the PC is insecure, which means that an attacker also has access to the device, e.g., through malware.

Three security properties are required to hold for this system. Firstly, only tickets issued by *ETickerServer* are valid and can be "punched". Secondly, a paid ticket can not be lost (i.e., a bought ticket is stored on the server until the card has received the ticket and has sent a delete ticket confirmation to the server), even if the *UserDevice* crashes, the *ETicketCard* is removed from the card reader or because of an attacker. Thirdly, a ticket can not be "punched" twice.

4   Translation of a SecureMDD Model into ASLan++ Specification

This section describes the transformation from a SecureMDD model (using deployment diagrams (see Fig. 2), class diagrams and activity diagrams) into ASLan++. The focus is on the correct translation without regard to the execution time of model checking. The transformations are application-independent but are illustrated using the electronic ticketing example.

SecureMDD uses UML that is tailored on security-critical applications. The static view is modeled by class diagrams and a deployment diagram, and the dynamic view is modeled by activity diagrams. The class diagrams define the participants, their attributes and the messages classes. The deployment diagram defines the communication structure as well as the attacker abilities. The activity diagrams contain the message exchange as well as the actions that will be executed after receiving a message (e.g., decrypting of messages, comparing of values or debiting a credit card). A platform-independent and domain-specific language called MEL [17] [6] is used. It supports assignments, object creation, local variables, comparisons and predefined operation (e.g., encrypt, sign, hash, generateNonce, etc.).

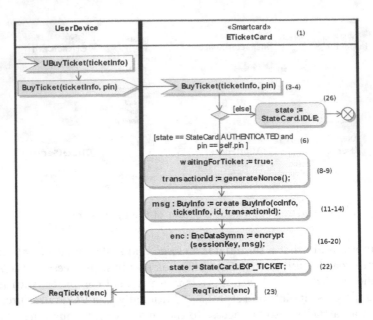

Fig. 3. A part of the activity diagram used by SecureMDD to describe the behavior of ETicketCard

Fig. 3 depicts a snippet of an activity diagram that describes a part of *ETicket-Card's* behavior. It describes the first step of the protocol to buy a ticket (which is initiated by the user) after a successful authentication between *ETicketCard* and *ETickerServer*. The activity diagram shows two partitions. The left one describes the participant *UserDevice* and the right one (1) represents the participant *ETicketCard*. *UserDevice* sends the message *BuyTicket* with *ticketInfo* and *pin* to an *ETicketCard*. After *ETicketCard* receives the message *BuyTicket* (3-4) it checks its state to ensure that an authentication has previously occurred and compares the received *pin* with the correct one stored in the *pin* attribute of the card(6). If the check fails, the state will be reset to *StateCard.IDLE* and the protocol step is finished (26). *StateCard* is an enumeration defined in a class diagram that can be *IDLE, AUTHENTICATED, EXP_TICKET*, etc. After a successful check *waitingForTicket* is set to true and a new *transactionId* (of type *Nonce*) is generated (8-9). *waitingForTicket, transactionId, state* and *pin* are class attributes of *ETicketCard* defined in the class diagram. After creating the local variable *msg* of type *BuyInfo* (11-14) this message is encrypted with a session key (16-20) which was exchanged in a previous authentication protocol. At the end, the state is set to *EXP_Ticket* (22) and the message *ReqTicket* with the encrypted content is sent to *UserDevice* (23).

ASLan++[20] is a textual language used by AVANTSSAR for specifying security-critical applications. The major building blocks are *entities*. They declare *types, symbols*, a *body* and other items. Each participant modeled as class in SecureMDD is translated into an ASLan++ entity. These entities are called agents. The local variables as well as class attributes are translated to *symbols* inside the resulting *entities*. The types of the attributes that are described by classes or primitives in SecureMDD are defined as *types* in ASLan++. A *body* section contains the dynamic part of the application as well as the communication structure and the attacker abilities on the individual communication channels.

```
1   entity ETicketCard (...){
2    ...
3    on( UserDevice -> Actor  :
4    buyTicket.( ticketInfo .(...).? M_buyTicket_pin )) :
5    {
6      if ( State = statecard_authenticated & M_buyTicket_pin = Pin )
7      {
8        WaitingForTicket := t;
9        TransactionId := fresh ();
10
11       L_buyTicket_msg_ccInfo ...
12       L_buyTicket_msg_ticketInfo ...
13       L_buyTicket_msg_cardID_id := Id_id;
14       L_buyTicket_msg_transactionId := TransactionId;
15
16       L_buyTicket_enc := scrypt (SessionKey , buyInfo.(
17         cCInfo.(...). ticketInfo .(...).
18         iD.( L_buyTicket_msg_cardID_id ).
19         L_buyTicket_msg_transactionId
20       ));
21
22       State := statecard_exp_ticket;
23       Actor -> UserDevice : reqTicket.( L_buyTicket_enc );
24     }
25     else{
26       State := statecard_idle;
27  } } }
```

Listing 1. A part of the ASLan++ specification that describes the behavior of ETicketCard

List. 1 shows the ASLan++ representation of the protocol step depicted in Fig. 3. The participant *ETicketCard* is described by an *entity* (1). The ability to receive the message *BuyTicket* from *UserDevice* is specified by the *on(...)* statement (3-4). It describes a conditional branch without *else* case. If the condition *UserDevice → Actor : buyTicket...* (3-4) inside the *on* statement is true then the actor (*ETicketCard*) receives the message *buyTicket...* from the *UserDevice*. → describes that the attacker can read, send and suppress messages on this connection. In ASLan++ it is not possible to define complex data types (e.g., a class that contains some attributes). Hence, for sending or receiving the message *BuyTicket*, only the attributes and the type information specified by constants to avoid type confusion are used. After *ETicketCard* receives the message *BuyTicket* (3-4) it checks its *State* and the received *pin* (6). If the check fails, the state will be set to *statecard_idle* (26). If the check was successful *WaitingForTicket* is set to true (8). After that *TransactionId* is set to a "fresh" value (this value is new and unique) (9). In SecureMDD we used for this the predefined function *generateNonce*. The assignment of complex data types has to be customized. Therefore, an object assignment has to be fragmented in several assignments for existing data types. The instantiation of complex data types, in this case *BuyInfo*, needs several statements because each attribute has to be assigned separately (11-14). After the instantiation *msg* is encrypted symmetrically with *SessionKey* (16-20). Finally, the state is set to *statecard_exp_ticket* (22) and the encrypted message is sent to *UserDevice* (23). The complete SecureMDD model and ASLan++ specification of eTicket is available on our website[1].

In the following some interesting aspects of the transformation of the UML application model into ASLan++ are described. In SecureMDD a participant is able to receive any known message type while he is waiting for a message. In our ASLan++ specification this behavior is formalized with an infinite loop and a non-deterministic choice of receiving messages inside the body of each agent (see List. 2). A non-deterministic choice is defined by the *select* statement that contains conditional branches without an *else* case (*on(...)*). $A \rightarrow Actor : M1$ means that the actor receives the message *M1* from the agent *A*.

```
1    while(true)
2    {
3      select
4      {
5        on(A->Actor  :  M1):{...}
6        on(A->Actor  :  M2):{...}
7        ...
8        on(B->Actor  :  Mn):{...}
9    } }
```

Listing 2. Definition of agent behavior

If/else statements, equality checks, logical expressions (e.g., AND, OR) as well as encrypt and sign operations can be directly mapped to existing equivalent ASLan++ language constructs. SecureMDD supports lists and key-value containers, whereas ASLan++ only supports sets. For example, lists in SecureMDD contain following operations:

- *add(Element e) : void* Adds the element *e* to the end of the list.
- *remove(Element e) : void* Deletes the element *e* from the list.

Therefore, SecureMDD lists are emulated using ASLan++ sets. Each ASLan++ list element is defined as a tuple consisting of the original list element and a unique index, while the set maintains an index counter. *Add* and *remove* have been translated in a simple and efficient way into ASLan++. The add operation increases this counter and inserts a new tuple into the set consisting of the original element and the new counter value as index. This allows us to insert duplicate elements into a set. The *remove* operation for a SecureMDD list is translated to an existing remove operation on ASLan++ sets. For this operation the index can be ignored.

Arithmetic operations like addition and multiplication are supported in SecureMDD but not in ASLan++. For some examples like eTicket they are not necessary but we have also examples modeled with SecureMDD that use arithmetic operations. Currently, SecureMDD applications that use arithmetic will not be translated into ASLan++. This is a severe limitation of AVANTSSAR and the used model checkers. However, we are not aware of a model checker that supports arithmetic and is tailored on security applications.

---

[1] http://www.informatik.uni-augsburg.de/lehrstuehle/swt/se/projects/
  secureMDD/

SecureMDD and ASLan++ support a full Dolev-Yao attacker [10] who is able to read, send, and suppress messages on the fly. Secure devices in SecureMDD like an *InspectorDevice* are translated to ASLan++ as an honest agent and an insecure device like *UserDevice* becomes a dishonest agent. Dishonest means that an attacker can play the role of such an agent.

SecureMDD uses invariants to specify security properties. The invariants can be translated into ASLan++ *goals*. The validated goals for our eTicket example are described in section 6.

5   Automatic Abstractions

SecureMDD models like eTicket are too large for the model checkers integrated in AVANTSSAR. The eTicket case study has 52 different protocol steps (where one protocol step can lead to several transition rules in ASLan). More precisely, an eTicket ASLan++ specification that is translated one-to-one without any abstractions leads to 162 transition rules. This is a lot compared to the average 20 transition rules that are considered by the AVANTSSAR examples.

The execution time of model checking depends on several factors. One of those factors is the number of agents as well as the complexity of their behavior. The behavior of system participants can be specified in ASLan++ primarily using guards and statements (e.g., the sending or receiving of a message, a conditional branch or an assignment). ASLan++ is translated into ASLan by AVANTSSAR. ASLan uses transition rules with pre- and postconditions to define the participants' behavior. A transition rule transfers a state machine from one state to another if the precondition is true. The number of such transition rules as well as their interconnectivity is also crucial for the complexity of the system specification. The attacker capabilities are just as important. If an attacker is able to generate and send messages to a system agent, it is checked at every transition whether the attacker is capable of generating a message that could lead to a security property being violated. If loops or more than one session are specified, the complexity of the specification depends on the number of transition rule executions and on the maximum trace length. A trace contains a list of transition rules and represents one possible execution order of the specified system.

Since model checkers need a lot of computing resources which are not always available, the application models need to be abstracted. This is usually done manually [2] and only by security experts. A manually abstracted version of the full eTicket example leads to 55 transition rules. In the following some automatic abstractions are mentioned with that the generated specification has only 65 transition rules against the 162 without any abstractions. This is very close to the manually abstracted version and can not be significantly reduced further without omitting some of the applications functionality.

1. **Removing participants that are not security-critical**

   An honest agent such as a terminal in SecureMDD which only forwards messages between other agents can be omitted in the abstract specification. In order for all communication options to be preserved, new communication paths have to be created. The attacker abilities on a new communication path is the most permissive combination of his abilities on the paths that are replaced by the new, direct communication path. If, however, such an agent that only forwards messages is dishonest (e.g., an "insecure" PC), the attacker abilities on a new communication path are "read, send, suppress". In the eTicket case study (see Fig. 2) the agent *UserDevice* can be removed. A new communication path is created between *User* and *ETicketServer*, between *User* and *ETicketCard* as well as between *ETicketCard* and *ETicketServer*. The attacker capabilities on the new created communication paths are "read, send, suppress". Using this abstraction, the resulting specification for the eTicket case study has 10% less transition rules.

2. **Deleting unused class attributes**
   Some class attributes are necessary for the implemented application but are never used in the protocols. For example the attributes of *TicketInfo* (departure, destination, expiration, ...) are relevant for the real users and inspectors but not for the formal specification. Hence, if the attributes of a class are never used by the protocols (especially no constructor call of the class) and if the security properties do not refer to those class attributes, they don't need to be specified in ASLan++. Consequently, such a SecureMDD class with unused attributes is translated to an ASLan++ type. Model checking a simplified eTicket version with the model checker Cl-AtSe using this abstraction, is five times faster than a version of eTicket that does not use this abstraction.

3. **Reducing conditional branches**
   In SecureMDD, the section between receiving a message and sending the next is called a protocol step and is considered to be atomic. If all steps in ASLan++ could be specified to be atomic each step could be translated into a single transition rule. However, in ASLan++ steps that contain branches are translated into several transition rules in ASLan, which increases the complexity of the specification. It is possible to merge several nested conditional branches into one by combining the branch conditions with a logical AND if only the innermost branch contains other statements. By doing so one can eliminate transition rules from the resulting ASLan specification. This abstraction can be used quite often with SecureMDD models and is executed automatically on the UML model.

   In SecureMDD, any system participant can receive any modeled message after having executed a step. For the state machine in ASLan this results in a large number of possible transition combinations. In most protocols, however, the message order is fixed by using explicit state variables that are usually checked in a branch condition immediately after receiving a message (see Fig. 3 (6)). But as already mentioned, conditional branches are to be avoided in ASLan++. Because for receiving a message a conditional branch without *else* case (on(...) see List. 1 (3-4)) is used, the mentioned abstraction would not be applicable. But because usually, in SecureMDD, all *else* cases from the state checks are the same (e.g. only set the state to idle), it is possible to get the required behavior by adding *on(true) state:= idle;* to the ASLan++ *select* statement inside the infinite loop of an entity depicted in List. 2. This is done automatically if the assumptions hold. This abstraction reduces the number of transition rules of the eTicket case study by 50% compared to a version of eTicket that does not use this abstraction.

4. **Assuming a fixed message order**
Another abstraction is to specify the message receive order statically in ASLan++. This means that the dynamic state check while receiving a message has to be translated into cascading receive blocks in the ASLan++ specification where the inner one can only receive a message if the outer one has received and executed a message. To guarantee that such abstraction does not lead to false positives the dynamic state checks remains. The static receive order is implemented very efficiently by the AVANTSSAR tools and leads to a major speed up that makes it possible for the first time to find security flaws in the eTicket case study.

The aforementioned abstractions are done automatically during the transformations and leads to a significant reduction of the system complexity and make model checking of medium-sized systems like eTicket with ASLan++ and a model-driven approach feasible in the first place. However, the execution time of model checking rises exponential with the number of transition rules. Therefore, larger systems like an electronic health card [16] which has 105 different protocol steps (translated and abstracted to approx. 130 transition rules) are too big for model checking application-specific properties for the whole application.

6   Security Flaws

AVANTSSAR is a project about "Automated VAlidatioN of Trust and Security of Service-oriented ARchitectures". It integrates three model checkers (Cl-AtSe, OFMC and SATMC) which use the same input language called ASLan++. But not all model checkers support its full syntax. Because only Cl-AtSe[19] covers all needed syntax elements and because speed tests illustrate that all three model checkers are comparably fast [19] we decided to use Cl-AtSe for our tests. Cl-AtSe is a "Constraint Logic based Attack Searcher" for security protocols. To find attacks it uses rewriting and constraint solving techniques as well as different kinds of backward strategies. Cl-AtSe supports a *split* function to split a specification into subtasks that can be executed in parallel. The tests were performed on a 3GHz quad core computer. Without using the split function, the CPU load was constantly at 13%, with the split function we were able to use the full capacity.

For the eTicket example we have defined three application-specific security properties in ASLan++. They are used to test which kind of protocol flaws can be found, which assumptions are necessary as well as how long it takes to find those flaws.

1. **Only tickets that were issued by the eTicket server can be "punched"**
To ensure this application-specific security property it is also necessary that only tickets that are stored on a valid card can be "punched". Hence, before an inspector "punches" a ticket, the card has to authenticate itself with the

inspector device. This is done using certificates. Then, it is ensured that the incoming messages were sent by the authenticated participant. This is done using nonces. The inspector device has to send a nonce encrypted with the certified card public key to the card and the card has to answer with the received nonce encrypted with the public key of the inspector device. If such a nonce is not used, the attacker can inject an answer message and a ticket that is not stored on a card will be "punched". That would lead to the fact that the mentioned security property does not hold. For testing the model checker we have removed the nonce. This security flaw has been detected with the abstracted version in a few seconds. The split function was not used and the assumptions were that each transition rule can be executed only once in a trace.

2. **A paid ticket cannot be lost (i.e., a bought ticket is stored on the server until it has been received by the card)**

Before a ticket can be bought, an authentication has to take place and a valid PIN has to be provided. If the user buys a ticket but does not receive it because the attacker has suppressed the message that contains the ticket, then the ticket is paid for but not stored on the buyer's card. Hence, a recovery protocol is used to be able to receive the last paid ticket until it can be stored successfully on the card. Therefore, a previously processed authentication and a boolean flag *waitingForTicket* set to true are necessary. *WaitingForTicket* is set to true before the *ReqTicket* message is sent out (see Fig. 3) and it is set to false after the ticket is received. However, after a ticket is bought but has not been received yet, it is possible that the card owner buys a new one. In this case, the first bought ticket which is stored on the server will be overwritten by the new one and the old ticket is lost. But that is against the security property. To find the flaw it is necessary that a ticket can be bought two times. Hence, for Cl-AtSe it is necessary that each transition rule can occur in a trace at least two times. This value has to be set manually and leads to a higher complexity and a higher execution time. With the abstracted version and the split function that allows a full CPU load the flaw could not be found even after a week. To ensure that this attack exists in the ASLan++ specification, we predetermined the attack trace. Then the attack was found. Another way to find the attack but without giving the full attack trace, is to omit protocol steps that are not necessary for the security property. This abstraction needs expert knowhow and can cause that some attacks can not be found. But it also reduces the complexity and raises the chance to find an attack. In this way we delete the inspector, the inspector device, all protocol steps that receive messages from the inspector device as well as the show ticket and delete ticket functionality. Then we were able to find the attack with the split function in 30 minutes.

3. **A ticket cannot be "punched" multiple times**

After a long time of analyzing the eTicket case study we have manually found a security flaw (security property is violated) that was actually hard to find and can only occur if almost all protocol steps are considered and the handshake is executed three times. Taking this knowledge into consideration we have tried to find the attack using model checking. Despite the abstraction, elimination of all not used protocol steps and the *split* function that allows a full CPU load the flaw could not be found even after a week. For the attack a handshake between card and server has to be processed and a ticket has to be bought, stored on the card and the delete ticket confirmation that should be sent to the server has to be suppressed. Then the ticket has to be stamped by an inspector device. For that the public keys have to be exchanged between card and inspector device and their certificates has to be verified. Additionally, a ticket has to be chosen and then stamped. After that a new Ticket has to be bought to set the *WaitingForTicket* flag to true. This means that a new handshake has to be processed but this time the message to buy the ticket has to be suppressed. After that the first bought ticket that is still stored on the server can be recovered by processing a handshake and the recovery. That replaces the stamped ticket with the same ticket but it is not stamped. After that the ticket can be stamped a second time. This attack requires 73 steps, which is a lot.

7   Comparison: Model Checking vs Interactive Verification

Existing ASLan++ specifications that consider security applications can often be checked within a few minutes. But to achieve this in the first place, the real applications are abstracted manually. In case of a real application not the whole system is considered but only a manually chosen part. For example, for our eTicket case study that has 52 different protocol steps (whereby one protocol step can lead to several transition rules in ASLan) the ASLan++ specification also considers that a user is able to view his purchased tickets. Because the exchanged messages to view purchased tickets are not relevant for the considered properties, a manual abstracted specification would omit those messages. But this has to be done by an expert because it is non-trivial which parts of the application can be omitted. Additionally, the assumptions (e.g., only one or maybe two protocol runs are considered) are too restrictive.

   In contrast to classic model checking, with interactive verification it is possible to verify security properties of an application that uses cryptographic protocols for an arbitrary number of agents and protocol runs. The formal model for interactive verification with KIV is based on algebraic specifications and Abstract State Machines (ASMs) [7]. It specifies a world in which agents exchange messages according to the protocols, and an attacker tries to break the security. The interactive verification of the mentioned security properties for eTicket (see 6) by an expert requires approx. three weeks to verify the properties for all possible protocol runs and for an arbitrary but finite number of agents. For model checking of medium-sized applications the application model has to be abstracted to reduce the search space. If these abstractions are done manually they are time-consuming, error-prone and require expert know-how. Interactive verification is also time-consuming and requires expert know-how but with "simplifier rules" that are generated automatically by KIV some verification steps can be automated. Arithmetic is also a difficult task for most model checkers. For example, ASLan++ only provides a *successor* as well as an *equal* function. Other model checkers like NuSMV[8] provide basic arithmetic like addition, subtraction, multiplication, comparison etc. But in those model checkers, a fixed range of values has to be specified. Model checkers that are able to verify properties for an arbitrary number of agents and protocol runs are currently work in progress. OFMC[15] is a model checker that implements a fixpoint module which uses an over-approximation of the search space to allow a verification for an unbounded number of transitions. To cope with the infinite set of traces, OFMC uses some abstractions that are not safe, which can lead to false attacks. It is also possible that the abstractions run into non-termination and nothing can be proved with the fixpoint module. Although OFMC is integrated in AVANTSSAR, it only supports a subset of full ASLan, which is not enough to specify our eTicket example. Hence, we were not able to test the fixpoint module of OFMC.

8   Related Work

Model checking is still used with a manual abstraction of an existing application [2]. Such abstractions can be done systematically and fault-preserving [13] but they are still time-consuming and need expert know-how. In our model-driven approach, runnable code as well as formal specifications are generated automatically from a model. To ensure that the generated code and the formal specification fit together, the resulting formal specification must not be adjusted manually. Hence, abstractions have to be done automatically. There are model-driven approaches that already generate formal specifications automatically for model checking.

The approach developed by Deubler et al. [9] considers the model-driven development of secure service-based systems and uses SMV to automatically check role-based access control policies. SecureUML [5] is also a model-driven approach that defines application behavior with UML. It uses Maude and Spin for model checking and Isabelle for interactive verification. However, it is tailored to role-based access control applications. Arsac et al. [3] use BPMN for modeling security-critical business processes and AVANTSSAR for model checking of security properties like role-based access control.

But all these approaches are not able to check or verify application-specific security properties. That is because they focus on the interaction between agents and do not model the full application behavior. Hence, by using those approaches one is only able to validate high level security properties like secrecy, integrity, authentication, authorization and role-based access control. But many system requirements are application-specific like "only tickets that were issued by a valid ticket server can be punched". Additionally, a few of them also generate code from the application model automatically but this code has to be extended by logic that is usually also security-critical. By combining our approach called SecureMDD with AVANTSSAR it is possible to model check the full system behavior for application-specific properties automatically.

UMLsec [14] describes another model-driven approach that uses sequence diagrams or state charts to model the system behavior and integrates model checkers (e.g., Spin) and automated theorem provers (e.g., SPASS) to check security properties like secrecy and integrity but are not restricted to those. UMLsec does not integrate AVANTSSAR and has not demonstrated the limitations of model checking in a model-driven approach.

9   Conclusion

Model checking can be used to find protocol flaws in security-critical systems. In this paper we successfully integrate model checking using AVANTSSAR into SecureMDD, a model-driven approach for security-critical applications. We have written model-transformations to automatically transform a SecureMDD model into ASLan++. The transformation automatically does abstractions on the UML input model to reduce the complexity of the resulting specification. The generated specification is very close to a manually written one that specifies the full application functionality. We have defined application-specific security properties for an eTicket application and have shown that within one week and a 3GHz quad core computer some attacks could be found but not all. The properties are checked for the whole system that has 52 protocol steps and represents a real and medium-sized application. Because the system complexity rises exponential with each protocol step, even larger applications than our eTicket case study are too big for model checking of application-specific properties for the whole system without omitting functionality. Finally, we have shown the difference between interactive verification and model checking. Future work could be to annotate protocol parts in the SecureMDD model that should be omitted in the resulting ASLan++ specification to reduce the system complexity.

We come to the conclusion that model checking enriches a model-driven approach for security-critical applications greatly. Such an approach with automatic generation and abstraction of formal specifications avoids expert know-how about formal methods as needed for interactive verification. But for large systems the complexity of model checking the whole system is too big. Furthermore, classic model checking is suitable to find application-specific security flaws but for verification (arbitrary number of agents and protocol runs) of large systems, interactive theorem proving is needed.

References

1. Armando, A., et al.: The AVANTSSAR platform for the automated validation of trust and security of service-oriented architectures. In: Flanagan, C., König, B. (eds.) TACAS 2012. LNCS, vol. 7214, pp. 267–282. Springer, Heidelberg (2012)
2. Armando, A., Carbone, R., Compagna, L., Cuellar, J., Tobarra, L.: Formal analysis of saml 2.0 web browser single sign-on: breaking the saml-based single sign-on for google apps. In: Proceedings of the 6th ACM Workshop on Formal Methods in Security Engineering, pp. 1–10. ACM (2008)
3. Arsac, W., Compagna, L., Pellegrino, G., Ponta, S.E.: Security validation of business processes via model-checking. In: Erlingsson, Ú., Wieringa, R., Zannone, N. (eds.) ESSoS 2011. LNCS, vol. 6542, pp. 29–42. Springer, Heidelberg (2011)
4. Balser, M., Reif, W., Schellhorn, G., Stenzel, K., Thums, A.: Formal system development with KIV. In: Maibaum, T. (ed.) FASE 2000. LNCS, vol. 1783, pp. 363–366. Springer, Heidelberg (2000)

5. Basin, D., Doser, J., Lodderstedt, T.: Model Driven Security: From UML Models to Access Control Infrastructures. ACM Transactions on Software Engineering and Methodology, 39–91 (2006)
6. Borek, M., Moebius, N., Stenzel, K., Reif, W.: Model-driven development of secure service applications. In: 2012 35th Annual IEEE Software Engineering Workshop (SEW), pp. 62–71. IEEE (2012)
7. Börger, E., Stärk, R.F.: Abstract State Machines—A Method for High-Level System Design and Analysis. Springer (2003)
8. Cimatti, A., Clarke, E., Giunchiglia, F., Roveri, M.: NuSMV: A new symbolic model verifier. In: Halbwachs, N., Peled, D.A. (eds.) CAV 1999. LNCS, vol. 1633, pp. 495–499. Springer, Heidelberg (1999)
9. Deubler, M., Grünbauer, J., Jürjens, J., Wimmel, G.: Sound development of secure service-based systems. In: Proceedings of the 2nd International Conference on Service Oriented Computing, pp. 115–124. ACM (2004)
10. Dolev, D., Yao, A.C.: On the Security of Public Key Protocols. In: Proc. 22nd IEEE Symposium on Foundations of Computer Science. IEEE (1981)
11. Hinton, A., Kwiatkowska, M., Norman, G., Parker, D.: PRISM: A tool for automatic verification of probabilistic systems. In: Hermanns, H., Palsberg, J. (eds.) TACAS 2006. LNCS, vol. 3920, pp. 441–444. Springer, Heidelberg (2006)
12. Holzmann, G.: The model checker spin. IEEE Transactions on Software Engineering 23(5), 279–295 (1997)
13. Hui, M.L., Lowe, G.: Fault-preserving simplifying transformations for security protocols. Journal of Computer Security 9(1), 3–46 (2001)
14. Jürjens, J.: Model-based security engineering with UML. In: Aldini, A., Gorrieri, R., Martinelli, F. (eds.) FOSAD 2004/2005. LNCS, vol. 3655, pp. 42–77. Springer, Heidelberg (2005)
15. Mödersheim, S., Viganò, L.: The open-source fixed-point model checker for symbolic analysis of security protocols. In: Foundations of Security Analysis and Design V. LNCS, vol. 5705, pp. 166–194. Springer, Heidelberg (2009)
16. Moebius, N., Stenzel, K., Borek, M., Reif, W.: Incremental development of large, secure smart card applications. In: Proceedings of the Workshop on Model-Driven Security. ACM (2012)
17. Moebius, N., Stenzel, K., Reif, W.: Modeling Security-Critical Applications with UML in the SecureMDD Approach. International Journal on Advances in Software 1(1) (2008)
18. Moebius, N., Stenzel, K., Reif, W.: Formal verification of application-specific security properties in a model-driven approach. In: Massacci, F., Wallach, D., Zannone, N. (eds.) ESSoS 2010. LNCS, vol. 5965, pp. 166–181. Springer, Heidelberg (2010)
19. Turuani, M.: The CL-atse protocol analyser. In: Pfenning, F. (ed.) RTA 2006. LNCS, vol. 4098, pp. 277–286. Springer, Heidelberg (2006)
20. von Oheimb, D., Mödersheim, S.: ASLan++ — A formal security specification language for distributed systems. In: Aichernig, B.K., de Boer, F.S., Bonsangue, M.M. (eds.) FMCO 2010. LNCS, vol. 6957, pp. 1–22. Springer, Heidelberg (2011)
21. ZDNet. Attackers hit google single sign-on password system (2010)
22. ZDNet. Chip and pin is broken, say researchers (2010)

Lifting Verification Results
for Preemption Statements

Manuel Gesell, Andreas Morgenstern, and Klaus Schneider

Embedded Systems Group, Department of Computer Science,
University of Kaiserslautern, Germany

Abstract. The normal operation of synchronous modules may be temporarily suspended or finally aborted due to requests of their environment. Hence, if a temporal logic specification has already been verified for a synchronous module, then the available verification result can typically only be used if neither suspension nor abortion will take place. Also, the simulation of synchronous modules has to be finally aborted so that temporal logic specifications referring to infinite behaviors cannot be completely answered. In this paper, we therefore define transformations on temporal logic specifications to lift available verification results for synchronous modules without suspension or abortion to refined temporal logic specifications that take care of these preemption statements. This way, one can establish simulation and modular verification of synchronous modules in contexts where preemptions are used.

1 Introduction

Reactive systems have been introduced as a special class of systems that have an ongoing interaction with their environment [11]. Their execution is divided into reaction steps, where the system reads inputs from the environment and reacts by computing the corresponding outputs. In contrast to interactive systems, the environment is allowed to initiate the interactions at any time, so that reactive systems usually have to work under real-time constraints. Typical examples are synchronous hardware circuits, many protocols, and many embedded and cyber-physical systems.

For the design of reactive systems, synchronous languages have been developed [9,3] whose paradigm directly reflects the reactive nature of the systems they describe. In addition to the explicit notion of reaction steps, languages like Esterel [4] and Quartz [15] offer many convenient statements for the design of reactive systems. One class of such statements are preemption statements for abortion and suspension that overwrite the normal behavior of the system when a specified condition holds. For example, the abortion statement **abort** S **when**(σ) behaves as its body statement S as long as the condition σ is false, and immediately terminates when σ holds. The suspension statement **suspend** S **when**(σ) also behaves as its body statement S as long as the condition σ is false, and suspends the computation in each step where σ holds. Both preemption statements can moreover be weak or strong which makes a difference on their

R.M. Hierons, M.G. Merayo, and M. Bravetti (Eds.): SEFM 2013, LNCS 8137, pp. 91–105, 2013.

influence on the control and data flow of the controlled statement S: While the weak versions allow the data flow actions to take place even if the condition σ holds, the strong versions also block the data flow.

Since reactive systems are often used in safety-critical applications, their functional correctness is of essential importance. For this reason, simulation and formal verification are routine steps in their design flows, and in particular, model checking is often used for these systems. However, due to the well-known state space explosion problem, a modular or compositional verification [7,6] is desired where modules can be replaced by their already verified properties. Large reactive systems can only be verified by modular or compositional approaches despite the tremendous progress on model checking procedures we have seen in the past two decades. Another reason for modular verification is that modules are defined for being reused later on, and therefore the effort for formal verification amortizes when one can simply reuse also the already verified properties.

However, it is clear that calling a module S in a preemption statement changes the behavior, so that temporal properties that hold for S may no longer be valid for the entire statement. It is therefore unclear how one can reuse available verification results for the statement S, which leads to the central question answered by this paper: 'What can we say about temporal properties of **(weak)abort** S **when**(σ) or **(weak)suspend** S **when**(σ), when we know that S satisfies a temporal property φ?'

In this paper, we therefore define transformations to map a temporal logic formula φ to modified temporal logic formulas $\Theta_{ab}^{wk}(\varphi, \sigma)$, $\Theta_{ab}^{st}(\varphi, \sigma)$, $\Theta_{sp}^{wk}(\varphi, \sigma)$, $\Theta_{sp}^{st}(\varphi, \sigma)$ such that these formulas hold for **weak abort** S **when**(σ), **abort** S **when**(σ), **weak suspend** S **when**(σ), and **suspend** S **when**(σ), respectively, provided that S satisfies φ. It is clear that these formulas are equivalent to φ if σ is false, and that 'as much as possible' of φ should be retained.

The results we present in this paper are not only useful for modular verification, which is our main interest. In [2], the authors considered the problem to make specifications for the simulation of reactive systems, which is difficult since the simulation has to be aborted after some finite time, so that properties that refer to the infinite behavior of the system cannot be completely answered. Our results can be also used for simulation in preemption contexts.

In [8], we already established modular verification techniques for synchronous programs. There a preemption context was simulated by introducing new input variables for the verification task. Hence, some assumptions about the context were made during the verification of a module. In this paper, however, we lift a given verification result $M \models \varphi$ where M does not consider any preemption statement to new results $\Theta_{ab}^{wk}(M, \sigma) \models \Theta_{ab}^{wk}(\varphi, \sigma)$, $\Theta_{ab}^{st}(M, \sigma) \models \Theta_{ab}^{st}(\varphi, \sigma)$, $\Theta_{sp}^{wk}(M, \sigma) \models \Theta_{sp}^{wk}(\varphi, \sigma)$, $\Theta_{sp}^{st}(M, \sigma) \models \Theta_{sp}^{st}(\varphi, \sigma)$ where $\Theta_{ab}^{wk}(M, \sigma)$, $\Theta_{ab}^{st}(M, \sigma)$, $\Theta_{sp}^{wk}(M, \sigma)$, $\Theta_{sp}^{st}(M, \sigma)$ are **weak abort** M **when**(σ), **abort** M **when**(σ), **weak suspend** M **when**(σ), and **suspend** M **when**(σ), respectively. Thus, concerning preemption statements, the results presented here are stronger since they allow us to introduce preemption in the module even if it has not been considered there from the beginning.

The outline of our paper is as follows: Section 2 explains the syntax and semantics of the linear temporal logic (LTL), the representation of synchronous systems by guarded actions and transition systems, and defines the preemptions $\Theta_{ab}^{wk}(\mathcal{G},\sigma)$, $\Theta_{ab}^{st}(\mathcal{G},\sigma)$, $\Theta_{sp}^{wk}(\mathcal{G},\sigma)$, and $\Theta_{sp}^{st}(\mathcal{G},\sigma)$ for a set of guarded actions $\mathcal{G}$. Then, in Section 3 the transformations $\Theta_{ab}^{wk}(\varphi,\sigma)$, $\Theta_{ab}^{st}(\varphi,\sigma)$, $\Theta_{sp}^{wk}(\varphi,\sigma)$, and $\Theta_{sp}^{st}(\varphi,\sigma)$ are defined and correctness proofs are given. Section 4 illustrates our approach.

2 Preliminaries

This section introduces the temporal logic LTL, the representation of synchronous systems by synchronous guarded actions, and their represented state transition systems as foundations for our transformations.

2.1 Syntax and Semantics of LTL

For specifications, we consider linear temporal logic, since it is well-known that branching time logics like CTL do not lend themselves well for modular verification [12]. Given a finite set of variables $\mathcal{V}$, the following grammar rules with starting symbol S define the formulas of the temporal logic LTL.

$$S ::= A\,P \qquad P ::= 0 \mid 1 \mid \mathcal{V} \mid \neg P \mid P \wedge P \mid P \vee P \mid XP \mid [P \underline{U} P] \mid [P \cup P]$$

The symbol S represents thereby state formulas and P represents the path formulas. Similar to preemption statements, $[\varphi \underline{U} \psi]$ is often called the 'strong until' while $[\varphi \cup \psi]$ is called the 'weak until' operator. It is well-known that these operators are sufficient to define LTL, but for convenience, we may also introduce further operators like $G\varphi := [\varphi \cup 0]$ (always), $F\varphi := [1 \underline{U} \varphi]$ (eventual), $[\varphi \, W \, \psi] := [\neg\psi \cup \varphi \wedge \psi)]$ (weak when), and $[\varphi \, \underline{W} \, \psi] := [\neg\psi \underline{U} (\varphi \wedge \psi)]$ (strong when). Their meaning is defined on state transition systems.

Definition 1 (Transition Systems). *A transition system* $\mathcal{T} = (\mathcal{S}, \mathcal{I}, \mathcal{R}, \mathcal{L})$ *for a finite set of variables* $\mathcal{V}$ *is given by a finite set of states* $\mathcal{S} \subseteq 2^{\mathcal{V}}$, *a set of initial states* $\mathcal{I} \subseteq \mathcal{S}$, *a transition relation* $\mathcal{R} \subseteq \mathcal{S} \times \mathcal{S}$, *and a label function* $\mathcal{L} : \mathcal{S} \to 2^{\mathcal{V}}$ *that maps each state to the set of variables that hold in this state.*

An infinite path is a function $\pi : \mathbb{N} \to \mathcal{S}$ with $(\pi^{(t)}, \pi^{(t+1)}) \in \mathcal{R}$, where we denote the t-th state of the path π as $\pi^{(t-1)}$ for $t \in \mathbb{N}$. The semantics of path formulas of a transition system $\mathcal{T}$ is defined by the relation $(\mathcal{T}, \pi, t) \models \varphi$ that defines if a path formula φ holds on position t of a path π of a transition system $\mathcal{T}$ (see e. g. [14] for a full definition).

- $(\mathcal{T}, \pi, t) \models p$ holds iff $p \in \mathcal{L}(\pi^{(t)})$ for every $p \in \mathcal{V}$
- $(\mathcal{T}, \pi, t) \models X\varphi$ holds iff $(\mathcal{T}, \pi, t+1) \models \varphi$
- $(\mathcal{T}, \pi, t) \models [\varphi \underline{U} \psi]$ holds iff there is a δ such that $(\mathcal{T}, \pi, t+\delta) \models \psi$ and for all $x < \delta$, we have $(\mathcal{T}, \pi, t+x) \models \varphi$
- $(\mathcal{T}, \pi, t) \models [\varphi \cup \psi]$ holds iff $(\mathcal{T}, \pi, t) \models [\varphi \underline{U} \psi]$ or for all x, we have $(\mathcal{T}, \pi, t+x) \models \varphi$.

$A\varphi$ holds in a state s of $\mathcal{T}$ if all paths π starting in s satisfy $(\mathcal{T}, \pi, 0) \models \varphi$. Finally, a transition system $\mathcal{T}$ satisfies a LTL formula $A\Phi$ if all initial states satisfy Φ, in this case, we write $\mathcal{T} \models A\Phi$.

2.2   The Synchronous Model of Computation

The execution of synchronous languages [9,3] is divided into a discrete sequence of reaction steps that are also called macro steps. Within each macro step, the system reads all inputs and instantaneously generates all outputs depending on the current state and the read inputs. Also, the next state is computed in parallel to the current outputs. There are many synchronous languages including Esterel [4], Quartz [15], Lustre [10], Signal [13], and SyncCharts [1]. In the following, we do not focus on a particular synchronous language, and therefore use synchronous guarded actions as an intermediate representation for any synchronous language. An example for generating guarded actions for a Quartz program is presented in [8] while [5,15] describes the general compilation.

Definition 2 (Synchronous Guarded Actions). *A synchronous system over input $\mathcal{V}_i$, label $\mathcal{V}_l$, state $\mathcal{V}_s$, and output variables $\mathcal{V}_o$ is defined by a set of guarded actions. A guarded action is thereby a pair $\gamma \Rightarrow \alpha$ consisting of a boolean condition γ called the trigger of the guarded action and its action α. Actions are either immediate assignments $x = \tau$ or delayed assignments $\mathbf{next}\,(x) = \tau$ where $x \in \mathcal{V}_l \cup \mathcal{V}_s \cup \mathcal{V}_o$.*

The intuitive meaning of synchronous guarded actions is a *state transition system* over the variables $\mathcal{V} := \mathcal{V}_i \cup \mathcal{V}_l \cup \mathcal{V}_s \cup \mathcal{V}_o$ (see Definition 1). A state s is thereby a valuation of variables to their respective values and the transition relation will be formally defined below. Intuitively, the meaning is that whenever the guard is true in a state s, the action is fired, which means that the corresponding equation must be true. In case of an immediate assignment $x = \tau$ this means that in state s, variable x must have the same value as τ, and for a delayed assignment $\mathbf{next}\,(x) = \tau$, it means that in all successor states s', variable x must have the value that τ has on s. Whenever there is no guarded action that determines the value of a variable, a default action takes place. This default reaction assigns a default value for event variables, and the previous value for memorized variables. Input and label variables are always event variables, while state and output variables may be event or memorized variables. Both kinds of variables are important for the convenient modeling of reactive systems.

Furthermore, we partition the set of guarded actions into *control and data flow* actions, which will be important for defining strong and weak preemptions.

Definition 3 (Control and Data Flow). *The control flow are guarded actions writing a label variable $\mathcal{V}_l$, while the data flow are guarded actions writing a state variable $\mathcal{V}_s$ or an output $\mathcal{V}_o$. We assume that guarded actions of the control flow have the form $\gamma \Rightarrow \mathbf{next}(\ell) = \mathbf{true}$.*

Label variables $\mathcal{V}_l$ correspond with places in the program where the control flow can rest between the macro steps, i.e., these labels denote places in the program code where a macro step ends and where another one starts. By construction, these labels are translated to boolean variables where only guarded actions as shown above are obtained. Since labels are event variables, they will be automatically reset to *false* if there is no assignment making them *true*.

The above informal remarks lead to the following formal definition of a state transition system. The aim is to generate boolean formulas for the initial state condition and the transition relation that can be directly used for model checking. To this end, we first define some auxiliary functions.

Definition 4 (Reactions per Variable). *Assume that for a variable $x \in \mathcal{V}$, we have the guarded actions $(\gamma_1, x = \tau_1), \ldots, (\gamma_p, x = \tau_p)$ with immediate and $(\chi_1, \textbf{next}(x) = \pi_1), \ldots, (\chi_q, \textbf{next}(x) = \pi_q)$ with delayed assignments. Then, we define the following boolean formulas over $\mathcal{V} \cup \mathcal{V}'$, where $v' \in \mathcal{V}'$ represents the variable $v \in \mathcal{V}$ in the next step/state and $\mathsf{Initial}(x)$ denotes the initial value of variable x that is 0 for integers and $\textbf{false}$ for booleans. Additionally, we make use of the substitution $\langle \varphi \rangle_{\mathcal{V}}^{\mathcal{V}'}$ that replaces all occurrences of a variable $v \in \mathcal{V}$ in φ by the corresponding variable $v' \in \mathcal{V}'$.*

- $\mathsf{Default}(x) := \begin{cases} \mathsf{Initial}(x) & : \textit{if } x \textit{ is an event variable} \\ x & : \textit{if } x \textit{ is a memorized variable} \end{cases}$
- $\mathsf{ImmActs}(x) := \bigwedge_{j=1}^{p} (\gamma_j \rightarrow x = \tau_j)$
- $\mathsf{DelActs}(x) := \bigwedge_{j=1}^{q} (\chi_j \rightarrow x' = \pi_j)$
- $\mathsf{InitDefActs}(x) := \left(\bigwedge_{j=1}^{p} \neg\gamma_j \right) \rightarrow x = \mathsf{Initial}(x)$
- $\mathsf{NextDefActs}(x) := \left\langle \bigwedge_{j=1}^{p} \neg\gamma_j \right\rangle_{\mathcal{V}}^{\mathcal{V}'} \wedge \left(\bigwedge_{j=1}^{q} \neg\chi_j \right) \rightarrow x' = \mathsf{Default}(x)$

We will use the above formulas to construct now an initial state condition $\mathcal{I}$ and the transition relation $\mathcal{R}$ of a transition system.

Definition 5 (Symbolic Representation of Systems). *For a synchronous system over the variables $\mathcal{V}$ consisting of input $\mathcal{V}_i$, label $\mathcal{V}_l$, state $\mathcal{V}_s$, and output variables $\mathcal{V}_o$, the transition system $\mathcal{T} := (\mathcal{S}, \mathcal{I}, \mathcal{R}, \mathcal{L})$ is defined by the states $\mathcal{S} = 2^{\mathcal{V}}$, $\mathcal{L}(s) := s$, the following initial state condition $\mathcal{I}$, and the state transition relation $\mathcal{R}$, where $\mathcal{V}_{\mathsf{write}} := \mathcal{V}_l \cup \mathcal{V}_s \cup \mathcal{V}_o$ denotes the writable variables.*

- $\mathcal{I} := \bigwedge_{x \in \mathcal{V}_{\mathsf{write}}} \mathsf{ImmActs}(x) \wedge \bigwedge_{x \in \mathcal{V}_{\mathsf{write}}} \mathsf{InitDefActs}(x)$
- $\mathcal{R} := \bigwedge_{x \in \mathcal{V}_{\mathsf{write}}} \mathsf{ImmActs}(x) \wedge \bigwedge_{x \in \mathcal{V}_{\mathsf{write}}} \mathsf{DelActs}(x) \wedge \bigwedge_{x \in \mathcal{V}_{\mathsf{write}}} \mathsf{NextDefActs}(x)$

Whenever one of the guards γ_i of an immediate assignment $\gamma_i \Rightarrow x = \tau_i$ holds in the definition of $\mathcal{R}$, then the equation $x = \tau_i$ must hold, since the assignment has an immediate effect. Analogously, if a guard χ_i of a delayed assignment $\chi_i \Rightarrow \textbf{next}(x) = \pi_i$ holds, then the equation $x' = \pi_i$ that defines the value for x in the next step must hold. The value of x is determined by the default action if no guard χ_i held in the previous step and no guard γ_i holds in the current step.

2.3   Preemption Statements

In the following, we describe the semantics of the four different preemption statements (*(weak)abort*, *(weak)suspend*) used in Quartz[1].

---

[1] We only consider the *immediate* variants of these statements in this paper that observe the preemption condition also in the first macro step of the statement while other variants omit the starting point of time. All results presented here can be easily transferred to the omitted delayed variants as well.

Definition 6 (Preemption of Synchronous Systems). *Given guarded actions $\mathcal{G}$ of a synchronous system over input $\mathcal{V}_i$, label $\mathcal{V}_l$, state $\mathcal{V}_s$, and output variables $\mathcal{V}_o$. Then, the weak/strong abortion and weak/strong suspension with a condition σ is obtained by modifying the guarded actions as follows to obtain synchronous systems $\Theta_{ab}^{st}(\mathcal{G}, \sigma)$, $\Theta_{ab}^{wk}(\mathcal{G}, \sigma)$, $\Theta_{sp}^{st}(\mathcal{G}, \sigma)$, and $\Theta_{sp}^{wk}(\mathcal{G}, \sigma)$, respectively.*

preemption		control flow $(\gamma \Rightarrow \textbf{next}(\ell) = \text{true}) \in \mathcal{G}$	data flow $(\gamma \Rightarrow \alpha) \in \mathcal{G}$
strong abort σ	$\Theta_{ab}^{st}(\mathcal{G}, \sigma)$	$\neg\sigma \wedge \gamma \Rightarrow \textbf{next}(\ell) = \text{true}$	$\neg\sigma \wedge \gamma \Rightarrow \alpha$
weak abort σ	$\Theta_{ab}^{wk}(\mathcal{G}, \sigma)$	$\neg\sigma \wedge \gamma \Rightarrow \textbf{next}(\ell) = \text{true}$	$\gamma \Rightarrow \alpha$
strong suspend σ	$\Theta_{sp}^{st}(\mathcal{G}, \sigma)$	$(\neg\sigma \wedge \gamma) \vee (\ell \wedge \sigma) \Rightarrow \textbf{next}(\ell) = \text{true}$	$\neg\sigma \wedge \gamma \Rightarrow \alpha$
weak suspend σ	$\Theta_{sp}^{wk}(\mathcal{G}, \sigma)$	$(\neg\sigma \wedge \gamma) \vee (\ell \wedge \sigma) \Rightarrow \textbf{next}(\ell) = \text{true}$	$\gamma \Rightarrow \alpha$

The table shows that the guarded actions of the data flow are only modified by the strong preemption statements since weak preemption allows data actions to take place at the time of preemption. Moreover, weak and strong abortions have the same effect on the control flow. Abortion statements disable all assignments to control flow labels ℓ so that the control flow leaves the system in case of abortion. During a suspension, the control flow is kept and does not move to other labels.

In addition, any preemption context represented by the transition system $\mathcal{T}' := (\mathcal{S}', \mathcal{I}', \mathcal{R}', \mathcal{L}')$ changes the behavior only if σ holds. Hence on a path π where no preemption takes place $(\forall i. \pi^{(i)} \not\models \sigma)$, the behavior of $\mathcal{T}'$ is equivalent to the original transition system $\mathcal{T} := (\mathcal{S}, \mathcal{I}, \mathcal{R}, \mathcal{L})$. Hence, it is clear that we have $\mathcal{S} \subseteq \mathcal{S}'$, $\mathcal{I} \subseteq \mathcal{I}'$ and $\mathcal{R} \subseteq \mathcal{R}'$, which allows us to apply the following lemma:

Lemma 1. *Let $\mathcal{T} = (\mathcal{S}, \mathcal{I}, \mathcal{R}, \mathcal{L})$ and $\mathcal{T}' = (\mathcal{S}', \mathcal{I}', \mathcal{R}', \mathcal{L}')$ be two transition systems where $\mathcal{S} \subseteq \mathcal{S}'$, $\mathcal{I} \subseteq \mathcal{I}'$, $\mathcal{R} \subseteq \mathcal{R}'$, and $\mathcal{L}(\vartheta) = \mathcal{L}'(\vartheta)$ holds for any state $\vartheta \in \mathcal{S}$. Then, there exists a simulation relation $\preceq$ between $\mathcal{T}$ and $\mathcal{T}'$.*

Proof. Simply define the simulation relation $\preceq$ as follows: $\vartheta_1 \preceq \vartheta_2 :\Leftrightarrow \vartheta_1 = \vartheta_2$, i.e. $\preceq$ is the identity relation that satisfies the simulation relation properties. ■

3   Making LTL Specifications Preemptive

In general, a temporal logic formula φ that holds in a synchronous system given by its guarded actions $\mathcal{G}$ will no longer be valid in one of the systems $\Theta_{ab}^{st}(\mathcal{G}, \sigma)$, $\Theta_{ab}^{wk}(\mathcal{G}, \sigma)$, $\Theta_{sp}^{st}(\mathcal{G}, \sigma)$, and $\Theta_{sp}^{wk}(\mathcal{G}, \sigma)$. For example, the system $\mathcal{G} = \{\text{true} \Rightarrow \textbf{next}(\ell) = \text{true}, \ell \Rightarrow c = i\}$ with $\mathcal{V}_i = \{i\}$, $\mathcal{V}_l = \{\ell\}$, and $\mathcal{V}_o = \{c\}$ is modified to $\Theta_{ab}^{st}(\mathcal{G}, abrt) = \{\neg abrt \Rightarrow \textbf{next}(\ell) = \text{true}, \neg abrt \wedge \ell \Rightarrow c = i\}$. Therefore, the LTL specification **A G** *(c↔i)* that holds on $\mathcal{G}$ is no longer satisfied in $\Theta_{ab}^{st}(\mathcal{G}, abrt)$. However, a specification like **A** $[(c \leftrightarrow i)$ U $abrt]$ holds, which states that c is equivalent to i until an abortion takes place.

In the following, we define transformations $\Theta_{ab}^{st}(\varphi, \sigma)$, $\Theta_{ab}^{wk}(\varphi, \sigma)$, $\Theta_{sp}^{st}(\varphi, \sigma)$, and $\Theta_{sp}^{wk}(\varphi, \sigma)$ for temporal logic formulas φ so that we establish the following modular proof rules. These rules allow us to reason about a satisfied temporal logic property (e.g. $\Theta_{ab}^{st}(\varphi, \sigma)$) of a system in a preemption context (e.g. $\Theta_{ab}^{st}(\mathcal{G}, \sigma)$), in case the property φ has already been proved for $\mathcal{G}$. Since we want to use our rules in an interactive verification tool that considers systems defined by guarded actions, we define these rules directly on guarded actions. Nevertheless, the correctness proofs will use the equivalent representation of transition systems that we defined in the previous section.

$$\frac{\mathcal{G} \models \varphi}{\Theta_{ab}^{st}(\mathcal{G}, \sigma) \models \Theta_{ab}^{st}(\varphi, \sigma)} \qquad\qquad \frac{\mathcal{G} \models \varphi}{\Theta_{ab}^{wk}(\mathcal{G}, \sigma) \models \Theta_{ab}^{wk}(\varphi, \sigma)}$$

$$\frac{\mathcal{G} \models \varphi \quad \mathsf{DFNxtEvtFree}(\mathcal{G})}{\Theta_{sp}^{st}(\mathcal{G}, \sigma) \models \Theta_{sp}^{st}(\varphi, \sigma)} \qquad\qquad \frac{\mathcal{G} \models \varphi}{\Theta_{sp}^{wk}(\mathcal{G}, \sigma) \models \Theta_{sp}^{wk}(\varphi, \sigma)}$$

The upper part defines the assumptions of the rule, the lower part defines the conclusions that hold by the rule. The condition $\mathsf{DFNxtEvtFree}(\mathcal{G})$ and the transformation $\Theta_{sp}^{st}(\varphi, \sigma)$ are explained in Section 3.2.

To this end, we assume without loss of generality that the given specification φ is in negation normal form and the next operators are shifted inwards such that next operators only occur in front of a variable, its negation or a next operator.

3.1 Transformation for Strong Abortion

An abortion can stop the execution of a system in every step. Hence, a preemptive specification should express that either the specification φ has already been satisfied or that the execution was aborted in a step before the specification was fulfilled (or violated). These thoughts lead to the following definition.

Definition 7 (Transformation $\Theta_{ab}^{st}(\varphi, \sigma)$). *The transformation $\Theta_{ab}^{st}(\varphi, \sigma)$ that generates an **abort**-sensitive specification for $A\varphi$ is defined recursively as*

$$\Theta_{ab}^{st}(\varphi, \sigma) := \begin{cases} \sigma \vee \varphi, & \textit{if } \varphi \textit{ is propositional} \\ \sigma \vee \mathbf{X}(\Theta_{ab}^{st}(\psi, \sigma)), & \textit{if } \varphi = \mathbf{X}\psi \\ [\Theta_{ab}^{st}(\psi, \sigma) \otimes \Theta_{ab}^{st}(\gamma, \sigma)], & \textit{if } \varphi = \psi \otimes \gamma \textit{ with } \otimes \in \{\underline{\mathsf{U}}, \mathsf{U}\} \\ \Theta_{ab}^{st}(\psi, \sigma) \otimes \Theta_{ab}^{st}(\gamma, \sigma), & \textit{if } \varphi = \psi \otimes \gamma \textit{ with } \otimes \in \{\wedge, \vee\}. \end{cases}$$

The crucial point of the definition is that we have to forbid the use of a variable after an abortion took place, which is achieved in that all recursive calls will finally introduce a disjunction with σ. The definition states that for the next operator, the specification $\varphi = \mathbf{X}\psi$ must lead to a specification that requires that the execution is aborted in the current or next step since σ holds or ψ holds in the next step. Thus, the specification $\varphi := [\psi \mathrel{\mathsf{U}} \gamma]$ (and $[\psi \mathrel{\underline{\mathsf{U}}} \gamma]$ respectively) requires that ψ holds in every step until (eventually) γ or σ holds (the condition σ is added implicitly by the recursive calls). Note that it is impossible to abort the left-hand side of a (strong) until without aborting the right-hand side, too. The same is valid for the Boolean operators because σ is added simultaneously on both sides. For a propositional formula φ, we have for example $\Theta_{ab}^{st}(G\varphi, \sigma) = [\varphi \mathrel{\mathsf{U}} \sigma]$ and $\Theta_{ab}^{st}(F\varphi, \sigma) = F(\varphi \vee \sigma)$.

Correctness. To prove the correctness of the proof rule related to the above transformation, we will make use of the following lemmata.

Lemma 2 (Containment of φ). *The transformation preserves the original specification if no preemption takes place, i.e., $\Theta_{ab}^{st}(\varphi, \text{false}) = \varphi$ holds.*

Proof. The lemma can be easily proved by induction over φ. ∎

The following lemma states that the transformed specifications are vacuously satisfied if σ holds.

Lemma 3. *For an arbitrary but fixed condition σ and a path π' through $\Theta_{ab}^{st}(\mathcal{G}, \sigma)$ and a position m such that $\pi'^{(m)} \vdash \sigma$ holds, we have*

$$(\Theta_{ab}^{st}(\mathcal{G}, \sigma), \pi', m) \models \Theta_{ab}^{st}(\varphi, \sigma).$$

Proof. The proof can be easily shown by an induction over the structure of φ.

The following theorem ensures the correctness of the modular proof rule for strong abortion, and even that the assumption and conclusion of the rule are equivalent.

Theorem 1. *For any set of guarded actions $\mathcal{G}$ and any condition σ, the following holds*

$$\Theta_{ab}^{st}(\mathcal{G}, \sigma) \models \Theta_{ab}^{st}(\varphi, \sigma) \leftrightarrow \mathcal{G} \models \varphi.$$

Proof. The '$\rightarrow$' direction states that we retained 'as much as possible' in our transformation and it follows directly from Lemma 2 and Lemma 1. The '$\leftarrow$' direction directly proves the correctness of the proof rule.

Let $\mathcal{T}$ be the original transition system for $\mathcal{G}$ and $\mathcal{T}'$ be the transition system for $\Theta_{ab}^{st}(\mathcal{G}, \sigma)$. Obviously, if σ does not occur on a path π' through $\mathcal{T}'$, then the original system $\mathcal{T}$ already contained π' and we can conclude from Lemma 2 that $(\mathcal{T}', \pi') \models \Theta_{ab}^{st}(\varphi, \sigma) = \varphi$.

Assume we have a path $\pi \in \mathcal{T}$ through the original system and $\pi' \in \mathcal{T}'$ is a path that is equivalent to π up to a minimal position t_σ where σ holds. We show by finite induction on the number of temporal operators ($\|\varphi\|$) in an arbitrary formula φ, that $\forall m \leq t_\sigma$: if $(\mathcal{T}, \pi, m) \models \varphi$ we have $(\mathcal{T}', \pi', m) \models \Theta_{ab}^{st}(\varphi, \sigma)$.

Base Case: $\|\varphi\| = 0$, hence φ is propositional and $\Theta_{ab}^{st}(\varphi, \sigma)$ is equivalent to $\varphi \vee \sigma$. A case distinction for $\pi'^{(m)}$ solves the case: for $\pi'^{(m)} \vdash \sigma$ we have $(\mathcal{T}', \pi', m) \models \sigma$ and for $\pi'^{(m)} \nvdash \sigma$ we have $(\mathcal{T}', \pi', m) \models \varphi$ following from the definition of π and π'. Hence, $(\mathcal{T}', \pi', m) \models \varphi \vee \sigma = \Theta_{ab}^{st}(\varphi, \sigma)$ holds.

Inductive Step: $\|\varphi\| = m + 1$, hence, $\Theta_{ab}^{st}(\varphi, \sigma)$'s result is besides the trivial boolean combinations either $\sigma \vee \mathbf{X}\Theta_{ab}^{st}(\psi, \sigma)$, $[\Theta_{ab}^{st}(\psi, \sigma) \underline{\mathsf{U}} \Theta_{ab}^{st}(\gamma, \sigma)]$, or $[\Theta_{ab}^{st}(\psi, \sigma) \underline{\mathsf{U}} \Theta_{ab}^{st}(\gamma, \sigma)]$.

For the next operator we have $(\mathcal{T}, \pi, m) \models \mathbf{X}\psi \stackrel{def}{\Rightarrow} (\mathcal{T}, \pi, m+1) \models \psi$. If $m + 1 < t_\sigma$, we can apply the inductive hypothesis to conclude $(\mathcal{T}', \pi', m + 1) \models \Theta_{ab}^{st}(\psi, \sigma)$. Otherwise, σ holds at position $m + 1$, and one can conclude from Lemma 3 that $(\mathcal{T}', \pi', m + 1) \models \Theta_{ab}^{st}(\psi, \sigma)$

Now we turn to the strong-until-operator, i. e. we consider the case that $(\mathcal{T}, \pi, m) \models [\psi \underline{\mathsf{U}} \gamma]$, hence there exists a t_γ such that $\forall m \leq t' < t_\gamma$. $(\mathcal{T}, \pi, t') \models \psi$ and $(\mathcal{T}, \pi, t_\gamma) \models \gamma$. Hence, if $t_\gamma < t_\sigma$, we can use our inductive hypothesis to conclude that $\forall m \leq t' < t_\gamma.(\mathcal{T}', \pi', t') \models \Theta_{ab}^{st}(\psi, \sigma)$

and $(\mathcal{T}', \pi', t_\gamma) \models \Theta^{st}_{ab}(\gamma, \sigma)$. For the other case, we apply Lemma 3 to conclude that $(\mathcal{T}', \pi', t_\sigma) \models \Theta^{st}_{ab}(\gamma, \sigma)$ and we can apply the I.H. to prove that $\forall m \leq t' < t_\sigma.(\mathcal{T}', \pi', t') \models \Theta^{st}_{ab}(\psi, \sigma)$. Hence $(\mathcal{T}', \pi', m) \models \Theta^{st}_{ab}([\psi \underline{\mathsf{U}} \gamma], \sigma)$ holds in both cases. The case for weak until is shown analogously.   ∎

3.2   Transformation for Strong Suspension

A suspension can postpone the current execution of the guarded actions to a later point of time. Hence, no guarded action is executed during the suspension, but the delayed assignments of the previous step still take place. The **suspend-**sensitive specification must ensure that either the execution of the system is suspended, and a violation of the specification is secondary (because no step of the original system is executed) or the next macro step of the system is executed, and as a consequence, the specification must be satisfied for this step. Note that it is possible to suspend the system infinitely often and that this case must be covered as well.

Unfortunately, the transformation defined below is not applicable if the *data flow* contains **next** assignments to *event* variables, because such an assignment may get lost during a suspension. The problem is explained in detail in Theorem 2. Hence, we exclude systems violating this requirement by adding the assumption DFNxtEvtFree($\mathcal{G}$) to the rule. This condition checks that the *data flow* is free of **next** assignments to *event* variables.

Definition 8 (Transformation $\Theta^{st}_{sp}(\varphi, \sigma)$). *For a given specification $\mathsf{A}\varphi$, the transformation $\Theta^{st}_{sp}(\varphi, \sigma)$ is defined as*

$$\Theta^{st}_{sp}(\varphi, \sigma) := \begin{cases} [\varphi \ \mathsf{W} \ \neg\sigma], & \text{if } \varphi \text{ is propositional} \\ [(\boldsymbol{X}\Theta^{st}_{sp}(\psi, \sigma)) \ \mathsf{W} \ \neg\sigma], & \text{if } \varphi = \boldsymbol{X}\psi \\ [\Theta^{st}_{sp}(\psi, \sigma) \otimes \Theta^{st}_{sp}(\gamma, \sigma)], & \text{if } \varphi = \psi \otimes \gamma \text{ with } \otimes \in \{\underline{\mathsf{U}}, \mathsf{U}\} \\ \Theta^{st}_{sp}(\psi, \sigma) \otimes \Theta^{st}_{sp}(\gamma, \sigma), & \text{if } \varphi = \psi \otimes \gamma \text{ with } \otimes \in \{\wedge, \vee\}. \end{cases}$$

The crucial point is again that we have to forbid the use of a variable whenever the suspension takes place. Note again that all recursive calls will finally introduce a weak when operator. A module satisfying a specification $\varphi := \boldsymbol{X}\psi$ is suspendable in two macro steps. The definition states that the evaluation is postponed to the first point of time where σ becomes false. Thus, the specifications $\varphi := [\psi \ \mathsf{U} \ \gamma]$ (and $[\psi \ \underline{\mathsf{U}} \ \gamma]$ respectively) must lead to a specification that requires that ψ holds in every step until (eventually) γ holds or an (in)finite suspension takes place (covered by the weak when operator introduced by recursive calls).

We have $\Theta^{st}_{sp}(\mathsf{G}\varphi, \sigma) = \mathsf{G}[\varphi \ \mathsf{W} \ \neg\sigma]$ and $\Theta^{st}_{sp}(\mathsf{F}\varphi, \sigma) = \mathsf{F}[\varphi \ \mathsf{W} \ \neg\sigma]$, for a propositional φ.

An interesting fact is that an infinite suspension is equivalent to an abortion, hence only a special case of it. Hence, the transformation for abort can be also obtained from the suspension transformation.

Correctness. The following theorem ensures the correctness of the modular proof rule for strong suspension.

Theorem 2. *For any set of guarded actions* $\mathcal{G}$, *where* DFNxtEvtFree($\mathcal{G}$) *holds for* $\mathcal{G}$ *and any condition* σ, *we have* $\Theta_{\mathsf{sp}}^{\mathsf{st}}(\mathcal{G}, \sigma) \models \Theta_{\mathsf{sp}}^{\mathsf{st}}(\varphi, \sigma) \leftrightarrow \mathcal{G} \models \varphi$.

Since the already proved rule for **abort** is a special case of the suspension rule, we only have to extend the proof of Theorem 1 at the appropriate places. We will omit this here and only describe the proof idea with help of Figure 1. There, the effect of a suspension on a simple Quartz program (given in Figure 2) is described in Figure 1. We consider three important points of time t_0, t_1 and t_{1s}: t_0 corresponds to a not suspended macro step starting in l_0, where the next assignment to x takes place. The time step t_1 is the intended execution of the macro step starting in l_1, but this step is now suspended. Nevertheless, the assignment to the variable x from the previous step takes place (v_0), but the immediate assignment to y is postponed until t_{1s}, which is the first point of time where the suspension is released. The assertion $\varphi(x, y)$ intended to be evaluated at point t_1 is postponed as well. It is no problem to evaluate $\varphi(x, y)$ in t_{1s}, since the immediate assignment is executed in the same step and for the delayed assignment the default reaction transfers the value v_0 to the step t_{1s} (indicated by the dashed box). Unfortunately, this holds only for memorized variables, since event variables are set to the type's default value and so the value v_0 gets lost during suspension. Hence, the example shows that a **next** assignment to an *event* variable in the data flow may completely change the behavior of the system. Hence, nothing can be deduced from the original specification. The delayed assignments to the control flow events are not problematic, i.e., are handled correctly.

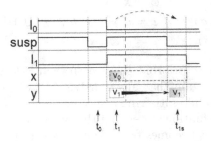

Fig. 1. Time Table for Suspend

```
l_0: pause;
next (x) = v0;
l_1: pause;
y = v1;
assert(φ(x,y));
```

Fig. 2. Quartz Program

3.3   Transformation for Weak Abortion

The weak preemption statements differ from their strong variants by allowing the execution of the data flow when the preemption takes place. If the abortion should take place at the termination point, it will therefore not modify the behavior. A **weak abort**-sensitive specification should express that either the specification φ is already satisfied or the execution was aborted in a state not violating the specification, but before it was ultimately fulfilled.

Definition 9 (Transformation $\Theta_{ab}^{wk}(\varphi, \sigma)$). *For a given specification $A\varphi$, the transformation $\Theta_{ab}^{wk}(\varphi, \sigma)$ is defined as*

$$\Theta_{ab}^{wk}(\varphi, \sigma) := \begin{cases} \varphi, & \text{if } \varphi \text{ is propositional} \\ \sigma \vee \mathbf{X}\Theta_{ab}^{wk}(\psi, \sigma), & \text{if } \varphi = \mathbf{X}\psi \\ [\Theta_{ab}^{wk}(\psi, \sigma) \otimes (\Theta_{ab}^{wk}(\gamma, \sigma) \vee \sigma \wedge \Theta_{ab}^{wk}(\psi, \sigma))], & \text{if } \varphi = [\psi \otimes \gamma] \text{ for } \otimes \in \{\underline{U}, U\} \\ \Theta_{ab}^{wk}(\psi, \sigma) \otimes \Theta_{ab}^{wk}(\gamma, \sigma), & \text{if } \varphi = \psi \otimes \gamma \text{ and } \otimes \in \{\wedge, \vee\} \end{cases}$$

The crucial point of the definition is that the specification must not be violated in a step where a weak abortion takes place. Hence, for the evaluation of a variable the value of σ is unimportant and only influences reads to the variable in a later step. This requires a different treatment of the until operators: Their evaluation must stop in a step where σ is satisfied. Furthermore, in such a step also one side of the operator must be satisfied. Hence, $\Theta_{ab}^{wk}(\psi, \sigma) \vee \Theta_{ab}^{wk}(\gamma, \sigma)$ must hold, but the right-hand side of this disjunction is already covered by

$$\Theta_{ab}^{wk}(\gamma, \sigma) \vee \sigma \wedge (\Theta_{ab}^{wk}(\psi, \sigma) \vee \Theta_{ab}^{wk}(\gamma, \sigma)) = \Theta_{ab}^{wk}(\gamma, \sigma) \vee \sigma \wedge \Theta_{ab}^{wk}(\psi, \sigma)$$

and so it is enough to additionally demand $\sigma \wedge \Theta_{ab}^{wk}(\psi, \sigma)$ to successfully stop the evaluation of the operator. For the next operator, the specification $\varphi = \mathbf{X}\psi$ must lead to a specification that requires that the execution is aborted in the first step (without restrictions) or ψ holds in the next step (with/without abortion).

Regarding the examples, we have $\Theta_{ab}^{wk}(G\varphi, \sigma) = [\varphi \cup (\sigma \wedge \varphi)]$ and $\Theta_{ab}^{wk}(F\varphi, \sigma) = F(\sigma \vee \varphi)$ for a propositional φ.

Correctness. The following theorem ensures the correctness of the modular proof rule for weak abortion.

Theorem 3. *For any set of guarded actions $\mathcal{G}$ and any condition σ, the following holds: $\Theta_{ab}^{wk}(\mathcal{G}, \sigma) \models \Theta_{ab}^{wk}(\varphi, \sigma) \leftrightarrow \mathcal{G} \models \varphi$.*

The proof is similar to the proof of Theorem 1: the used Lemma 2 is analogous for the weak abortion case, but Lemma 3 must be replaced by the following lemma:

Lemma 4. *Let $\mathcal{T}$ be the original transition system for $\mathcal{G}$ that satisfis φ and $\mathcal{T}'$ be the transition system for $\Theta_{ab}^{wk}(\mathcal{G}, \sigma)$. Assume we have paths $\pi \in \mathcal{T}$ and $\pi' \in \mathcal{T}'$ that is equivalent to π up to a minimal position where σ holds. For an arbitrary position m such that $\pi'^{(m)} \vdash \sigma$ holds, we have $(\Theta_{ab}^{wk}(\mathcal{G}, \sigma), \pi', m) \models \Theta_{ab}^{wk}(\varphi, \sigma)$.*

Proof. The proof can be made by an induction over the structure of φ and the fact $(\Theta_{ab}^{wk}(\mathcal{G}, \sigma), \pi', m) \models \varphi$ which follows from the definition of Θ_{ab}^{wk}.

With this lemma and the fact inferred from Definition Θ_{ab}^{wk} that the considered paths π and π' are equivalent up to t_σ, the proof is analogous to Theorem 1.

3.4   Transformation for Weak Suspension

A weak suspension freezes the control flow, but the data flow is not affected. Hence, the **weak suspend**-sensitive specification must express that in case of a suspension, the current state is not left which motivates the following definition.

Definition 10 (Transformation $\Theta_{\mathsf{sp}}^{\mathsf{wk}}(\varphi, \sigma)$). *Given* $\Omega := \mathsf{G}(\sigma \wedge \Theta_{\mathsf{sp}}^{\mathsf{wk}}(\gamma, \sigma))$ *and* $\otimes \in \{\wedge, \vee, \mathsf{U}\}$, *then we define*

$$\Theta_{\mathsf{sp}}^{\mathsf{wk}}(\varphi, \sigma) := \begin{cases} [(\sigma \wedge \varphi) \; \mathsf{U} \; (\neg\sigma \wedge \varphi)], & \text{if } \varphi \text{ is propositional} \\ [\sigma \; \mathsf{U} \; \neg\sigma \wedge \boldsymbol{X}\Theta_{\mathsf{sp}}^{\mathsf{wk}}(\psi, \sigma)], & \text{if } \varphi = \boldsymbol{X}\psi \\ [\Theta_{\mathsf{sp}}^{\mathsf{wk}}(\psi, \sigma) \; \underline{\mathsf{U}} \; (\Theta_{\mathsf{sp}}^{\mathsf{wk}}(\gamma, \sigma) \vee \Omega)], & \text{if } \varphi = [\psi \; \underline{\mathsf{U}} \; \gamma] \\ \Theta_{\mathsf{sp}}^{\mathsf{wk}}(\psi, \sigma) \otimes \Theta_{\mathsf{sp}}^{\mathsf{wk}}(\gamma, \sigma), & \text{if } \varphi = \psi \otimes \gamma. \end{cases}$$

Regarding the examples, we have $\Theta_{\mathsf{sp}}^{\mathsf{wk}}(\mathsf{G}\varphi, \sigma) = \mathsf{G}\left[(\sigma \wedge \varphi \; \mathsf{U} \; (\neg\sigma \wedge \varphi)]\right)$ and that $\Theta_{\mathsf{sp}}^{\mathsf{wk}}(\mathsf{F}\varphi, \sigma) = \mathsf{F}\left[(\sigma \wedge \varphi) \; \mathsf{U} \; (\neg\sigma \wedge \varphi \vee \mathsf{G}\sigma)\right]$ holds for a propositional φ.

It is again provable that the weak abortion is equivalent to an infinite weak suspension. The only difference to the strong case is that the weak until operator in $\Theta_{\mathsf{sp}}^{\mathsf{wk}}(\varphi, \sigma)$ is not changed, because both sides already cover the changes made in $\Theta_{\mathsf{ab}}^{\mathsf{wk}}(\varphi, \sigma)$. The term $\left[\Theta_{\mathsf{sp}}^{\mathsf{wk}}(\psi, \sigma) \; \mathsf{U} \; \Theta_{\mathsf{sp}}^{\mathsf{wk}}(\gamma, \sigma) \vee \mathsf{G}(\sigma \wedge (\Theta_{\mathsf{sp}}^{\mathsf{wk}}(\psi, \sigma) \vee \Theta_{\mathsf{sp}}^{\mathsf{wk}}(\gamma, \sigma)))\right]$ is reducible to $\left[\Theta_{\mathsf{sp}}^{\mathsf{wk}}(\psi, \sigma) \; \mathsf{U} \; \Theta_{\mathsf{sp}}^{\mathsf{wk}}(\gamma, \sigma)\right]$.

Correctness. The following theorem ensures the correctness of the modular proof rule for weak suspension.

Theorem 4. *For any set of guarded actions $\mathcal{G}$ and any condition σ, the following holds:* $\Theta_{\mathsf{sp}}^{\mathsf{wk}}(\mathcal{G}, \sigma) \models \Theta_{\mathsf{sp}}^{\mathsf{wk}}(\varphi, \sigma) \leftrightarrow \mathcal{G} \models \varphi.$

Proof. The proof for the **weak suspend** case is analogous to the proof of Theorem 2, but the exclusion of delayed assignments to event variables (checked by DFNxtEvtFree($\mathcal{G}$)) is not necessary, because all data flow assignments are executed in case of a weak suspension. Hence, the assignments to y and $\boldsymbol{x}$'s take place at t_1 and $\varphi(\boldsymbol{x}, \boldsymbol{y})$ can be evaluated there, too. We illustrate this situation in Figure 3 in analogy to Figure 1. Nevertheless, a set of guarded actions containing next assignments to event variables may only satisfy $\varphi(\boldsymbol{x}, \boldsymbol{y})$ during suspension, since the assignment to $\boldsymbol{x}$ is lost after t_1.

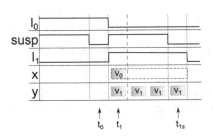

Fig. 3. Time Table for Weak Suspend

4   Example

In this section, we show how to apply the developed proof rules. To this end, let us assume that we have an already implemented traffic light controller, like the one represented by the (simplified) set of guarded actions in Figure 4 obtained from the Quartz file in Figure 5. Note that during compilation a *boot flag bf* is added that is **false** in the first macro step and **true** in all other steps. This is necessary for initialization purposes. The traffic light controller has one input

```
control flow:
  True ⇒ next(bf)
  ¬req∧(¬bf∨10) ⇒ next(10)
  req∧(¬bf∨10) ⇒ next(11)
  11 ⇒ next(12)
data flow:
  req∧(¬bf∨10∨12) ⇒ ylw
  11 ⇒ grn = True
specifications:
  A G (req→grn∨ylw∧(X grn))
```

```
module TrafficLightController
  (event ?req, !ylw, !grn){
  loop{
    while (¬req){
      10: pause;
    }
    emit (ylw);
    11: pause;
    emit (grn);
    12: pause;
  }
} satisfies {
  A G (req→grn∨ylw∧X grn);
}
```

Fig. 4. Compiled Guarded Actions   **Fig. 5.** Quartz Source Code

variable *req* and two output variables ylw and grn (indicated by **?** and **!** respectively), which are Boolean events. Thus, the outputs are **false** for macro steps not assigning a value to them. A traffic light usually has three lights, we will model these lights with the two output variables: ylw=**true** means that the yellow light is on, grn=**true** means that the green light is on, and grn=**false** means that the red light is on. The behavior of the controller is very simple, as long as the environment does not request a green light by req=**true**, the controller will respond by not setting any output (hence, the red light is on). A request is answered by enabling the yellow light (and the red light, since grn=**false**) in the current step, and the green light in the next step. Furthermore, it is easily provable that the controller implements the specification **A G** *(req → grn ∨ ylw ∧ **X** grn)*.

Assume, we want to extend the traffic light controller to operate additionally lights for a crossing pedestrian (with priority). To this end, we reuse the already existing controller, like it is done in Figure 7[2]. In Figure 6, we added the guarded actions for the compiled version where we simplified the Quartz compiler's output and for a better readability, we replaced the term *(C. 10 ∨ C. 11 ∨ C. 12)* by *inC* and *(P. 10 ∨ P. 11 ∨ P. 12)* by *inP*. The original module was used twice, but embedded in two different **abort** statements (in the second call the output for the yellow light is ignored, which is indicated by the underscore). It is not obvious that this implementation is correct, but we will see that our rules help to determine this.

---

[2] We omitted the **immediate** modifier for both **abort** statements to be consistent with the defined rules.

```
control flow:
  True ⇒ next(bf)
  ¬reqP∧¬reqC∧(bf∨(C.12∨C.10)∨inP)
    ⇒ next(C.10)
  ¬reqP∧reqC∧(bf∨(C.12∨C.10)∨inP)
    ⇒ next(C.11)
  ¬reqP∧C.11∧¬reqP ⇒ next(C.12)
  reqP∧(bf∨inC∨(P.10∨P.12))
    ⇒ next(P.11)
  reqP∧P.11 ⇒ next(P.12)
data flow:
  bf∧reqC∧¬reqP ⇒ ylwC
  ¬reqP∧reqC∧C.10 ⇒ ylwC
  C.11∧¬reqP ⇒ grnC
  reqC∧C.12∧¬reqP ⇒ ylwC
  P.11 ⇒ grnP
  reqP∧P.12 ⇒P.ylw
  reqP∧(C.10∨C.11∨C.12) ⇒P.ylw
  reqC∧¬reqP∧(P.10∨P.11∨P.12) ⇒ ylwC
```

Fig. 6. Compiled Guarded Actions

```
module TrafficLightController2
  (event ?reqC, !ylwC, !grnC,
         ?reqP, !grnP,){
  loop{
    abort{
      C: TrafficLightController
         (reqC, ylwC, grnC);
    }when (reqP);
    weak abort{
      P: TrafficLightController
         (reqP, _, grnP);
    }when(¬reqP);
  }
}
```

Fig. 7. Quartz Source Code

Applying our rules for the two **abort** statements after renaming the variables to the specification $\varphi(req, ylw, grn) = \mathbf{G}(req \to grn \vee ylw \wedge \mathbf{X}\ grn)$ leads to $\Theta^{st}_{ab}(\varphi(reqC, ylwC, grnC), reqP)$. Hence, we have to evaluate

$$\Theta^{st}_{ab}([(\neg reqC \vee grnC \vee ylwC \wedge \mathbf{X}\ grnC)\ \mathsf{U}\ false], reqP) =$$
$$\mathbf{G}\ (reqC \to reqP \vee grnC \vee ylwC \wedge \mathbf{X}\ (grnC \vee reqP))$$

Using the same steps we deduce the specification for the **weak abort** as $\Theta^{wk}_{ab}(\varphi(reqP, \_, grnP), \sigma) = [reqP \to grnP \vee \mathbf{X}\ grnP\ \mathsf{U}\ \neg reqP]$.

Hence, we know that the module calls of the *TrafficLightController* together with the surrounding **abort** statement satisfies the corresponding specification (without having to verify it).

Additionally, the first specification tells us that we reached the goal prioritizing the pedestrian's lights, because *reqP* is able to shadow a green light for the cars. The second specification shows that in every step, we are inside the second **abort** either $reqP \to grnP \vee \mathbf{X}\ grnP$ or $\neg reqP$ holds. Additionally, we know that the statement before the second **abort** terminates if and only if *reqP* holds. Hence, in the first step of the second **abort** statement, the property $grnP \vee \mathbf{X}\ grnP$ must hold. Hence, the reuse of the traffic-light controller lead to a correct implementation.

Nevertheless, we have to define similar rules for the other Quartz statements, e.g. a rule for sequences, to determine a property that is valid for the whole *TrafficLightController2* module.

5   Conclusion

In this paper, we defined transformations to modify given verification results such that these will take care of preemptions of the system. These transformations allow us to define modular proof rules for preemption statements to reason about their correctness. We are thereby able to introduce preemption statements even though these have not been considered in the available verification results, and our transformations automatically derive new specifications that hold under the preemption contexts.

References

1. André, C.: SyncCharts: A visual representation of reactive behaviors. Research Report tr95-52, University of Nice, Sophia Antipolis, France (1995)
2. Armoni, R., Bustan, D., Kupferman, O., Vardi, M.Y.: Resets vs. Aborts in linear temporal logic. In: Garavel, H., Hatcliff, J. (eds.) TACAS 2003. LNCS, vol. 2619, pp. 65–80. Springer, Heidelberg (2003)
3. Benveniste, A., Caspi, P., Edwards, S., Halbwachs, N., Le Guernic, P., de Simone, R.: The synchronous languages twelve years later. Proceedings of the IEEE 91(1), 64–83 (2003)
4. Berry, G., Gonthier, G.: The Esterel synchronous programming language: Design, semantics, implementation. Science of Computer Programming 19(2), 87–152 (1992)
5. Brandt, J., Schneider, K.: Separate compilation for synchronous programs. In: Falk, H. (ed.) Software and Compilers for Embedded Systems (SCOPES), Nice, France. ACM International Conference Proceeding Series, vol. 320, pp. 1–10. ACM (2009)
6. de Boer, F.S., de Roever, W.-P.: Compositional proof methods for concurrency: A semantic approach. In: de Roever, W.-P., Langmaack, H., Pnueli, A. (eds.) COMPOS 1997. LNCS, vol. 1536, pp. 632–646. Springer, Heidelberg (1998)
7. de Roever, W.-P.: The need for compositional proof systems: A survey. In: de Roever, W.-P., Langmaack, H., Pnueli, A. (eds.) COMPOS 1997. LNCS, vol. 1536, pp. 1–22. Springer, Heidelberg (1998)
8. Gesell, M., Schneider, K.: Modular verification of synchronous programs. In: Application of Concurrency to System Design (ACSD), Barcelona, Spain. IEEE Computer Society (2013)
9. Halbwachs, N.: Synchronous programming of reactive systems. Kluwer (1993)
10. Halbwachs, N.: A synchronous language at work: the story of Lustre. In: Formal Methods and Models for Codesign (MEMOCODE), Verona, Italy, pp. 3–11. IEEE Computer Society (2005)
11. Harel, D., Pnueli, A.: On the development of reactive systems. In: Apt, K. (ed.) Logic and Models of Concurrent Systems, pp. 477–498. Springer (1985)
12. Kupferman, O., Vardi, M.Y.: On the complexity of branching modular model checking (extended abstract). In: Lee, I., Smolka, S.A. (eds.) CONCUR 1995. LNCS, vol. 962, pp. 408–422. Springer, Heidelberg (1995)
13. Le Guernic, P., Gauthier, T., Le Borgne, M., Le Maire, C.: Programming real-time applications with SIGNAL. Proceedings of the IEEE 79(9), 1321–1336 (1991)
14. Schneider, K.: Verification of Reactive Systems – Formal Methods and Algorithms. Texts in Theoretical Computer Science (EATCS Series). Springer (2003)
15. Schneider, K.: The synchronous programming language Quartz. Internal Report 375, Department of Computer Science, University of Kaiserslautern, Kaiserslautern, Germany (December 2009)

Rule-Level Verification of Graph Transformations for Invariants Based on Edges' Transitive Closure*

Christian Percebois, Martin Strecker, and Hanh Nhi Tran

IRIT (Institut de Recherche en Informatique de Toulouse)
Université de Toulouse, France
{Christian.Percebois,Martin.Strecker,Hanh-Nhi.Tran}@irit.fr

Abstract. This paper develops methods to reason about graph transformation rules for proving the preservation of structural properties, especially global properties on reachability. We characterize a graph transformation rule with an applicability condition specifying the matching conditions of the rule on a host graph as well as the properties to be preserved during the transformation. Our previous work has demonstrated the possibility to reason about a graph transformation at rule-level with applicability conditions restricted to Boolean combinations of edge expressions. We now extend the approach to handle the applicability conditions containing transitive closure of edges, which implicitly refer to an unbounded number of nodes. We show how these can be internalized into a finite pattern graph in order to enable verification of global properties on paths instead of local properties on edges only.

Keywords: graph transformations, verification, formal methods, transitive closure, global property.

1 Introduction

Graph transformations have numerous applications in computer science. Many of them can be considered safety critical and therefore have to satisfy stringent correctness requirements. Verifying the correctness of a transformation involves formulating a property to be verified using a suitable logic and providing a method for proving the correctness of a given transformation. Although many efforts have been made to prove properties about transformation systems, like confluence or termination, there is only little work on ensuring the correctness of transformations. One challenge here is that many verification problems turn out to be hard to express, or worse, to be undecidable on graphs.

Two popular strategies can be used for verification of graph transformations: model checking and theorem proving. Works on model checking involve exploring the set of reachable states of a graph transformation system with respect to

---

* Part of this research has been supported by the *Climt (Categorical and Logical Methods in Model Transformation)* project (ANR-11-BS02-016).

R.M. Hierons, M.G. Merayo, and M. Bravetti (Eds.): SEFM 2013, LNCS 8137, pp. 106–121, 2013.

a start graph to ensure that the required conditions holds. This technique is in particular possible if the graph is small enough but puts immediate limits on the state space of problems, potentially enormous, that can be explored by model checkers. In contrast to the model checking approach, the theorem proving approach reasons about constraints on states, not about instances of states. The search space of a theorem prover is thus typically infinite, whereas the search space of model checkers are usually finite (though large). One drawback of the theorem proving approach is that it is typically done interactively with advanced proof skills and not automatically, as in model checking.

The work described in this paper adopts the theorem proving approach to prove that a transformation rule is correct when applied to an arbitrary graph, provided certain applicability conditions are met. Our aim is to develop methods allowing to demonstrate the preservation of a given structural property during a graph transformation. A fundamental question underlying our approach is: is it possible to reason about a graph transformation by just taking into account the elements appearing in the rule itself, without having to consider others that might exist in the graph where the rule is applied?

This paper homogenizes and continues the strands developed by the authors in previous papers [17,18], in which we have shown that reasoning about a transformation applied to an arbitrary graph can be essentially reduced to reasoning about a bounded portion of the graph, namely the image of the transformation rule in the target graph. However, in this previous work, the verifiable properties are restricted to those that can be formulated by Boolean combinations of simple edge relations, encompassing properties that hold for vertices or constant-size vertex-neighborhoods. Consequently, the proposed solution could not handle global properties that hold for the graph as a whole, thus concern possibly an infinite number of edges which are outside of the rule, as acyclicity and connectivity. Generally, global properties must be expressed and verified at a global level [3]. The challenges here are how to express those global properties in the rule's applicability condition and how to reason about a possibly infinite number of nodes and edges with a finite number of computations. In this paper, we extend our approach to deal with global properties on paths in the rules' applicability conditions, especially connectivity and separation, thus allow verifying global properties at the rule-level.

First we introduce *transitive closure patterns* to express that the rule can be applied provided that two nodes are connected via the transitive closure of an edge relation. Then we show that this pattern, even though referring to a possibly unbounded number of nodes, can be reduced to a verification on simple edges, thus allows automation in this case. We also point out that sometimes one has to stipulate the non-existence of a connection in the underlying graph. Reasoning about these negative connectivity patterns turns out to be much more difficult, and we cannot give a complete calculus. We present however some reasoning patterns that allow a simplification in common situations.

We have used the interactive proof assistant Isabelle to model the transformations and to carry out the proofs described in this paper.

The rest of the paper is structured as follows: after a summary of our graph transformation representation in Section 2, we give some introductory examples in Section 3. Then in Section 4 we describe the background of our approach for rule-level verification. Section 5 presents the main contributions of this paper to handle the applicability conditions having transitive closure patterns in order reduce them to a finite case. In Section 6 we discuss some significant related work. Then we conclude with a perspective on future work.

2   Graphs and Graph Transformations

In order to facilitate the understanding of the rest of this article, we summarize our way of representing graphs and graph transformations.

In its simplest form, a graph gr is a datatype with two functions $nodes$ (yielding the set of the nodes of the graph) and $edges$ (yielding the set of edges of the graph). An edge is just an ordered pair of nodes. The node set of a graph is assumed to be finite (and, consequently, is the edge set).

A graph transformation rule gt is characterized by the following elements:

- **Transfo** gives the rule's name, followed by a list of $parameters$ that designate nodes of the graph that the rule is applied to.
- **Appcond** specifies under which $applicability\ condition$ the rule can be applied to a given graph. This condition, having as only free variables the rule's parameters, is a $path\ formula$ whose structure will be defined later.
- **Action** describes which nodes and edges are to be deleted or added during the transformation.

Visually represented, a graph transformation rule consists of a left-hand side graph (LHS) and a right-hand side graph (RHS). The rule's LHS presents the rule's applicability condition and the rule's RHS presents the result of the rule's actions.

The specification of the transformation in Figure 1 is given as follows. The transformation $Refactoring$ is applicable to three nodes c_1, c_2 and c_3. The applicability condition is that there is an edge between c_1 and c_3 (written as $\ll c_1, c_3 \gg$) and another between c_2 and c_3. The action is to delete the edge $\ll c_1, c_3 \gg$ and to add one between c_1 and c_2.

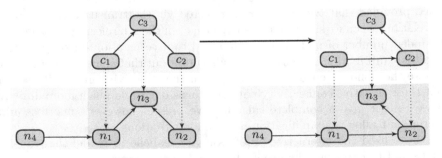

Fig. 1. Application of a graph transformation rule

Transfo $Refactoring(c_1, c_2, c_3)$
Appcond $\ll c_1, c_3 \gg \wedge \ll c_2, c_3 \gg$
Action $delete\text{-}edges: \ll c_1, c_3 \gg$
$add\text{-}edges: \ll c_1, c_2 \gg$

When applying the transformation rule gt to a host graph gr, we need the notion of *morphism* which maps the variables of the rule to nodes of the target graph. For example, in Figure 1 the morphism is the mapping $[c_1 \mapsto n_1, c_2 \mapsto n_2, c_3 \mapsto n_3]$. Quite naturally, some nodes of the graph gr might not be in the image of the morphism, e.g. node n_4.

For a transformation rule gt, its applicability condition *appcond gt* is represented by a path formula pf built on path expressions pe which are defined as follows:

$$pe ::= \ll n_1, n_2 \gg \qquad \text{- edge between nodes } n_1 \text{ and } n_2$$
$$\mid n_1 \rightsquigarrow n_2 \qquad \text{- path between nodes } n_1 \text{ and } n_2$$
$$pf ::= pe \qquad \text{- elementary path formula}$$
$$\mid \neg pf$$
$$\mid pf \wedge pf$$

Given a graph transformation gt, a host graph gr, a graph morphism gm:

- the predicate *path-form-interp* defines what it means for the applicability condition of gt, i.e. the path formula pf, to be satisfied under gm in gr.
- the application *apply-graphtrans-rel* performs the modifications specified in the action part of the transformation rule gt, by adding (respectively deleting) nodes and edges. The precise definition is technically more complex because it has to take deletion of dangling edges into account (c.f. [16]).

With these preliminaries, we can define *apply-transfo-rel*, the relation between a graph gr and the graph gr' resulting from applying the transformation gt to gr.

$$\frac{\exists gm.path\text{-}form\text{-}interp\ gr\ gm\ pf \quad \wedge \quad apply\text{-}graphtrans\text{-}rel\ gt\ gr\ gr'}{apply\text{-}transfo\text{-}rel\ gt\ gr\ gr'}$$

This definition is entirely descriptive and not executable, because it imposes no choice as to which morphism gm (among several applicable morphisms) is selected. The graph gr' thus appears as a function of gr.

3 Illustrating Examples

To illustrate the motivations of our work, we use the example of refactoring navigation models to reorganize the set of web pages included in a web application and the links between those pages.

The rule displayed in Figure 2 describes a refactoring step that might be carried out on a navigation model. This rule refers explicitly to three pages c_1, c_2 and c_3. The solid arrow $\longrightarrow$ presents a direct navigation link r and the dashed arrow $-\rightarrow$ presents a navigation path r^* (reflexive-transitive closure of direct navigation links). The refactoring step consists in cutting the direct navigation link between c_1 and c_3 and introducing one between c_1 and c_2. As explained in

Fig. 2. Reorganizing a navigation model

Section 2, the rule's LHS presents the applicability condition. The application context might require that this refactoring only extends, but does not restrict the previous navigation possibility, for example in order to avoid that pages become unreachable. For example, the transformation keeps c_3 accessible from c_1 thanks to the navigation path $c_2- \to c_3$. If r is the navigation relation before and r' the navigation relation after refactoring, we can express this preservation property more formally by the requirement $r^* \subseteq (r')^*$.

The delicate point about this transformation is the navigation path $c_2- \to c_3$ in the rule's applicability condition, because it might be composed of some edges inside the rule, or might refer to an arbitrary number of intermediate nodes that are not explicitly mentioned in the rule. The next sections discuss three possible patterns of such a path and point out the problems to resolve for reducing the reasoning of graph transformation application to reasoning about the graph transformation rule.

3.1 Edge Conditions

The first example, displayed in Figure 1, describes the refactoring rule where the navigation path $c_2- \to c_3$ contains just one edge (c_2, c_3). This example represents a more general case of transformation rules whose applicability condition includes only the elements described inside the rule. In other words, the applicability conditions of such rules can be expressed with path formulae that are essentially Boolean combinations of simple edge relations.

In our previous work [17], we have proposed a solution to reason locally about this kind of transformation rules to prove the preservation of reachability properties. We will briefly recapitulate the approach in Section 4.

3.2 Positive Path Conditions

Figure 3 shows the second example illustrating a more complicated case of applicability condition where the navigation path $c_2- \to c_3$ is a reflexive-transitive closure of direct navigation links. Thus, this path might pass through nodes that are not described explicitly in the rule but appear in the host graph where the rule is applied. For example, when applying the rule on the graph in the lower part of Figure 3, we can see that the nodes in the image of the morphism (the dark-shaded area), namely n_2 and n_3, are connected by a path running through the outside node n_4.

Suppose that the transformation preserves the navigation path $c_2- \to c_3$, this example typifies transformation rules requiring the existence of transitive closure

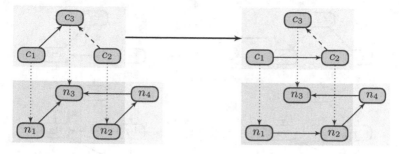

Fig. 3. Positive path condition ($n_2 \rightsquigarrow n_3$)

patterns in the rule's applicability condition. We call such conditions *"positive path conditions"*.

The first representation of the rule defined in Figure 2 is given in Figure 4a. The applicability condition, which is restricted to positive path condition in this example, is that there is an edge between c_1 and c_3 (written as $\ll c_1, c_3 \gg$) and a path between c_2 and c_3 (written as $c_2 \rightsquigarrow c_3$).

Transfo	$Refactoring(c_1, c_2, c_3)$		**Transfo**	$Refactoring(c_1, c_2, c_3)$
Appcond	$\ll c_1, c_3 \gg \wedge (c_2 \rightsquigarrow c_3)$		**Appcond**	$\ll c_1, c_3 \gg \wedge (c_2 \rightsquigarrow c_3)$
				$\wedge \neg (c_2 \rightsquigarrow c_1)$
Action	*delete-edges:* $\ll c_1, c_3 \gg$		**Action**	*delete-edges:* $\ll c_1, c_3 \gg$
	add-edges: $\ll c_1, c_2 \gg$			*add-edges:* $\ll c_1, c_2 \gg$

    (a) positive path condition   **(b)** positive and negative path conditions

Fig. 4. Definition of the rule *Refactoring*

The question here is how to reduce reasoning about the transitive closure relation r^* in the rule's LHS to reasoning about the direct edge relation r.

In Section 5.1, we will propose a solution to eliminate positive path conditions in order to enable a rule-level verification of reachability properties.

3.3 Negative Path Conditions

Unfortunately, defined as in Figure 2, an application of the rule might lead to an incorrect result if the navigation path $c_2- \rightarrow c_3$ is affected by the transformation. Figure 5 shows an example of such situations. As one can see in this example, the path between the images of c_2 and c_3, namely the navigation path $n_2- \rightarrow n_3$, runs through nodes n_4 and n_1. While n_4 is outside the image of the rule in the graph, n_1 and n_3 are inside the rule's image. The transformation deletes the image of edge (c_1, c_3) on the graph, i.e. the edge (n_1, n_3) and the navigation path $n_2- \rightarrow n_3$ is not preserved. Consequently, n_1 is no more connected to n_3 after application of the rule, contrary to the intention of the rule.

Specifically for this example, a (very strict) solution is to forbid a path between c_2 and c_1: $\neg (c_2- \rightarrow c_1)$. This solution introduces a *"negative path condition"*

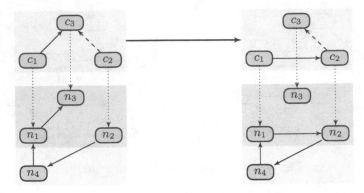

Fig. 5. Positive path condition $(n_2 \leadsto n_3)$; Negative path condition $\neg(n_2 \leadsto n_1)$

into the rule's applicability condition besides the positive one and makes the local reasoning about the rule more difficult to deal with.

Figure 4b shows the rule in Figure 2 reinforced by forbidding the path between c_2 and c_1 to guarantee its correct applications on any graph. This second applicability contains then a negative path condition $\neg(c_2 \leadsto c_1)$.

In Section 5.1, we will outline where negative path conditions come into play during elimination of positive path conditions.

4   Rule-level Verification Based on Graph Decomposition

In this section, first we formalize the problem of graph transformation verification. Then, we briefly recapitulate our approach for reasoning about graph transformation at rule-level.

The properties that we want to prove are properties of global preservation of reachability or non-reachability (separation), formalized in the form

 - $(edges\ gr)^* \subseteq (edges\ gr')^*$ for reachability or
 - $(edges\ gr')^* \subseteq (edges\ gr)^*$ for non-reachability (separation).

where $edges\ gr$ is the edge relation of the original graph and $edges\ gr'$ is the edge relation of the transformed graph.

In [17], we have shown that if we restrict the applicability conditions to path formulae that are essentially Boolean combinations of simple edge relations, it is possible to reason about a graph transformation by just taking into account the nodes appearing in the rule itself, without having to consider other nodes that might exist in the graph where the rule is applied. We explain the main points of our approach in the following.

In a transformation, nodes included in a rule, denoted as node set A, represent free variables of the transformation's application condition, i.e. the possible images of the transformation under a given graph morphism. Embedding these conditions into a larger graph leads us to split the graph into an interior zone of A which is involved in the transformation, and an exterior zone of A which is a priori unaltered.

Since the properties of interest in this paper are mostly concerned with the edge relations of a graph, we define the *interior* and *exterior* of a relation r with respect to a node set A as follows:

definition *interior* $A\, r = r \cap (A \times A)$
definition *exterior* $A\, r = r \setminus (A \times A)$

So an edge belongs to the interior if both of its endpoints are in A; otherwise it belongs to the exterior.

An example is depicted in Figure 1: when choosing $A = \{n_1, n_2, n_3\}$ and $r = (edges\ gr)$, the interior zone is the dark-shaded part in Figure 1, i.e. $\{(n_1, n_3), (n_2, n_3)\}$, and the exterior zone is the light-shaded part, i.e. $\{(n_4, n_1)\}$.

The interior and exterior of a relation are disjoint and add up to the whole relation again:

$$interior\ A\ r \cap exterior\ A\ r = \emptyset \qquad (1)$$
$$interior\ A\ r \cup exterior\ A\ r = r \qquad (2)$$

Similar lemmas hold for transitive closure and reflexive-transitive closure; in the following we give those of reflexive-transitive closure:

$$((interior\ A\ r)^* \cap (exterior\ A\ r)^*)^* = \emptyset \qquad (3)$$
$$((interior\ A\ r)^* \cup (exterior\ A\ r)^*)^* = r^* \qquad (4)$$

The following two lemmas are at the heart of the decomposition method that we propose. When applied from right to left, they split up a goal into an exterior and an interior that can then be further simplified.

$$(interior\ A\ r \subseteq interior\ A\ s) \wedge (exterior\ A\ r \subseteq exterior\ A\ s) = (r \subseteq s) \quad (5)$$
$$((interior\ A\ r)^* \subseteq (interior\ A\ s)^*) \wedge ((exterior\ A\ r)^* \subseteq (exterior\ A\ s)^*)$$
$$\implies (r^* \subseteq s^*) \quad (6)$$

However, the converse of the last lemma does not hold in general. In fact, we will choose A to be the largest set of nodes i.e. nodes of the interior occurring in both relations r and s. We call *field* this and so we have:

$$field\ s \subseteq A \wedge r^* \subseteq s^* \implies (interior\ A\ r)^* \subseteq (interior\ A\ s)^* \qquad (7)$$
$$field\ r \subseteq A \wedge r^* \subseteq s^* \implies (exterior\ A\ r)^* \subseteq (exterior\ A\ s)^* \qquad (8)$$

The detail proofs of the above lemmas are given in [16]. Examining the above subset containments of interior and exterior enables us to have a sound and also complete decomposition for a class of graphs where the region A has been chosen large enough.

Concretely, considering the edge relation *edges gr* (or variants with transitive closures *(edges gr)**) of a graph *gr*, to prove the preservation of reachability properties after the transformation on the graph gr', we replace the goal $(edges\ gr) \subseteq (edges\ gr')$ with two new goals:

$$(exterior\ A\ (edges\ gr)) \subseteq (exterior\ A\ (edges\ gr'))$$
$$\text{and}\ (interior\ A\ (edges\ gr)) \subseteq (interior\ A\ (edges\ gr'))$$

where in practice A will be the largest set of nodes whose existence is ascertained in the actual proof goal.

If the rules only have preconditions that are Boolean combinations of edge relations, it is sufficient to split the graph into an interior (the subgraph which lies entirely within the image of the rule's free variables under the graph morphism) and an exterior (the rest of the graph). The exterior of the graph can henceforth be disregarded; it is sufficient to verify the desired property on the interior of the graph, which can be done by a Boolean satisfiability check or, in the simplest case, by a symbolic computation.

Let us conclude this section by applying the above procedure to our example in Figure 1 to prove the preservation of all the paths in gr' after the transformation. The operational description of the rule specifies the addition of the edge (n_1, n_2) and the deletion of the edge (n_1, n_3) in the graph gr'. The injective morphism *injective-morphism* maps the variables of the rule to the nodes of the target graph gr. The initial goal is $(edges\ gr)^* \subseteq (edges\ gr')^*$. After expansion of definitions and some tidying of the proof state, this goal is derived into:

$$[\![\ n_1 \in nodes\ gr; n_2 \in nodes\ gr; n_3 \in nodes\ gr;$$
$$injective\text{-}morphism[c_1 \mapsto n_1, c_2 \mapsto n_2, c_3 \mapsto n_3];$$
$$(n_1, n_3) \in edges\ gr; (n_2, n_3) \in edges\ gr;$$
$$nodes\ gr' = nodes\ gr; edges\ gr' = \{(n_1, n_2)\} \cup (edges\ gr - \{(n_1, n_3)\})]\!]$$
$$\implies (edges\ gr)^* \subseteq (\{(n_1, n_2)\} \cup (edges\ gr - \{(n_1, n_3)\}))^*$$

Since the variables n_1, n_2 and n_3 are free in our goal, we choose $A = \{n_1, n_2, n_3\}$, and obtain two new subgoals:

$$(exterior\ \{n_1, n_2, n_3\}\ (edges\ gr))^*$$
$$\subseteq (exterior\ \{n_1, n_2, n_3\}\ (\{(n_1, n_2)\} \cup (edges\ gr - \{(n_1, n_3)\})))^*$$
$$\wedge\ (interior\ \{n_1, n_2, n_3\}\ (edges\ gr))^*$$
$$\subseteq (interior\ \{n_1, n_2, n_3\}\ (\{(n_1, n_2)\} \cup (edges\ gr - \{(n_1, n_3)\})))^*$$

We develop the first goal by using the definition of exterior and the distributive property and get the refined goal:

$$(exterior\ \{n_1, n_2, n_3\}\ (edges\ gr)) \subseteq (\{(n_1, n_2)\} \setminus (\{n_1, n_2, n_3\} \times \{n_1, n_2, n_3\})) \cup$$
$$(exterior\ \{n_1, n_2, n_3\}\ (edges\ gr) \setminus (\{(n_1, n_3)\} \setminus (\{n_1, n_2, n_3\} \times \{n_1, n_2, n_3\})))$$

In this first goal, we have $(\{(n_1, n_2)\} \setminus (\{n_1, n_2, n_3\} \times \{n_1, n_2, n_3\})) = \emptyset$ and $(\{(n_1, n_3)\} \setminus (\{n_1, n_2, n_3\} \times \{n_1, n_2, n_3\})) = \emptyset$. Thus, the goal can be eliminated.

The second goal, after reductions by using the definition of interior, becomes

$\{(n_1, n_3), (n_2, n_3)\}^* \subseteq \{(n_1, n_2), (n_2, n_3)\}^*$ which can be verified by a simple symbolic computation.

5   Local Reasoning about Path Conditions

The question about local reasoning becomes more complex in the presence of transitive closures in the applicability conditions of a rule, as in the relation $c_2- \rightarrow c_3$ in Figure 2. Dealing with transitive closure is a difficult problem that quickly becomes undecidable [8]. The existence of transitive closure patterns might be in the form of positive path conditions (as in Figure 4a) or negative path conditions (as in Figure 4b) that is considered as the adequate applicability condition of the rule in Figure 2:

$$\textbf{Appcond} \ll c_1, c_3 \gg \wedge\, (c_2 \rightsquigarrow c_3) \wedge \neg(c_2 \rightsquigarrow c_1)$$

This applicability condition requires the presence of the edge (c_1, c_3), the existence of a path between c_2 and c_3, but forbids a path between c_2 and c_1.

In the following, we outline:

- how to eliminate positive path conditions (Section 5.1);
- where negative path conditions come into play during elimination of positive paths (Section 5.1);
- after the reductions of transitive closure patterns, how to reason about graph transformations by applying the decomposition approach presented in Section 4 (Section 5.2).

We recall that we are mainly interested in problems of preservation of *reachability* of the form $(edges\ gr)^* \subseteq (edges\ gr')^*$. Slightly rewritten, this is the problem of showing $(x, y) \in (edges\ gr)^* \Rightarrow (x, y) \in (edges\ gr')^*$, for arbitrary x, y.

Lastly, the problems of preservation of *separation* are symmetric and can be handled with identical methods, so we only concentrate on the first kind of problem. To simplify the discussion and avoid complicated case distinctions, we furthermore make the assumption that graph morphisms are injective.

5.1   Materialization of Paths

The first step in our simplification procedure consists in replacing paths in our applicability conditions by edges in order to reduce reasoning about paths to reasoning about edges only. The following property justifies this step:

Lemma 1 (Path replacement)
$$(a, b) \in r^* \implies (\{(a, b)\} \cup r)^* = r^*$$
and similarly for transitive closure $(.)^+$ *instead of reflexive-transitive closure* $(.)^*$.

The lemma expresses that a path $a \rightsquigarrow b$ known to exist in a graph can be materialized by adding the edge $\ll a, b \gg$ without changing the path relation.

Proof. In the following, we show the property for transitive closure only; reflexive-transitive closure is similar, but slightly more involved.

One direction of this equation is trivial by using monotonicity of the transitive closure relation:

$$r \subseteq r \cup \{(a,b)\} \implies r^+ \subseteq (r \cup \{(a,b)\})^+$$

The direction $(\{(a,b)\} \cup r)^+ \subseteq r^+$ can be seen by expanding $(v,w) \in (\{(a,b)\} \cup r)^+$ into $(v,w) \in r^+ \vee ((v = a \vee (v,a) \in r^+) \wedge (b = w \vee (b,w) \in r^+))$ and then showing $(v,w) \in r^+$ by case distinction. These steps lead to four situations automatically resolved:

$$[\![(a,b) \in r^+; v = a; b = w]\!] \implies (v,w) \in r^+,$$
$$[\![(a,b) \in r^+; v = a; (b,w) \in r^+]\!] \implies (v,w) \in r^+,$$
$$[\![(a,b) \in r^+; (v,a) \in r^+; b = w]\!] \implies (v,w) \in r^+,$$
$$[\![(a,b) \in r^+; (v,a) \in r^+; (b,w) \in r^+]\!] \implies (v,w) \in r^+. \qquad \square$$

In Lemma 1, we have dealt with the addition of a new edge; we need a related lemma for removal of an edge, as the edge $\ll c_1, c_3 \gg$ in the rule presented in Figure 4.

Lemma 2 (Deletion of unreachable edge)

$$(v,a) \notin r^* \implies ((v,w) \in (r - \{(a,b)\}))^* \Leftrightarrow ((v,w) \in r^*)$$

This lemma expresses that if a node a is not reachable from a node v in a graph, then any edge (a,b) starting from a can be removed without influencing the reachability from v.

Proof. The left to right direction is trivial: as $(r - \{(a,b)\}) \subseteq r$, so $(r - \{(a,b)\})^* \subseteq r^*$ by monotonicity of transitive closure.

To prove the other direction, we define the set *reach v r* of nodes reachable from node v under relation r: $reach\ v\ r = \{w/(v,w) \in r^*\}$.
– The definition of *reach* allows us to conclude :
$$(v,w) \in r^* \implies (v,w) \in (r \cap (reach\ v\ r) \times (reach\ v\ r))^* \qquad (a)$$
– By assumption we have $(v,a) \notin r^*$ which means $a \notin reach\ v\ r$ and implies:
$$(a,b) \notin ((reach\ v\ r) \times (reach\ v\ r))^* \qquad (b)$$
– From (a) and (b) we can conclude that $(r \cap (reach\ v\ r) \times (reach\ v\ r))^* \subseteq (r - \{(a,b)\})^*$ and therefore $(v,w) \in (r - \{(a,b)\})^*$. $\qquad \square$

5.2   Proving Preservation of Paths

Lemma 1 and Lemma 2 are used as conditional rewrite rules in the process of materialization. The starting point is to show that $(\{(a,b)\} \cup r)^* = r^*$, if there is a path $a \rightsquigarrow b$ in the applicability condition of a rule. During simplification, we may obtain subgoals of the form $(x,y) \in r^*$, which may be simplified by

– recursive use of Lemma 1,
– recursive use of Lemma 2,
– monotonicity rules of the form $(x,y) \in r^* \implies (x,y) \in s^*$, for $r \subseteq s$.

To ensure termination, we do not try to simplify or to prove goals of the form $(x, y) \notin r^*$. Rather, these negative path conditions have to be directly given as hypotheses.

$$(x, y) \in (edges\ gr)^* \implies (x, y) \in (edges\ gr')^*$$

where $edges\ gr$ is the edge relation of the original graph and $edges\ gr'$ is the edge relation of the transformed graph, possibly after addition of some edges that materialize paths.

To get rid of the abstract set $edges\ gr$ and $edges\ gr'$, we perform the graph decomposition presented in Section 4. By choosing A is the set of all nodes found in the transformation rule, $(interior\ A\ (edges\ gr))^*$ is the image of the rule LHS and $(exterior\ A\ (edges\ gr))^* = \emptyset$. Consequently, this process leaves us with the only goal:

$$(interior A\ (edges\ gr))^* \subseteq (interior A\ (edges\ gr'))^*$$

We can therefore reduce the global reasoning on gr and gr' to the local reasoning on the images of LHS and RHS.

With these observations, we can verify the transformation in our example in Figure 4b. In this example, we have the preconditions: $(x, y) \in (edges\ gr)^*$; $(n_1, n_3) \in edges\ gr$ and $(n_2, n_3) \in (edges\ gr)^*$. We furthermore have $(n_2, n_1) \notin (edges\ gr)^*$. Under these preconditions, we have to show

$$(x, y) \in (\{(n_1, n_2)\} \cup (edges\ gr - \{(n_1, n_3)\}))^*$$

We now materialized the path $n_2 \rightsquigarrow n_3$ by the edge (n_2, n_3), then showing that this goal is equivalent to

$$((x, y) \in (\{(n_2, n_3), (n_1, n_2)\} \cup (edges\ gr - \{(n_1, n_3)\}))^*$$

Proof. Indeed,

- By assumption we have $(n_2, n_1) \notin (edges\ gr)^*$. By Lemma 2 we can write:

$$(n_2, n_3) \in (edges\ gr - \{(n_1, n_3)\})^* \Leftrightarrow (n_2, n_3) \in (edges\ gr)^* \qquad \text{(a)}$$

- Then by monotonicity of reflexive-transitive closure we have:
$$(n_2, n_3) \in (edges\ gr - \{(n_1, n_3)\})^* \implies$$
$$(n_2, n_3) \in (\{(n_1, n_2)\} \cup (edges\ gr - \{(n_1, n_3)\}))^* \qquad \text{(b)}$$

- From (b) and using Lemma 1 to add the edge (n_2, n_3) to the set in (b), we have $(n_2, n_3) \in (\{(n_1, n_2)\} \cup (edges\ gr - \{(n_1, n_3)\}))^* \implies$

$$(\{(n_2, n_3), (n_1, n_2)\} \cup (edges\ gr - \{(n_1, n_3)\}))^*$$
$$= (\{(n_1, n_2)\} \cup (edges\ gr - \{(n_1, n_3)\}))^* \qquad \text{(c)}$$

Thanks to (c), we have the new equivalent proof goal $((x, y) \in (\{(n_2, n_3), (n_1, n_2)\} \cup (edges\ gr - \{(n_1, n_3)\}))^*$ which can then be tackled with the methods of Section 4.

Choosing $A = \{n_1, n_2, n_3\}$, after decomposing the graph, we get the goal

$$\{(n_1, n_3)\}^* \subseteq \{(n_2, n_3), (n_1, n_2)\}^*$$

which can be verified by a simple symbolic computation.   □

6   Related Work

There are two main approaches in formal verification of graph transformations: solutions based on category theory and solutions based on a logical framework. The first one uses an underlying algebraic formalism as a framework for specifying and executing transformations. The second one defines a suitable logical framework to encode graphs and their properties, then uses inference methods to verify the properties on graphs as logical structures. While the category approach can propose efficient solutions, its level of generalization is rather low. Logical frameworks present general solutions but have to dealt with the problem of decidability and computational complexity. Some recent work on verification of graph transformations tries to take advantage of both of the above approaches.

In this paper we have followed the logical approach, however without defining a new logic, and focus on the verification of global properties. In the same spirit, Basil Becker et al. [1,2] proposed an automatic verification of invariants by creating symbolic representations for possible violations of the rule's properties. Then every transformation rule is inspected with respect to well-formedness constraints expressed either as a forbidden or a conditional forbidden pattern of the modeling language's meta-model. This work encodes graph patterns as first-order predicates, therefore it has to define additional maintenance rules in order to ensure global properties which cannot be expressed by forbidden or conditional forbidden patterns. In comparison with [2], we try to encapsulate global properties at the rule level by replacing paths with edges (see Lemma 1 and Lemma 2) without adding extra-predicates on nodes and edges which have to be analyzed during the verification process.

In [3] the authors analyzed global graph properties as connectivity, acyclicity and the Eulerian and Hamiltonian properties which are not definable in a basic modal logic. Then they proposed using a basic hybrid logic for some of these properties, a hybrid logic with a specific operator for Hamiltonian property and a hybrid logic together with a graded modal logic in order to handle numerical conditions for Eulerian property.

The work in [12] adds proposition graphs to transformation rules in order to compactly described feature connectivity patterns required during the transformation. The invariants to be verified are expressed in Computation Tree Logic (CTL). The main result of this paper states a satisfaction condition theorem for a transformation rule which preserves a given property. Close to us, [10] introduced the *-labelled edge notation as a replacement for a set of paths, each representing a possible sequence of edges. On the opposite, forbidden paths using regular expressions is proposed in the tool Augur2 [11].

In [9], the authors verified graph transformations written in Core UnCAL against the specified input/output graph structural constraints (schemes) in Monadic Second-Order logic (MSO). They first represented both Core UnCAL transformations and schemes by MSO formulas and then developed an algorithm to reduce the graph transformation verification problem to the validity of MSO over trees. The efficiency of this work relies on the algorithm to map the type-annotated Core UnCAL to a MSO-definable graph transduction, in conjunction with the decision procedure to verify MSO formulas.

The traditional algebraic approach has been also explored for reasoning on graph transformations. In this context, graph structures and properties are logically interpreted [13,5]. In [14,6] Pennemann et al. introduced the notion of nested graph conditions to describe structural properties. Since these conditions are first-order logic on graphs with a graphical representation of the nodes and edges, they cannot describe non-local graph properties. This approach extracts graph conditions and feeds them into SAT solvers or first-order theorem provers. However, there is no tight coupling between the semantics (expressed in categorical terms) and the proof obligation generator, and thus there is a dependency on a larger trusted code base.

In [7], the authors generalized the concept of nested graph conditions to Hyperedge Replacement conditions (HR) as conditions over graphs with variables. HR+ [15], the extension of HR, have been proposed as counterpart to MSO formulas to deal with global properties. The authors investigated the expressiveness of HR+ conditions and show that graphs with variables and replacement morphisms form a weak adhesive HLR category. Their conditions allow to express non-local properties of graphs.

In [4] the authors generalized Courcelle's notion of recognizable graph languages. They defined the logic on subobjects together with a procedure for translating MSO graph formulas into automaton functors for a class of categories including the category of graphs. This work allows defining complex properties such as "a subgraph is closed under reachability", or "there exists a path from x to y". However, this theoretical approach has practical consequences: graph decomposition into smaller units leads to a complex translation of graph formulas and more troublesome is the explosion of the state sets of automata which is still an open problem.

7   Conclusion

Expressive transformation patterns (such as transitive closure) that go beyond what is commonly used in graph rewriting systems are useful in some application domains, and they are amenable to a formal analysis. In this sense, we have presented simplification strategies that reduce reasoning about paths to reasoning about edges. These strategies can be understood as preprocessing steps carried out before verification procedures applicable to more restricted graph transformations.

The simplification method we have presented is sound, but not complete. Also, our approach is currently geared towards the preservation of particular properties (reachability and separation). However, for dealing with the challenge of transitive closures, we think that our heuristic approach is a good compromise that we try to extend to other common reasoning patterns. We will also investigate more systematic sound and complete procedures, but for weaker logics.

As witnessed by our examples, it is difficult to get rules right; in particular, this means that some preconditions covering unsuspected special cases are usually missing. Another interesting line of research is therefore to help developers of rules find the right applicability patterns for transformations that are supposed to satisfy particular correctness conditions.

References

1. Becker, B., Beyer, D., Giese, H., Klein, F., Schilling, D.: Symbolic invariant verification for systems with dynamic structural adaptation. In: Proceedings of the 28th International Conference on Software Engineering, ICSE 2006 pp. 72–81. ACM (2006)
2. Becker, B., Lambers, L., Dyck, J., Birth, S., Giese, H.: Iterative development of consistency-preserving rule-based refactorings. In: Cabot, J., Visser, E. (eds.) ICMT 2011. LNCS, vol. 6707, pp. 123–137. Springer, Heidelberg (2011)
3. Benevides, M.R.F., Menasché Schechter, L.: Using modal logics to express and check global graph properties. Logic Journal of IGPL 17(5), 559–587 (2009)
4. Sander Bruggink, H.J., König, B.: A logic on subobjects and recognizability. In: Calude, C.S., Sassone, V. (eds.) TCS 2010. IFIP Advances in Information and Communication Technology, vol. 323, pp. 197–212. Springer, Heidelberg (2010)
5. Ehrig, H., Golas, U., Habel, A., Lambers, L., Orejas, F.: M-adhesive transformation systems with nested application conditions. Part 2: Embedding, critical pairs and local confluence. Fundam. Inf. 118(1-2), 35–63 (2012)
6. Habel, A., Pennemann, K.-H.: Correctness of high-level transformation systems relative to nested conditions. Mathematical Structures in Computer Science 19(02), 245–296 (2009)
7. Habel, A., Radke, H.: Expressiveness of graph conditions with variables. In: Electronic Communications of the EASST (2010)
8. Immerman, N., Rabinovich, A., Reps, T., Sagiv, M., Yorsh, G.: The boundary between decidability and undecidability for transitive-closure logics. In: Marcinkowski, J., Tarlecki, A. (eds.) CSL 2004. LNCS, vol. 3210, pp. 160–174. Springer, Heidelberg (2004)
9. Inaba, K., Hidaka, S., Hu, Z., Kato, H., Nakano, K.: Graph-transformation verification using monadic second-order logic. In: Proceeding of the 13th International ACM SIGPLAN Symposium on Symposium on Principles and Practice of Declarative Programming. ACM Press (July 2011)
10. Koch, M., Mancini, L.V., Parisi-Presicce, F.: Graph-based specification of access control policies. J. Comput. Syst. Sci. 71(1), 1–33 (2005)
11. König, B., Kozioura, V.: Augur 2 — a new version of a tool for the analysis of graph transformation systems. Electron. Notes Theor. Comput. Sci. 211, 201–210 (2008)
12. Langari, Z., Trefler, R.: Application of graph transformation in verification of dynamic systems. In: Leuschel, M., Wehrheim, H. (eds.) IFM 2009. LNCS, vol. 5423, pp. 261–276. Springer, Heidelberg (2009)

13. Orejas, F., Ehrig, H., Prange, U.: Reasoning with graph constraints. Formal Aspects of Computing 22, 385–422 (2010)
14. Pennemann, K.-H.: Resolution-like theorem proving for high-level conditions. In: Ehrig, H., Heckel, R., Rozenberg, G., Taentzer, G. (eds.) ICGT 2008. LNCS, vol. 5214, pp. 289–304. Springer, Heidelberg (2008)
15. Radke, H.: Correctness of graph programs relative to hr+ conditions. In: Ehrig, H., Rensink, A., Rozenberg, G., Schürr, A. (eds.) ICGT 2010. LNCS, vol. 6372, pp. 410–412. Springer, Heidelberg (2010)
16. Strecker, M.: Interactive and automated proofs for graph transformations. Technical report, IRIT/Université de Toulouse (2012), http://www.irit.fr/
~Martin.Strecker/Publications/proofs_graph_transformations.html
17. Strecker, M.: Locality in reasoning about graph transformations. In: Schürr, A., Varró, D., Varró, G. (eds.) AGTIVE 2011. LNCS, vol. 7233, pp. 169–181. Springer, Heidelberg (2012)
18. Tran, H.N., Percebois, C.: Towards a rule-level verification framework for property-preserving graph transformations. In: Proceeding of the IEEE ICST Workshop on Verification and Validation of Model Transformations (April 2012)

Sound Symbolic Linking
in the Presence of Preprocessing

Gijs Vanspauwen and Bart Jacobs

iMinds-DistriNet, KU Leuven, 3001 Leuven, Belgium
{gijs.vanspauwen,bart.jacobs}@cs.kuleuven.be

Abstract. Formal verification enables developers to provide safety and
security guarantees about their code. A modular verification approach
supports the verification of different pieces of an application in separation.
We propose symbolic linking as such a modular approach, since it allows
to decide whether or not earlier verified source files can be safely linked
together (i.e. earlier proven properties remain valid).

If an annotation-based verifier for C source code supports both symbolic linking and preprocessing, care must be taken that symbolic linking
does not become unsound. The problem is that the result of a header
expansion depends upon the defined macros right before expansion.

In this paper, we describe how symbolic linking affects the type checking process and why the interaction with preprocessing results in an
unsoundness. Moreover, we define a preprocessing technique which ensures soundness by construction and show that the resulting semantics
after type checking are equivalent to the standard C semantics. We implemented this preprocessing technique in VeriFast, an annotation-based
verifier for C source code that supports symbolic linking, and initial experiments indicate that the modified preprocessor allows most common
use cases. To the extent of our knowledge, we are the first to support
both modular and sound verification of annotated C source code.

Keywords: modular program verification, verification of C programs,
C preprocessor.

1   Introduction

One of the means to create safe and secure software is the formal verification of
source code. Formal verification allows a developer to prove certain properties of
his source code, so that he in turn can rigorously provide guarantees to the users
of his software. There are many different tools available to verify source code.
Tools that allow to show arbitrary properties of code, require some hints to be
provided. Indeed, the validity of arbitrary properties of code is undecidable. For
many verifiers these hints must be provided as annotations added to the source
code. We only consider annotation-based verifiers [1–5] in this paper.

Proving security properties of code is most often a daunting task. A modular
verification approach allows a developer to concentrate on the security sensitive
parts of his application. We propose symbolic linking as such a modular approach.

R.M. Hierons, M.G. Merayo, and M. Bravetti (Eds.): SEFM 2013, LNCS 8137, pp. 122–136, 2013.

After having verified different source files in isolation, symbolic linking allows to show whether or not the source files can be safely (i.e. earlier proven properties remain valid) linked together into an application without having to reverify them. As far as we can see, we are the first to report on a both modular and sound verification technique for annotated C source code. To support sound modular verification with symbolic linking, we modified the lexical and semantical analysis phases of verification. However, we show that the resulting semantics of these modifications are equivalent to the standard C semantics.

The first modification impacts the type checking procedure of the semantical analysis phase. Symbolic linking requires that for each C source file there is a header file containing forward declarations that describe the functionality from the source file. Besides that, it also requires that the verification of a single source file is performed with the assumption that the annotations in the header files of other source files are valid. Since header files can textually include each other using the C preprocessor, this last requirement implies, as explained further on, that the type checking procedure of the verifier must be recursive to type check every header file in isolation.

The second modification is concerned with lexical analysis, in particular preprocessing. Allowing the full functionality of the C preprocessor during verification renders symbolic linking unsound. Indeed, the result of including a header file depends on the context (i.e. the set of defined macros) at the point of inclusion. This can trick symbolic linking into thinking that earlier verified files can be safely linked together, while it is not safe to do so. A possible solution is to modify the behavior of the C preprocessor: if a header inclusion is encountered during preprocessing, expand it with an empty set of defined macros so that a header is always expanded in the same way. This resolves the verification hazard, but this context-free preprocessor differs from the normal C preprocessor. This can be solved by running both preprocessors in parallel and signaling an error if they diverge. To define this parallel preprocessor, precautions must be taken to support header files that use a macro as guard to prevent double inclusions.

In Section 2, we discuss symbolic linking and recursive type checking in more detail. The unsoundness problem caused by preprocessing is clarified in Section 3. Our solution to this problem is presented in Section 4 and in Section 5 we show that for the verification of a given source file, the semantics of recursive type checking after parallel preprocessing are equivalent to the standard C semantics. We implemented symbolic linking and the parallel preprocessing technique in VeriFast [4], an annotation-based verifier for single- and multi-threaded C programs. The implementation and some findings of initial experiments are described in Section 6. Finally, we end this paper with a discussion on related work and some conclusions in Section 7.

2 Symbolic Linking

Verifying an existing application with an annotation-based verifier is a nontrivial task. If a lot of source code must be annotated to prove correctness of a small piece of security-sensitive functionality, the verifier is not modular and verification would become unmanageable for applications with a large code base. A modular verifier allows the verification of smaller pieces of code in isolation.

To build a modular application, a linker can be used to combine different compiled object files into an executable program. Symbolic linking is the verification counterpart of this compilation stage. Instead of object files, manifest files are created during verification. These manifest files describe the essential contents of the source files from the point of view of the verifier. During the symbolic linking process the manifest files are inspected to decide whether or not the original verified source files can be safely linked together.

This process imposes some conditions on the structure of the source files. First, we describe these conditions. Then we elaborate on the contents of the generated manifest files and how they are used by the symbolic linking process. We finish our discussion on symbolic linking with the necessity of a recursive type checking process for the verifier.

2.1   Source File Structure

An abstract view of a source file is one in which the file simply declares some program elements and these declarations may use program elements from other files. Symbolic linking requires that these dependencies are explicitly recorded in interfaces. In the context of the C language, for each source file a header file is used as its interface. The function headers of the functions implemented in a C source file are recorded in its corresponding header file together with annotations. Without going into the details of the VeriFast annotation language, here is an example of a C source file `abs.c` implementing the function `abs()`, which returns the absolute value of its only argument, together with its interface `abs.h`:

abs.c

```
#include "abs.h"

int abs(int x)
//@ requires true;
//@ ensures 0 <= x ?result == x:
                 result == 0 - x;
{ if(0<=x) { return x;}
  else    {return 0 - x;} }
```

abs.h

```
#ifndef ABS_H
#define ABS_H

int abs(int x);
//@ requires true;
//@ ensures 0 <= x ?result == x:
                 result == 0 - x;
#endif
```

The verification of another source file that uses the function `abs()`, has to include the header `abs.h` (as would be necessary for compilation too) so the verifier can find the annotation. That source file must then be verified with the assumption that the annotation found in the header `abs.h` is true.

2.2   Manifest Files

The implementation in a source file is thus verified with the assumption that annotated declarations (without implementation) in interface files are valid. During verification of a source file, all the declarations that were used but not implemented by the file, should be recorded in the manifest. These *requires*-records from the manifest file contain the name of the interface where the declaration was found and the name of the declaration itself. Besides the *requires*-records, there are also *provides*-records included in the manifest. These records describe all implemented constructs from the source file, together with the name of the interface where the construct was declared. Of course the verifier must check that an annotation of a declaration in an interface conforms with the annotation of its implementation in the source file.

The symbolic linking process uses the manifest files to decide if the earlier verified files can be safely linked together. The process checks that there exists some matching *provides*-record for each *requires*-record in the manifest files of the earlier verified files. This ensures that all necessary functionality is correctly implemented somewhere. Due to the annotations in the interface, the linking process knows that a declaration has the same meaning in all source files (ignoring preprocessing for now) and thus earlier proven properties remain valid.

2.3   Recursive Type Checking

An important issue was ignored when describing manifest files and the symbolic linking process. For the verification of C source code with VeriFast, header files (i.e. interfaces) can contain auxiliary constructs (inductive data types, pure functions over these data types, predicates, ...) for specifying annotations. These constructs can then be used in the annotations in the rest of the header file as well as in the source file. Of course a header file can also use annotation constructs from another header. If this is the case, it must be made sure that the first header file includes the second. Otherwise the semantics of an inclusion depends upon the type checking context in which the header file was included and thus its meaning can be different for different source files that included it. The following unsound example illustrates this requirement:

main.c

```
#include "true.h"
#include "unsafe.h"

int main()
//@ requires true;
//@ ensures true;
{ unsafe();
  return 0; }
```

unsafe.c

```
#include "false.h"
#include "unsafe.h"

void unsafe()
//@ requires false;
//@ ensures true;
{ void **p;
  *p = 0;     }
```

unsafe.h

```
void unsafe();
//@ requires pre();
//@ ensures true;
```

true.h

```
/*@
fixpoint bool pre(){
  return true;
} @*/
```

false.h

```
/*@
fixpoint bool pre(){
  return false;
} @*/
```

The `fixpoint` functions from `true.h` and `false.h` specify pure functions that can be used in other VeriFast annotations and can be considered to be synonyms for `true`, respectively `false` in the rest of this example. The file `unsafe.h` is an interface containing the forward declaration of the function `unsafe()` annotated with a contract. In file `unsafe.c`, the header file `unsafe.h` is included after including the file `false.h`. The expansion of `unsafe.h` will be a forward declaration of the function `unsafe()` with the same contract as its implementation in `unsafe.c`. Again without going into the details of the annotation language of VeriFast, the contract in `unsafe.c` trivially holds since the precondition is false. So verification succeeds even if there clearly is a memory violation in the function `unsafe()`. A function with `false` as a precondition may never be used of course or verification will fail. Verification of the function `main()` in `main.c` also succeeds since by including the file `true.h` before including `unsafe.h`, the precondition of `unsafe()` is trivially satisfied (i.e. it is simply `true`) so the function may be used anywhere. These files verify correctly in isolation, but they should not be compiled together into an application. It is clear from this example that the semantics of the forward declaration of the function `unsafe()` from the included header `unsafe.h` is dependent upon previous includes.

A way to ensure that includes are independent from previous includes, is to type check each (directly or indirectly) included header file recursively in isolation: type check an included header with an empty set of declarations before using its declarations to type check the file that included the header. If an included header file is well-typed in isolation, we know it includes all the necessary constructs for the semantics of its contents. In our previous example the recursive type checking of `unsafe.h` will fail, since the pure function `pre()` is not defined there. To ensure that this kind of type checking preserves the semantics of a language, the language must exhibit the following property which we consider an axiom for the C language:

Axiom 1
A declaration that is well-typed according to two sets of type checked declarations, has the same semantics relative to the two sets if one is a subset of the other.

Since in the C programming language a declaration cannot be hidden by a subsequent declaration in the same scope and we only allow includes at global scope (this follows from the definitions of a preprocessor tree in Section 4 and the fact that a proper prefix of a declaration in C is itself not a valid declaration), the C language has this property.

3   Unsoundness Caused by Preprocessing

In the context of the C programming language, header files are used as interfaces for symbolic linking and these have to be included in a source file by using the preprocessor. However, an annotation-based verifier for C source code that supports symbolic linking, cannot allow full C preprocessor functionality[1] without becoming unsound.

The problem is that the C preprocessor performs textual inclusion and also allows to define textual macros. The earlier described symbolic linking process implicitly assumes that interfaces contain the same annotations for different

---

[1] C11 - ISO/IEC 9899:2011: standard for the C programming language.

source files being verified. But the result of a header file inclusion, depends on the context (i.e. defined macros) at the point of inclusion. We clarify this problem by an example and end this discussion with possible alternative solutions.

3.1 Unsound Example

The unsound example presented here is quite similar to the one from Section 2. Consider the following files annotated for verification with VeriFast:

main.c	unsafe.c	unsafe.h
| ```c
#define PRE true
#include "unsafe.h"

int main()
//@ requires true;
//@ ensures true;
{ unsafe();
  return 0; }
``` | ```c
#define PRE false
#include "unsafe.h"

void unsafe()
//@ requires false;
//@ ensures true;
{ void **p;
  *p = 0;      }
``` | ```c
#ifndef UNSAFE_H
#define UNSAFE_H

void unsafe();
//@ requires PRE;
//@ ensures true;

#endif
``` |

The file unsafe.h is an interface containing the forward declaration of the function unsafe() annotated with a contract. In file unsafe.c, the header file unsafe.h is included after defining the preprocessor symbol PRE to false. After preprocessing, the expansion of unsafe.h will be a forward declaration of the function unsafe() with the same contract as its implementation. So verification unsafe.c of will succeed since the precondition is false. Verification of the function main() in main.c also succeeds since by defining preprocessor symbol PRE to true before including unsafe.h, the precondition of unsafe() is trivially satisfied. Like before, these files verify correctly in isolation, but they should not be compiled together into an application.

Unfortunately, the symbolic linking process concludes that they can be safely linked together. This is clear from the manifest files generated for main.c and unsafe.c, i.e. main.vfmanifest, respectively unsafe.vfmanifest:

main.vfmanifest	unsafe.vfmanifest
`.requires .\unsafe.h#unsafe` `.provides main : prelude.h#main()`	`.provides .\unsafe.h#unsafe`

The manifest file for unsafe.c only contains a *provides*-record for function unsafe() and the manifest file for main.c only contains a *requires*-record for the same function and a *provides*-record for the function main(). Since all required functionality is provided, symbolic linking decides that the files can be linked together.

The problem of combining preprocessing with symbolic linking, was shown here for the contract of a simple function inside a header file. The same problem can emerge if macro symbols are used for function names, function parameters or other parts of declarations.
```

3.2 Alternative Solutions

There are different possible solutions for the unsoundness problem introduced by preprocessing, each with their advantages and disadvantages. One solution could be to include annotations after preprocessing in the manifest files and check during symbolic linking that corresponding annotations are identical. However, in VeriFast annotations can be specified using inductive data types, primitive recursive pure functions over these data types and predicates. For this solution to work, these construct also have to be included in the manifest file and will make it bloated.

Another possible solution would be to reverify the source files during symbolic linking. In many cases this solution is unacceptable (e.g. it deteriorates modularity) or even impossible (e.g. linking with a library when only the header files of that library are available and not the source code).

Finally, the solution presented in the rest of this paper makes use of a modified (context-free) preprocessor. This context-free preprocessor does the trick by processing each included header with an empty set of defined macros. Thus the inclusion is not dependent on the context in which the include occurs (i.e. context-free). The context-free preprocessor should then be executed in parallel with the normal preprocessor and if their outputs diverge, an error is reported. This ensures that a correct execution of the resulting parallel preprocessor is context-free and compliant with the normal C preprocessor.

4 Preprocessing for Sound Symbolic Linking

Here, we describe our solution to the unsoundness problem. First, we formalize the preprocessor by describing its behavior with a set of inference rules. Then, based on this formalization, a parallel preprocessing process is explained that resolves the unsoundness by construction. We conclude this discussion of our solution with a formal definition of the resulting semantics of the verification process as compared to a normal compilation process.

4.1 Preprocessing Formalized

Before presenting our solution, it is instructive to formalize the behavior of the preprocessor. Using the unspecified sets W and H we define in Definition 1 a token which represents the contents of a source file. Representing a source file by a single token simplifies the definitions that follow. A token can be a list of words

Definition 1.
$w \in W$ and $h \in H$
$t \in T ::=$
$\quad | \ \bar{w} \qquad | \ \pmb{def} \ w \ \bar{w}$
$\quad | \ t \ t \qquad | \ \pmb{undef} \ w$
$\quad | \ h \qquad | \ \pmb{ifdef} \ w \ t \ \pmb{else} \ t \ \pmb{endif}$

Definition 2.
$m \in H \to T$

Definition 3.
$d \in W \rightharpoonup W^*$

Definition 4.
$\tau ::=$
$\quad | \ []$
$\quad | \ w :: \tau$
$\quad | \ (h, \tau) :: \tau$

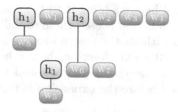

Fig. 1. Graphical representation of the preprocessor tree
$[(h_1, [w_5]), w_1, (h_2, [(h_1, [w_5]), w_6, w_7]), w_2, w_3, w_4]$

($\bar{w} \in W^*$), a sequence of other tokens (t t) or a preprocessor directive. In this simplified setting there are directives for header inclusion (h), macro definition (**def** w $\bar{w}$), macro removal (**undef** w) and conditional compilation (**ifdef** w t **else** t **endif**). During preprocessing, a header map m is used to retrieve the contents of header files and the partial function d is used to remember the defined macros. The output of the preprocessor is a preprocessor tree τ, which is in fact a list of words augmented with the original include structure of the source file as illustrated in Fig. 1.

The behavior of the C preprocessor can then be captured by the (incomplete) inference rules rules in Definition 5 using big-step semantics. The complete set of rules can be found in a technical report [6]. Only the rules for macro definition, macro expansion and header expansion are shown here. The judgment $m \vdash (d, t) \Downarrow (d', \tau)$ defined by Definition 5, indicates that, given a certain header map m, the formal preprocessor will accept a token t and a set of defined macros d and it returns a resulting preprocessor tree τ and an updated set of defined macros d'.

In rule P-DEFINE the function update is used to add the defined macro to d. Since a premise in the rule P-WORDS-UNDEFINED states that w is not in the domain of d, the word is just copied to the resulting preprocessor tree. In the rule P-WORDS-DEFINED on the other hand, w is in the domain of d and its

Definition 5. *Inference rules for preprocessing*

$$\frac{}{m \vdash (d, \mathbf{def}\ w\ \bar{w}) \Downarrow (d[w := \bar{w}], [])}\ \text{P-DEFINE}$$

$$\frac{w \notin dom(d) \qquad m \vdash (d, \bar{w}) \Downarrow (d, \tau)}{m \vdash (d, w :: \bar{w}) \Downarrow (d, w :: \tau)}\ \text{P-WORDS-UNDEFINED}$$

$$\frac{\begin{array}{c} w \in dom(d) \\ d(w) = \bar{w}_1 \qquad m \vdash (d, \bar{w}_2) \Downarrow (d, \tau_2) \\ m \vdash (d|_{dom(d) \setminus \{w\}}, \bar{w}_1) \Downarrow (d|_{dom(d) \setminus \{w\}}, \tau_1) \end{array}}{m \vdash (d, w :: \bar{w}_2) \Downarrow (d, \tau_1\ \tau_2)}\ \text{P-WORDS-DEFINED}$$

$$\frac{m \vdash (d, m(h)) \Downarrow (d', \tau)}{m \vdash (d, h) \Downarrow (d', [(h, \tau)])}\ \text{P-HEADER-EXP}$$

expansion $\bar{w}$ is preprocessed before adding it to the resulting preprocessor tree. The domain restriction of a function is used there to indicate that the expansion of a macro is preprocessed without the macro itself as a defined macro. Finally, the problematic rule P-WORDS-EXP describes how a header is expanded. It is clear from this rule that the header is preprocessed with the current partial function of defined macros d before the expansion is returned.

4.2   Parallel Preprocessing

As mentioned before, it is the context-dependency of the inclusion of a header in rule P-HEADER-EXP that renders symbolic linking unsound. To overcome this problem we define the context-free preprocessor. The context-free preprocessor works exactly the same as the normal preprocessor except that when it encounters an include directive, the expansion of the included file is calculated by a recursive call with an empty set of defined macros. This is done by replacing the rule P-HEADER-EXP with the rule CFP-HEADER-CF-EXP from Definition 6 (for the complete set of rules see [6]), which results in the definition of the judgment $m \vdash (d, t) \Downarrow_{cf} (d', \tau)$. Since the defined macros at the point of inclusion are the only source of variability in the resulting expansion, the context-free preprocessor always expands an included file in the same way. So the context of defined macros does not influence the result of an inclusion. Note that the macros that are defined during preprocessing of the header file, are added to the preexisting macros.

Definition 6. *Inference rule for context-free header expansion*

$$\frac{m \vdash (\varnothing, m(h)) \Downarrow_{cf} (d', \tau)}{m \vdash (d, h) \Downarrow_{cf} (d \cup d', [(h, \tau)])} \text{ CFP-HEADER-CF-EXP}$$

The context-free preprocessor clearly behaves differently from the normal preprocessor, but its context-freeness ensures that symbolic linking is sound. However, the compliance to the C standard of the normal preprocessor is also required. Our solution is to run both preprocessors in parallel and signal an error if they diverge. Care must be taken with the inclusion of header files that protect themselves from double inclusions by using a macro as guard (i.e. guarded headers). Since the inference rule CFP-HEADER-CF-EXP calls the preprocessor recursively with an empty set of defined macros, the macro guarding a header file is never defined at that point during preprocessing. Thus the second time a guarded header is included, it is expanded anyway by the context-free preprocessor. The normal preprocessor will not expand the second include of that guarded header. So a naive parallel preprocessing technique, would fail here.

To make parallel preprocessing succeed for guarded headers, we remove the secondary occurrences of header includes during context-free preprocessing. Only thereafter are the produced normal preprocessor tree and context-free preprocessor tree checked for equality during parallel preprocessing. This is safe to do, since the context-free preprocessor always expands a header to the same parse tree. To formalize this we first need the function I_h that does nothing more than collecting all the header names that occur in an outputted preprocessor tree τ or in a set $\bar{\bar{h}}$ containing header nodes (i.e. ordered pairs of header names and preprocessor trees).

Definition 7. *Function I_h collects header names*

$$
\begin{aligned}
I_h([]) &= \varnothing \\
I_h(b :: \tau) &= I_h(\tau) \\
I_h((h, \tau_h) :: \tau) &= \{h\} \cup I_h(\tau_h) \cup I_h(\tau) \\
&\quad and \\
I_h(\bar{\bar{h}}) &= \bigcup_{\bar{h} \in \bar{\bar{h}}} I_h([\bar{h}])
\end{aligned}
$$

Having defined the function I_h, we now can specify the function RSO which removes secondary occurrences from a preprocessor tree. As shown in Definition 8, this function expects a preprocessor tree τ and a set of already encountered header names $\bar{h}$. Only the case for $\tau = (h, \tau_h) :: \tau_r$ and $h \notin \bar{h}$ is worth discussing. Secondary occurrences from the tree τ_h are removed first and only then are they removed from τ_r. Note that the header names encountered while processing τ_h must be added to the set of already encountered headers names $\bar{h}$ before processing τ_r. This is the reason for adding the set $I_h([(h, \tau_{h'})])$ to $\bar{h}$ before RSO is called recursively.

Definition 8. *Function RSO removes secondary occurrences*

$$
\begin{aligned}
RSO([], \bar{h}) &= [] \\
RSO(b :: \tau_r, \bar{h}) &= b :: RSO(\tau_r, \bar{h}) \\
RSO((h, \tau_h) :: \tau_r, \bar{h}) &= (h, []) :: RSO(\tau_r, \bar{h}) &&(if\ h \in \bar{h}) \\
RSO((h, \tau_h) :: \tau_r, \bar{h}) &= \textbf{let } \tau_{h'} = RSO(\tau_h, \bar{h} \cup \{h\}) \textbf{ in} &&(if\ h \notin \bar{h}) \\
&\quad (h, \tau_{h'}) :: RSO(\tau_r, \bar{h} \cup I_h([(h, \tau_{h'})]))
\end{aligned}
$$

Finally, we can formalize the parallel preprocessing technique. Let the judgment $m, t \blacktriangleright \tau_p, \tau_{cfp}$ as defined in Definition 9 indicate that parallel preprocessing succeeded and produced the normal preprocessor tree τ_p and the context-free preprocessor tree τ_{cfp} for a specific token t and header map m (and an empty set of defined macros). Thus the implementation of the parallel preprocessing technique (see Section 6) must ensure that if it was successful, then $\tau_p = RSO(\tau_{cfp}, \varnothing)$ holds. Notice that this means that we do not support unguarded headers.

Definition 9. *Semantics of parallel preprocessing*

$$
\forall\, m, t, \tau_p, \tau_{cfp}.\ m, t \blacktriangleright \tau_p, \tau_{cfp} \Leftrightarrow \exists\, d_p, d_{cfp}.\
\begin{cases}
m \vdash (\varnothing, t) \Downarrow (d_p, \tau_p) \ \wedge \\
m \vdash (\varnothing, t) \Downarrow_{cf} (d_{cfp}, \tau_{cfp}) \ \wedge \\
\tau_p = RSO(\tau_{cfp}, \varnothing)
\end{cases}
$$

4.3 Resulting Semantics

Our sound approach to modular verification we call symbolic linking requires a modified (i.e. context-free) preprocessing phase and a modified semantic analysis phase (i.e. recursive type checking). While the behavior of each phase separately differs from the C standard, we prove in Section 5 that their combined semantics are equivalent to the semantics defined by the C standard.

In order to state the soundness theorem for our approach, we need a way to specify the semantics of normal compilation and the semantics of a verification process with parallel preprocessing and recursive type checking. For this reason we introduce the following concepts:

- a declaration block ($b \in W^*$):
    a list of declarations that is not interrupted by an include directive
- a type checked declaration block ($b_{tc} \in W^* \times E$):
    an ordered pair of a declaration block and its type checking environment
- a type checking environment ($e \in E = \mathbb{N}_0^{W^* \times E}$):
    a multiset of declaration blocks

Strictly speaking E is the smallest set for which $E = \mathbb{N}_0^{W^* \times E}$ holds. Now we can express the semantics of compilation and verification in terms of a type checking environment. We will discuss these in turn.

Compilation. Let the function CP from Definition 10 represent the normal type checking procedure in the compilation process. The input to CP is a normal preprocessor tree τ and a current global type checking environment e_g, and the output is the resulting type checking environment which represents the semantics of the source file during compilation. This resulting type checking environment is a multiset containing all the declaration blocks found in the preprocessor tree together with the environment in which they are to be type checked. For a one-pass compile language like C every declaration is type checked given all the previous encountered declarations. This is the reason that e_g is called the global environment. So the rule for CP($b :: \tau, e_g$) in Definition 10 correctly includes the previous global environment as the type checking environment of the encountered declaration block b. Note that b is used here to implicitly indicate the longest match of consecutive words in the tree that is not interrupted by an include.

Definition 10. *Function CP computes semantics of compilation*

$$CP([], e_g) = e_g$$
$$CP(b :: \tau, e_g) = CP(\tau, e_g \uplus \{|(b, e_g)|\})$$
$$CP((h, \tau_h) :: \tau, e_g) = CP(\tau, CP(\tau_h, e_g))$$

Verification. The function VF specified in Definition 11 (and named VF_s in [6]) represents the recursive type checking process of a verifier that supports our solution for sound symbolic linking. The output of VF is again a type checking environment and represents the semantics of the corresponding source file as seen by the verification process.

In contrast to CP, VF does recursive type checking and so the type checking environment e_d expected by VF is not global. It only contains declarations directly declared in the current expansion. Besides a context-free preprocessor tree τ and a direct type checking environment e_d, the function VF also expects

Definition 11. *Function VF computes semantics of verification*

$$VF([], \bar{\bar{h}}_t, e_d) = e_d$$
$$VF(b :: \tau, \bar{\bar{h}}_t, e_d) = \mathbf{let}\ e := e_d \uplus MH(\bar{\bar{h}}_t)\ \mathbf{in}$$
$$VF(\tau, \bar{\bar{h}}_t, e_d \uplus \{|(b, e)|\})$$
$$VF(\tilde{h} :: \tau, \bar{\bar{h}}_t, e_d) = VF(\tau, \bar{\bar{h}}_t \cup I_\tau([\tilde{h}]), e_d)$$

Definition 12. *Function I_τ collects header nodes*

$$I_\tau([]) = \varnothing$$
$$I_\tau(b :: \tau) = I_\tau(\tau)$$
$$I_\tau((h, \tau_h) :: \tau) = \{(h, \tau_h)\} \cup I_\tau(\tau_h) \cup I_\tau(\tau)$$
$$and$$
$$I_\tau(\bar{\bar{h}}) = \bigcup_{\tilde{h} \in \bar{\bar{h}}} I_\tau([\tilde{h}])$$

a set of transitively encountered header nodes $\bar{\bar{h}}_t$. In this set the occurrences of included headers are collected together with their transitive includes. As for e_d, this multiset only contains headers from the current expansion. To calculate the transitive includes of the encountered header in the rule for $VF(\tilde{h} :: \tau, \bar{\bar{h}}_t, e_d)$, the function I_τ from Definition 12 is used before adding the result to $\bar{\bar{h}}_t$.

The rule for $VF(b :: \tau, \bar{\bar{h}}_t, e_d)$ does all the work to get the correct recursive type checking environment for type checking the encountered declaration block. The recursive type checking environment is the direct type checking environment together with all the declaration blocks occurring in $\bar{\bar{h}}_t$. But the declaration blocks from $\bar{\bar{h}}_t$ must be type checked before they are to be added to the type checking environment of the encountered declaration block. So the auxiliary function MH from Definition 13 is used in the let expression of rule $VF(b :: \tau, \bar{\bar{h}}, e_d)$ to calculate these type checked declaration blocks from $\bar{\bar{h}}_t$. Function MH simply calculates the resulting type checking environment of all the header nodes in $\bar{\bar{h}}_t$ using the function VF. These type checking environments are then merged and the final resulting type checking environment is returned.

Definition 13. *Function MH merges header nodes into type checking environment*

$$MH(\bar{\bar{h}}) = \biguplus_{(h, \tau) \in \bar{\bar{h}}} VF(\tau, \varnothing, \varnothing)$$

5   Proof of Equivalence

In the previous section we formalized the semantics of compilation and verification with sound symbolic linking. We now must make sure that their semantics are equivalent. Otherwise a successful verification would be meaningless, since the verification is then performed on a semantically different program. So we need a way to compare type checking environments which represent the semantics of compilation and verification.

Comparing type checking environments can be done using the two mutually recursive judgments from Definition 14 and Definition 15. The (asymmetric)

Definition 14. *Equivalence of type checking environments*

$$\frac{}{\varnothing \gtrsim \varnothing} \text{ENV-EQ-EMPTY}$$

$$\frac{e_1 \gtrsim e_2 \qquad e_{11} \succeq e_{21}}{\{|(b, e_{11})|\} \uplus e_1 \gtrsim \{|(b, e_{21})|\} \uplus e_2} \text{ENV-EQ-NOT-EMPTY}$$

Definition 15. *Subsumption of type checking environments*

$$\forall e_1, e_2. \ (e_1 \succeq e_2 \Leftrightarrow \exists e_3. e_1 \gtrsim e_2 \uplus e_3)$$

judgment $\gtrsim$ from Definition 14 means equivalence between two type checking environments. Clearly two empty environments are equivalent. If two environments are equivalent, adding a type checked declaration block to each of them where the type checking environment of the first subsumes the one of the second as defined by the judgment $\succeq$ from Definition 15, preserves this equivalence.

To see why the judgment from Definition 14 indeed implies that equivalent type checking environments have the same semantics according to the C language, note that the C language has the property mentioned in Axiom 1: declarations can not be hidden by subsequent ones.

If we can prove that (when parallel preprocessing succeeds) for a preprocessor tree τ_p generated from a specific source file by the normal preprocessor and a preprocessor tree τ_{cfp} generated form the same file by the context-free preprocessor, the semantics of $CP(\tau_p, \varnothing)$ are the same as that of $VF(\tau_{cfp}, \varnothing, \varnothing) \uplus \mathrm{MH}(I_\tau(\tau_{cfp}))$, we know that the verification has the same semantics as compilation. This main property of our approach is expressed in Theorem 1.

Theorem 1. *Soundness theorem*

$$\forall m, t, \tau_p, \tau_{cfp}. \ m, t \blacktriangleright \tau_p, \tau_{cfp} \ \Rightarrow \ CP(\tau_p, \varnothing) \gtrsim VF(\tau_{cfp}, \varnothing, \varnothing) \uplus MH(I_\tau(\tau_{cfp}))$$

We proved this theorem by first showing the validity of Lemma 1 from which Theorem 1 can be straightforwardly deduced. The proof of Lemma 1 is omitted here for space reasons but can be found in [6].

Lemma 1. *Main lemma*

$$\forall \tau_p, \tau_{cfp}, e_g, e_d, e_o, \bar{\bar{h}}_t, \bar{\bar{h}}_o. \begin{cases} \bar{\bar{h}}_t = I_\tau(\bar{\bar{h}}_t) \wedge \\ \bar{\bar{h}}_o = I_\tau(\bar{\bar{h}}_o) \wedge \\ (\forall h, \tau_h. \ (h, \tau_h) \in I_\tau(\tau_{cfp}) \Rightarrow (h, \tau_h) \notin I_\tau(\tau_h)) \wedge \\ (\forall h, \tau_1, \tau_2. \ ((h, \tau_1) \in I_\tau(\tau_{cfp}) \wedge \\ \qquad (h, \tau_2) \in I_\tau(\tau_{cfp}) \cup \bar{\bar{h}}_t \cup \bar{\bar{h}}_o) \Rightarrow \tau_1 = \tau_2) \wedge \\ \tau_p = RSO(\tau_{cfp}, I_h(\bar{\bar{h}}_t \cup \bar{\bar{h}}_o)) \wedge \\ e_g \gtrsim e_d \uplus MH(\bar{\bar{h}}_t \cup \bar{\bar{h}}_o) \uplus e_o \end{cases}$$

$$\Rightarrow CP(\tau_p, e_g) \gtrsim VF_s(\tau_{cfp}, \bar{\bar{h}}_t, e_d) \uplus MH(\bar{\bar{h}}_t \cup \bar{\bar{h}}_o \cup I_\tau(\tau_{cfp})) \uplus e_o$$

6   Implementation

The recursive type checking procedure as represented by the function VF from Subsection 4.3, was already implemented in VeriFast to support symbolic linking.

When performing recursive type checking in that implementation, the problem that occurs due to the removal of secondary occurrences of guarded headers by the C preprocessor, was solved by preprocessing, parsing and type checking all header files in isolation. Only then are the declarations a header contains added to the type checking environment of the file that included the header. The unsoundness introduced by preprocessing was addressed originally by only allowing includes and header guards, but nothing else of the capabilities of the C preprocessor.

The parallel preprocessing technique from Subsection 4.2 was straightforward to implement in VeriFast. An implementation of the C preprocessor and the context-free preprocessor are run in parallel and an error is reported if their outputs diverge. If a single header is included many times, the function VF is not very efficient. For every declaration block that needs the header for type checking its declarations, the function VF is recursively called for that header through the function MH. In the actual implementation the result for each header is remembered, so when it is needed again, it does not have to be recomputed. Another issue in the implementation was the use of lemma functions. To make sure during symbolic linking that these functions are correctly implemented, lemma functions are also recorded in the manifest files and their termination is ensured.

Since the verification process itself did not have to be updated, the necessary modifications were nicely isolated. Only the preprocessing stage and the type checking stage of the verifier had to be updated. Initial tests with the modified verifier, show we support most common use cases of the C preprocessor. To support this claim, these are the use cases we currently support: the use of header guards, using macro definitions as constants and enumerations, and using macros for abbreviating repetitive code. Although not supported in the current implementation, we can extend it to support parameterized headers. This can be done by introducing a new preprocessor directive that states which macros are the parameters of a header. The definitions of these macros at the point of inclusion must then be recorded in the manifest files during verification for an equality check during symbolic linking to ensure context-freeness. A theoretical foundation for this approach still has to be developed.

7   Related Work and Conclusion

There are several annotation-based verifiers available for C source code including Microsoft's Verifying C Compiler (VCC) [1], the Escher C Verifier [2] from Escher Technologies, the work of Claude Marché et al. resulting in the Caduceus [5] tool, and the Frama-C [3] platform and its plug-ins (e.g. WP [3] and Jessie [3]).

Microsoft states on its website that VCC is sound and modular. VCC indeed allows the verification of files in isolation, but the problem of linking earlier verified files together is not mentioned. Since the C preprocessor can be used before verification, a header file can have a different meaning for different include sites. However, there is no way to determine if properties of source files earlier proven by VCC remain valid if they are linked together in an application. So this seams to break modularity. The Escher C Verifier, the Caduceus tool and the Frama-C platform do not claim to be modular. The Frama-C platform does let you verify source files in isolation, but requires all the source files to be presented together if an entire application is to be soundly verified.

As for as we can see, no other verifier for C source code supports both modular verification and a mechanism for determining whether or not earlier proven properties remain valid when source files are linked together. The modular verification approach we implemented in VeriFast (i.e. symbolic linking with parallel preprocessing), does support this by limiting the capabilities of the preprocessor and these limitations are quite permissive. Moreover, we proved that the resulting semantics are equivalent to the standard C semantics; a property which is necessary when deviating from the C standard. Since our solution only impacts the lexical and semantical analysis phases, it is a valid candidate for implementation in other verifiers.

Acknowledgements. The research leading to these results has received funding from the European Union Seventh Framework Programme [FP7/2007-2013] under grant agreement n°317753, and more precisely from the STANCE project (a Source code analysis Toolbox for software security AssuraNCE).

This research is also partially funded by the EU FP7 project NESSoS, the Interuniversity Attraction Poles Programme Belgian State, the Belgian Science Policy, and by the Research Fund KU Leuven.

References

1. Cohen, E., Dahlweid, M., Hillebrand, M., Leinenbach, D., Moskal, M., Santen, T., Schulte, W., Tobies, S.: VCC: A practical system for verifying concurrent C. In: Berghofer, S., Nipkow, T., Urban, C., Wenzel, M. (eds.) TPHOLs 2009. LNCS, vol. 5674, pp. 23–42. Springer, Heidelberg (2009)
2. Crocker, D., Carlton, J.: Verification of C programs using automated reasoning. In: Proceedings of the Fifth IEEE International Conference on Software Engineering and Formal Methods, SEFM 2007, pp. 7–14. IEEE Computer Society, Washington, DC (2007)
3. Cuoq, P., Kirchner, F., Kosmatov, N., Prevosto, V., Signoles, J., Yakobowski, B.: Frama-c: a software analysis perspective. In: Eleftherakis, G., Hinchey, M., Holcombe, M. (eds.) SEFM 2012. LNCS, vol. 7504, pp. 233–247. Springer, Heidelberg (2012)
4. Jacobs, B., Smans, J., Philippaerts, P., Vogels, F., Penninckx, W., Piessens, F.: VeriFast: A powerful, sound, predictable, fast verifier for C and java. In: Bobaru, M., Havelund, K., Holzmann, G.J., Joshi, R. (eds.) NFM 2011. LNCS, vol. 6617, pp. 41–55. Springer, Heidelberg (2011)
5. Moy, Y., Marché, C.: Inferring local (non-)aliasing and strings for memory safety. In: Heap Analysis and Verification (HAV 2007), Braga, Portugal, pp. 35–51 (2007)
6. Vanspauwen, G., Jacobs, B.: VeriFast: Sound symbolic linking in the presence of preprocessing. CW Reports CW638, Department of Computer Science, KU Leuven (2013)

Inferring Physical Units in B Models

Sebastian Krings and Michael Leuschel

Institut für Informatik, Universität Düsseldorf*
Universitätsstr. 1, D-40225 Düsseldorf
sebastian.krings@uni-duesseldorf.de, leuschel@cs.uni-duesseldorf.de

Abstract. Most state-based formal methods, like B, Event-B or Z, provide support for static typing. However, these methods and the associated tools lack support for annotating variables with (physical) units of measurement. There is thus no obvious way to reason about correct or incorrect usage of such units. In this paper we present a technique that analyses the usage of physical units throughout a B machine, infers missing units and notifies the user of incorrectly handled units. The technique combines abstract interpretation with classical animation and model checking and has been integrated into the PROB validation tool, both for classical B and for Event-B. It provides source-level feedback about errors detected in the models. The plugin uses a combination of abstract interpretation and constraint solving techniques. We provide an empirical evaluation of our technique, and demonstrate that it scales up to real-life industrial models.

Keywords: B-Method, Event-B, Physical Units, Model Checking, Abstract Interpretation.

1   Introduction and Motivation

Static type checking is generally[1] considered to be very useful to catch obvious errors early on and most specification languages are strongly typed. In particular, the B language [1] and its successor Event-B [2] are strongly typed. However, their type systems are relatively simple. In particular, there is no way to subtype the integers: a variable holding natural numbers and a variable holding a negative integer have the same type: INTEGER. Moreover, there is no way to specify physical units for integers, which would have been useful to avoid illegal manipulations, such as adding a speed value to a time value. For safety critical systems such a static check would be highly desirable, but currently there is no obvious way to enforce correctness of physical unit manipulations within B models.

   In this paper we propose a solution to this problem, by integrating an abstract interpretation technique into the PROB animator [14,15]. More precisely:

---

* Part of this research has been sponsored by the EU funded FP7 project 287563 (ADVANCE).
[1] See, however, [13].

R.M. Hierons, M.G. Merayo, and M. Bravetti (Eds.): SEFM 2013, LNCS 8137, pp. 137–151, 2013.

- we provide an abstract semantics for B, where integers are represented by their physical units;
- the abstract semantics can be simulated using the PROB toolset, by switching from the concrete mode to the abstract mode;
- we can run PROB in abstract mode until a fixpoint is reached;
- the result (abstract values computed for variables, parameters, ...) of the fixpoint is analyzed and translated into source-level user feedback.

The technique has been implemented both for B and Event-B, and applied to several industrial safety critical models.

An introductory example can be found in Figure 1. It contains an extract of a simple B machine modeling a car. The current speed and position are stored in two variables. The duration of one tick is defined by a constant. Implicitly, the speed is measured in meters per second, the position in meters from a starting point and the length of a tick is defined in seconds. However, when updating the car's position in the keep_speed operation, a multiplication of the speed with the tick_length is missing. While this does not lead to an invariant violation, it leads to wrong results for the position of the car.

Analyzing the physical units of measurement, the error is easy to detect. Looking at the units of speed and tick_length, we see that the position should be in meters. Furthermore, we see that adding position (meters) to speed (meters per second) does not result in a well-formed unit of measurement. Hence, the missing multiplication is detected.

```
MACHINE Car
CONSTANTS tick_length
PROPERTIES tick_length = 2
VARIABLES speed, position
INVARIANT speed : INT & position : INT
INITIALISATION speed,position := 0,0
OPERATIONS
  keep_speed =
    PRE position + speed * tick_length : INT
    THEN position := position + speed END
  ...
END
```

Fig. 1. Introductory Example

2   Inference of Physical Units

Below, in Section 2.1 we will discuss how the syntax of the B language was extended in order to be able to declare physical units and reason about them. We will mainly use the international system of units (SI) [20], but a user can also declare additional non-SI units. Afterwards, how we use abstract interpretation will be explained in Section 2.2. Section 3 will explain why we had to improve the technique with constraint solving. Empirical results will be presented in Section 4. We conclude with alternative approaches and related work in Section 5 and a discussion of our results and future work in Section 6.

2.1 Syntactic Extension of the B Language

Initially, the user must provide the physical units for certain variables as a starting point of our analysis. For Event-B, this has been achieved by attaching new attributes to variables in the Rodin database [3]. In classical B, this association must be described within the B ASCII syntax[2]. We wanted to ensure that a B machine making use of the new syntax is still usable by other tools (such as Atelier-B). This requirement ruled out an extension involving keywords or constructs which are not part of the standard B language and could therefore not be parsed by tools other than PROB. Instead, we decided to implement the new functionality inside semantically relevant comments, i.e., *pragmas*. While the usual B block comment is enclosed in /* and */, a pragma is enclosed in /*@ and */. (Atelier-B will treat such a pragma as an ordinary comment.)

For our work we have introduced four pragmas to the B language:

1. "unit", the pragma used to attach a physical unit to a B construct. This can be done either by specifying it by a B expression in an SI-compatible form or by using a predefined alias like "cm" instead of "10**-2 * m". The given unit has to be a valid SI unit [20]; i.e., a derived unit such as "m * s**-2" is acceptable. The usage is shown in Figure 2.
2. "inferred_unit", which works similar to unit. It is included in the pretty print of a machine, attaching units inferred by PROB to variables and constants. This enables the user to generate a model containing the information gathered by our analysis.
3. "conversion", used to annotate operations meant as conversions between units. An example can be found in Figure 3.
4. "unit_alias", used to define new aliases for existing unit definitions.

2.2 Using Abstract Interpretation

Inferring units of measurement has a strong connection to type checking, which can be seen as a special kind of abstract interpretation [8]. In consequence, inference of units throughout a B machine can be done by abstract interpretation of the operations of a machine and abstract evaluation of invariants, guards, etc.

Regarded as an abstract interpretation, type checking in B can be performed with the abstract domain outlined in Figure 4. Initially, any type is still possible, represented by the bottom element $\perp$. Upon type checking, the type of each construct is inferred as one of the following inductively defined B types:

---

[2] Screenshots of input, output and errors messages can be found on http://www.stups.uni-duesseldorf.de/models/sefm2013/screenshots.

```
MACHINE UnitExample
VARIABLES
  /*@ unit 10 * m */ x,
  y
INVARIANT x:NAT & y:NAT & x>y
INITIALISATION x,y := 0,0
OPERATIONS
  n <-- addToX = BEGIN n := x + y END;
END
```

Fig. 2. Example Usage of the Unit Pragma

```
MACHINE ConversionExample
VARIABLES
  /*@ unit 10**-2 * m */ x,
  /*@ unit 10**-3 * m */ y
INVARIANT x:NAT & y:NAT
INITIALISATION x,y := 0,0
OPERATIONS
  mmToCm = x := /*@ conversion */ (10*y)
END
```

Fig. 3. Example Usage of the Conversion Pragma

- $\bot \in Types$
- $Bool \in Types$
- $String \in Types$
- $\mathbb{Z} \in Types$
- $Given \subseteq Types$ where $Given$ contains all the user-defined deferred, enumerated or parameter sets
- $x \in Types \wedge y \in Types \Rightarrow x \times y \in Types$
- $t \in Types \Rightarrow \mathcal{P}(t) \in Types$ [3]

Furthermore, if multiple types are inferred, there is a type error. This is denoted by the special type $\top$[4]. We define $Types_\top = Types \cup \{\top\}$. Note, that for Event-B, the Rodin tool also generates a type error if the inferred type still contains $\bot$. This can occur for a predicate such as $\{\} = \{\}$, where the type of $\{\}$ would be inferred as $\mathcal{P}(\bot)$.

Basically, types are ordered using the relation $\sqsubseteq$, forming the lattice in Fig. 4 and defined using the following five rules. (We define $\sqsubset$ in the usual way: $s \sqsubset t$ iff $s \sqsubseteq t \wedge s \neq t$.)

---

[3] Functions and relations are stored as sets of couples.

[4] As the top element represents the least upper bound that matches two different types. However, only one type is acceptable for a correct model.

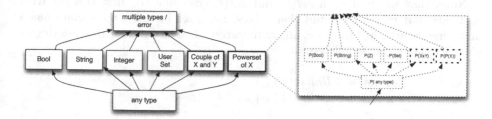

Fig. 4. B Type System and the relation $\sqsubseteq$

- $\bot \sqsubseteq t$ for any $t \in Types_T$
- $t \sqsubseteq \top$ for any $t \in Types_T$
- $t \sqsubseteq t$ for any $t \in Types_T$
- $s \times t \sqsubseteq s' \times t'$ iff $s \sqsubseteq s' \wedge t \sqsubseteq t'$.
- $\mathcal{P}(t) \sqsubseteq \mathcal{P}(t')$ iff $t \sqsubseteq t'$.

The abstract domain used to perform unit analysis is an extension of the abstract domain used for type checking. While the types for boolean, string and the construction of sets, sequences and couples remain, the integer type is replaced by an entire subdomain. An abstract integer value is now represented by a set of triples of the form $[10^c \times u^e]$ where $c \in \mathbb{Z}$ is the exponent of the coefficient, u a SI base unit symbol and $e \in \mathbb{Z}$ the exponent of the unit.[5]

Definition 1. *A unit is a set of triples* $\{[10^{c_1} \times u_1{}^{e_1}], \ldots, [10^{c_k} \times u_k{}^{e_k}]\}$ *such that for all $i \in 1..k$ we have $c_i \in \mathbb{Z}$, $e_i \in \mathbb{Z}$, u_i being a base SI unit and $\forall j \bullet j \in 1..k \wedge j \neq i \Rightarrow u_i \neq u_j$.*

With the definition above, $\frac{m}{s}$ would be expressed as $\{[10^0 \times m^1], [10^0 \times s^{-1}]\}$. The empty set of triples denotes a dimensionless integer value.

Definition 2. *The set of all valid units is denoted by* Units.

As in the type checking domain, we add an element $\bot_U$ to *Units* denoting that initially any unit is possible. Additionally, we define $\top_U$ representing the fact that multiple units were inferred. Again, this should not occur in a correct model.

Summarizing, our abstract interpretation framework for B uses the set of all possible B values as the concrete domain $\mathcal{C}$ and maps it to the abstract domain $\mathcal{A}$, which is recursively defined by

- $boolean \in \mathcal{A}$
- $string \in \mathcal{A}$
- $\forall u \in Units \cup \{\bot_U, \top_U\} \Rightarrow int(u) \in \mathcal{A}$
- $\forall S \in Given, u \in Units \cup \{\bot_U, \top_U\} \Rightarrow set(S, u) \in \mathcal{A}$
- $x \in \mathcal{A} \wedge y \in \mathcal{A} \Rightarrow couple(x, y) \in \mathcal{A}$
- $t \in \mathcal{A} \Rightarrow set(t) \in \mathcal{A}$.

---

[5] For convenience, some SI derived units and units accepted for use with the SI standard (see [20]) are stored on their own rather than converting them.

Note, that we need both $set(t)$ and $set(t, u)$: While the first is a set with elements that may hold a unit themselves, i.e. a set integers, the second has a unit directly attached to it, i.e. an enumerated set. The rules for the ordering of abstract values are as follows:

- $\bot_U \sqsubseteq_U u$ for any $u \in Units \cup \{\top_U\}$
- $u \sqsubseteq_U \top_U$ for any $u \in Units \cup \{\bot_U\}$
- $\bot_U \sqsubseteq_U \top_U$
- $t \sqsubseteq t$ for any $t \in \mathcal{A}$
- $\bot \sqsubseteq t$ for any $t \in \mathcal{A}$
- $t \sqsubseteq \top$ for any $t \in \mathcal{A}$
- $int(u) \sqsubseteq int(u')$ iff $u \sqsubseteq u'$
- $set(t, u) \sqsubseteq set(t, u')$ iff $u \sqsubseteq u'$
- $couple(s, t) \sqsubseteq couple(s', t')$ iff $s \sqsubseteq s' \wedge t \sqsubseteq t'$
- $set(t) \sqsubseteq set(t')$ iff $t \sqsubseteq t'$

To perform abstract interpretation the abstraction and concretization functions $\alpha : \mathcal{C} \rightarrow \mathcal{A}$ and $\gamma : \mathcal{A} \rightarrow \mathcal{P}(\mathcal{C})$ need to be defined. These functions have to be recursively defined, as the B type system contains arbitrarily nested data types. The following definitions of α and γ are used:

$$
\alpha(x) = \begin{cases}
boolean & \text{if } x \in \{true, false\} \\
string & \text{if type of } x \text{ is string} \\
int(unit) & \text{if } x \in \mathbb{Z} \text{ with an annotated unit} \\
int(\bot_U) & \text{if } x \in \mathbb{Z} \text{ without an annotated unit} \\
set(S, unit) & \text{if } x \in S, S \text{ annotated with unit} \\
set(S, \bot_U) & \text{if } x \in S, S \text{ without an annotated unit} \\
couple(\alpha(x_1), \alpha(x_2)) & \text{if } x \text{ is of type } x_1 \times x_2 \\
set(\alpha(x_1)) & \text{if } x \in \mathcal{P}(x_1)
\end{cases}
$$

with $S \in Given$ and

$$
\gamma(y) = \begin{cases}
\{true, false\} & \text{if } y = boolean \\
\{s | \text{type of } s \text{ is string}\} & \text{if } y = string \\
S & \text{if } y = set(S, unit), \text{ with any unit} \\
\mathbb{Z} & \text{if } y = int(unit), \text{ with any unit} \\
\gamma(y_1) \times \gamma(y_2) & \text{if } y = couple(y_1, y_2) \\
\mathcal{P}(\gamma(y_1)) & \text{if } y = set(y_1).
\end{cases}
$$

The B instructions the abstract interpreter needs to implement can be categorized by their effect on the units of measurement:

1. Instructions like addition of integers or concatenation of sequences expect all operands and the result to hold the same unit.

2. Instructions that work on abstract elements which are composed in a different way while still holding the same units. The Cartesian product for example maps two sets to a set of couples.
3. Instructions like multiplication or division are able to generate new units based on the units of their operands.

Data: Factors $x_1 \in Units, x_2 \in Units$
Result: Product $p \in Units$
$p := \emptyset$ **foreach** *triple* $[10^{c_1} \times u^{e_1}] \in x_1$ **do**
$\quad$ **if** *there is a triple* $[10^{c_2} \times u^{e_2}] \in x_2$ **then**
$\quad\quad$ $p := p \cup \{[10^{c_1+c_2} \times u^{e_1+e_2}]\}$
$\quad\quad$ $x_2 := x_2 \setminus \{[10^{c_2} \times u^{e_2}]\}$
$\quad$ **else**
$\quad\quad$ add $[10^{c_1} \times u^{e_1}]$ to p
$\quad$ **end**
end
$p := p \cup x_2$

Algorithm 1. Abstract Multiplication

The first and second kind of operations can be implemented by unification or returning $\top$ if incompatible units are found. This could be achieved by a classical type inference algorithm (e.g., Hindley-Milner). The third kind however needs more work, and is one justification for using abstract interpretation rather than (unification-based) type inference. On the representation outlined above, multiplication is implemented by addition of the exponents of triples holding the same unit symbol. See Algorithm 1 for an outline. With the multiplication in place, $\frac{a}{b}$ can easily be implemented as $a \times b^{-1}$.

A few operations were not immediately obvious, in particular modulo division. It was not clear what the correct operation on the unit domain had to be. The B Book [1] (page 164) defines the result as

$$n \bmod m = n - m * \left\lfloor \frac{n}{m} \right\rfloor.$$

Consequently, for the unit of $n \bmod m$

$$unit(n \bmod m) = unit\left(n - m * \left\lfloor \frac{n}{m} \right\rfloor\right) = unit(n).$$

Following the above reasoning, in the current implementation of the unit interpreter the unit of $n \bmod m$ is the unit of n. However, other definitions are certainly possible. Up to now, our empirical evaluation did not reveal any problems with the given definition.

We perform a fixpoint search by executing all operations of a B machine. Additionally, we evaluate properties and invariants in every iteration. Pseudocode can be found in Algorithm 2. For the example machine in Figure 2, the fixpoint search would perform the following steps:

1. Initialize the machine: If a unit is attached to an identifier, the unit is stored. Otherwise, $\perp_U$ is used. In the example, we set the initial state σ_0 to $\{(x, int(\{[10^1 \times m^1]\})), (y, int(\perp_U))\}$.
2. Evaluate the invariant on σ_0. The predicate $x > y$ allows us to infer the unit of y, updating $\sigma_0 = \{(x, int(\{[10^1 \times m^1]\})), (y, int(\{[10^1 \times m^1]\}))\}$. No incorrect usage of units is detected.
3. Execute addToX on σ_0:
   (a) Generate local state $\sigma_{IN} = \{(n, int(\perp_U))\} \cup \sigma_0$.
   (b) Evaluate $x + y = int(\{[10^1 \times m^1]\})) + int(\{[10^1 \times m^1]\})) = int(\{[10^1 \times m^1]\}))$
   (c) Substitute n by calculating the least upper bound of $\perp_U$ and $int(\{[10^1 \times m^1]\}))$. The resulting output state is
   $\sigma_{OUT} = \{(n, int(\{[10^1 \times m^1]\})), (x, int(\{[10^1 \times m^1]\})), (y, int(\{[10^1 \times m^1]\}))\}$.
4. Again, no incorrect usage of units is detected.
5. The next iteration executes addToX a second time. However, the state does not change and the fixpoint is reached.

3 Extending Abstract Interpretation with Constraints

Below we show that our abstract interpretation scheme on its own still has some limitations. Consider the B machine in Figure 5, where the variable x contains a length in meters and t holds a time interval in seconds. The unit of y should be inferred. Evaluating the expression $t := (x * y) * t$ needs several interpretation steps:

1. The interpreter computes the product of x and y. As $y = int(\perp_U)$, the interpreter can only return $int(\perp_U)$ as a result.
2. In consequence, the interpreter finds that $(x * y) * t = int(\perp_U) * t = int(\perp_U) * int(\{[10^0 \times s^1]\}) = int(\perp_U)$.
3. The assignment $t := (x * y) * t$ is evaluated by computing the least upper bound of t and $int(\perp_U)$, i.e., $int(\{[10^0 \times m^1]\})$. No information is propagated back to the inner expressions; we are thus unable to infer the unit of y.

The example shows that it is necessary to attach some kind of constraints to the resulting variables containing $\perp_U$. Inside, the operation and the operands that lead to $\perp_U$ are stored. We implemented constraints for multiplication, division and exponentiation, as those can not be handled by unification alone.

In the example given in Fig. 5 two constraints are used to infer the unit of variable y. First, a constraint containing x and y is attached to the result of the inner multiplication. The result of the outer multiplication is annotated in the same way. When computing the assignment to t, we know the unit that the outer multiplication has to return. We can use the domain operation for division of units to reverse the multiplications and compute the value of y.

In general, once a variable with an attached constraint is unified with another variable, the unit plugin has different ways to react:

```
σ = {(identifier of x, α(x)) : x variable or constant}
evaluate properties / invariant (might replace ⊥_U by units in σ)
repeat
 │  foreach operation / event do
 │   │  update σ by executing operation / event:
 │   │    evaluate preconditions / guards (might replace ⊥_U by units in σ)
 │   │    perform substitutions x := x' by setting x to lub(x, x') in σ
 │   │  if parameter or return value contains ⊤_U then
 │   │  │  report error
 │   │  end
 │   │  evaluate properties / invariant (might replace ⊥_U by units in σ)
 │   │  if σ contains ⊤_U then
 │   │  │  report error
 │   │  end
 │   │  if invalid unit usage detected then
 │   │  │  report error
 │   │  end
 │   │  foreach variable holding a constraint do
 │   │  │  evaluate constraint if possible
 │   │  end
 │  end
until σ did not change in loop
```

Algorithm 2. Fixpoint Search

- The other variable does not hold a physical unit at the moment. Hence, we can not solve the constraint.
- The other variable contains a physical unit. Now, we have to look at the variables inside:
  - If both variables are currently unset, there are multiple possible solutions. We again delay the computation to the next iteration of the fixpoint algorithm.
  - If one of the variables is unknown and the other one contains a unit, we can compute the missing unit.
  - If both are set, the constraint is dropped without further verification.
- Further unifications in the second step may trigger this process on another variable.

We do not perform error handling when evaluating constraints. If a new unit has been inferred, the state has changed and the next iteration of the fixpoint search will eventually discover new errors. If the state did not change, the constraint could only detect an error already reported. See Algorithm 2 for details.

4   Empirical Results

Our empirical evaluation was based on three key aspects:

- the effort needed to annotate the machines and debug them if necessary;

```
MACHINE InvolvedConstraintUnits
VARIABLES /*@ unit m */ x, y, /*@ unit s */ t
INVARIANT
 x:NAT & y:NAT & t:NAT
INITIALISATION x,y,t := 1,1,1
OPERATIONS
 Op = BEGIN t := (x*y)*t END
END
```

Fig. 5. Machine requiring involved constraint solving

- additionally, the number of iterations performed and the time spent in search for a fixpoint was of particular interest;
- the accuracy of the abstract interpretation.

The first case study is based on an intelligent traffic light warning system. The traffic light broadcasts information about its current status and cycle to oncoming cars using an ad-hoc wireless network. The system should warn the driver and eventually trigger the brakes, in case the car approaches a traffic light and will not be able to pass when it would be still allowed[6].

After the annotations were done, the plugin reported an incorrect usage of units. The underlying cause was the definition

$$ceil\_div(a, b) == \frac{a}{b} + \frac{b - 1 + a \bmod b}{b},$$

a ceiling division that rounds the result up to the next integer value. It was introduced to keep the approximation of breaking distances sound.

The expected result for the unit of ceil_div is the unit of a regular division, that is the unit of a divided by the unit of b. However, the definition above does not lead to a consistent unit. Thus, the former definition of ceil_div was not convenient for use with the unit plugin. It was changed to

$$ceil\_div(a, b) == \frac{a}{b} + \frac{\min(1, a \bmod b)}{(b + 1) \bmod b},$$

which leads to the expected result.

Furthermore, the speed of the car was stored as a length and implicitly used as a "distance per tick". Our plugin discovered that the speed variable could not be associated with any suitable unit without giving further errors.

Regarding the performance factors mentioned above, the number of iterations and the computation time was measured. Furthermore we timed annotating the machine and correcting unit errors if necessary. The results are listed in benchmarks 1 to 3 in Table 1. For comparison purposes, the table also lists the number

---

[6] The machines used in this case study can be downloaded from
http://www.stups.uni-duesseldorf.de/models/sefm2013/.

of lines of code and the number of operations for each machine[7]. No variables contained T_U, so the abstract interpretation did not lead to a loss of precision.

The effort needed to annotate and correct the model was reasonably low, in particular when compared with the time needed to create the model in the first place. The evaluation also showed that it is easy to split developing the model and performing unit analysis.

The second case study used a ClearSy tutorial on modeling in B[8]. It contains both abstract and implementation machines (all in all seven B machines). The system uses several sensors to estimate the remaining amount of fuel in a tank.

The first step was to annotate all variables with their respective units. When no error was found, the number of pragmas was gradually reduced, to measure the efficiency of our approach with less user input available. Eventually, we only needed one pragma for the abstract and one for the implementation machine. All other units could be inferred[9]. In the process, no unit reached T_U. The benchmarks are presented in Table 1, rows 4 to 10: again, the computation time is very low and only two iterations are needed to fully infer the units of all variables. The additional step of introducing an implementation level did not lead to longer computation times. No significant annotation work was needed on the implementation machine, once the abstract machine had been analyzed.

To evaluate the performance of the unit plugin on large scale examples, several B railway models from Alstom were used as benchmarks. As most of these machines are confidential, neither source code nor implementation details can be provided.

During the evaluation, the plugin showed some difficulties in handling large B functions or relations of large cardinality. Mainly, this is because for every new element that is added to a relation, the plugin tries to infer new units for range and domain. In almost all cases this does not modify the currently inferred units. In a future revision, the plugin might rely more on information from the type checker to reduce the number of inferences.

Furthermore, lookup of global variables and their units slowed the interpreter down. When accessing elements of deferred or enumerated sets, the machine had to be unpacked frequently. To overcome this limitation, certain units are now cached to reduce the lookup time.

Currently, there is no way to annotate both range and domain of a function or relation at once, as this would require another pragma or at least a second variant of the unit pragma. Therefore, they have to be annotated on their own. Our evaluation shows that this is possible without substantial rewriting of a machine.

---

[7] Both were counted on the internal representation of the machines. Thus, the metrics include code from imported machines. Comments are not counted, as they are not in the internal representation. However, new lines used for pretty printing are counted.

[8] The tutorial including the machines can be found at
http://www.tools.clearsy.com/wp1/?page_id=161.

[9] The exception being variables and sets belonging to the system's status. Here, no unit of measurement applies and no unit was inferred.

Examples 11 to 13 in Table 1 shows the benchmark results for some of the Alstom machines. Total lines of code and number of operations are again given to ease comparison with the former case studies. As can be seen, our analysis scales to these large, industrial examples.

As a last case study, we used some of the Event-B hybrid machines described in [4]. Hybrid systems usually consist of a controller working on discrete time intervals, while the environment evolves in a continuous way. To deal with the challenge of analyzing both a discrete and a continuous component simultaneously, time is modeled by a variable called "now". It can be used as input to several functions mapping it to a real-world observation, taken from the environment at that moment in time. Hence, this approach is an addition to the former case studies using different techniques.

From the three models described in [4], two were used as case studies: the hybrid_nuclear model and the hybrid_train model. The hybrid_nuclear model was originally introduced in [6]. It models a temperature control system for a heat producing reactor that can be cooled by inserting one of two cooling rods once a critical temperature is reached. The hybrid_train example was originally developed in [18]. It features one or more trains running on the same line. Each train receives a point m on the track where it should stop at the least.

The machines with less abstraction introduced hybrid components by using functions as explained above. The unit plugin stores these functions as mappings from one unit to another. Hence, to be able to fully analyze the usage of units inside a machine, there have to be annotations on both the discrete and the continuous variables.

In the train models, the variables holding speed and position were annotated in the abstract model. In the more concrete model, the acceleration was stored as $\frac{m}{s}$ while one of the time variables was annotated as seconds. Both configurations lead to full inference of the used units through all variables and constants. No unset variables or variables with multiple inferred units occurred.

In the hybrid_nuclear models, different combinations of annotating one of the temperatures and one of the time variables were tried. Regardless of the combination, once both a temperature and a time were annotated, all other units could be inferred. The belonging benchmarks are 14 to 19 in Table 1.

5   Alternative Approaches and Related Work

Aside from the idea to use abstract interpretation, an extension of the type checking capabilities of ProB was initially considered. This approach would act more like a static analysis of the B machine, rather than interpreting it (abstractly) while observing the state space. Note, however, that simple classical unification-based type inference (Hindley-Milner style) is not powerful enough due to the generation of new units, e.g., during multiplication.

A type checking approach for a modeling language is followed in [10]. The authors describe a language extension for Z adding physical units. The correct usage of units is verified by static analysis. Support for physical units is also present in the specification languages Modelica [16] and CHARON [5].

Table 1. Benchmarks

No.	machine	LOC	operations	iterations	time analysis	time annotating
1	Car	74	4	2	< 10 ms	≈ 30 min
2	TrafficLight	81	2	1	< 10 ms	≈ 20 min
3	System	322	20	2	50 ms	≈ 60 min
4	measure	42	2	1	< 10 ms	≈ 5 min
5	utils	24	2	1	< 10 ms	≈ 5 min
6	utils_i	38	2	1	< 10 ms	≈ 5 min
7	ctx	16	0	1	< 10 ms	≈ 5 min
8	ctx_i	16	0	1	< 10 ms	≈ 5 min
9	fuel0	64	2	2	< 10 ms	≈ 5 min
10	fuel_i	106	6	2	< 10 ms	≈ 5 min
11	compensated_gradient	3079	20	3	620 ms	≈ 45 min
12	vital_gradient	986	4	3	160 ms	≈ 45 min
13	sgd	773	0	2	170 ms	≈ 90 min
14	T_m0	115	6	3	20 ms	≈ 15 min
15	T_m1	179	11	3	30 ms	≈ 15 min
16	C_m0	108	4	3	20 ms	≈ 15 min
17	C_m1	141	4	3	20 ms	≈ 15 min
18	C_m2	162	4	3	40 ms	≈ 15 min
19	C_m3	228	7	3	90 ms	≈ 15 min

Aside from specification languages, several extensions for general purpose language exist. Among others there are solutions for Lisp [9], C [11], C++ [21], Java [22] and F# [12].

In [12] and [23] the limitations of unification-based type inference mentioned above are solved by inferring new units as the solutions of a system of linear equations. In our approach these equations can be found in the constraints mentioned in Section 3.

In contrast to the interpreter based approach, implementing an extended type checker would possibly have resulted in less implementation work. On the downside, it would not be able to animate or to reason about intermediate states. In contrast, the interpreter based approach can also be used as an interactive aid while debugging errors.

Another approach is followed in [19] and [17], providing an expressive type system containing physical units for Simulink, a modeling framework based on Matlab. The approach followed in [19] differs from the one implemented in this paper. Instead of using abstract interpretation, the problem is translated into an SMT problem [7], which can be solved by a general purpose solver. In the approach presented in [17], the SMT backend is replaced by a set of constraints solvable by Gauss-Jordan elimination.

In addition to performing unit analysis, an SMT or constraint based approach makes it easier to generate test cases that verify the required properties. In particular, calculating the unsatisfiable core makes it possible to generate minimal test cases for certain errors. However, in contrast to the abstract interpreter based approach, verifying intermediate states and performing animation involve multiple reencodings of the problem to SMT-LIB.

6   Discussion and Conclusion

In conclusion, our first set of goals could be fulfilled. The newly developed plugin extends PROB by the ability to perform unit analysis for formal models developed in B or Event-B. We provide source-level error feedback to the user and usually a small number of annotations is sufficient to infer the units of all variables and check the consistency of a machine. In future, we plan to support other languages, in particular TLA$^+$ and Z.

As anticipated, the plugin is able to infer units of constants and variables and handle their conversions. Additionally, user controlled unit conversions can be performed and are fully integrated with the analysis tools.

Furthermore, the extension of B by pragmas leaves all machines usable by the different tools and tool sets without limitations. Deploying unit analysis does not interfere with any step of a user's usual B workflow.

Most machines only needed a few iterations inside the fixpoint algorithm. Furthermore, the top element was only reached in machines containing errors. Thus, the selected abstract domain seems fitting for the desired analysis results.

While the overall performance generally matches the expectations, there is still room for improvement. Especially on large machines, computations should be refined. Yet, more input from industrial users is needed first, both in form of reviews and test reports as well as in form of case studies and sample machines.

We plan to further investigate the usage of constraints to speed up unit inference. In particular, an in-depth comparison with the SMT and constraint based approaches will be performed. This comparison will focus both on speed as well as on the completeness of the resulting unit information.

All in all, the unit analysis plugin extends the capabilities of B and PROB and is a useful addition to the existing B tools. It should be able to find errors which are not easily discoverable by the existing tools and might lead to errors in a future implementation. The technique scales to real-life examples and the animation capabilities aid in identifying the causes of errors.

References

1. Abrial, J.-R.: The B-Book: Assigning Programs to Meanings. Cambridge University Press (1996)
2. Abrial, J.-R.: Modeling in Event-B: System and Software Engineering. Cambridge University Press (2010)
3. Abrial, J.-R., Butler, M., Hallerstede, S., Voisin, L.: An open extensible tool environment for Event-B. In: Liu, Z., Kleinberg, R.D. (eds.) ICFEM 2006. LNCS, vol. 4260, pp. 588–605. Springer, Heidelberg (2006)

4. Abrial, J.-R., Su, W., Zhu, H.: Formalizing hybrid systems with Event-B. In: Derrick, J., Fitzgerald, J., Gnesi, S., Khurshid, S., Leuschel, M., Reeves, S., Riccobene, E. (eds.) ABZ 2012. LNCS, vol. 7316, pp. 178–193. Springer, Heidelberg (2012)
5. Anand, M., Lee, I., Pappas, G., Sokolsky, O.: Unit & dynamic typing in hybrid systems modeling with CHARON. In: Computer Aided Control System Design, pp. 56–61. IEEE (2006)
6. Back, R.-J., Seceleanu, C.C., Westerholm, J.: Symbolic simulation of hybrid systems. In: Proceedings APSEC 2002, pp. 147–155. IEEE Computer Society (2002)
7. Barrett, C., Stump, A., Tinelli, C.: The SMT-LIB Standard: Version 2.0. Technical report, Department of Computer Science, University of Iowa (2010), http://www.SMT-LIB.org
8. Cousot, P., Cousot, R.: Abstract interpretation: A unified lattice model for static analysis of programs by construction or approximation of fixpoints. In: Proceedings POPL 1977, pp. 238–252. ACM (1977)
9. Cunis, R.: A package for handling units of measure in Lisp. ACM SIGPLAN Lisp Pointers 5, 21–25 (1992)
10. Hayes, I.J., Mahony, B.P.: Using units of measurement in formal specifications. Formal Aspects of Computing 7 (1994)
11. Jiang, L., Su, Z.: Osprey: a practical type system for validating dimensional unit correctness of C programs. In: Proceedings ICSE 2006, pp. 262–271. ACM (2006)
12. Kennedy, A.: Types for units-of-measure: Theory and practice. In: Horváth, Z., Plasmeijer, R., Zsók, V. (eds.) CEFP 2009. LNCS, vol. 6299, pp. 268–305. Springer, Heidelberg (2010)
13. Lamport, L., Paulson, L.C.: Should your specification language be typed. ACM Trans. Program. Lang. Syst. 21(3), 502–526 (1999)
14. Leuschel, M., Butler, M.: ProB: A model checker for B. In: Araki, K., Gnesi, S., Mandrioli, D. (eds.) FME 2003. LNCS, vol. 2805, pp. 855–874. Springer, Heidelberg (2003)
15. Leuschel, M., Butler, M.: ProB: an automated analysis toolset for the B method. Int. J. Softw. Tools Technol. Transf. 10(2), 185–203 (2008)
16. Modelica Association. The Modelica Language Specification version 3.0 (2007)
17. Owre, S., Saha, I., Shankar, N.: Automatic dimensional analysis of cyber-physical systems. In: Giannakopoulou, D., Méry, D. (eds.) FM 2012. LNCS, vol. 7436, pp. 356–371. Springer, Heidelberg (2012)
18. Platzer, A.: Logical Analysis of Hybrid Systems: Proving Theorems for Complex Dynamics. Springer (2010)
19. Roy, P., Shankar, N.: SimCheck: An expressive type system for Simulink. In: Proceedings NFM 2010, pp. 149–160. NASA (2010)
20. Thompson, A., Taylor, B.N.: The International System of Units (SI). Nist Special Publication (2008)
21. Umrigar, Z.: Fully static dimensional analysis with C++. ACM SIGPLAN Notices 29, 135–139 (1994)
22. van Delft, A.: A Java extension with support for dimensions. Software: Practice and Experience 29(7), 605–616 (1999)
23. Wand, M., O'Keefe, P.: Automatic dimensional inference. In: Computational Logic: Essays in Honor of Alan Robinson, pp. 479–483 (1991)

A Tool for Behaviour-Based Discovery of Approximately Matching Web Services*,**

Mahdi Sargolzaei[1], Francesco Santini[2],
Farhad Arbab[3], and Hamideh Afsarmanesh[1]

[1] Universiteit van Amsterdam, Amsterdam, Netherlands
{H.Afsarmanesh,M.Sargolzaei}@uva.nl
[2] EPI Contraintes, INRIA - Rocquencourt, France
francesco.santini@inria.fr
[3] Centrum Wiskunde & Informatica, Amsterdam, Netherlands
Farhad.Arbab@cwi.nl

Abstract. We present a tool that is able to discover stateful Web Services in a database, and to rank the results according to a similarity score expressing the affinities between each of them and a user-submitted query. To determine these affinities, we take behaviour into account, both of the user's query and of the services. The names of service operations, their order of invocation, and their parameters may differ from those required by the actual user, which necessitates using similarity scores, and hence the notion of soft constraints. The final tool is based on Soft Constraint Automata and an approximate bisimulation among them, modeled and solved as a Constraint Optimisation Problem.

1 Introduction

Web Services (WSs) [1] constitute a typical example of the *Service Oriented Computing* (SOC) paradigm. WS discovery is the process of finding a suitable WS for a given task. To enable a consumer use a service, its provider usually augments a WS endpoint with an interface description using the *Web Service Description Language (WSDL)*. In such loosely-coupled environments, automatic discovery becomes even more complex: users' decisions must be supported by taking into account a similarity score that describes the affinity between a user's requested service (the query) and the specifications of actual services available in the considered database.

Although several researchers have tackled this problem and some search tools (e.g., [16]) have achieved good results, very few of them (see Sec. 6) consider the

---

* This work was carried out during the second author's tenure of the ERCIM "Alain Bensoussan" Fellowship Programme, which is supported by the Marie Curie Cofunding of Regional, National and International Programmes (COFUND) of the European Commission.

** The first and fourth authors are partially supported by the FP7 project GLONET, funded by the European Commission.

R.M. Hierons, M.G. Merayo, and M. Bravetti (Eds.): SEFM 2013, LNCS 8137, pp. 152–166, 2013.
© Springer-Verlag Berlin Heidelberg 2013

behavioural signature of a service, which describes the sequence of operations a user is actually interested in. This is partly due to the unavoidable limitations of today's standard specifications, e.g., WSDL, which do not encompass such aspects. Despite this, the behaviour of stateful services represents a very important issue to be considered during discovery, to provide users with an additional means to refine the search in such a diverse environment.

In this paper, we first describe a formal framework (originally introduced in [4]) that, during the search procedure, considers both a description of the requested (stateful) service behaviour, and a global similarity score between services and queries. This underlying framework consists of *Soft Constraint Automata* (*SCA*), where semiring-based soft constraints (see Sec. 2) enhance classical (not soft) CA [5] with a parametric and computational framework that can be used to express the optimal desired similarity between a query and a service.

The second and the main contribution of the work reported in this paper is an implementation of such a framework using approximate bisimulation techniques [11] between two SCA: we implement this inexact comparison between a query and a service as a *Constraint Optimisation Problem* (*COP*), by using Ja-CoP libraries[1]. In the end, we are able to rank all search results according to their similarity with a proposed query. In this way, we can benefit from off-the-shelf techniques with roots in *Artificial Intelligence* (*AI*), in order to tackle the search complexity over large databases. To evaluate a similarity score we use different metrics to measure the syntactical distance between operations and between parameter names (see Sec. 4), e.g., between "*getWeather*" and "*g_weather*". These values are then automatically cast into soft constraints as semiring values (see Sec. 2), with the purpose of being parametrically composed and optimised for the sake of discovery. Thus, a user may eventually choose a service that adheres to her/his needs more than the other ones in a database.

The exploitation of the behaviour during a search process represents the main feature of our tool. SCA represent the formal model we use to represent behaviours: the different states of an SCA represent the different states of a stateful service/query. Relying on SCA allows us to have a framework that comes along with sound operators for composition and hiding of queries [4]. Our plan is to integrate this search tool with the tool presented in [14]. In this comprehensive tool it will be possible, first to search for the desired WSs (or components), and then to compose them into a more complex structured service [14].

The rest of this paper is structured as follows. In Sec. 2 we summarise the background on semiring-based soft constraints [7], as well as the background on SCA [4]. Section 3 shows some examples of how to use SCA to represent the behaviour of services and the similarity between their operation and parameter names. Section 4 describes our tool which implements the search introduced in Sec. 3, while Sec. 5 focuses on how we measure the similarity between two different behavioural signatures. Section 4 introduces the first experimental results evaluating the precision of this tool. In Sec. 6 we report on the related work. Finally, in Sec. 7 we draw our conclusions and explain our future work.

---

[1] Java Constraint Programming solver (JaCoP): http://www.jacop.eu

2   Soft Constraint Automata

Semring-based Soft Constraints. A *c-semiring* [7] (simply semiring in the sequel) is a tuple $S = \langle A, +, \times, \mathbf{0}, \mathbf{1} \rangle$, where A is a possibly infinite set with two special elements $\mathbf{0}, \mathbf{1} \in A$ (respectively the bottom and top elements of A) and with two operations $+$ and $\times$ that satisfy certain properties over A: $+$ is commutative, associative, idempotent, closed, with $\mathbf{0}$ as its unit element and $\mathbf{1}$ as its absorbing element; $\times$ is closed, associative, commutative, distributes over $+$, $\mathbf{1}$ is its unit element, and $\mathbf{0}$ is its absorbing element. The $+$ operation defines a partial order $\leqslant_S$ over A such that $a \leqslant_S b$ iff $a + b = b$; we say that $a \leqslant_S b$ if b represents a value *better* than a. Moreover, $+$ and $\times$ are monotone on $\leqslant_S$, $\mathbf{0}$ is the min of the partial order and $\mathbf{1}$ its max, $\langle A, \leqslant_S \rangle$ is a complete lattice and $+$ is its *least upper bound* operator (i.e., $a + b = lub(a, b)$) [7].

Some practical instantiations of the generic semiring structure are the *boolean* $\langle \{false, true\}, \vee, \wedge, false, true \rangle$, *fuzzy* $\langle [0..1], max, min, 0, 1 \rangle$, *probabilistic* $\langle [0..1], max, \hat{\times}, 0, 1 \rangle$ and *weighted* $\langle \mathbb{R}^+ \cup \{+\infty\}, min, \hat{+}, \infty, 0 \rangle$ (where $\hat{\times}$ and $\hat{+}$ respectively represent the arithmetic multiplication and addition).

A *soft constraint* [7] may be seen as a constraint where each instantiation of its variables has an associated preference. An example of two constraints defined over the *Weighted* semiring is given in Fig. 2. Given $S = \langle A, +, \times, \mathbf{0}, \mathbf{1} \rangle$ and an ordered finite set of variables V over a domain D, a soft constraint is a function that, given an assignment $\eta : V \rightarrow D$ of the variables, returns a value of the semiring, i.e., $c : (V \rightarrow D) \rightarrow A$. Let $\mathcal{C} = \{c \mid c : D^{|I \subseteq V|} \rightarrow A\}$ be the set of all possible constraints that can be built starting from S, D and V: any function in $\mathcal{C}$ depends on the assignment of only a (possibly empty) finite subset I of V, called the *support*, or *scope*, of the constraint. For instance, a binary constraint $c_{x,y}$ (i.e., $\{x, y\} = I \subseteq V$) is defined on the support $supp(c) = \{x, y\}$. Note that $c\eta[v = d]$ means $c\eta'$ where η' is η modified with the assignment $v = d$. Note also that $c\eta$ is the application of a constraint function $c : (V \rightarrow D) \rightarrow A$ to a function $\eta : V \rightarrow D$; what we obtain is, thus, a semiring value $c\eta = a$. The constraint function $\bar{a}$ always returns the value $a \in A$ for all assignments of domain values, e.g., the $\bar{\mathbf{0}}$ and $\bar{\mathbf{1}}$ functions always return $\mathbf{0}$ and $\mathbf{1}$ respectively.

Given the set $\mathcal{C}$, the combination function $\otimes : \mathcal{C} \times \mathcal{C} \rightarrow \mathcal{C}$ is defined as $(c_1 \otimes c_2)\eta = c_1\eta \times c_2\eta$ [7]; $supp(c_1 \otimes c_2) = supp(c_1) \cup supp(c_2)$. Likewise, the combination function $\oplus : \mathcal{C} \oplus \mathcal{C} \rightarrow \mathcal{C}$ is defined as $(c_1 \oplus c_2)\eta = c_1\eta + c_2\eta$ [7]; $supp(c_1 \oplus c_2) = supp(c_1) \cup supp(c_2)$. Informally, $\otimes/\oplus$ builds a new constraint that associates with each tuple of domain values for such variables a semiring element that is obtained by multiplying/summing the elements associated by the original constraints to the appropriate sub-tuples. The partial order $\leqslant_S$ over $\mathcal{C}$ can be easily extended among constraints by defining $c_1 \sqsubseteq_S c_2 \iff \forall \eta, c_1\eta \leqslant_S c_2\eta$.

The search engine of the tool we present in Sec. 4 relies on the solution of *Soft Constraint Satisfaction Problems (SCSPs)* [7], which can be considered as COPs. An SCSP is defined as a quadruple $P = \langle S, V, D, C \rangle$, where S is the adopted semiring, V the set of variables with domain D, and C is the constraint set. $Sol(P) = \bigotimes C$ collects all solutions of P, each associated with a similarity value $s \in S$. Soft constraints are also used to define SCA (see Sec 2).

Soft Constraint Automata. Constraint Automata were introduced in [5] as a formalism to describe the behaviour and possible data flow in coordination models (e.g., Reo [5]); they can be considered as acceptors of *Timed Data Streams* (*TDS*) [3,5]. In [4] we paved the way to the definition of *Soft Constraint Automata* (SCA), which represent the theoretical fundament behind our tool.

SCA [4] use a finite set $\mathcal{N}$ of names, e.g., $\mathcal{N} = \{n_1, \ldots, n_p\}$, where n_i ($i \in 1..p$) is the i-th input/output port. The transitions of SCA are labeled with pairs consisting of a non-empty subset $N \subseteq \mathcal{N}$ and a soft (instead of crisp as in [5]) data-constraint c. Soft data-constraints can be viewed as an association of data assignments with a preference for that assignment. Formally,

Definition 1 (Soft Data-Constraints). *A soft data-constraint is a function* $c : (\{d_n \mid n \in N\} \to Data) \to A$ *defined over a semiring* $S = \langle A, +, \times, \mathbf{0}, \mathbf{1} \rangle$, *where* $\{d_n \mid n \in N\} \to Data$ *is a function that associates a data item with every variable* d_n *related to port name* $n \in N \subseteq \mathcal{N}$, *and* Data *is the domain of data items that pass through ports in* $\mathcal{N}$. *The grammar of soft data-constraints is:*

$$c_{\{d_n \mid n \in N\}} = \bar{\mathbf{0}} \mid \bar{\mathbf{1}} \mid c_1 \oplus c_2 \mid c_1 \otimes c_2$$

where $\{d_n \mid n \in N\}$ *is the support of the constraint, i.e., the set of variables (related to port names) that determine its preference.*

Informally, a soft data-constraint is a function that returns a preference value $a \in A$ given an assignment for the variables $\{d_n \mid n \in N\}$ in its support. In the sequel, we write $SDC(N, Data)$, for a non-empty subset N of $\mathcal{N}$, to denote the set of soft data-constraints. We will use SDC as an abbreviation for $SDC(\mathcal{N}, Data)$. Note that in Def. 1 we assume a global data domain $Data$ for all names, but, alternatively, we can assign a data domain $Data_n$ for every variable d_n.

We state that an assignment η for the variables $\{d_n \mid n \in N\}$ satisfies c with a preference of $a \in A$, if $c\eta = a$.

In Def. 2 we define SCA. Note that by using the *boolean* semiring, thus within the same semiring-based framework, we can exactly model the "crisp" data-constraints presented in the original definition of CA [5]. Therefore, CA are subsumed by Def. 2. Note also that weighted automata, with weights taken from a proper semiring, have already been defined in the literature [10]; in SCA, weights are determined by a constraint function instead.

Definition 2 (Soft Constraint Automata). *A Soft Constraint Automaton over a domain* Data, *is a tuple* $\mathcal{T}_S = (\mathcal{Q}, \mathcal{N}, \longrightarrow, \mathcal{Q}_0, S)$ *where i)* S *is a semiring* $\langle A, +, \times, \mathbf{0}, \mathbf{1} \rangle$, *ii)* $\mathcal{Q}$ *is a finite set of states, iii)* $\mathcal{N}$ *is a finite set of names, iv)* $\longrightarrow$ *is a finite subset of* $\mathcal{Q} \times 2^{\mathcal{N}} \times SDC \times \mathcal{Q}$, *called the transition relation of* $\mathcal{T}_S$, *and v)* $\mathcal{Q}_0 \subseteq \mathcal{Q}$ *is the set of initial states. We write* $q \xrightarrow{N,c} p$ *instead of* $(q, N, c, p) \in \longrightarrow$. *We call* N *the name-set and* c *the guard of the transition. For every transition* $q \xrightarrow{N,c} p$ *we require that i)* $N \neq \varnothing$, *and ii)* $c \in SDC(N, Data)$ *(see Def. 1).* $\mathcal{T}_S$ *is called finite iff* $\mathcal{Q}, \longrightarrow$ *and the underlying data-domain* Data *are finite.*

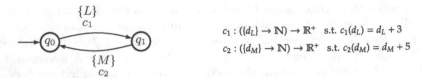

$$c_1 : (\{d_L\} \to \mathbb{N}) \to \mathbb{R}^+ \text{ s.t. } c_1(d_L) = d_L + 3$$
$$c_2 : (\{d_M\} \to \mathbb{N}) \to \mathbb{R}^+ \text{ s.t. } c_2(d_M) = d_M + 5$$

Fig. 1. A Soft Constraint Automaton   **Fig. 2.** c_1 and c_2 in Fig 1

The intuitive meaning of an SCA $\mathcal{T}_S$ as an operational model for service queries is similar to the interpretation of labeled transition systems as formal models for reactive systems. The states represent the configurations of a service. The transitions represent the possible one-step behaviour, where the meaning of $q \xrightarrow{N,c} p$ is that, in configuration q, the ports in $n \in N$ have the possibility of performing I/O operations that satisfy the soft guard c and that leads from configuration q to p, while the ports in $\mathcal{N} \backslash N$ do not perform any I/O operation. Each assignment of variables $\{d_n \mid n \in N\}$ represents the data associated with ports in N, i.e., the data exchanged by the I/O operations through ports in N.

In Fig. 1 we show an example of a (deterministic) SCA. In Fig. 2 we define the *weighted* constraints c_1 and c_2 that describe the preference (e.g., a monetary cost) for the two transitions in Fig. 1, e.g., $c_1(d_L = 2) = 5$.

In [4] we have also softened the synchronisation constraints associated with port names in $\mathcal{N}$ over the transitions. This allows for different service operations to be considered somehow similar for the purposes of a user's query. Note that a similar service can be used, e.g., when the "preferred" one is down due to a fault, or when it offers bad performances, e.g., due to the high number of requests. Definition 3 formalises the notion of soft synchronisation-constraint.

Definition 3 (Soft Synchronization-constraint). *A soft synchronization-constraint is a function* $c : (V \to \mathcal{N}) \to A$ *defined over a semiring* $S = \langle A, +, \times, 0, 1 \rangle$, *where* V *is a finite set of variables for each I/O ports, and* $\mathcal{N}$ *is the set of I/O port names of the SCA.*

3   Representing the Behaviour of Services with SCA

In this section we show how the formal framework presented in Sec. 2 (e.g., SCA) can be used to consider a similarity score between a user's query and the service descriptions in a database, in oder to find the best possible matches for the user.

We begin by considering how parameters of operations can be associated with a score value that describes the similarity between a user's request and an actual service description in a database. We suppose to have two different queries: the first, `getByAuthor(Firstname)`, which is used to search for conference papers using the `Firstname` (i.e., the parameter name) of one of its authors; the name of the invoked service operation is, thus, `getByAuthor`. The second query, `getByTitle(Conference)`, searches for conference papers, using the title of the `Conference` wherein the paper has been published; the name of the invoked operation is `getByTitle`. These two queries are represented as the SCA

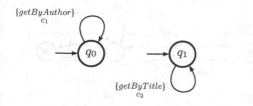
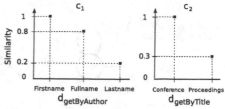

Fig. 3. Two soft Constraint Automata representing two different queries

Fig. 4. The definitions of c_1 and c_2 in Fig. 3

(see Sec. 2) q_0 and q_1, in Fig. 3. Soft constraints c_1 and c_2 in Fig. 4, define a similarity score between the parameter name used in a query and all parameter names in the database (for the same operation name, i.e., either `getByAuthor` or `getByTitle`). These similarity scores can be modeled with the *fuzzy* semiring $\langle[0..1], \max, \min, 0, 1\rangle$ wherein the aim is to maximise the similarity ($+ \equiv \max$) between a request and a service returned as a matching result. Constraint c_1 in Fig. 4 states that similarity is full if a `getByAuthor` operation in the database takes `Firstname` as parameter (since 1 is the top preference of the *fuzzy* semiring), less perfect, that is 0.8, if it takes `Fullname` (usually, `Fullname` includes `Firstname`), or even less perfect, that is 0.2, if it takes `Lastname` only. Similar considerations apply to the operation name `getByTitle` (see Fig. 3) and c_2 in Fig. 4. Similarity scores are automatically extracted as explained in Sec. 4.

Suppose now that our database contains the four services represented in Fig. 5. All these services are stateless, i.e., their SCA have a single state each. For instance, service a has only one invocable operation whose name is `getByAuthor`, which takes `Lastname` as parameter. Service d has two distinct operations, `getByAuthor` and `getByTitle`.

According to the similarity scores expressed by c_1 and c_2 in Fig. 4, queries q_0 and q_1 in Fig. 3 return different result values for each operation/service, depending on the instantiation of variables $d_{getByAuthor}$ and $d_{getByTitle}$. Considering q_0, services a, b, and d have respective preferences of 0.2, 1, and 0.8. If query q_1 is used instead, the possible results are operations c and d, with respective preferences of 1 and 0.3. When more than one service is returned as the result of a search, the end user has the freedom to choose the best one according to his preferences: for the first query q_0, the user can opt for service b, which corresponds to a preference of 1 (i.e., the top preference), while for query q_1 the user can opt for c (top preference as well).

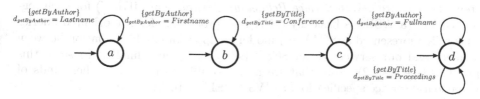

Fig. 5. A database of services for the queries in Fig. 3; d perfoms both kinds of search

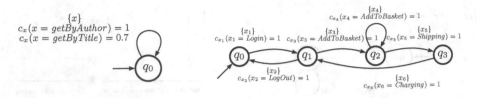

Fig. 6. A similarity-based query for the *Author/Title* example

Fig. 7. A similarity-based query for the on-line purchase service

We now move from parameter names to operation names, and show that by using soft synchronisation constraints (see Def. 3), we can also compute a similarity score among them. For example, suppose that a user queries q_0 in Fig. 3. The possible results are services a, b and d in the database of Fig. 5, since service c has an operation named `getByTitle`, different from `getByAuthor`. However, the two services are somehow similar, since they both return a paper even if the search is based either on the author or on the conference. As a result, a user may be satisfied also by retrieving (and then, using) service c. This can be accomplished with the query in Fig. 6, where $c_x(x = getByAuthor) = 1$, and $c_x(x = getByTitle) = 0.7$. Note that we no longer deal with constraints on parameter names, but on operation names. Then, we can also look for services that have similar operations, not only similar parameters in operations.

However, the main goal of this paper is to compute a similarity score considering also the behaviour of queries and services. For instance (the query in Fig. 7), a user may need to find an on-line purchase service satisfying the following requirements: *i*) charging activity comes before shipping activity, *ii*) to purchase a product, the requester first needs to log into the system and finally log out of the system, and *iii*) filling the electronic basket of a user may consist of a succession of "add-to-basket" actions. In Sec. 5 we will focus on this aspect.

Constraints on parameter (their data-types as well) and operation names can be straightforwardly mixed together to represent a search problem where both are taken into account simultaneously for optimization. The tool in Sec. 4 exploits this kind of search: the similarity functions represented by constraints are computed through the composition of different syntactic similarity metrics.

4   Tool Description

Conceptually, our behaviourally-based WS discovery proceeds in four successive steps: *i*) generate a *Web Service Behaviour Specification* (*WSBS*) for each registered WS (a WSBS is basically a CA), *ii*) process preference-oriented queries (basically represented as SCA), *iii*) model an approximate bisimulation between a query and our services as an SCSP (see Sec. 2), and finally, *iv*) solve this problem (see Sec. 2). Note that we are also able to translate other kinds of behavioural service specification, as WS-BPEL[2], into (S)CA [8].

---

[2] WS-Business Process Execution Language, 2.0: http://tinyurl.com/czkoolw

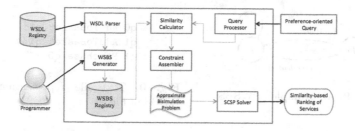

Fig. 8. General architecture of the tool

Step i is needed because no standard language or tool exists to specify the behaviour of stateful WSs. Therefore, we have to define our internal WSBS as a behavioural specification for WSs, using WSDL and some extra necessary annotations. In step ii, we obtain a query from a user and we process it to find the similarities between the request and the actual services in the database. In the third step, we set up an SCSP (see Sec. 2), where soft-constraint functions are assembled by using the similarity scores derived from step ii; at the same time, we define those constraints that compare the two behavioural signatures (query/service), and measure their similarity. Finally, we find the best solutions for this SCSP, and we return them to the user. All these steps are implemented by different software modules, whose global architecture is defined in Fig. 8.

WSDL Parser. We rely on a repository of WSDL documents that are captured in a registry, i.e., the *WSDL Registry* (see Fig. 8). WSDL is an XML-based standard for syntactical representation of WSs, which is currently the most suitable for our purpose. First, we parse these XML-based documents to extract the names and interfaces of service operations using the *Axis2* technology.[3]

WSBS Generator. While a WSDL document specifies the syntax and the technical details of a service interface, it lacks the information needed to convey its behavioural aspects. In fact, a WSDL document only reveals the operation names and the names and data types of their arguments. Hence, we must indicate the permissible operation sequences of a service. If we know that a WS is stateless, then all of its operations are permissible in any order. For a stateful service, however, we need to know which of its operations is (not) allowed in each of its states. In [14], some of the authors of this paper have already formalised the behaviour of a WS (i.e., the WSBS) in terms of CA [5]. Therefore, we adopt the *Extensible Coordination Tools* (*ECT*) [2], which consist of a set of plug-ins for the *Eclipse* platform[4], as the core of the *WSBS Generator*, in order to generate a CA to specify the externally observable behaviour of a service. Normally, the ECT is used to give a semantics to Reo circuits [5]. The resulting CA are captured as XML documents, where the <*states*> and <*transitions*> tags identify the structure of each automaton. It is also possible to indicate the

---

[3] http://axis.apache.org/axis2/java/core/
[4] ECT webpage: http://reo.project.cwi.nl/reo/wiki/Tools

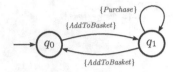

Fig. 9. An example of WSBS

```
q0 AddToBasket q1;
q1 AddToBasket q1;
q1 Purchase q0.
```

Fig. 10. Text file representing the WSBS in Fig. 9

behaviour of WSs in text files, in a simplified form. The file in Fig. 10 describes the service represented in Fig. 9. In our architecture, all WSBSs are stored in a *WSBS Registry* (see Fig. 8).

We can automatically extract a single-state automaton from the operations defined in a WSDL document describing a stateless WS: we use this support-tool to extract the automata for the real-world WSs used in our following experiment. For stateful WSs, we developed an interactive tool that (using a GUI) allows a programmer (see Fig. 8) to visually create the automaton states describing the behavior of a service, and tag its transitions with the operations defined in its WSDL document.

Query Processor. At search time, a user specifies a desired service by means of a text file, and feeds it to this module. An example of our query is represented in Fig. 11. The query format allows to specify all desired transitions among states, including operation names, and the names and data types of their arguments. It enables to search for multiple similar services (separated by "or" operators) at the same time while the tool ranks all the results in the same list. Finally, the tool assigns to each service description a preference score prescribed by the user. A user may use a score (e.g., fuzzy preferences in [0..1]) to weigh all the results, as represented in Fig. 11. Each query is represented as an SCA [4] (see Sec. 2), since preferences can be represented by soft constraints. This textual representation resembles a list of WSBSs, each of them associated with a preference score (see Fig. 11 and Fig. 10 for a comparison).

Similarity Calculator. As Fig. 8 shows, this module requires two inputs: the WSBSs and the processed query. It returns three different kinds of similarity scores, which reflect the similarities between one service and one query *i*) operations names, *ii*) names of input-parameters of operations, and *iii*) data types of input-parameters. We use different string similarity-metrics (also known as *string distance functions*) as the functions to measure the similarity between two text-strings. We have chosen three of the most widely known metrics, including the *Levenshtein Distance*, the *Matching Coefficient*, and the *QGrams Distance*. Each of these metrics operates with two input strings, and return a score estimating their similarity. Since each function returns a value in [0..1], we average these three scores to merge them into a single value still in [0..1].

These similarity scores are subsequently used by the *Constraint Assembler* in Fig. 8, in order to define the similarity functions that are translated into soft constraints, as explained in Sec. 3. The representation of the search problem q0 Weather(City:string) q0, [1.0] or q0 Weather(Zipcode:string) q0, [0.8]

Fig. 11. A single-state query asking for the weather conditions over a `City`, or using a `Zipcode`. Different user's preference scores are represented within square brackets.

in terms of constraints is completely constructed by the *Constraint Assembler* module, while the *Similarity Calculator* only provides it with similarity scores.

Constraint Assembler. This module produces a model of the discovery problem, in the form of approximate bisimulation (see Sec. 5), as an SCSP (see Sec. 2). To do so, it represents all preference and similarity requirements as soft constraints. In order to assemble these constraints, we used *JaCoP*, which is a Java library that provides a finite-domain constraint programming paradigm. We have made ad-hoc extensions to the crisp constraints offered by JaCoP in order to equip them with weights, and we have exploited the possibility to minimise/maximise a given cost function to solve SCSPs. Specifically, we have expressed the WSs discovery problem as a fuzzy optimisation problem, by implementing the *fuzzy* semiring, i.e., $\langle [0..1], max, min, 0, 1 \rangle$ (see Sec. 2).

For instance, *SumWeight* is a JaCoP constraint that computes a weighted sum as the following pseudo-code: $w_1 \cdot x_1 + w_2 \cdot x_2 + w_3 \cdot x_3 = sum$, where *sum* represents the global syntactic similarity between two operation names (x_1), considering also their argument names (x_2) and types (x_3). These scores are provided by the *Similarity Calculator*. Moreover, we can tune the weights w_1, w_2, and w_3 to give more or less importance to the three different parameters. In the experiments in Sec. 4 we use equal weights. We leave to Sec. 5 a discussion on how to compute how much two behavioural signatures (query/service) are similar, and how the general constraint-based model is designed.

SCSP Solver. Finally, after the specification of the model consisting of variables and constraints, a search for a solution of the assembled SCSP can be started. This represents the final step (see Fig. 8). The result can be generalised as a ranking of services in the considered database: at the top positions we find the services that are more similar to a user's request.

Experimental Results on a Stateless Scenario. In this section we show the precision results of our tool through a scenario involving stateless real WSs. Figure 11 shows a single-state query that searches for WSs that return the "weather" forecast for a location indicated by the name of a "city" (with a user's preference of 1) or its "zip-code" (preference of 0.8). We retrieved 14 different WSDL documents by querying the word "Weather" on *Seekda*[5], which is a public WS search-engine. These documents list a total of 58 different operations, which populate our *WSDL Registry* (see Fig. 8).

Table 1 reports a part of the experiment results. From left to right the columns respectively report the position in the final ranking, the obtained fuzzy score, the WS name, and, lastly, the matched service operation.

---

[5] http://webservices.seekda.com

5   On Comparing Behaviour Signatures

In this section we zoom inside the *Constraint Assembler* component that we introduced in Sec. 4. We describe how we can approximate the behaviour of a posed query with that of a service, since a perfect match can be uncommon.

The basic idea is to compute an approximate bisimulation [11] between the two automata respectively representing a query, and a WS in a database. The notion of approximate bisimulation relation is obtained by relaxing the equality of output traces: instead of requiring them to be identical, we require that they remain "close". Metrics (represented as semirings, in our case) essentially quantify how well a system is approximated by another based on the distance between their observed behaviours. In this way, we are able to consider different transition-labels by estimating a similarity score between their operation interfaces, and different numbers of states. To model approximate bisimulation with constraints, we exploited constraint-based graph matching techniques [17]; thus, we are able to "compress" or "dilate" one automaton structure into another.

In the following, we use the query example in Fig 12, and the service example in Fig. 13 to describe our constraint-based model for the search. We subdivide this description by considering how we match the different elements of automata (transitions or states), and how we finally measure their overall similarity.

States. To represent our signature-match problem, for each of the query-automaton states (cardinality Q) we define a variable that can be assigned to one or several states of a service (cardinality S). For this purpose, we use *SetVar*, i.e., JaCoP variables defined as ordered collections of integers. Considering our running example, one of the possible matches between these two signatures can be given by $M \equiv q_0 = \{s_0, s_1, s_3\}, q_1 = \{s_2\}$. This matching is represented in Fig. 12 and Fig. 13 using gray and black labels for states. Clearly, the proposed modelling solution represents a relationship and not a function, since a query state can be associated with one or more service-states; on the other hand, different query states can be associate with the same service state, in case a query has more states than a service. Thus, to match the two automata we allow to "merge" together those states that are connected by a transition (e.g., s_0, s_1

Table 1. The ranking of the top-ten matched WSs, based on the query represented in Fig. 11, out of a database of 14 different WSDL documents

Rank	Score	Name of WS	Interface of the operation
1	0.82	weather	$GetWeather(City : string)$
2	0.69	globalweather	$GetWeather(CityName : string)$
3	0.5	Weather	$Get\_Weather(ZIP : string)$
4	0.48	WeatherWS	$getWeather(theCityCode : string, theUserID : string)$
5	0.47	WeatherWebService	$getWeatherbyCityName(theCityName : string)$
6	0.44	usweather	$GetWeatherReport(ZipCode : string)$
7	0.42	WeatherForecast	$GetWeatherByZipCode(ZipCode : string)$
8	0.4	WeatherForecast	$GetWeatherByPlaceName(PlaceName : string)$
9	0.4	weatherservice	$GetLiveCompactWeathe(cityCode : string, ACode : string)$
10	0.36	weatherservice	$GetLiveCompactWeatherByStationID(stationid : string, un : UnitType, ACode : string)$

and s_3 in Fig. 13) into a single state (e.g., q_0) at the cost of incurring a certain penalty.

Transitions. In our running example, if we match the two behaviours as defined by $\mathcal{M}$, we consequently obtain a match for the transitions (and their labels) as well. Our model has a variable (*IntVar*, in JacoP) for each of the transitions in a query automaton; considering the example in Fig. 12, we have three variables l_1, l_2, l_3. In Fig. 12 and Fig. 13 we label each transition with its identifier $(l_1, \ldots, l_3, m_1, \ldots, m_5)$, and a string that represents its related operation-name (in this example, we ignore parameter names and types for the sake of brevity). Thus, the full match-characterisation is now $\mathcal{M} \equiv q_0 = \{s_0, s_1, s_3\}, q_1 = \{s_2\}, l_1 = m_2, l_2 = m_3, l_3 = m_5$. Note that, if a query has more transitions than a service, it may happen to be impossible to match all of them; for this reason, since we need to assign each of the variables in order to find a solution, we assign a mark *NM* (i.e., *Not Matched*) to unpaired transitions.

Match Cost. In this paragraph we show how to compute a global similarity score Γ for a match $\mathcal{M}$ (i.e., $\Gamma(\mathcal{M})$). We consider two different kinds of scores, *i*) a state similarity-score, $\sigma(\mathcal{M})$, is derived from how much we need to (de)compress the behaviour (in terms of number of states) to pass from one signature to another, and *ii*) a transition similarity-score, $\theta(\mathcal{M})$, is derived from a comparison between matched labels. In a simple case, we can consider the mean value $\Gamma(\mathcal{M}) = (\sigma(\mathcal{M}) + \theta(\mathcal{M}))/2$, or we can imagine more sophisticated aggregation functions. A rather straightforward function is $\sigma(\mathcal{M}) = \min(\#\mathsf{S}_\mathcal{M}, \#\mathsf{Q}_\mathcal{M})/\max(\#\mathsf{S}_\mathcal{M}, \#\mathsf{Q}_\mathcal{M})$ (if $\#\mathsf{S}_\mathcal{M} = \#\mathsf{Q}_\mathcal{M}$, our match is perfect), but we can think of non-linear functions as well, for instance. The score $\theta(\mathcal{M})$ is computed by aggregating the individual *ssim* syntactic similarity-scores (computed by the *Similarity Calculator* in Sec. 4) obtained for each label match, and then averaging on the number of matched labels. For our example, $\theta(\mathcal{M}) = (ssim(label_{l_1}, label_{m_2}) + ssim(label_{l_2}, label_{m_4}) + ssim(label_{l_3}, label_{m_5}))/3$.

An Experiment with Stateful Services. Since all current WS standards are stateless, for this experiment we hand-crafted four stateful WSs (see Tab. 2). We use the following query against this database. The ideal service matching the query first retrieves the weather forecast for a city based on its name, and then retrieves the forecasts for its neighbouring cities:

    q0 GetWeather(SetCity : string) q1; q1 GetNeighbourhoodWeather() q0 [1.0].

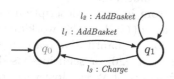

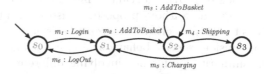

Fig. 12. A query example

Fig. 13. A possible service in a database related to the query in Fig. 12

Table 2. Our registry of hand-crafted stateful WSs, and the obtained similarity scores

ID	WSBS	θ	σ	Γ	Rk
S_1	q0 getweather(city:string) q0	.76	.5	.63	4
S_2	q0 getweather(city:string) q1 ; q1 getneighborsweather q0	.8	1	.9	1
S_3	q0 login(password:string) q1; q1 getweather(city:string) q2 ; q2 getneighborsweather q0	.8	.66	.73	3
S_4	q0 GetWeather(myCity:string) q1; q1 getNeighWeather q0	.69	1	.84	2

Table 2 shows the results of this experiment: the transition similarity-score $\theta(\mathcal{M})$, the state similarity-score $\sigma(\mathcal{M})$, the global similarity-score $\Gamma(\mathcal{M})$, and the rank Rk of each service. These results match our expectations, since the behaviour of S_2 and S_4 each is identical to the behaviour of our query, while the operation interface of S_2 is more similar to the query compared to that of S_4.

6   Related Work

Compared to the work reported in the literature, the solution in this paper seems more general, compact, and comprehensive, because it can encompass any semiring-like metrics, and the whole framework is expressively modeled and solved using Constraint Programming. Moreover, elaborating on a formal framework allows us to easily check properties of services/queries (e.g., to model-check or bi/simulate them [4]), and to have join and hide operators to work on them [4]. Most of the literature seems to report more ad-hoc engineered and specific solutions, instead, which consequently, are less amenable to formal reasoning.

In [18] the authors propose a new behaviour model for WSs using automata and logic formalisms. Roughly, the model associates messages with activities and adopts the IOPR model (i.e., Input, Output, Precondition, Result) in OWL-S^6 to describe activities. The authors use an automaton structure to model service behaviour. However, similarity-based search is not mentioned in [18]. In [21] the authors present an approach that supports service discovery based on structural and behavioural service models, as well as quality constraints and contextual information. Behaviours are matched through a subgraph isomorphism algorithm. In [12] the problem of behavioural matching is translated to a graph matching problem, and existing algorithms are adapted for this purpose.

The model presented in [19] relies on a simple and extensible keyword-based query language and enables efficient retrieval of approximate results, including approximate service compositions. Since representing all possible compositions can result in an exponentially-sized index, the authors investigate clustering methods to provide a scalable mechanism for service indexing.

In [6], the authors propose a crisp translation from interface description of WSs to classical crisp *Constraint Satisfaction Problems* (*CSPs*). This work does not consider service behaviour and it does not support a quantitative reasoning on similarity/preference involving different services. In [20], a semiring-based framework is used to model and compose QoS features of WSs. However, no notion of similarity relationship is given in [20].

---

[6] OWL-S: Semantic Markup for Web Services, 2004: www.w3.org/Submission/OWL-S/

In [9], the authors propose a novel clustering algorithm that groups names of parameters of WS operations into semantically meaningful concepts. These concepts are then leveraged to determine similarity of inputs (or outputs) of web-service operations. In [15] the authors propose a framework of fuzzy query languages for fuzzy ontologies, and present query answering algorithms for these query languages over fuzzy *DL-Lite* ontologies. In [13] the authors propose a metric to measure the similarity of semantic services annotated with an *OWL ontology*. They calculate similarity by defining the intrinsic information value of a service description based on the "inferencibility" of each of *OWL Lite* constructs. The authors in [16] show a method of WS retrieval called *URBE* (*UDDI Registry By Example*). The retrieval is based on the evaluation of similarity between the interfaces of WSs. The algorithm used in *URBE* combines the analysis of the structure of a WS and the terms used inside it.

7 Conclusions

We have presented a tool for similarity-based discovery of WSs that is able to rank the service descriptions in a database, in accordance with a similarity score between each of them and the description of a service desired by a user. The formal framework behind the tool consists of SCA [4], which can represent different high-level stateful software services and queries. Thus, we can use SCA to formally reason on queries (e.g., bisimulation for SCA is introduced in [4]). The tool is based on implementing approximate bisimulation [11] with constraints (see Sec. 5), which allows to quantitatively estimate the differences between two behaviours. Defining this problem as an SCSP makes it parametric with respect to the chosen similarity metric (i.e., a semiring), and allows using efficient AI techniques for solving it: subgraph isomorphism is not known to be in P.

Our main intent has been to propose a formal framework and a tool with an approximate bisimulation of behaviours at its heart, not to directly compete against tools such as [16], which although show higher precision than what we have summarised in Sec. 4, do not support behaviour specification in their matching. Nevertheless, in the future we plan to refine the performance of our tool by also evaluating a semantic similarity-score between the operation and parameter names, using an appropriate ontology for services as OWL-S.

References

1. Alonso, G., Casati, F., Kuno, H.A., Machiraju, V.: Web Services - Concepts, Architectures and Applications. Data-Centric Systems and Applications. Springer (2004)
2. Arbab, F., Koehler, C., Maraikar, Z., Moon, Y., Proença, J.: Modeling, testing and executing Reo connectors with the Eclipse Coordination Tools. Tool demo session at FACS 8 (2008)
3. Arbab, F., Rutten, J.J.M.M.: A coinductive calculus of component connectors. In: Wirsing, M., Pattinson, D., Hennicker, R. (eds.) WADT 2003. LNCS, vol. 2755, pp. 34–55. Springer, Heidelberg (2003)

4. Arbab, F., Santini, F.: Preference and similarity-based behavioral discovery of services. In: ter Beek, M.H., Lohmann, N. (eds.) WS-FM 2012. LNCS, vol. 7843, pp. 118–133. Springer, Heidelberg (2013)
5. Baier, C., Sirjani, M., Arbab, F., Rutten, J.J.M.M.: Modeling component connectors in Reo by constraint automata. Sci. Comput. Program. 61(2), 75–113 (2006)
6. Benbernou, S., Canaud, E., Pimont, S.: Semantic web services discovery regarded as a constraint satisfaction problem. In: Christiansen, H., Hacid, M.-S., Andreasen, T., Larsen, H.L. (eds.) FQAS 2004. LNCS (LNAI), vol. 3055, pp. 282–294. Springer, Heidelberg (2004)
7. Bistarelli, S., Montanari, U., Rossi, F.: Semiring-based constraint satisfaction and optimization. J. ACM 44(2), 201–236 (1997)
8. Changizi, B., Kokash, N., Arbab, F.: A Unified Toolset for Business Process Model Formalization. In: Proceedings of FESCA 2010 (2010)
9. Dong, X., Halevy, A., Madhavan, J., Nemes, E., Zhang, J.: Similarity search for web services. In: Proceedings of Very Large Data Bases, vol. 30, pp. 372–383, VLDB Endowment (2004), http://dl.acm.org/citation.cfm?id=1316689.1316723
10. Droste, M., Kuich, W., Vogler, H.: Handbook of Weighted Automata, 1st edn. Springer Publishing Company, Incorporated (2009)
11. Girard, A., Pappas, G.J.: Approximation metrics for discrete and continuous systems. IEEE Trans. Automat. Contr. 52(5), 782–798 (2007)
12. Grigori, D., Corrales, J.C., Bouzeghoub, M.: Behavioral matchmaking for service retrieval. In: IEEE International Conference on Web Services (ICWS), pp. 145–152. IEEE Computer Society (2006)
13. Hau, J., Lee, W., Darlington, J.: A semantic similarity measure for semantic web services. In: Web Service Semantics Workshop at WWW (2005)
14. Jongmans, S.-S.T.Q., Santini, F., Sargolzaei, M., Arbab, F., Afsarmanesh, H.: Automatic code generation for the orchestration of web services with Reo. In: De Paoli, F., Pimentel, E., Zavattaro, G. (eds.) ESOCC 2012. LNCS, vol. 7592, pp. 1–16. Springer, Heidelberg (2012)
15. Pan, J.Z., Stamou, G., Stoilos, G., Taylor, S., Thomas, E.: Scalable querying services over fuzzy ontologies. In: Proceedings of World Wide Web, WWW 2008, pp. 575–584. ACM, New York (2008), http://doi.acm.org/10.1145/1367497.1367575
16. Plebani, P., Pernici, B.: Urbe: Web service retrieval based on similarity evaluation. IEEE Trans. on Knowl. and Data Eng. 21(11), 1629–1642 (2009), http://dx.doi.org/10.1109/TKDE.2009.35
17. le Clément, V., Deville, Y., Solnon, C.: Constraint-based graph matching. In: Gent, I.P. (ed.) CP 2009. LNCS, vol. 5732, pp. 274–288. Springer, Heidelberg (2009)
18. Shen, Z., Su, J.: Web service discovery based on behavior signatures. In: Proceedings of the 2005 IEEE International Conference on Services Computing, SCC 2005, vol. 01, pp. 279–286. IEEE Computer Society, Washington, DC (2005)
19. Toch, E., Gal, A., Reinhartz-Berger, I., Dori, D.: A semantic approach to approximate service retrieval. ACM Trans. Internet Technol. 8(1) (November 2007)
20. Zemni, M.A., Benbernou, S., Carro, M.: A soft constraint-based approach to QoS-aware service selection. In: Maglio, P.P., Weske, M., Yang, J., Fantinato, M. (eds.) ICSOC 2010. LNCS, vol. 6470, pp. 596–602. Springer, Heidelberg (2010)
21. Zisman, A., Dooley, J., Spanoudakis, G.: Proactive runtime service discovery. In: Proceedings of the 2008 IEEE International Conference on Services Computing, SCC 2008, vol. 1, pp. 237–245. IEEE Computer Society, Washington, DC (2008), http://dx.doi.org/10.1109/SCC.2008.60

A Type System for Components*

Ornela Dardha[1], Elena Giachino[1], and Michaël Lienhardt[2]

[1] INRIA Focus Team / University of Bologna, Italy
{dardha,giachino}@cs.unibo.it
[2] University of Paris Diderot, France
lienhar@inria.fr

Abstract. In modern distributed systems, dynamic reconfiguration, i.e., changing at runtime the communication pattern of a program, is challenging. Generally, it is difficult to guarantee that such modifications will not disrupt ongoing computations. In a previous paper, a solution to this problem was proposed by extending the object-oriented language ABS with a component model allowing the programmer to: *i*) perform updates on objects by means of *communication ports* and their *rebinding*; and *ii*) precisely specify when such updates can safely occur in an object by means of *critical sections*. However, improper rebind operations could still occur and lead to runtime errors. The present paper introduces a type system for this component model that extends the ABS type system with the notion of ports and a precise analysis that statically enforces that no object will attempt illegal rebinding.

1 Introduction

In modern complex distributed scenarios, unplanned dynamic reconfiguration, i.e., changing at runtime the communication pattern of a program, is challenging as it is difficult to ensure that such modifications will not disrupt ongoing computations. In [14] the authors propose to solve the problem by integrating notions coming from component models [2–4,8] within the actor-based *Abstract Behavioral Specification* programming language (ABS) [13]. ABS is designed for distributed object-oriented systems and integrates concurrency and synchronization mechanisms to solve data races. Actors, called *cog*s or simply *group*s, are dynamic collections of collaborating objects. Cogs offer consistency by guaranteeing that at most one method per cog is executing at any time. Within a cog, objects collaborate using (*synchronous*) method calls and *collaborative concurrency* with the **suspend** and **await** operations which can suspend the execution of the current method, and thus allow another one to execute. Between cogs, collaboration is achieved by means of *asynchronous* method calls that return *future*, i.e., a placeholder where the result of the call is put when its computation finishes.

---

* This research is partly funded by the EU project FP7-231620 HATS and by the French National Research Agency (ANR), projects REVER ANR 11 INSE 007.

R.M. Hierons, M.G. Merayo, and M. Bravetti (Eds.): SEFM 2013, LNCS 8137, pp. 167–181, 2013.
© Springer-Verlag Berlin Heidelberg 2013

On top of the ABS language, [14] adds the notions of *ports*, *bindings* and *safe state* to deal with dynamic reconfiguration. Ports define variability points in an object and can be *rebound* (i.e., modified) from outside the object (on the contrary, fields, which represent the inner state of the object, can only be modified by the object itself). To ensure consistency of the **rebind** operation, [14] enforces two constraints on its application: *i*) it is only possible to rebind an object's port when the object is in a *safe state*; and *ii*) it is only possible to rebind an object's port from *any* object within the *same* cog. Safe states are modeled by annotating methods as **critical**, specifying that while one or more **critical** methods are executing, the object is *not* in a safe state. The resulting language offers a consistent setting for dynamic reconfigurations, which means performing modifications on a program at runtime while still ensuring consistency of its execution. Consistency is based on two constraints: both synchronous method calls and rebinding operations must involve two objects in the same cog. These constraints are enforced at runtime; therefore, programs may encounter unexpected runtime errors during their execution.

In this paper, we define a type system for the component model that statically ensures the legality of both synchronous method calls and port rebindings, guaranteeing that well-typed programs will always be consistent. Our approach is based on a static tracking of group membership of the objects. The difficulty in retrieving this kind of information is that cogs as well as objects are dynamic entities. Since we want to trace group information statically, we need a way to identify and track every group in the program. To this aim, we define a technique that associates to each group creation a fresh *group name*. Then, we keep track of which cog an object is allocated to, by associating to each object a *group record*. The type system checks that objects indeed have the specified group record, and uses this information to ensure that synchronous calls and rebindings are always performed locally to a cog. The type system is proven to be sound with respect to the operational semantics. We use this result to show that well-typed programs do not violate consistency during execution.

Motivating Example. In the following we present a running example that gives a better understanding of the ABS language and the component extension, and most importantly, motivates our type system. Consider the following typical distributed scenario: suppose that we have several clients working together in a specific workflow and using a central server for their communications. Updating the server is a difficult task, as it requires to update its reference in all clients at the same time in order to avoid communication failures.

First, in Fig. 1 we consider how this task is achieved in ABS. The programmer declares two interfaces **Server** and **Client** and a class **Controller**. Basically, the class **Controller** updates the server in all the clients c_i by synchronously calling their setter method. All the clients are updated at the same time: since they are in the same cog as the controller they cannot execute until the execution of method **updateServer** has terminated.

```
interface Server { ... }
interface Client { Unit setServer(Server s); ... }

class Controller {
  Client c1, c2, ... cn;

  Unit updateServer(Server s2) {
    c1.setServer(s2);
    c2.setServer(s2);
    ...
    cn.setServer(s2);
  }}
```

Fig. 1. Workflow in ABS

However, this code does not ensure that the update is performed when the clients are in a safe state. This can lead to inconsistencies because clients that are using the server are not aware of the modification taking place. This problem can be solved by using the notions of **port** and **rebind** [14] as shown in Fig. 2. Here, the method `updateServer` first waits for all clients to be in a safe state (**await** statement performed on the conjunction of all clients) and then updates their reference one by one (**rebind** server s which is declared to be a **port**).

```
interface Server { ... }
interface Client { port Server s; ... }

class Controller {
  Client c1, c2, ... cn;
    ...
  Unit updateServer(Server s2) {
    await ||c1|| ∧ ||c2|| ∧ ... ∧ ||cn||;
    rebind c1.s = s2;
    rebind c2.s = s2;
    ...
    rebind cn.s = s2;
  }}
```

Fig. 2. Workflow using the Component Model

However, runtime errors can still occur. For instance, if the clients and the controller are not in the same cog, the update will fail. Consider the code in Fig. 3. Method `main` instantiates classes `Client` and `Controller` –and possibly other classes, like `Server`, present in the program– by creating objects $c_1, c_2, \ldots, c_n, c$. These objects are created in the same cog by the **new** command, except for client c_1, which is created and placed in a new cog by the **new cog** command.

Now, suppose that the code in Fig. 2 is executed. At runtime, the program will check if the controller and the client belong to the same cog to respect the consistency constraints on rebinding. In case of c_1 this check will fail by leading to a runtime error.

The present paper addresses this problem in order to avoid these runtime errors and the overhead in dealing with them. We present a type system that tracks cog membership of objects thus permitting to typecheck only programs where rebinding is consistent. So, the code presented above would not typecheck, as shown in § 3, thus discarding the program at compile time instead of leading to a runtime error.

```
Unit main () {          ...
    Client c₁ = new cog Client (s);
    Client c₂ = new Client (s);
        ...
    Client cₙ = new Client (s);
    Controller c = new Controller (c₁, c₂, ... cₙ);
}
```

Fig. 3. Client and Controller objects creation

Roadmap. The rest of the paper is structured as follows: § 2 introduces the calculus, types and terms; § 3 presents our type system and its properties; and § 4 concludes the paper and discusses future and related works.

2   The Calculus

In this section we present the calculus underlying our approach, which is a component extension of the ABS language[1]. We present formally only the syntax of the calculus which is necessary for specifying the type system. We already gave some intuitions about the operational semantics of the calculus in the introduction and through the example, whereas for the formal definition we refer to the original paper [14] and the extended version of this paper [9].

The syntax of the calculus is given in Fig. 4 and corresponds to the original one, except for types, which are here extended in order to store also group information. This syntax is based on several categories of names: I and C range over interface and class names; V ranges over type variables for polymorphism; G ranges over cog names, which will be explained thoroughly in § 3; D, Co and fun range respectively over data type, constructor and function names; m, f and p

---

[1] For the sake of readability, the calculus we consider is a subset of [14]. The notion of *location* has been dropped, since it is orthogonal to ports and rebinding. The validity of our approach and of our type system still holds for the full calculus.

$$P ::= \overline{Dl} \{ s \}$$ Program
$$Dl ::= D \mid F \mid I \mid C$$ Declarations
$$T ::= \mathtt{V} \mid \mathtt{D}[\langle \overline{T} \rangle] \mid (\mathtt{I}, \mathtt{r})$$ Type
$$\mathtt{r} ::= \bot \mid \mathtt{G}[\overline{f : T}] \mid \alpha \mid \mu\alpha.\mathtt{r}$$ Record
$$D ::= \mathbf{data} \; \mathtt{D}[\langle \overline{T} \rangle] = \mathtt{Co}[(\overline{T})] | \mathtt{Co}[(\overline{T})];$$ Data Type
$$F ::= \mathbf{def} \; T \; \mathbf{fun}[\langle \overline{T} \rangle](\overline{T \; x}) = e;$$ Function
$$I ::= \mathbf{interface} \; \mathtt{I} \; [\mathbf{extends} \; \overline{\mathtt{I}}] \; \{ \; \overline{\mathbf{port} \; T \; x}; \overline{S} \; \}$$ Interface
$$C ::= \mathbf{class} \; \mathtt{C} \; [(\overline{T \; x})] \; [\mathbf{implements} \; \overline{\mathtt{I}}] \; \{ \; \overline{Fl} \; \overline{M} \; \}$$ Class
$$Fl ::= [\mathbf{port}] \; T \; x$$ Field Declaration
$$S ::= [\mathbf{critical}] \; (\mathcal{G}, \mathtt{r}) \; T \; \mathtt{m}(\overline{T \; x})$$ Method Header
$$M ::= S \{ \; s \; \}$$ Method Definition
$$s ::= \mathbf{skip} \mid s; s \mid T \; x \mid x = z \mid \mathbf{await} \; g$$ Statement
$$\mid \mathbf{if} \; e \; \{ \; s \; \} \; \mathbf{else} \; \{ \; s \; \} \mid \mathbf{while} \; e \; \{ \; s \; \} \mid \mathbf{return} \; e$$
$$\mid \mathbf{rebind} \; e.p = z$$
$$z ::= e \mid \mathbf{new} \; [\mathbf{cog}] \; \mathtt{C} \; (\overline{e}) \mid e.\mathtt{m}(\overline{e}) \mid e!\mathtt{m}(\overline{e}) \mid \mathbf{get}(e)$$ Expression with Side Effects
$$e ::= v \mid x \mid \mathbf{fun}(\overline{e}) \mid \mathbf{case} \; e \; \{\overline{p \Rightarrow e_p}\}$$ Expression
$$v ::= \mathbf{null} \mid \mathtt{Co}[(\overline{v})]$$ Value
$$p ::= \_ \mid x \mid \mathbf{null} \mid \mathtt{Co}[(\overline{p})]$$ Pattern
$$g ::= x \mid x? \mid \|x\| \mid g \wedge g$$ Guard

Fig. 4. Core ABS Language and Component Extension

range respectively over method, field and port names (in order to have a uniform presentation, we will often use f for both fields and ports); and x ranges over variables, with the addition of the special variable **this** indicating the current object. For the sake of readability, we use the following notations: an overlined element corresponds to any finite, possibly empty, sequence of such element; and an element between square brackets is optional.

A program P consists of a sequence of declarations ended by a main block, namely a statement s to be executed. Declarations include data type declarations D, function declarations F, interface declarations I and class declarations C. A type T can be: a type variable $\mathtt{V}$; a data type D like $\mathtt{Bool}$ or futures $\mathtt{Fut}\langle T \rangle$, used to type data structures; or a pair consisting of an interface name $\mathtt{I}$ and a *record* $\mathtt{r}$ to type objects. Note that the ABS type system only uses interface names to type objects, but here we add records to track in which cog an object is located. Records can be: $\bot$, meaning that the structure of the object is unknown; $\mathtt{G}[\overline{f : T}]$, meaning that the object is in the cog $\mathtt{G}$ and its fields $\overline{f}$ are typed with $\overline{T}$; or regular terms, using the standard combination of variables α and the μ-binder. Data types D have at least one constructor, with name $\mathtt{Co}$, and possibly a list of type parameters $\overline{T}$. Functions F are declared with a return type T, a name $\mathtt{fun}$, a list of parameters $\overline{T \; x}$ and a code e. Interfaces I declare methods and ports that can be modified at runtime. Classes C implement interfaces; they have a list of fields and ports Fl and implement all declared methods. Method headers S are used to declare methods with their classic type annotation, and i) the possible annotation **critical** that ensures that no rebinding will be performed on that object during the execution of that method; and ii) a *method signature* $(\mathcal{G}, \mathbf{r})$ which will be described and used in our type system section. Method declarations M consist of a header and a body, the latter being a sequential composition of local variables and commands. Statements s are standard except for **await** g, which suspends the execution of the method until the guard g is **true**, and **rebind** $e.p = z$, which rebinds the port p of the object e to the value stored in z. Expressions z include: expressions without side effects e; **new** C $(\bar{e})$ and **new cog** C $(\bar{e})$ that instantiate a class C and place the object in the current cog and in a new cog, respectively; synchronous $e.\mathtt{m}(\bar{e})$ and asynchronous $e!\mathtt{m}(\bar{e})$ method calls, the latter returning a future that will hold the result of the method call when it will be computed; and **get**(e) which gives the value stored in the future e, or actively waits for it if it is not computed yet. Pure expressions e include values v, variables x, function call $\mathtt{fun}(\bar{e})$ and pattern matching **case** e $\{\overline{p \Rightarrow e_p}\}$ that tests e and execute e_p if it matches p. Patterns p are standard: _ matches everything, x matches everything and binds it to x, **null** matches a null object and $\mathtt{Co}(\bar{p})$ matches a value $\mathtt{Co}(\overline{e_p})$ where p matches e_p. Finally, a guard g can be: a variable x; x? which is **true** when the future x is completed, **false** otherwise; $\|x\|$ which is **true** when the object x is in a safe state, i.e., it is not executing any **critical** method, **false** otherwise; and the conjunction of two guards $g \wedge g$ has the usual meaning.

3   Type System

The goal of our type system is to statically check whether synchronous method calls and rebindings are performed locally to a cog. Since cogs and objects are entities created at runtime, we cannot know statically their identity. We address this issue by using a *linear* type system approach on names of cogs $\mathtt{G}, \mathtt{G}', \mathtt{G}'' \ldots$ that abstracts the runtime identity of cogs. This type system associates to every cog creation a unique cog name, which makes it possible to check if two objects are in the same cog or not. Precisely, we associate objects to their cogs using records $\mathbf{r}$, having the form $\mathtt{G}[\overline{f:T}]$, where $\mathtt{G}$ denotes the cog in which the object is located and $[\overline{f:T}]$ maps any object's fields $\bar{f}$ to its type $\bar{T}$. In order to correctly track cog membership of each expression, we also need to keep information about the cog of the object's fields in a record. This is needed, for instance, when an object stored in a field is accessed within the method body and then returned by the method; in this case one needs a way to bind the cog of the accessed field to the cog of the returned value. Let us now explain the method signature $(\mathcal{G}, \mathbf{r})$ annotating a method header. The record $\mathbf{r}$ is used as the record of **this** during the typing of the method, i.e., $\mathbf{r}$ is the binder for the cog of the object **this** in the scope of the method body, as we will see in the typing rules in the following. The set of cog names $\mathcal{G}$ is used to keep track of the fresh cogs that

S:DATA
$$\frac{\forall i \quad T_i \leq T_i'}{D\langle \overline{T} \rangle \leq D\langle \overline{T'} \rangle}$$

S:BOT
$$(L, \mathtt{r}) \leq (L, \bot)$$

S:FIELDS
$$\frac{\forall i \quad T_i \leq T_i' \qquad f \notin ports(L)}{(L, \mathtt{G}[f : T; \overline{f : T}]) \leq (L, \mathtt{G}[\overline{f : T'}])}$$

S:PORTS
$$\frac{\forall i \quad T_i \leq T_i' \qquad f \in ports(L)}{(L, \mathtt{G}[\overline{f : T}]) \leq (L, \mathtt{G}[f : T; \overline{f : T'}])}$$

S:TYPE
$$\frac{L \leq L' \in CT}{(L, \mathtt{r}) \leq (L', \mathtt{r})}$$

Fig. 5. Subtyping Relation[2]

the method creates. In particular, when we deal with recursive method calls, the set $\mathcal{G}$ gathers the fresh cogs of every call, which is then returned to the main execution. Moreover, when it is not necessary to keep track of cog information about an object, because the object is not going to take part in any synchronous method call or any rebind operation, it is possible to associate to this object the *unknown* record $\bot$. This special record does not keep any information about the cog where the object or its fields are located, and it is to be considered different from any other cog, thus to ensure the soundness of our type system. Finally, note that data types also can contain records: for instance, a list of objects is typed with List$\langle T \rangle$ where T is the type of the objects in the list and it includes also the record of the objects.

A *typing environment* Γ is a partial function from names to typings, which assigns types T to variables, a pair $(\mathtt{C}, \mathtt{r})$ to **this**, and arrow types $\overline{T} \to T'$ to function symbols like Co or fun.

3.1 Subtyping Relation

The subtyping relation $\leq$ on types is a preorder and is presented in Fig. 5. Rule S:DATA states that data types are covariant in their type parameters. Rule S:BOT states that every record $\mathtt{r}$ is a subtype of the unknown record $\bot$. Rules S:FIELDS and S:PORTS use *structural* subtyping on records. Fields, like methods, are what the object provides, hence it is sound to forget about the existence of a field in an object. This is why the rule S:FIELDS allows to remove fields from records. Ports on the other hand, model the *dependencies* the objects have on their environment, hence it is sound to consider that an object may have more dependencies than it actually has during execution. This is why the rule S:PORTS allows to add ports to records. Notice that in the standard object-oriented setting this rule would not be sound, since trying to access a non-existing attribute would lead to a null pointer exception. Therefore, to support our vision of port behavior, we add a REBIND-NONE reduction rule to the component calculus semantics which simply permits the rebind to succeed without modifying anything if the port is not available. Finally, rule S:TYPE adopts *nominal* subtyping between classes and interfaces.

---

[2] For readability, we let L be either a class name C or an interface name I.

$$\text{tmatch}(T, T) = id \qquad \text{tmatch}(\mathtt{r}, \mathtt{r}) = id \qquad \text{tmatch}(V, T) \triangleq [V \mapsto T]$$

$$\frac{\forall i.\ \text{tmatch}(T_i, T_i') = \sigma_i \qquad \forall i, j,\ \sigma_{i|\text{dom}(\sigma_j)} = \sigma_{j|\text{dom}(\sigma_i)}}{\text{tmatch}(D\langle \overline{T}\rangle, D\langle \overline{T'}\rangle) \triangleq \bigcup_i \sigma_i} \qquad \frac{\text{tmatch}(\mathtt{r}, \mathtt{r}') = \sigma}{\text{tmatch}((\mathtt{I}, \mathtt{r}), (\mathtt{I}, \mathtt{r}')) \triangleq \sigma}$$

$$\frac{\forall i.\ \text{tmatch}(T_i, T_i') = \sigma_i \qquad \forall i, j,\ \sigma_{i|\text{dom}(\sigma_j)} = \sigma_{j|\text{dom}(\sigma_i)} \qquad \forall i,\ \sigma(\mathtt{G}) \in \{\mathtt{G}, \mathtt{G}'\}}{\text{tmatch}(\mathtt{G}[\overline{f:T}], \mathtt{G}'[\overline{f:T'}]) \triangleq [\mathtt{G} \mapsto \mathtt{G}'] \bigcup_i \sigma_i}$$

$$\text{pmatch}(\_, T) \triangleq \emptyset \qquad \text{pmatch}(x, T) \triangleq \emptyset; x:T \qquad \text{pmatch}(\mathbf{null}, (\mathtt{I}, \mathtt{r})) \triangleq \emptyset$$

$$\frac{\Gamma(\mathtt{Co}) = \overline{T} \rightarrow T' \qquad \text{tmatch}(T', T'') = \sigma \qquad \forall i.\ \text{pmatch}(p_i, \sigma(T_i)) = \Gamma_i}{\text{pmatch}(\mathtt{Co}(\overline{p}), T'') \triangleq \biguplus_i \Gamma_i}$$

$$\frac{\mathtt{C} \leq \mathtt{I} \in CT \qquad \text{dom}(\sigma') \cap \text{dom}(\sigma) = \emptyset \qquad \textit{fields}(\mathtt{C}) = (\overline{f:(\mathtt{I},\mathtt{r})}; \overline{f':D(\dots)})}{(\mathtt{I}, \mathtt{G}[\sigma \uplus \sigma'(\overline{f:(\mathtt{I},\mathtt{r})})]) \in \text{crec}(\mathtt{G}, \mathtt{C}, \sigma)}$$

$$\frac{\text{equals}(\mathtt{G}, \mathtt{G}')}{\text{coloc}(\mathtt{G}[\dots], (\mathtt{C}, \mathtt{G}'[\dots]))}$$

$$\frac{\textit{ports}(\mathtt{C}) \subseteq \textit{ports}(\mathtt{I}) \text{ and } \forall p \in \textit{ports}(\mathtt{C}).\ \textit{ptype}(p, \mathtt{C}) \leq \textit{ptype}(p, \mathtt{I})}{\textit{heads}(\mathtt{I}) \subseteq \textit{heads}(\mathtt{C}) \text{ and } \forall \mathtt{m} \in \mathtt{I}.\ \textit{mtype}(\mathtt{m}, \mathtt{I}) = \textit{mtype}(\mathtt{m}, \mathtt{C})}{\text{implements}(\mathtt{C}, \mathtt{I})}$$

$$\frac{\textit{ports}(\mathtt{I}) \subseteq \textit{ports}(\mathtt{I}') \text{ and } \forall p \in \textit{ports}(\mathtt{I}).\ \textit{ptype}(p, \mathtt{I}) \leq \textit{ptype}(p, \mathtt{I}')}{\textit{heads}(\mathtt{I}') \subseteq \textit{heads}(\mathtt{I}) \text{ and } \forall \mathtt{m} \in \mathtt{I}'.\ \textit{mtype}(\mathtt{m}, \mathtt{I}) = \textit{mtype}(\mathtt{m}, \mathtt{I}')}{\text{extends}(\mathtt{I}, \mathtt{I}')}$$

Fig. 6. Auxiliary functions and predicates

3.2 Functions and Predicates

The type system makes use of several auxiliary functions and predicates presented in Fig. 6 [3]. Function tmatch returns a substitution σ of the formal parameters to the actual ones. It is defined both on types and on records. The matching of a type T to itself, or of a record $\mathtt{r}$ to itself, returns the identity substitution id; the matching of a type variable V to a type T returns a substitution of V to T; the matching of data type D parameterized on formal types $\overline{T}$ and on actual types $\overline{T'}$ returns the union of substitutions that correspond to the matching of each type T_i with T_i' in such a way that substitutions coincide when applied to the same formal types; the matching of records follows the same idea as that of data types. Finally, tmatch applied on types $(\mathtt{I}, \mathtt{r}), (\mathtt{I}, \mathtt{r}')$ returns the same substitution obtained by matching $\mathtt{r}$ with $\mathtt{r}'$. Function pmatch, performs matchings on patterns and types by returning a typing environment Γ. In particular, pmatch returns an empty set when the pattern is $\_$ or **null**, or $x : T$ when applied on a variable x and a type T. Otherwise, if applied to a constructor expression $\mathtt{Co}(\overline{p})$ and a type T'' it returns the union of typing environments corresponding to patterns in $\overline{p}$. Function crec asserts that $(\mathtt{I}, \mathtt{G}[\sigma \uplus \sigma'(\overline{f:(\mathtt{I},\mathtt{r})})])$ is a member of $\text{crec}(\mathtt{G}, \mathtt{C}, \sigma)$ if class $\mathtt{C}$ implements interface $\mathtt{I}$ and σ' and σ are substitutions defined on disjoint sets of names. Function $\textit{fields}(\mathtt{C})$ returns the typed fields and ports of a class $\mathtt{C}$. Function $\textit{port}$ instead, returns only the typed

---

[3] For readability reasons, the lookup functions like $\textit{ports}$, $\textit{fields}$, $\textit{ptype}$, $\textit{mtype}$, $\textit{heads}$ are written in italics, whether the auxiliary functions and predicates are not.

$$\frac{\text{T:Var/Field}}{\Gamma(x) = T} \qquad \frac{\text{T:Null} \quad \textbf{interface } \text{I} \, [\cdots] \, \{ \, \cdots \, \} \in CT}{\Gamma \vdash \textbf{null} : (\text{I}, \text{r})}$$

$$\frac{\text{T:Constructor}}{\Gamma(\text{Co}) = \overline{T} \to T' \quad \text{tmatch}(\overline{T}, \overline{T'}) = \sigma \quad \Gamma \vdash \overline{v} : \overline{T'}}{\Gamma \vdash \text{Co}(\overline{v}) : \sigma(T')}$$

$$\frac{\text{T:Fun}}{\Gamma(\text{fun}) = \overline{T} \to T' \quad \text{tmatch}(\overline{T}, \overline{T'}) = \sigma \quad \Gamma \vdash \overline{v} : \overline{T'}}{\Gamma \vdash \text{fun}(\overline{v}) : \sigma(T')}$$

$$\frac{\text{T:Case}}{\Gamma \vdash e : (T, \text{r}) \quad \Gamma \vdash \overline{p \Rightarrow e_p} : (T, \text{r}) \to (T', \text{r}')}{\Gamma \vdash \textbf{case } e \, \{\overline{p \Rightarrow e_p}\} : (T', \text{r}')}$$

$$\frac{\text{T:Branch}}{\Gamma \vdash p : (T, \text{r}) \quad \Gamma; \text{pmatch}(p, (T, \text{r})) \vdash e_p : (T', \text{r}')}{\Gamma \vdash p \Rightarrow e_p : (T, \text{r}) \to (T', \text{r}')} \qquad \frac{\text{T:Sub}}{\Gamma \vdash e : T \quad T \leq T'}{\Gamma \vdash e : T'}$$

$$\frac{\text{T:FGuard}}{\Gamma \vdash x : \text{Fut}\langle T \rangle}{\Gamma \vdash x? : \text{Bool}} \qquad \frac{\text{T:CGuard}}{\Gamma \vdash x : (\text{I}, \text{r})}{\Gamma \vdash \|x\| : \text{Bool}} \qquad \frac{\text{T:LGuard}}{\Gamma \vdash g_1 : \text{Bool} \quad \Gamma \vdash g_2 : \text{Bool}}{\Gamma \vdash g_1 \wedge g_2 : \text{Bool}}$$

Fig. 7. Typing Pure Expressions and Guards

ports. Predicate coloc states the equality of two cog names. Predicates implements and extends check when a class implements an interface and an interface extends another one properly. A class C implements an interface I if the ports of C are at *most* the ones of I. This follows the intuition: since ports indicate services then an object has at most the services declared in its interface. Then, any port in C has a subtype of the respective port in I. Instead, for methods, C may define at *least* the methods declared in I having the same signature. The extends predicate states when an interface I properly extends another interface I' and it is defined similarly to the implements predicate.

3.3 Typing Rules

In this section we present the typing rules. Typing judgments use a typing environment Γ and possibly a set $\mathcal{G}$ which indicates the set of new cogs created by the term being typed. They have the following forms: $\Gamma \vdash g : \text{Bool}$ for guards, $\Gamma \vdash e : T$ for pure expressions, $\Gamma, \mathcal{G} \vdash z : T$ for expressions with side effects and $\Gamma, \mathcal{G} \vdash s$ for statements. Finally, typing judgments for method, class and interface declarations are $\Gamma \vdash M$, $\Gamma \vdash C$ and $\emptyset \vdash I$, respectively.

Pure Expressions. Typing rules for pure expressions are given in Fig. 7. Rule T:Var/Field states that a variable is of type the one assumed in the typing environment. Rule T:Null states that **null** is of type any interface I declared in the CT and any record r. Rule T:Constructor states that constructor Co applied to a list of values $\overline{v}$ is of type $\sigma(T')$ where the constructor is of a functional type $\overline{T} \to T'$ and the values are of type $\overline{T'}$ obtained by the auxiliary function tmatch. Rule T:Fun for function expressions is the same as the previous one for constructor expressions. Rule T:Case states that if all branches are well-typed and have the same type, then the case expression is also well-typed. Rule T:Branch states that a branch $p \Rightarrow e_p$ is well-typed if the pattern p is well-typed

$$
\begin{array}{c}
\text{T:Exp} \\
\dfrac{\Gamma \vdash e : T}{\Gamma, \emptyset \vdash e : T}
\end{array}
\qquad
\begin{array}{c}
\text{T:New} \\
\dfrac{params(\mathsf{C}) = \overline{T\ f} \quad \Gamma \vdash \overline{e : T'} \quad \mathrm{tmatch}(\overline{T}, \overline{T'}) = \sigma \quad T \in \mathrm{crec}(\mathsf{G}, \mathsf{C}, \sigma)}{\Gamma \vdash \mathbf{new}\ \mathsf{C}(\overline{e}) : T}
\end{array}
$$

$$
\begin{array}{c}
\text{T:Cog} \\
\dfrac{params(\mathsf{C}) = \overline{T\ f} \quad \Gamma \vdash \overline{e : T'} \quad \mathrm{tmatch}(\overline{T}, \overline{T'}) = \sigma \quad T \in \mathrm{crec}(\mathsf{G}, \mathsf{C}, \sigma)}{\Gamma, \{\mathsf{G}\} \vdash \mathbf{new\ cog}\ \mathsf{C}\ (\overline{e}) : T}
\end{array}
$$

$$
\begin{array}{c}
\text{T:SCall} \\
\dfrac{mtype(\mathtt{m}, \mathtt{I}) = (\mathcal{G}, \mathtt{r})(\overline{T\ x}) \to T \quad \Gamma \vdash e : (\mathtt{I}, \sigma(\mathtt{r})) \quad \Gamma \vdash \overline{e} : \overline{\sigma(T)} \quad \mathrm{coloc}(\sigma(\mathtt{r}), \Gamma(\mathbf{this}))}{\Gamma \vdash e.m(\overline{e}) : \sigma(T)}
\end{array}
$$

$$
\begin{array}{c}
\text{T:ACall} \\
\dfrac{mtype(\mathtt{m}, \mathtt{I}) = (\mathcal{G}, \mathtt{r})(\overline{T\ x}) \to T \quad \Gamma \vdash e : (\mathtt{I}, \sigma(\mathtt{r})) \quad \Gamma \vdash \overline{e} : \overline{\sigma(T)}}{\Gamma \vdash e!m(\overline{e}) : \mathtt{Fut}\langle \sigma(T) \rangle}
\end{array}
\qquad
\begin{array}{c}
\text{T:Get} \\
\dfrac{\Gamma \vdash e : \mathtt{Fut}\langle T \rangle}{\Gamma \vdash \mathbf{get}(e) : T}
\end{array}
$$

Fig. 8. Typing Expressions

and the expression e_p is well-typed in the extension of Γ with typing assertions for the pattern. Rule T:Sub is the standard subsumption rule.

Guards. Typing rules for guards are given in Fig. 7. Rule T:FGuard states that if a variable x has type $\mathtt{Fut}\langle T \rangle$, the guard $x?$ has type Bool. Rule T:CGuard states that $\|x\|$ has type Bool if x is an object. Rule T:LGuard states that if each g_i has type Bool for $i = 1, 2$ then the conjunction $g_1 \wedge g_2$ has type Bool.

Expressions. The typing rules for expressions with side effects are given in Fig. 8. These are different w.r.t. the previous ones as they keep track of the new cogs created. Rule T:Exp is a weakening rule which asserts that a pure expression e is well-typed in a typing context Γ and an empty set of cogs, if it is well-typed in Γ. Rule T:New assigns type T to the object $\mathbf{new}\ \mathsf{C}(\overline{e})$ if the actual parameters have types compatible with the formal ones, by applying function tmatch, the cogs of the object and **this** coincide and the type T is in the crec predicate. Rule T:Cog is similar to the previous one, except for the creation of a new cog G where the new object is placed. Rules T:SCall and T:ACall type synchronous and asynchronous method invocations, respectively. Both rules use $mtype$ to obtain the method signature as well as the method's typed parameters and the return type, i.e., $(\mathcal{G}, \mathtt{r})(\overline{T\ x}) \to T$. The group record $\mathtt{r}$, the parameters types and the return type of the method are the "formal" ones. In order to obtain the "actual" ones, we use σ that maps formal cog names to actual cog names. Consequently, the callee e has type $(\mathtt{I}, \sigma(\mathtt{r}))$ and the actual parameters $\overline{e}$ have types $\overline{\sigma(T)}$. Finally, the invocations are typed in the substitution $\sigma(T)$. The rules differ in that the former also checks whether the group of **this** and the group of the callee coincide, by using the auxiliary function coloc, and also the types of the returned value are $\sigma(T)$ and $\mathtt{Fut}\langle \sigma(T) \rangle$, respectively. Rule T:Get states that $\mathbf{get}(e)$ is of type T, if expression e is of type $\mathtt{Fut}\langle T \rangle$.

Statements. The typing rules for statements are presented in Fig. 9. Rule T:Skip states that **skip** is always well-typed. Rule T:Decl states that $T\ x$ is well-typed if variable x is of type T in Γ. Rule T:Semi types the composition of statements, if s_1 and s_2 are well-typed in the same typing environment and, like

$$\frac{}{\Gamma, \emptyset \vdash \textbf{skip}} \text{ T:Skip} \qquad \frac{\Gamma(x) = T}{\Gamma, \emptyset \vdash T\ x} \text{ T:Decl} \qquad \frac{\Gamma, \mathcal{G}_1 \vdash s_1 \qquad \Gamma, \mathcal{G}_2 \vdash s_2}{\Gamma, \mathcal{G}_1 \uplus \mathcal{G}_2 \vdash s_1; s_2} \text{ S:Semi} \qquad \frac{\Gamma(x) = T \qquad \Gamma, \mathcal{G} \vdash z : T}{\Gamma, \mathcal{G} \vdash x = z} \text{ S:Assign}$$

$$\frac{\Gamma \vdash g : \texttt{Bool}}{\Gamma, \emptyset \vdash \textbf{await}\ g} \text{ S:Await} \qquad \frac{\Gamma \vdash e : \texttt{Bool} \qquad \Gamma, \mathcal{G}_1 \vdash s_1 \qquad \Gamma, \mathcal{G}_2 \vdash s_2}{\Gamma, \mathcal{G}_1 \uplus \mathcal{G}_2 \vdash \textbf{if}\ e\ \{\ s_1\ \}\ \textbf{else}\ \{\ s_2\ \}} \text{ S:Cond} \qquad \frac{\Gamma \vdash e : \texttt{Bool} \qquad \Gamma, \mathcal{G} \vdash s}{\Gamma, \mathcal{G} \vdash \textbf{while}\ e\ \{\ s\ \}} \text{ S:While}$$

$$\frac{\Gamma \vdash e : T \qquad \Gamma(\textbf{destiny}) = T}{\Gamma, \emptyset \vdash \textbf{return}\ e} \text{ S:Return}$$

$$\frac{\Gamma(\textbf{this}) = (\texttt{C}, \texttt{G}[\ldots]) \qquad T\ p \in ports(\texttt{I}) \qquad \Gamma \vdash e : (\texttt{I}, \texttt{r}) \qquad \Gamma, \mathcal{G} \vdash z : T \qquad coloc(\texttt{r}, \Gamma(\textbf{this}))}{\Gamma, \mathcal{G} \vdash \textbf{rebind}\ e.p = z} \text{ Rebind}$$

Fig. 9. Typing Statements

$$\frac{\Gamma, \overline{x} : \overline{T}, \textbf{destiny} : \texttt{Fut}\langle T \rangle, \textbf{this} : (\texttt{C}, \texttt{r}), \mathcal{G} \vdash s}{\Gamma \vdash [\textbf{critical}]\ (\mathcal{G}, \texttt{r})\ T\ \texttt{m}(\overline{T\ x})\{\ s\ \}\ in\ \texttt{C}} \text{ T:Method}$$

$$\frac{\forall \texttt{I} \in \overline{\texttt{I}}.\ implements(\texttt{C}, \texttt{I}) \qquad \Gamma, \overline{x} : \overline{T} \vdash \overline{M}\ in\ \texttt{C}}{\Gamma \vdash \textbf{class}\ \texttt{C}\ (\overline{T\ x})\ \textbf{implements}\ \overline{\texttt{I}}\ \{\ \overline{Fl}\ \overline{M}\ \}} \text{ T:Class} \qquad \frac{\forall \texttt{I}' \in \overline{\texttt{I}}.\ extends(\texttt{I}, \texttt{I}')}{\vdash \textbf{interface}\ \texttt{I}\ \textbf{extends}\ \overline{\texttt{I}}\ \{\ \textbf{port}\ T\ x; \overline{S}\ \}} \text{ T:Interface}$$

Fig. 10. Typing Declarations

in linear type systems, they use distinct cog names. Hence, their composition uses the disjoint union $\uplus$ of the corresponding sets. Rule T:Assign asserts the well-typedness of the assignment $x = z$ if both x and z have the same type T. Rule T:Await asserts that **await** g is well-typed whenever the guard g has type Bool. Rules T:Cond and T:While are quite standard, except for the presence of the linear set of cog names. Rule T:Return asserts that **return** e is well-typed if expression e has the same type as the variable **destiny**. Finally, rule T:Rebind types statement **rebind** $e.p = z$ by checking that: $i)$ p is a port of the right type, and $ii)$ z is in the same group as **this**.

Method, Class and Interface Declarations. The typing rules are presented in Fig. 10. Rule T:Method states that method m is well-typed in class C if the method's body s is well-typed in a typing environment augmented with the method's typed parameters; type information about **destiny** and the current object **this**; and cog names as specified by the method signature. Rule T:Class states that a class C is well-typed when it implements all the interfaces $\overline{\texttt{I}}$ and all its methods are well-typed. Rule T:Interface states that an interface I is well-typed if it extends all interfaces in $\overline{\texttt{I}}$.

Remark. The typing rule for assignment requires the group of the variable and the group of the expression being assigned to be the same. This restriction applies to rule for rebinding, as well. To see why this is needed let us consider a sequence of two asynchronous method invocations $\texttt{x!m();x!n()}$, both called on the same object and both modifying the same field. Say m does $\textbf{this}.\texttt{f} = z_1$ and n does $\textbf{this}.\texttt{f} = z_2$. Because of asynchronicity, there is no way to know the order in which the updates will take place at runtime. A similar example may

$$\frac{\Gamma(\textbf{this}) = (\texttt{Controller}, \texttt{G}[\ldots]) \qquad (\texttt{Server}, \texttt{r}) \; s \in ports(\texttt{Client})}{\qquad \forall i = 2, \ldots, n \quad \Gamma \vdash \texttt{c}_i : (\texttt{Client}, \texttt{G}[\ldots, s : (\texttt{Server}, \texttt{r})])}$$

$$\frac{\Gamma, \emptyset \vdash s2 : (\texttt{Server}, \texttt{r}) \qquad coloc(\texttt{G}[\ldots, s : (\texttt{Server}, \texttt{r})], \Gamma(\textbf{this}))}{\forall i \; \Gamma, \emptyset \vdash \textbf{rebind} \; \texttt{c}_i.s = s2}$$

Fig. 11. REBIND derivation

be produced for the case of rebinding. Working statically, we can either force the two expressions z_1 and z_2 to have the same group as f, or keep track of all the different possibilities, thus the type system must assume for an expression a set of possible objects it can reduce to. In this paper we adopt the former solution, we let the exploration of the latter as a future work. We plan to relax this restriction following a similar idea to the one proposed in [11].

Example Revisited. We now recall the example of the workflow given in Fig. 2 and Fig. 3. We show how the type system works on this example: by applying the typing rule for **rebind** we have the derivation in Fig. 11 for any clients from c_2 to c_n. For client c_1, if we try to typecheck the rebinding, we would have the following typing judgments in the premise of REBIND:

$$\Gamma(\textbf{this}) = (\texttt{Controller}, \texttt{G}[\ldots]) \qquad \Gamma, \emptyset \vdash \texttt{c}_1 : (\texttt{Client}, \texttt{G}'[\ldots, s : (\texttt{Server}, \texttt{r})])$$

But then, the predicate $coloc(\texttt{G}'[\ldots, s : (\texttt{Server}, \texttt{r})], \Gamma(\textbf{this}))$ is false, since $equals(\texttt{G}, \texttt{G}')$ is false. Then one cannot apply the typing rule REBIND, by thus not typechecking **rebind** $\texttt{c}_1.s = s2$.

3.4   Properties of the Type System

In this section we briefly overview the properties of the type system and we outline the runtime system devised in order to provide the proofs of those properties. The full technical treatment with proofs can be found in [9]. Before stating the properties that our type system enjoys, we first introduce the following notions:

Runtime typing environments Δ are obtained by augmenting typing environments Γ with runtime information about objects and futures, namely $o : (C, \texttt{r})$ and $f : \texttt{Fut}\langle T \rangle$ where o and f are object and future variables, respectively.

Runtime configurations N extend the language with constructs used during execution, mainly with objects. An object $ob(o, \sigma, K_{\textbf{idle}}, Q)$ has a name o; a substitution σ mapping the object's fields, ports and special variables like **this**, **destiny**, to values; a running process $K_{\textbf{idle}}$, that is **idle** if the object is idle; and a queue of *suspended processes* Q. A process K is $\{ \sigma \mid s \}$ where σ maps the local variables to their values and s is a list of statements.

Reduction relation $N \to N'$ is defined over runtime configurations and follows the definition of such relation in [13, 14].

Runtime judgments are of the form $\Delta, \mathcal{G} \vdash_R N$ meaning that the configuration N is well-typed in the typing context Δ by using a set $\mathcal{G}$ of new cogs.

Our type system enjoys the classical properties of subject reduction and type correction stated in the following.

Theorem 1 (Subject Reduction). *If $\Delta, \mathcal{G} \vdash_R N$ and $N \to N'$ then $\exists \Delta', \mathcal{G}'$ such that $\Delta' \supseteq \Delta$, $\mathcal{G}' \subseteq \mathcal{G}$ and $\Delta', \mathcal{G}' \vdash_R N'$.*

Proof. The proof is done by induction over the operational semantics rules.   □

Theorem 2 (Correction). *If $\Delta, \mathcal{G} \vdash_R N$, then for all objects $ob(o, \sigma, \{ \sigma_k \mid s \}, Q) \in N$ with either $s = \mathbf{rebind}\ x.f_i = x'; s'$ or $s = x.\mathtt{m}(\overline{x}); s'$, there exists an object $ob(o', \sigma', K_{\mathbf{idle}}, Q') \in N$ such that $\sigma \circ \sigma_k(x) = o'$ and $\sigma(\mathbf{cog}) = \sigma'(\mathbf{cog})$. Where $\circ$ defines the composition of substitutions.*

Proof. The proof is done by induction over the structure of N.   □

As a consequence of the previous results, rebinding and synchronous method calls are always performed between objects of the same cog:

Corollary 1. *Well-typed programs do not perform i) an illegal rebinding or ii) a synchronous method call outside the cog.*

4   Conclusions, Future and Related Works

This paper presents a type system for a component-based calculus [14], an extension of ABS [13] with **ports** and **rebind** operations. Ports denote the access point to the functionalities provided by the environment and can be modified by performing a rebind operation. There are two consistency issues involving ports: *i)* ports cannot be modified while in use; this problem is solved in [14] by combining the notions of ports and critical section; *ii)* it is forbidden to modify a port of an object outside the cog; this problem is solved in the present paper by designing a type system that guarantees the above requirement. The type system tracks an object's membership to a certain cog by adopting group records. Rebind statement is well-typed if there is compatibility of groups between objects involved in the operation.

Regarding future work, we want to investigate several directions. First, as discussed in Section 3 our current approach imposes a restriction on assignments, namely, it is possible to assign to a variable/field/port only an object belonging to the same cog. We plan to relax this restriction following an idea similar to the one proposed in [11], where instead of having just one group associated to a variable, it is possible to have a set of groups. Second, we want to deal with runtime misbehavior. For instance, deadlocks are intrinsically related to the semantic model, which requires a component to be in a safe state when rebinded, thus introducing synchronization points between the rebinder and the rebindee. For this reason deadlocks may arise. How to detect and avoid this kind of misbehavior is left as future work, possibly following [10]. Moreover, in this paper we showed how to use our technique for a very specific safety problem in the context of a component-based language, but we believe the tracking of object/-group identities/memberships is useful for other problems (deadlock detection, race detection, resource consumption) and other settings (business processes and web-services languages). We plan to investigate this direction further.

Related Works. Most component models [2–4, 8] have a notion of component distinct from that of object. The resulting language is structured in two separate layers, one using objects for the main execution of the program and the other using components for the dynamic reconfiguration. This separation makes it harder for the reconfiguration requests to be integrated in the program's workflow. The component model used in the present paper has a unified description of objects and components by exploiting the similarities between them. This bring several benefits w.r.t. previous component models: i) the integration of components and objects strongly simplifies the reconfiguration requests handling, ii) the separation of concepts (component and object, port and field) makes it easier to reason about them, for example, in static analysis, and iii) ports are useful in the deployment phase of a system by facilitating, for example, the connection to local communication. Various type systems have been designed for components. The type system in [15] categorizes references to be either Near (i.e., in the same cog), Far (i.e., in another cog) or Somewhere (i.e., we don't know). The goal is to automatically detect the distribution pattern of a system by using the inference algorithm, and also control the usage of synchronous method calls. It is more flexible than our type system since the assignment of values of different cogs is allowed, but it is less precise than our analysis: consider two objects o_1 and o_2 in a cog c_1, and another one o_3 in c_2; if o_1 calls a method of o_3 which returns o_2, the type system will not be able to detect that the reference is Near. In [1] the authors present a tool to statically analyze concurrency in ABS. Typically, it analyses the concurrency structure, namely the cogs, but also the synchronization between method calls. The goal is to get tools that analyze concurrency for actor-like concurrency model, instead of the traditional thread-based concurrency model. On the other hand, our type system has some similarities with the type system in [5] which is designed for a process calculus with *ambients* [6], the latter roughly corresponding to the notion of components in a distributed scenario. The type system is based on the notion of group which tracks communication between ambients as well as their movement. However, groups in [5] are a "flat" structure whether in our framework we use group records defined recursively; in addition, the underlying language is a process calculus, whether ours is a concurrent object-oriented one. As object-oriented languages are concerned, another similar work to ours is the one on *ownership types* [7], where basically, a type consists of a class name and a context representing object ownership: each object owns a context and is owned by the context it resides in. The goal of the type system is to provide alias control and invariance of aliasing properties, like role separation, restricted visibility etc. [12].

References

1. Albert, E., Flores-Montoya, A.E., Genaim, S.: Analysis of may-happen-in-parallel in concurrent objects. In: Giese, H., Rosu, G. (eds.) FMOODS/FORTE 2012. LNCS, vol. 7273, pp. 35–51. Springer, Heidelberg (2012)
2. Alliance, O.: Osgi Service Platform, Release 3. IOS Press, Inc.(2003)
3. Bhatti, N.T., Hiltunen, M.A., Schlichting, R.D., Chiu, W.: Coyote: A system for constructing fine-grain configurable communication services. ACM Trans. Comput. Syst. 16(4) (1998)
4. Bruneton, E., Coupaye, T., Leclercq, M., Quema, V., Stefani, J.-B.: The Fractal Component Model and its Support in Java. Software - Practice and Experience 36(11-12) (2006)
5. Cardelli, L., Ghelli, G., Gordon, A.D.: Types for the ambient calculus. Information and Computation 177(2), 160–194 (2002)
6. Cardelli, L., Gordon, A.D.: Mobile ambients. Theor. Comput. Sci. 240(1), 177–213 (2000)
7. Clarke, D.G., Potter, J., Noble, J.: Ownership types for flexible alias protection. In: OOPSLA, pp. 48–64 (1998)
8. Coulson, G., Blair, G., Grace, P., Joolia, A., Lee, K., Ueyama, J.: A component model for building systems software. In: Proc. IASTED Software Engineering and Applications, SEA 2004 (2004)
9. Dardha, O., Giachino, E., Lienhardt, M.: A Type System for Components. Full version (2013), http://www.cs.unibo.it/~giachino/
10. Giachino, E., Crazia, C.A., Laneve, C., Lienhardt, M., Wong, P.Y.H.: Deadlock analysis of concurrent objects: Theory and practice. In: Johnsen, E.B., Petre, L. (eds.) IFM 2013. LNCS, vol. 7940, pp. 394–411. Springer, Heidelberg (2013)
11. Giachino, E., Lascu, T.A.: Lock Analysis for an Asynchronous Object Calculus. Presented at ICTCS (2012), http://www.cs.unibo.it/~giachino/
12. Hogg, J., Lea, D., Wills, A., de Champeaux, D., Holt, R.: The geneva convention – on the treatment of object aliasing. OOPS Messenger (1992)
13. Johnsen, E., Hähnle, R., Schäfer, J., Schlatte, R., Steffen, M.: Abs: A core language for abstract behavioral specification. In: Aichernig, B.K., de Boer, F.S., Bonsangue, M.M. (eds.) FMCO 2010. LNCS, vol. 6957, pp. 142–164. Springer, Heidelberg (2011)
14. Lienhardt, M., Bravetti, M., Sangiorgi, D.: An object group-based component model. In: Margaria, T., Steffen, B. (eds.) ISoLA 2012, Part I. LNCS, vol. 7609, pp. 64–78. Springer, Heidelberg (2012)
15. Welsch, Y., Schäfer, J.: Location types for safe distributed object-oriented programming. In: Bishop, J., Vallecillo, A. (eds.) TOOLS 2011. LNCS, vol. 6705, pp. 194–210. Springer, Heidelberg (2011)

Early Fault Detection in DSLs
Using SMT Solving and Automated Debugging[*]

Sarmen Keshishzadeh[1], Arjan J. Mooij[2], and Mohammad Reza Mousavi[3]

[1] Eindhoven University of Technology, Eindhoven, The Netherlands
[2] Embedded Systems Innovation by TNO, Eindhoven, The Netherlands
[3] Center for Research on Embedded Systems, Halmstad University, Sweden
s.keshishzadeh@tue.nl, arjan.mooij@tno.nl, m.r.mousavi@hh.se

Abstract. In the context of Domain Specific Languages (DSLs), we study ways to detect faults early in the software development cycle. We propose techniques that validate a wide range of properties, classified into basic and advanced. Basic validation includes syntax checking, reference checking and type checking. Advanced validation concerns domain specific properties related to the semantics of the DSL. For verification, we mechanically translate the DSL instance and the advanced properties into Satisfiability Modulo Theory (SMT) problems, and solve these problems using an SMT solver. For user feedback, we extend the verification with automated debugging, which pinpoints the causes of the violated properties and traces them back to the syntactic constructs of the DSL. We illustrate this integration of techniques using an industrial case on collision prevention for medical imaging equipment.

Keywords: Early Fault Detection, Formal Verification, Domain Specific Language (DSL), Satisfiability Modulo Theories (SMT), Delta Debugging.

1 Introduction

Domain specific languages (DSLs, [20,15]) are used to specify software at a higher level of abstraction than implementation code, and to mechanically generate code afterwards. By trading generality for expressiveness in a limited domain, DSLs offer substantial gains in ease of use compared with general-purpose programming and specification languages in their domain of application [15]. Hence, DSLs bring formality closer to domain requirements.

Our goal is to investigate ways to provide early fault detection (see, e.g., [11]) when developing industrial software using DSLs. Program verification techniques often focus on implementation code, and heavily depend on abstraction techniques. Since DSLs are based on domain specific abstractions, we aim to integrate verification at the level of the DSL, i.e., before generating any code.

---

[*] This research was supported by the Dutch national program COMMIT and carried out as part of the Allegio project.

R.M. Hierons, M.G. Merayo, and M. Bravetti (Eds.): SEFM 2013, LNCS 8137, pp. 182–196, 2013.
© Springer-Verlag Berlin Heidelberg 2013

Meta-modelling frameworks, such as the Eclipse Modelling Framework (EMF, [19]), XText [7], and MontiCore [14], provide support for developing editors, performing validation, and generating code. The validation for DSLs often concerns basic validation, such as syntax checking, reference checking, and type checking. In this paper, we focus on techniques for more advanced kinds of validation.

Our investigation is based on a prototype DSL for collision prevention, developed in collaboration with Philips Healthcare; see [16]. The main objective of this DSL is to facilitate the reuse of software among different product configurations. The primary goals are hence to reach a convenient abstraction level, and to generate implementation code. Since correct and timely functioning is vital for medical systems, this prototype DSL is an interesting study case for advanced validation.

Through our interaction with the software developers, we have identified two important user requirements for the integration of advanced validation in industrial DSLs. These have guided our selection of formal techniques.

The first requirement is to hide the validation techniques from the user of the DSL. This implies that a push-button technology should be used, such as model-checking [1] or satisfiability checking [3]. It also implies that we should not rely on user knowledge about applying verification techniques and analyzing their outputs. To this end we mechanically generate the validation input from the DSL instance; this input includes both the formal model and the formal properties. We also translate any property violations back to the abstraction level of the DSL. To detect the syntactic constructs that cause the property violations, we have used an automated debugging technique called delta debugging [23,4,22]. Thus the detected causes are presented in the DSL editor.

The second requirement is to provide feedback to the users in a short amount of time (in the order of seconds to minutes). This often rules out model-checking techniques based on explicit state-space exploration [9], and generic numerical analysis techniques for hybrid systems [8]. We aim to use existing tools as they are, and therefore we refrain from developing ad-hoc abstraction techniques for our specific DSL. We have used Satisfiability Modulo Theories (SMT) [2,6] solving. SMT solvers check satisfiability of first order logic formulae with respect to a combination of background theories, e.g., on integer arithmetic. In recent years, SMT solvers have been extensively applied as an efficient means for program verification [6].

Thus we propose an integration of three techniques, viz., domain-specific languages, SMT solving and delta debugging. Fig. 1 gives an overview of our approach; we refer to it throughout this paper. The traditional use of DSLs is depicted at the left, starting with a system specification which is formalized as a DSL instance. The DSL instance is used for basic validation, and for generating implementation code in languages such as C++. In addition, we introduce advanced validation by automatically generating a set of SMT problems that express some system properties for the DSL instance. Finally the verification results are linked back to the DSL instance.

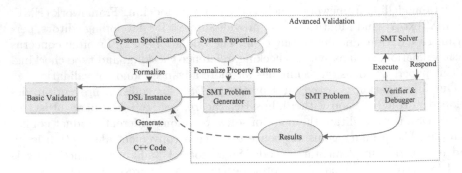

Fig. 1. Overview of the Automated Approach

Although the SMT problems are generated from the DSL instance, the verification results do not change the DSL instance; so Fig. 1 is not a round-trip engineering environment. Instead, the verification results are displayed in the DSL editor. Automated debugging is used to determine a fault location.

Related work. Delta-debugging has initially been developed for debugging programs. We are aware of a few research works [12,21] that apply this technique to more abstract domains. In this paper, we apply it to a declarative DSL.

Integrations of satisfiability checking and debugging have been studied in both hardware and software domains. [18] applies such an integration in the context of logic circuits. [13] proposes a method that, given a C program with an assert statement and a set of failing test cases, provides a list of potential fault locations in an interactive process. This method analyzes a failure trace by encoding the definition and use relation for program variables as MAX-SAT problems. Unlike C programs there is no definition-use relation among the statements of our DSL. Hence, this approach is not applicable in our case.

An integration of verification techniques and DSLs is reported in [17]. Their goal is to maximize reusability among different DSLs. They extract commonalities shared between different DSLs (e.g., a Boolean expressions module) and encapsulate them as analysis-DSLs. Analysis tools, such as model checkers and SMT solvers, are applied to instances of analysis-DSLs. Their validation is limited to properties shared between various domains, e.g., completeness of a set of specified restrictions, and consistency of simultaneously activated restrictions.

Overview. In Section 2, we introduce the industrial prototype DSL, its syntax and informal semantics. Subsequently, we describe the kinds of properties that we aim to validate in Section 3. The translation to SMT is presented in Section 4. Automated debugging for determining the causes of property violations is presented in Section 5, whereas the integration with the DSL editor is reported in Section 6. In Section 7 we draw some conclusions and suggest future research.

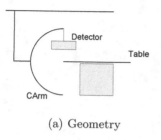

(a) Geometry

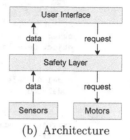

(b) Architecture

Fig. 2. Industrial Study Case

2   A Prototype DSL for Collision Prevention

To illustrate our approach, we consider the interventional X-ray scanners of
Philips Healthcare. These systems consist of several moving objects with shapes
as sketched in Fig. 2(a). For example, the Table can be moved horizontally, the
Detector can be moved vertically, and the CArm can be rotated.

To prevent collisions between these objects, the architecture contains a safety
layer as depicted in Fig. 2(b). All movement requests from the user to the motors
pass this layer. For making decisions on user requests, this layer stores data from
the sensors in internal structures called "geometric models". In particular each
geometric model stores the (shortest) distance between each pair of objects.

To describe the safety layer, we consider a simplified prototype DSL that
focuses on decision rules for collision prevention. We illustrate the syntax and
the intuitive meaning of the syntactic constructs using the example instance in
Fig. 3. For confidentiality reasons, numbers and details have been changed.

2.1   Physical Objects and Geometric Models

Each DSL instance declares the physical objects in the system. The example in
Fig. 3 corresponds to the geometry in Fig. 2(a) with three objects, viz., Table,
CArm and Detector. The shapes of the objects are not specified in the DSL.

This example DSL instance declares a *predefined* geometric model and a *user-dependent* geometric model:

- Actuals: current object distances, as given by the sensors;
- LookAhead: predicted object distances, based on Actuals and user requests.

The definitions of these models are internal, and not specified in the DSL.

2.2   Movement Restrictions

The user requests consist of a vector for each object movement (translation and
rotation). The collision prevention logic is specified in terms of restrictions on
these object movements. Each restriction contains an activation condition, which

```
// --- Context Declarations -------
object Table
object CArm
object Detector


model Actuals        predefined
model LookAhead      userdependent

// --- Restrictions -------
restriction ApproachingTableAndCArm
  activation
    Distance[Actuals](Table, CArm) < 35 mm + 15 cm
  effect
    absolute limit CArm[Rotation]
      at ((Distance[Actuals](Table, CArm) - 35 mm) / 15 cm) * 10 dgps


restriction ApproachingTableAndDetector
  activation
    Distance[LookAhead](Table, Detector) < 35 mm + 15 cm
 && Distance[LookAhead](Table, Detector) <
                                Distance[Actuals](Table, Detector)
  effect
    relative limit Detector[Translation]
      at ((Distance[LookAhead](Table, Detector) - 35 mm) / 15 cm)
```

Fig. 3. Example Instance of the DSL

is a boolean expression, and an effect that is only considered when the activation condition evaluates to true. The effect specifies a speed limitation for a specific object movement; to be more precise, a limitation on the (Euclidean) norm of the movement vector. An *absolute* speed limit specifies a maximum speed that may be requested to the motors. A *relative* limit indicates the maximum percentage of the user request that may be requested to the motors.

The example restrictions in Fig. 3 illustrate that the expressions can refer to the (shortest) distance between two objects in a specific geometric model. Constants can be annotated with measurement units, or otherwise a default unit is assumed. Further processing of a DSL instance unifies the applied units.

For each object movement, multiple restrictions can specify absolute and relative limits. In this case, for each object movement, only the most-restrictive activated limits are considered, i.e., the minimum of the absolute limits and the minimum of the relative limits; the other limits are masked. Given the incoming request vector $\overrightarrow{inRequest}$ for an object movement, we first compute the requested speed *inSpeed*. Using the most-restrictive activated limits *absLimit* and *relLimit* for this object movement, we compute the resulting speed *outSpeed* and the outgoing movement request vector to the motors $\overrightarrow{outRequest}$ as follows:

$$inSpeed = \mathbf{norm}(\overrightarrow{inRequest})$$
$$outSpeed = \mathbf{min}(absLimit, relLimit \times inSpeed)$$
$$\overrightarrow{outRequest} = \frac{outSpeed}{inSpeed} \times \overrightarrow{inRequest}$$

3 Validation Properties

In this section we describe several kinds of properties, that can be analysed early in the software development cycle, in particular before generating code.

3.1 Basic Validation

Practically all modern editors for programming languages and domain-specific languages offer some basic types of validation:

- based on the language (context-free analysis):
  - parsing: syntactic constructs are in accordance with the DSL grammar;
- based on the parse tree (context-dependent analysis):
  - referencing: references refer to elements that have been defined;
  - type checking: expressions have a well-defined type.

In addition, there can be domain-specific constraints like acyclic dependencies. There can also be warnings for correct fragments that are probably not intended, such as, in our DSL, the distance between an object and itself.

3.2 Advanced Validation

Our aim is to offer validation that goes beyond basic validation. In this section we consider the system properties focusing on collision prevention, which include value ranges, safety properties, and absence of deadlocks.

In our example DSL, such checks often require additional knowledge about the environment, including the geometric models and the timing. We try to keep these details to a minimum in order to make the verification feasible and to give quick feedback to the user. In our analyses this has an impact on the following:

- distances: We only assume that the distance function on pairs of objects is symmetric and gives non-negative values. We ignore whether the distances are feasible in practice.
- timing: We ignore the acceleration characteristics of the physical objects, and any time delays between sensing and acting.

However, this can result in false positive reponses for well-definedness of expressions and safety properties and false positive/negative responses for deadlock. The challenge is to balance the number of false positive/negative results with the number of additional details that need to be provided. In what follows, we categorize the kind of checks that could be useful for our DSL users.

Well-definedness of Expressions. There are some general conditions that can be checked. For example, a potential division by zero, or a potential exponentiation resulting in a complex number. (Similarly, for DSLs allowing for case analysis, we can check whether the cases are complete and non-overlapping.) Such checks are more involved than basic type checking, because they involve the valuation of distance variables and arithmetic operations on them.

Ranges. The minimum of activated absolute limits of each object movement should be a non-negative real number; similarly, the minimum of activated relative limits should be a real number between 0 and 1.

Safety. The ultimate goal of the safety layer is to prevent collisions. We check specific speed limits when two objects are "very close" and "approaching". We also check monotonicity properties (with respect to each distance parameter), e.g., the closer two objects, the stricter the speed limits. The notion of "approaching" can be expressed by comparing object distances in the Actuals (current distances) and the LookAhead (predicted distances) geometric models; see also the activation condition of `ApproachingTableAndDetector` in Fig. 3.

Deadlock. Sometimes objects can reach a deadlock position. Consider for example restriction `ApproachingTableAndCArm` in Fig. 3. Suppose we move the Table and the CArm towards each other. If the remaining distance is exactly 35 mm, then the speed of the CArm is limited to 0, independently of any (future) user request for the CArm. Unless there is another way to move the CArm, this object has reached an individual deadlock.

We aim to warn the DSL-user for such situations, where certain sensor inputs can stop an object independently of any future user request. As we abstract from the dependencies between distance parameters in different geometric models, our possibilities to formulate this property are limited. We formulate it as "for each object, and for each valuation of the Actuals geometric model, there exist a valuation of the LookAhead geometric model (a user dependent geometric model), such that the object can move". This can result in false positive/negative responses. The false negative responses may sound serious in our context, but this check is still useful as a warning for typical domain errors.

4   From DSL Instances and Properties to SMT

In this section we describe the SMT problem generator from Fig. 1. We describe the advanced validation properties from Section 3.2 using examples, but for each property also a formal pattern is defined. Given any DSL instance, these properties are mechanically instantiated to a set of SMT problems in the common SMT-LIB format, which is supported by various SMT solvers.

In Section 4.1 we address well-definedness of expressions, and in Section 4.2 we address the other properties, which need to take all restrictions into account. Finally, in Section 4.3 we report on our experiences with SMT solvers.

Note that all SMT expressions are written in the prefix style. As a convention, in our examples any SMT variable `GeoModel_Object1_Object2` represents the expression **Distance[GeoModel](Object1,Object2)** in the DSL instance. So we can assume that `GeoModel_Object1_Object2` is non-negative. The SMT problem generator (Fig. 1) guarantees that **Distance[GeoModel](Object1,Object2)** and **Distance[GeoModel](Object2,Object1)** are represented by the same variable. For brevity we use **ahead** instead of **LookAhead** in our naming convention.

4.1   Well-definedness of Expressions

Since users can specify complicated activation conditions or speed limits, we provide mechanisms to warn for mathematically undefined expressions. As an example we focus on potential divisions by zero, which can occur at two places. First, any divisions in the activation condition are checked in isolation. Second, divisions appearing in effect clauses are checked under the assumption that the corresponding activation condition holds.

Consider the following restriction which contains division at both locations:

```
restriction DivByZeroSample
    activation 1 / (1 + Distance[Actuals](Table,CArm)) > 0  &&
               Distance[Actuals](Table,CArm) < 5
    effect absolute limit CArm[Rotation] at
               1 / (6 - Distance[Actuals](Table,CArm))
```

Assuming non-negative distances, both checks are satisfied in our example. The following assertion statement encodes the check for the effect clause in SMT.

```
(assert (forall ((actuals_Table_CArm Real))
    (implies  (and  (>= actuals_Table_CArm 0.0)
                    (> (/ 1.0 (+ 1.0 actuals_Table_CArm)) 0.0)
                    (< actuals_Table_CArm 5.0)  )
              (not  (= (- 6.0 actuals_Table_CArm) 0.0))  )))
```

In this example, the SMT variable actuals_Table_CArm corresponds to **Distance**[Actuals](Table,CArm), and condition (>= actuals_Table_CArm 0.0) encodes the domain knowledge that the used distances are non-negative.

4.2   Ranges, Safety, and Deadlock

The remaining properties need to take all restrictions into account. We first introduce a procedure to translate the speed limits enforced by the restrictions to SMT expressions. Each restriction is mapped to a single SMT expression, and afterwards they are combined. This allows for tracing the detected faults back to the corresponding DSL constructs in Section 5. For each identified pattern for these properties we give an example from Fig. 3. To keep the formulae simple, we omit the information that each distance is non-negative (see Section 4.1).

Consider the following general template of a restriction:

```
restriction [restriction]
    activation [act_restriction]
    effect
        relative/absolute limit [object_movement] at [eff_restriction]
```

Each **restriction** is translated to a function definition with as parameters the distances it depends on. We encode restrictions as functions with an if-then-else (ite) structure with [act_restriction] and [eff_restriction] specified as the condition and the **then** part of the conditional statement, respectively.

```
(define-fun func_restriction ((arg_1 Real)...(arg_n Real)) Real
   (ite [act_restriction]
        [eff_restriction]
        infinity ))
```

We define a sufficiently large number as `infinity`. If the activation condition is not satisfied, then `infinity` is returned, implying that there is no speed limit.

Multiple active restrictions can affect the same absolute/relative limit of an object movement. In this case, if at least one of the effects is active, we take the minimum of the activated effects as the overall effect for this limit. Otherwise, there is no restriction on the object movement. In SMT, the overall effect is specified again as a function with an `ite` structure. The parameter set of this function is the union of the parameter sets of the contributing functions.

```
(define-fun Object_Movement_Limit ((arg_1 Real)...(arg_n Real)) Real
   (ite  (or [act_restriction_1] [act_restriction_2] ...)
         (min  (func_restriction_1 arg_11 arg_12 ... arg_1k)
               (func_restriction_2 arg_21 arg_22 ... arg_2l)
               ...   )
         ([DEFAULT_VALUE]) ))
```

The value of `[DEFAULT_VALUE]` is determined by the limit type. For relative limits, 1 is used; for absolute limits, `infinity` is used.

Let `RelDetTrans` be the SMT function that specifies the overall relative translation limit for *Detector*. In our example, the only restriction that contributes to this overall limit is `ApproachingTableAndDetector`, which is specified in terms of the two parameters `actuals_Table_Detector` and `ahead_Table_Detector`. These are also the parameters of the overall function `RelDetTrans`.

Ranges. For functions specifying the overall relative limit we check that the return value is between 0 and 1 for any valuation of distance parameters. The pattern for absolute limits is similar. For example, the following property will be generated for Fig. 3. Given the function `RelDetTrans` that specifies the overall relative translation limit for *Detector*, this property specifies that the relative limit for the *Translation* movement of *Detector* is at most 1:

```
(assert (forall((actuals_Table_Detector Real)(ahead_Table_Detector Real))
   (<= (RelDetTrans actuals_Table_Detector ahead_Table_Detector) 1.0) ))
```

Safety. As an example, we consider the monotonicity properties for each relative/absolute limit and each rotation/translation movement with respect to each distance parameter. Based on Fig. 3, the following property is generated to verify the monotonicity of the relative limit of the translation movement for *Detector* with respect to `actuals_Table_Detector`. This means that decreasing this distance parameter, while maintaining the other distance parameters, may not lead to a more relaxed limit.

```
(assert (forall ((actuals_Table_Detector Real)(ahead_Table_Detector Real)
                 (actuals_Table_Detector' Real))
```

```
(implies
  (<= actuals_Table_Detector actuals_Table_Detector')
  (<= (RelDetTrans actuals_Table_Detector  ahead_Table_Detector)
      (RelDetTrans actulas_Table_Detector' ahead_Table_Detector)) )))
```

Deadlock. We identified the following pattern to check for absence of rotation/translation deadlock: "for each valuation of distance parameters in Actuals, there exists a valuation of LookAhead (a user-dependent geometric model) such that relative and absolute limits are non-zero".

For the example in Fig. 3, the following property expresses deadlock freedom of the *Detector* translation movement. There is no absolute limit specified for this movement and this property only depends on the arguments of `RelDetTrans`.

```
(assert (forall ((actuals_Table_Detector Real))
 (exists ((ahead_Table_Detector' Real))
  (not (= (RelDetTrans actuals_Table_Detector ahead_Table_Detector') 0.0))
      )))
```

4.3   Feasibility of SMT Solving

Applying this translation to real examples has led to some observations. First of all, most state-of-the-art SMT solvers have limited support for non-linear constraints such as exponentiation. Thus the occurrence of complex non-linear expressions in a DSL specification may limit the analysis power of our method. In our examples, exponentiation was mainly applied to model brake patterns. We have temporarily isolated these patterns from the rest of the DSL. Approximating non-linear constraints remains as one of the issues that we want to investigate in our future work.

Secondly, in order to keep validation practically feasible, we have slightly modified the SMT expressions. Since `forall` is an expensive operation for SMT solvers [10], we follow a counterexample-based approach. Instead of showing that the expressions hold for all parameter values, we aim to find parameter values that violate the property; in other words, if the negated property cannot be satisfied by any valuation, the property itself holds for all possible valuations. We have not used specific facilities (such as quantifier instantiation) provided by specific SMT solvers (such as Z3) in our analyses.

5   Automated Debugging

Based on the SMT problems presented in Section 4, the "verifier and debugger" component in Fig. 1 checks the validity of the properties. Since we encode the DSL restrictions as SMT functions with distance parameters, for any violated property, SMT solvers provide a counterexample in terms of distance values.

We aim for a debugger that mechanically computes the location of any fault in terms of the DSL instance. In this section we first describe suitable locations to report faults for the different types of properties. Then we present a procedure to compute these locations. Finally we discuss how to avoid computing masked restrictions as locations.

5.1   Fault Location

In case of any property violation, we aim to indicate the location of any fault in the DSL instance. We distinguish three kinds of locations in the DSL:

Expression. The well-definedness property from Section 4.1 is defined for each expression in isolation. In case of a violation, the fault location is the expression itself.

Restriction. The properties from Section 4.2 are verified against the whole DSL instance. In these cases the fault locations are the restrictions that can be pivotal in causing the violation. We define this as follows:

> "A restriction r is a pivotal restriction for causing the violation of property P, if there exists a set of restrictions that does not violate property P, but after adding restriction r the property is violated."

Fixed. If a property is violated for all subsets of the restrictions, then there is no pivotal restriction. For our example properties, this can apply to safety properties that specify a certain speed limit. For such properties that do not (trivially) hold for the empty set of restrictions, we report any violations at a fixed location in the DSL instance.

Debugging is only needed when restrictions should be identified as fault location. In the remainder of this section, we focus on the properties from Section 4.2 that are trivially valid for the empty set of restrictions and violated by the full set of restrictions.

5.2   Procedure to Locate a Single Pivotal Restriction

Our debugging procedure is based on the delta-debugging approach of [22]. In [22] the delta-debugging procedure is introduced for isolating the relevant part of a failure inducing program input. We adapt this procedure to our setting to detect restrictions that cause property violations. In particular, for a violated property we aim to find a pivotal restriction by narrowing down the difference between sets of passing (satisfying the property) and failing (violating the property) restrictions. Our procedure can be summarized as follows:

1. Choose a passing (R^+) and a failing (R^-) set, i.e., a set of restrictions that satisfies the property and a set that violates the property, such that $R^+ \subseteq R^-$. We choose R^+ as the empty set, and R^- as the set of all restrictions.
2. Repeatedly try to minimize the difference between sets R^+ and R^-:
   (a) Select a set R of restrictions such that $R^+ \subset R \subset R^-$;
   (b) Use the SMT solver to check whether R satisfies the property;
   (c) If set R satisfies the property, then replace the passing set R^+ by R, otherwise replace the failing set R^- by R.
3. The single restriction r that distinguishes the passing set R^+ from the failing set R^- is a pivotal restriction for the property violation.

Iteration	R^+	R^-	Step 2.(a) R	Step 2.(b) Status of R	Step 2.(c) Minimization	Step 3 Fault
1	$\{\}$	$\{r_1, r_2\}$	$\{r_1\}$	satisfies the property	$R^+ := R$	-
2	$\{r_1\}$	$\{r_1, r_2\}$	-	-	-	r_2

Fig. 4. Isolating a faulty restriction with delta-debugging

As an example, consider Fig. 3 where the relative limit for Detector translation can be negative. Fig. 4 illustrates the application of this fault isolation procedure to detect a faulty restriction. Restrictions r_1 and r_2 represent the first and second restriction in Fig. 3. Finally, in the second iteration, restriction r_2, i.e., `ApproachingTableAndDetector`, is identified as a fault location.

From the description of Step 2(a) one can easily deduce that the fault isolation procedure is non-deterministic. In the presence of multiple faulty restrictions, each execution of this procedure can identify a different restriction.

Regarding the performance, in the worst case the number of iterations of Step 2 is linear in the total number of restrictions. One can constrain the choice of R in Step 2(a) to make it logarithmic. Moreover, the debugging considers only subsets of the original specification, for which SMT solving has a lower complexity (i.e., typically consuming much less time and memory).

5.3 Masked Restrictions

The procedure from Section 5.2 can also report restrictions as faults at points where they are masked (see the DSL semantics in Section 2.2). To illustrate this, we consider three example restrictions r_1, r_2, and r_3 based on a single distance parameter. Fig. 5(a) represents the individual relative limits for a specific object movement in terms of the distance parameter. The overall effect is defined as the minimum of the individual effects, as depicted in Fig. 5(b).

The effect of a restriction r is masked for a given set of distance values, if there exists at least one restriction r' for which the effect is less than the effect of r for the same combination of distance values. In this example, the effect of restriction r_3 is masked by another restriction for every distance value.

Considering the range property "relative limits should be at most 1", restriction r_3 in isolation violates this property, and hence the procedure from Section 5.2 can indicate this masked restriction as the fault location. Masking is no issue for the verification, but it is undesired that debugging reports masked restrictions as fault location.

If the semantics of the DSL is correctly implemented throughout code generation, masked restrictions will never lead to failures and hence, are considered spurious by the domain experts. To avoid reporting masked restrictions as fault locations, we replace all restrictions by just their unmasked parts, as shown in Fig. 5(b). This requires a small modification of the SMT formulations from Section 4.2. For restriction $r3$ it results in the following SMT expression:

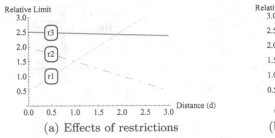

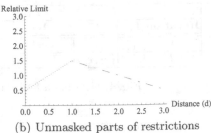

(a) Effects of restrictions   (b) Unmasked parts of restrictions

Fig. 5. Masked restriction

```
(define-fun r3 ((d Real)) Real
   (ite (and [act_r3]
             (not (and [act_r1] (< [eff_r1] [eff_r3]) ))
             (not (and [act_r2] (< [eff_r2] [eff_r3]) )) )
        [eff_r3]
        infinity ))
```

In comparison with the encoding from Section 4.2, the activation condition is extended with two conjuncts indicating that its effect is not masked by an active restriction $r1$ nor by an active restriction $r2$. We apply a similar encoding to restrictions $r1$ and $r2$. In this way masked restrictions have no effect any more, and hence, they cannot be identified as fault location.

6   Integration with DSL Editor

We have implemented the introduced verification and debugging approach using the Eclipse Modeling Framework (EMF, [19]). Xtext is the open-source framework that we have applied to specify the grammar of the DSL. It is integrated with Xtend for validation and code generation. Z3 [5] is the SMT solver that we have used in our experiments. To hide all the verification and debugging strategies from the user, we provide the user with a Python script that for a given DSL instance verifies the set of predefined properties through a sequence of calls to Z3. For any violated property the debugging procedure is automatically invoked.

Basic validators are continuously executed while editing an instance of the DSL. To avoid additional delays while editing, we have decided not to perform continuous validation using SMT checkers. We generate the SMT problems and the Python script using an Xtend code generator. The validation can be initiated on user request by invoking the Python script. The validation results are stored, interpreted by a validator and shown back in the editor.

The user is notified about the validation results using "warnings", which result in a yellow underlining of the problematic parts together with a textual message; see Fig. 6. We cannot use "errors", because they block future executions of all code generators (including the SMT problem generator). We also warn the user about verification or debugging attempts for which the corresponding SMT problem is not decidable (e.g., as a result of non-linear expressions).

```
restriction ApproachingTableAndCArm
  activation
    Distance[Actuals](Table, CArm) < 35 mm + 15 cm
  effect
    absolute limit CArm[Rotation]
      at ((Distance[Actuals](Table, CArm) - 35 mm) / 15 cm) * 10 dgps
```

```
Multiple markers at this line
- Potential (Rotation) deadlock for CArm
- Absolute limit for CArm rotation should be non-negative
```

Fig. 6. Debugging results displayed in the DSL editor

7   Conclusions and Future Work

We have used a Domain Specific Language (DSL) for collision prevention to study ways to support early fault detection in industrial applications. The goal is to add value to the use of DSLs beyond code generation. In particular we have focused on validation types that are more advanced than the usual basic types of validation that can be found in modern programming environments.

For this prototype DSL, we have shown a useful set of advanced properties that can be verified efficiently using the SMT solver Z3. Actual instances consisting of 16 distance parameters from geometric models, and 81 restrictions lead to 264 generated properties from 5 property patterns. In case of 226 violations, the whole advanced validation process (including a non-optimized generator of SMT problems and Python scripts (22 sec.), and verification and debugging (105 sec.)) takes about 2 minutes on a standard desktop computer. The results are displayed at logical locations in the DSL editor. To this end, we have integrated three techniques, viz., domain-specific languages, SMT solving and delta debugging.

In the studied DSL, restrictions can sometimes be masked by other restrictions and hence they have no observable effect. In particular, we have shown how to ensure that masked restrictions are not reported as fault location.

We envisage some possible extensions of the present work. The debugging procedure can be extended to detect all possible causes of a property violation. Moreover, we aim to investigating other abstraction levels in order to rule out false positive/negative responses.

References

1. Baier, C., Katoen, J.-P.: Principles of Model Checking. MIT Press (2008)
2. Barrett, C., Sebastiani, R., Seshia, S.A., Tinelli, C.: Satisfiability modulo theories. In: Handbook of Satisfiability, vol. 185, pp. 825–885 (2009)
3. Biere, A., Heule, M.J.H., van Maaren, H., Walsh, T. (eds.): Handbook of Satisfiability. Frontiers in Artificial Intelligence and Applications, vol. 185. IOS Press (2009)
4. Cleve, H., Zeller, A.: Locating causes of program failures. In: Proceedings of ICSE 2005, pp. 342–351. ACM (2005)

5. de Moura, L., Bjørner, N.: Z3: An efficient SMT solver. In: Ramakrishnan, C.R., Rehof, J. (eds.) TACAS 2008. LNCS, vol. 4963, pp. 337–340. Springer, Heidelberg (2008)
6. De Moura, L., Bjørner, N.: Satisfiability modulo theories: introduction and applications. Communications of the ACM 54(9), 69–77 (2011)
7. Eysholdt, M., Behrens, H.: Xtext: implement your language faster than the quick and dirty way. In: SPLASH/OOPSLA Companion, pp. 307–309. ACM (2010)
8. Frehse, G., Le Guernic, C., Donzé, A., Cotton, S., Ray, R., Lebeltel, O., Ripado, R., Girard, A., Dang, T., Maler, O.: SpaceEx: Scalable verification of hybrid systems. In: Gopalakrishnan, G., Qadeer, S. (eds.) CAV 2011. LNCS, vol. 6806, pp. 379–395. Springer, Heidelberg (2011)
9. Garavel, H., Lang, F., Mateescu, R., Serwe, W.: CADP 2010: A toolbox for the construction and analysis of distributed processes. In: Abdulla, P.A., Leino, K.R.M. (eds.) TACAS 2011. LNCS, vol. 6605, pp. 372–387. Springer, Heidelberg (2011)
10. Ge, Y., de Moura, L.: Complete instantiation for quantified formulas in satisfiabiliby modulo theories. In: Bouajjani, A., Maler, O. (eds.) CAV 2009. LNCS, vol. 5643, pp. 306–320. Springer, Heidelberg (2009)
11. Hooman, J., Mooij, A.J., van Wezep, H.: Early fault detection in industry using models at various abstraction levels. In: Derrick, J., Gnesi, S., Latella, D., Treharne, H. (eds.) IFM 2012. LNCS, vol. 7321, pp. 268–282. Springer, Heidelberg (2012)
12. Hwang, J.H., Xie, T., Chen, F., Liu, A.X.: Fault localization for firewall policies. In: Proceedings of SRDS 2009, pp. 100–106. IEEE Computer Society (2009)
13. Jose, M., Majumdar, R.: Cause clue clauses: error localization using maximum satisfiability. ACM SIGPLAN Notices 46(6), 437–446 (2011)
14. Krahn, H., Rumpe, B., Völkel, S.: MontiCore: a framework for compositional development of domain specific languages. J. STTT 12(5), 353–372 (2010)
15. Mernik, M., Heering, J., Sloane, A.M.: When and how to develop domain-specific languages. ACM Computing Surveys 37(4), 316–344 (2005)
16. Mooij, A.J., Hooman, J., Albers, R.: Gaining industrial confidence for the introduction of domain-specific languages. In: Proceedings of IEESD, 2013 (to appear, 2013)
17. Ratiu, D., Voelter, M., Molotnikov, Z., Schaetz, B.: Implementing modular domain specific languages and analyses. In: Workshop on MoDeVVa (2012)
18. Smith, A., Veneris, A., Ali, M.F., Viglas, A.: Fault diagnosis and logic debugging using boolean satisfiability. IEEE Transactions on Computer-Aided Design of Integrated Circuits and Systems 24(10), 1606–1621 (2005)
19. Steinberg, D., Budinsky, F., Paternostro, M., Merks, E.: Eclipse Modeling Framework. Pearson Education (2008)
20. van Deursen, A., Klint, P., Visser, J.: Domain-specific languages: an annotated bibliography. SIGPLAN Notices 35(6), 26–36 (2000)
21. Woehrle, M., Bakhshi, R., Mousavi, M.R.: Mechanized extraction of topology antipatterns in wireless networks. In: Derrick, J., Gnesi, S., Latella, D., Treharne, H. (eds.) IFM 2012. LNCS, vol. 7321, pp. 158–173. Springer, Heidelberg (2012)
22. Zeller, A.: Why Programs Fail? A Guide to Systematic Debugging. Morgan Kaufmann (2009)
23. Zeller, A., Hildebrandt, R.: Simplifying and isolating failure-inducing input. IEEE Transactions on Software Engineering 28(2), 183–200 (2002)

Static Detection of Implementation Errors Using Formal Code Specification

Iman Saleh[1], Gregory Kulczycki[2], M. Brian Blake[1], and Yi Wei[3]

[1] Department of Computer Science, University of Miami, Florida, USA
{iman,m.brian.blake}@miami.edu
[2] Cyber Innovation Unit, Battelle Memorial Institute, Virginia, USA
kulczycig@battelle.org
[3] Department of Computer Science and Engineering,
University of Notre Dame, Notre Dame, USA
yweil@nd.edu

Abstract. The software engineering community suggests that formal specification of source code facilitates the verification that can help to identify hidden functional errors. In this work, we investigate the impact of various levels of formal specification on the ability to statically detect errors in code. Our goal is to quantify the return on investment with regards to the effectiveness of identifying errors versus the overhead of specifying software at various levels of detail. We looked at common algorithms and data structures implemented using C# and specified using Spec#. We selectively omitted various parts of the specification to come up with five different levels of specification, from unspecified to highly-specified. For each level of specification, we injected errors into the classes using a fault injection tool. Experimentation using a verifier showed that over 80% of the errors were detected from the highest specification levels while the levels in between generated mixed results. To the best of our knowledge, our study is the first to quantitatively measure the effect of formal methods on code quality. We believe that our work can help convince skeptics that formal methods can be practically integrated into programming activities to produce code with higher quality even with partial specification.

Keywords: Formal Methods, Mutation Testing, Experimentation.

1 Introduction

Formal Methods used in developing computer systems are mathematically based techniques for describing and reasoning about system properties [1]. Ideally, formal methods can provide the means of statically proving that a system has been implemented correctly with respect to its specification. In other words – in theory at least – formal methods can be used to mathematically verify that the code is correct without ever having to run the program [2][3]. In this work, we use the Spec# verification system [4] to investigate how formal specification and verification can be practically employed to detect implementation errors. Our results demonstrate how writing specifications can potentially increase software correctness, and our experiment provides

R.M. Hierons, M.G. Merayo, and M. Bravetti (Eds.): SEFM 2013, LNCS 8137, pp. 197–211, 2013.

an insight into the usefulness of different specification constructs on improving the code implementation practices.

We adapt a methodology from the software testing fields where code mutation is used to assess the quality of a testing technique. Mutation testing [5][6][7] is carried out by injecting errors in the code and measuring the ability of a testing tool to detect these errors. The main assumption with this methodology is that the number of mutation errors detected by a tool is an indication of number of errors that this tool can detect in the future when unknown bugs are present in the code. We use a similar methodology to evaluate the ability of code specification in detecting mutation errors.

To the best of our knowledge, our study is the first to provide an empirical evidence of the benefits of using formal methods on writing bug-free code and to propose using mutation testing techniques to evaluate the quality of formal specifications. We believe that our work can help convince skeptics that formal methods can be practically integrated within programming practices to enhance code quality and that exhaustive code specification is not required to achieve that goal. We also make our dataset publicly available [8] to stimulate research in that direction.

2   Formal Specifications and Verification

Formal Methods used in developing computer systems are mathematically-based techniques for describing system properties [9]. A method is formal if it has a sound mathematical basis, typically given by a formal specification language. In our work, we use Hoare-style specification. The specification employs preconditions and postconditions to specify the behavior of a method [10]. A tool that statically verifies the correctness of the code with respect to the specifications is called a *verifying compiler*. The input and output of a verifying compiler is shown in Figure 1. The input is a set of mathematical specifications and code that is intended to implement those specifications. A compiler performs standard checks – such as syntax and type checking – on both the code and the specs, and then a verifier attempts to prove that the code correctly implements the specifications.

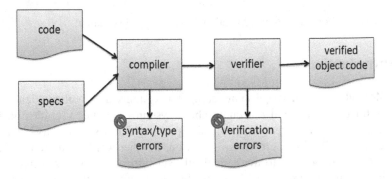

Fig. 1. Input and output of a verifying compiler

In this work, we choose Spec# [4] as our specification language as it represents a recent effort of integrating formal specification with current programming practices. Spec# uses constructs with similar syntax to the C# programming language. Consequently, it is easier for programmers to learn the languages over other specification languages that use special-purpose mathematical notations. We also use the Boogie verifier for Spec#. Boogie is a static verifier that uses a theorem prover to verify that a program or class satisfies its specification. All verifications in our experiments are done automatically using the Boogie tool. In the following paragraphs, we describe each construct used to write code specification along with examples that we adapt from the Spec# documentation [4].

- **Non-Null Types** are used to denote whether an expression may or may not evaluate to null. Such a mechanism helps programmers avoid null-dereference errors. For example, the notation `Transcript!` `t` declares an attribute *t* as a non-null type by using the exclamation point (!).

- **Preconditions** specify the conditions under which the method is allowed to be called, using a *requires* clause. Here is a simple example:

```
class ArrayList {
    public virtual void Insert(int index , object value)
    requires 0 <= index && index <= Count; { . . . }
```

- **Postconditions** specify the change in the system state after a method's execution using *ensures* clauses For example, the postconditions of *Insert* can be specified as:

```
ensures Count == old(Count) + 1;
ensures value == this[index];
ensures Forall{int i in 0 : index ; old(this[i]) == this[i]};
ensures Forall{int i in index : old(Count); old(this[i]) ==
this[i+1]};
```

The **old**(*Count*) denotes the value of *Count* on entry to the method. In the third line, the special function *Forall* is applied to the comprehension of the boolean expression *old(this[i])* == *this[i]*, where *i* ranges over the integer values in the half-open interval from 0 to less than *index* .

- **Frame Conditions** limit the parts of the program state that the method is allowed to modify. For example, the following method specification denotes that method *M* is permitted to have a net effect on the value of *x*.

```
void M() modifies x ; {…}
```

- **Class Contracts** are also called object invariants and spell out what is expected to hold for each object's data fields in the steady state of the object [4]. For example, the following class fragment declares that the lengths of the arrays students and absent are to be the same.

```
class AttendanceRecord {
    Student[ ]! students;
    bool[ ]! absent;
    invariant students.Length == absent.Length; … }
```

- **Loop Invariants** are logical assertions that must evaluate to true at the beginning and end of every iteration of the loop. The following code fragment shows an example of a loop invariant.

```
for (int n = i; n < j; n++)
  invariant i <= n && n <= j; {
  s += a[n];
}
```

- **Assertions** are boolean expressions that specify assumptions within a piece of code. Assertions are typically checked at runtime, however, they can also be used to help a code verifier statically prove that some other code conditions hold. As an example:

```
public int doubler(int x){
    int XX;
    XX = 2 * x;
    assert XX == 2 * x;
    return XX;
}
```

3   Research Hypothesis

We are interested in studying the effect of using formal code specification and verification in enabling the writing of bug-free code. Our research hypothesis can hence be stated as follows: *"Implementation errors based on common code mutations can be detected statically (without running the code) by using formal code specification and verification techniques. These errors are not detected using a non-verifying compiler. Furthermore, the number of errors detected increases as more comprehensive specification levels are used."*

In this experiment, specification levels are based on the inclusion or exclusion of the various formal constructs described above, such as non-null annotations, invariants, and pre and post conditions.

4   Data Set

Our dataset is comprised of a total of 248 program mutations generated out of a set of 13 formally specified C# classes. These classes are implemented and formally specified, using Spec#, by the authors of [11] based on a collection of textbook algorithms provided in [12]. The data set represents a set of general-purpose algorithms including search and sort algorithms, basic data structures, mathematical calculations and array manipulation functionalities. The classes are selected as a set of simple yet practical examples of using code specifications. Table 1 lists the classes along with short descriptions of their functionalities.

Note that classes 4 and 5 represent the same implementation of the Bubble Sort algorithm but with different specifications. The specification writers used this example to demonstrate different ways to express the same assertion using different Spec# constructs. We use this example in the experiment to show the effect of different specifications on the ability to discover errors, as will be detailed later. Our dataset is available at [8] for use in replicating results and conducting similar experiments.

Table 1. Data Set Description

	Class	Description
1	CircQueue	Circular array implementation of Queue.
2	IntStack	Non-Circular array implementation of Stack.
3	ArrayCount	Calculates the number of nulls in an array.
4	BubbleSort1	Implements the Bubble Sort to sort an array of integers.
5	BubbleSort2	Implements the Bubble Sort to sort an array of integers.
6	SegmentSum	Calculates the sum of the elements in an array segment
7	DutchNationalFlag	Given 'N' objects colored red, white or blue, sorts them so that objects of the same color are adjacent, with the colors in the order red, white and blue.
8	GCD	Calculates the Greatest Common Divisor of two numbers.
9	SumXValues	Sum the first x numbers in an array.
10	Reverse	Reverses the order of elements in an array.
11	Queue	Non-Circular array implementation of Queue.
12	BinarySearch	Implements the Binary Search to determine if an element is in an array.
13	SumEven	Sums values at the even indices of an array.

5   Methodology

We test our hypothesis by applying the following steps:

1. Each class in Table 1 is verified using the Boogie verifier to ensure that the implementation initially satisfies the formal specifications.
2. A fault injection tool, implemented by the authors of [6], is used to automatically introduce errors in each class. Software fault injection techniques are described in [5] and the authors of [6] extend these techniques for object-oriented code. These techniques simulate programmer errors by randomly applying mutation operators. A subset of these mutation operators, which could be generated for our code dataset, is used in our experiment and we describe them in Table 2.
3. The Boogie verifier is executed on each mutant of each class. If the verifier generates an error, than the mutant is said to be *killed* and the specification has enabled the error to be detected. Otherwise, the error has not been detected by the automatic verifier and the mutant is said to be *alive*.
4. Step (3) is repeated for different types of errors and the total number of errors detected using different specification levels is calculated.

The following specification levels are considered in the experiment:

- L0: No specification, this level acts as a baseline
- L1: Specifying only the non-null types
- L2: Adding assertions and both loop and class invariants to L1 specifications

- L3: Specifying only the methods preconditions in addition to L1 specifications
- L4: The highest available level of specification of a class including non-null types, methods contracts, frame conditions, loop and class invariants and assertions.

Table 2. Mutation Operators Used in the Experiment

Operator	Description	Example
AOR	Arithmetic Operator Replacement	a = b + c *to* a = b − c
ROR	Relational Operator Replacement	while(a < b) *to* while(a > b)
PRV	Reference assignment with other compatible type	a = b *to* a = c
EOC	Replace == with Equals()	x == 0 *to* x.Equals(0)
JID	Member variable initialization deletion	int[] a = new int[2] *to* int[] a
JTD	*this* keyword deletion	this.x *to* x

These levels are selected from a practicality standpoint as we believe they capture the different levels of efforts that can be invested by programmers in writing formal specifications. It is worth noting here that L4 is the highest specification level provided by the specification writers and does not necessarily imply a comprehensive specification of the code behavior.

The independent variable in the proposed experiment is the *specification level*. The specification level is a nominal variable that includes the five levels of specification L0 to L4. The dependent variable is a ratio value capturing the percentage of errors detected to the total number of errors injected into the code. This is also called the *mutation score* in the software testing terminology.

The main idea is that the number of errors detected using either of the specification levels studied in our experiment is an indication of the correctness of software produced using that level. Our goal is to measure the effectiveness of the formal

Table 3. Mutation operators applied to each class and the corresponding number of mutants

	Class	Mutation Operators	No. Of Mutants
1	CircQueue	AOR – ROR – EOC – JID	25
2	IntStack	ROR – EOC – JID	13
3	ArrayCount	ROR – JTD	7
4	BubbleSort1	AOR – ROR	22
5	BubbleSort2	AOR – ROR	22
6	SegmentSum	ROR	5
7	DutchNationalFlag	AOR – ROR	41
8	GCD	AOR – ROR - EOC – PRV	31
9	SumXValues	AOR – ROR	13
10	Reverse	ROR	5
11	Queue	ROR – EOC - JID	13
12	BinarySearch	AOR – ROR	35
13	SumEven	AOR – ROR – EOC – JID	16
		Total	248

specification in detecting design-time errors and hence maximizing software correctness. The mutation scores are used as a measure of that effectiveness. We would also like to study the effect of each level of specification on our ability to detect errors. A total of 248 mutants were generated and formally verified throughout the experiment. Table 3 gives a summary of number of mutants generated for each class and the mutation operators that they cover.

6   Results and Analysis

For each class used in our experiment, we calculated the mutation score at different levels of specifications. We then analyzed the results to test if there's a significant difference achieved at the different specification levels. The mutation score achieved for each of the 13 classes is depicted in Figure 2 at different levels of specifications.

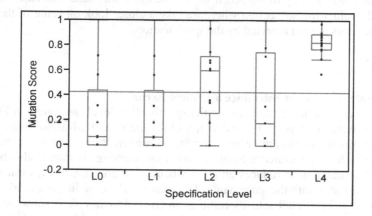

Fig. 2. The mutation scores achieved at different specification levels

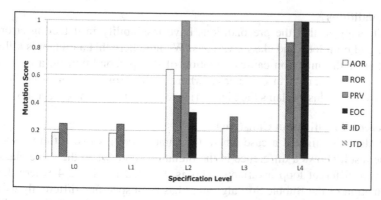

Fig. 3. The mutation scores achieved at different specification levels for different types of mutation operators

A boxplot [13] is a graphical way for depicting a set of data values. The bottom of the box is the 25th percentile and the top of the box the 75th percentile. The line across the middle of the box is the median or 50th percentile. The plot also displays outliers, which is a value that is significantly distant from the rest of the data. The plot is used to visualize the differences/similarities between data sets. It should be noted here that the mutation tool generates errors that are syntactically correct and hence none of these injected errors are detected by the C# non-verifying compiler. In other words, the mutation score of the non-verifying compiler is consistently equal to zero.   Our next set of results calculates the mutation scores achieved at different levels of specifications for different types of mutation errors. The results are depicted in Figure 3. As seen in the figure, L4 performs the best by detecting the highest number of errors across different error types while L2 comes at the second rank. There's no significant difference between L0, L1 and L3 in their ability to detect errors. Using preconditions at L3 fails to detect errors compared to invariants used at L2. This is due to the nature of the code employed by the experiment. We describe this case and others in more detail in the following subsection where we take a closer look on some of the examples where errors are not detected by the specification.

6.1   Observations

–   Mutants that do not Introduce a Logical Error

Some errors are not detected by any of the specification levels as shown in Figure 2. Mainly, the errors of type JID (the deletion of a variable initialization) and JTD (the deletion of *this* keyword) are never detected.   However, throughout our experiment, all JID errors have generated a Spec# compilation warning. It should also be noted that the JTD mutation introduces an error whenever a program has a local variable and class attributes with the same name. This was not the case in our experiment and hence the mutation did not actually result in an error. An example is shown in Listing 3. Mutants that remove the *this* keyword on lines 8 or on line 11 are not killed by the specification as they don't constitute a logical error in this case.

–   Preconditions

The results suggest that the preconditions have less ability in detecting errors than assertions and both loop and class invariants. We note here that a mutant is killed by a precondition if the mutation causes violation of this precondition on a method call. This case is not common in our dataset where many programs consisted of a class with one method. This explains the high variance of the mutation score at L3.

–   Different Specification Constructs

We have also investigated a case where the same code has two different specifications. The result shows a difference in the mutation score when the same class is annotated with different loop invariants. This is depicted in Figure 4 where the same implementation of the Bubble Sort algorithm has been specified differently using two different sets of loop invariants. As shown in the figure, there's a difference in number of error detected at L2 and L4. The *BubbleSort1* code is shown in Listing 1. The mutation score is enhanced, for *BubbleSort2*, when the loop invariant at line 13 is written using Spec# comprehension keyword *max* as follows:

```
invariant forall{int i in (n: a.Length);
                        a[i] == max{int k in (0..i); a[k]}}
```

According to the results, using the Spec# keyword enables better verification of the assertion and hence achieves higher mutation score. This is due to the fact that the Spec# verifier can smartly handle comprehension expressions, like *sum, min, max, count*, and *product*, and translates them into verification conditions that can be tackled by a first-order Satisfiability Modulo Theories (SMT) solver. It is hence recommended to use these expressions in writing the formal specifications, whenever it is feasible. More details about the verification of comprehension assertions can be found in [11].

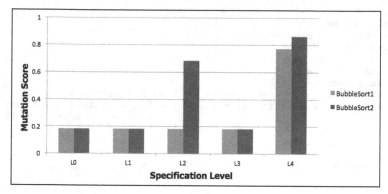

Fig. 4. The effect of different loop invariants on error detection

```
1   public class BubbleSort1 {
2
3     static void Sort_Forall(int[]! a)
4     modifies a[*];
5     ensures forall{int i in (0: a.Length), int j in (0: a.Length),
6                                   i <= j; a[i] <= a[j]}; {
7       for (int n = a.Length; 0 <= --n; )
8       invariant 0 <= n && n <= a.Length;
9       invariant forall{int i in (n: a.Length), int k in (0: i);
10          a[k] <= a[i]}; {
11          for (int j = 0; j < n; j++)
12          invariant j <= n;
13          invariant forall{int i in (n+1:a.Length), int k in (0: i);
14                                   a[k]<= a[i]};
15          invariant forall{int k in (0: j); a[k] <= a[j]}; {
16            if (a[j+1] < a[j]) {
17               int tmp = a[j];  a[j] = a[j+1];  a[j+1] = tmp;
18            }
19          }
20        }
21      }
22    }
```

Listing 1. An implementation of the Bubble Sort algorithm

Another example, shown in Listing 2, is the implementation of a GCD calculator. A mutant changing line 6 to be `while (i < a-b)` is not detected by the precondition at line 4 but can be detected by the invariant as it causes violation to the assertion at line 7.

– **Loop Invariants**

In some cases, the loop invariants have actually concealed an error that is detected when no invariant is added. This is due to the way the Boogie verifier handles loop unfolding. The verifier treats loops as if the only thing known at the beginning of an iteration is that the loop invariant holds. This means that loop invariants are used to rule out unreachable states that otherwise would cause the program verifier to generate an error message [14]. Figure 5 shows two examples where loop invariants at L2 and L4 cause some errors to be undetected by the verifier as they prevent the verifier from checking states that are specified as unreachable by the loop invariant. An example, for *ArrayCount* invariant, is shown in Listing 3.

```
1    public class GCD{
2       static int CalculateGCD(int a, int b)
3       requires a > 0 && b > 0; {
4          int i = 1; int res = 1;
5          while (i < a+b) {
6          invariant i <= a+b;
7          invariant res > 0 && a % res == 0 && b % res == 0;
8          invariant forall{int k in (1..i), a % k == 0 && b % k == 0;
9                                                          k <= res};{
10               i++;
11               if (a % i == 0 && b % i == 0) { res = i; }
12           }
13         return res;
14       }
15     }
```

Listing 2. An implementation of a GCD calculator

```
1    public class ArrayRefCount {
2       [Rep]public string []! a;
3       [SpecPublic] int count;
4       invariant 0 <= count && count <= a.Length;
5
6       public ArrayRefCount(string[]! input)
7       requires 0 < input.Length; {
8          this.count  = 0;
9          string[]! b = new string[input.Length];
10          input.CopyTo(b, 0);
11          this.a = b;
12       }
13
14      public void CountNonNull()
15      ensures count == count{int i in (0: a.Length); (a[i] != null)};
     {
16          expose(this){
17          int ct = 0;
18          for (int i = 0; i < a.Length; i++)
19          invariant i <= a.Length; //infers 0<=i
20          invariant 0 <= ct && ct <= i;
21          invariant ct == count{int j in (0: i); (a[j]!=null)}; {
22            if (a[i]!=null) ct++;
23          }
24          count = ct;
25          }
26        }
27     }
```

Listing 3. An implementation of a class used to count number of nulls in an array

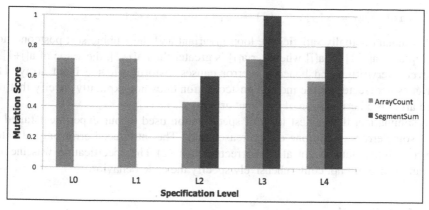

Fig. 5. The effect of loop invariants on error hiding

```
1    public class IntQueue {
2
3       [Rep][SpecPublic] int[]! elements = new int[10];
4       [SpecPublic] int head;
5       [SpecPublic] int tail;
6       invariant 0 <= head && head <= elements.Length;
7       invariant 0 <= tail && tail <= elements.Length;
8       invariant head <= tail;
9       ...
10         [Pure] public bool IsFull()
11         ensures result == (tail == elements.Length); {
12             return (tail == elements.Length);
13         }
14      ...
15      }
```

Listing 4. A code snippet of an implementation of a Queue data structure

–   Errors Undetected under the Highest Level of Specification

Theoretically, all mutation errors should be detected when code is fully specified, which is expected at L4. However, looking at the results, this is not the case. We take a closer look at some of the cases where errors in L4 go undetected by the Boogie verifier. Listing 4 for example shows the implementation of the *isFull()* method for a queue data structure class. The queue is implemented using a static array of integers. The *isFull()* method returns true if the tail of the queue is equal to number of elements in the array. One of the mutants generated for this class consisted of changing the return statement of the *isFull()* method at line 12 to be:

```
return (tail >= elements.Length);
```

This mutant is however not killed by the Boogie verifier. The reason is that, given the class invariant at line 7, the condition `tail >= elements.length` is equivalent to `tail == elements.length` which still satisfies the postcondition.

Another case where errors are not detected at L4 is the case when the specification is actually incomplete. Consider for example a mutant of the code is Listing 3 (b) that introduces an error in the swap operation at line 17 to be:

```
int tmp = a[j];  a[j] = a[j*1];  a[j+1] = tmp;
```

This mutant actually satisfies the loop invariant and the Bubble sort postcondition as it replaces a[j+1] by a[j] whenever a[j] is greater than a[j+1], the value of a[j+1] is however overwritten and hence this error causes distortion to the input array. The error goes undetected as the method postcondition does not explicitly specify that the sorted array is a permutation of the input array.

To summarize, the highest level of specification used in our experiment failed to detect some errors due to one of two reasons: (1) The introduced error only affected code readability but did not affect correctness, or (2) The specification was incomplete and hence did not comprehensively specify the code behavior.

7   Validity Discussion

7.1   Internal Validity

First, a core assumption in our experiment is that the mutation score measured at a certain level of specification is an accurate measure for predicting software reliability achieved at that level of specification. Our assumption stems from the fact that the set of mutation operators used in our experiment are based on the Mothra mutation testing system [15]. Mothra defines a set of mutation operators derived from studies of programmers' errors and correspond to mistakes that programmers typically make. This set of operators represents more than ten years of refinement through several mutation systems [5]. The authors of [16] extend these operators to support C# object orientation and syntax. They empirically evaluate the quality of these mutation operators and establish their relationship to actual programmers' errors [17]. We use the tool that they provide in our experiment. An alternative approach would be to have students or developers implement each algorithm, introducing a larger variety of errors into the code. Such an experiment would have to guard against other threats to validity, as results would largely depend on the population selected, their familiarity with the code specification practices and their level of programming expertise

Secondly, the asymmetry in number of mutants generated for mutation operator implies that, while we can draw results on the ability of specification to detect errors, we cannot however draw conclusive connection between the type of error and the mutation score. And third, the author of the specification is not an expert in Spec#, yet was helped by Spec# experts [11]. In real-life scenarios, it is expected that the specifier would undergo some kind of formal trainings to write the specification and hence we consider our experiment setting to simulate a real-life case. However, these specifications are not guaranteed to be comprehensive and hence we actually expect that better mutation could be achieved with more exhaustive specifications.

Finally, the high variance in the mutation scores achieved at L3 suggests that further study is needed before drawing conclusions on the effect of preconditions on detecting mutation errors.

7.2   External Validity

Threats to external validity are conditions that limit the ability to generalize the results of experiments to industrial practice [16]. The data set used consisted of basic algorithms whose implementations typically do not depend on object-oriented design such as the use of inheritance or method overloading. An extension of this research is needed to cover a broader and richer set of classes with different programming constructs and covering different object-oriented design patterns.

We have also used C# and Spec# as our programming and specification languages, respectively. Hence, care should be taken if results are to be generalized to other languages, especially if different verification techniques are used. Moreover, the Spec# verifier is neither sound nor complete. Consequently, the verifier can generate false positives as well as false negatives when verifying the code correctness.

8   Related Work

Since the early 1980s, the research community has recognized the need for rigorous engineering methods to face the increase in size and complexity of software systems. Consequently, formal methods have been developed and specification languages have been introduced such as the Vienna Definition Method (VDM) [18], the Z notation [19], Eiffel [20], SAL [21], the Java Modeling Language (JML) [22] for Java, and the Spec# language for C#. Additionally, there has been a significant progress in developing verification tools. The Isabelle [23] interactive theorem prover, the RESOLVE verifying compiler [26], the Boogie verifier [4] and the ESC/Java2 [24] are some examples. The authors of [25] present the challenges faced by current specification and verification techniques. The work proposes some partial solutions and promising approaches to the open problems. The myths and benefits of formal methods have been discussed by a large number of papers, a summary can be found in [26]. In related work [27][28][29], we proposed formal specification of data-centric Web services in order to enhance their reuse. The justification for using formal methods and annotating code with formal assertions remains however a major issue affecting their wide adaptation by programmers. In this work, we try to address this issue by quantitatively measuring the effect of formal methods on code quality. Our study also establishes an empirical methodology for evaluating the quality of the code specifications.

9   Conclusions

In this study, we empirically illustrate that formal specifications using Spec# can enable the detection of programmer's errors at design-time. We have shown by using statistical methods that the higher the level of specification, the higher the probability of detecting errors. Based on our results, we can sort the specification levels by their ability of detecting errors in the code:

1. Highest Available Specification Level.
2. Invariants and Assert statements.
3. Preconditions.
4. Non-null types or no specification.

It should be noted that, even though the highest available specifications in our experiments were not guaranteed to be exhaustive, these specifications have enabled the discovery of 83%, on average, of the injected errors. As shown in the results, some errors are detected by using a verifying-compiler without adding code specifications. This is due to the fact that a verifying-compiler applies some additional checks, e.g. array bound checking and possible divisions by zero. This can be a useful practice for developers that would like to enhance the quality of their code without adding the effort of formally specifying it. A study of the overhead of specifying code would be a valuable addition to the current study as it would enable developers to evaluate the cost of formally specifying code versus developing testing tools. Finally, studying the common specification errors and running mutation techniques on the contracts is another interesting area for experimentation.

References

[1] Marciniak, J.J.: Encyclopedia of Software Engineering, 2nd edn. Wiley Interscience (2001)
[2] Wing, J.M.: A Specifier's Introduction to Formal Methods. Computer 23(9), 8–22 (1990)
[3] Harton, H.K., Sitaraman, M., Krone, J.: Formal Program Verification. In: Wah, B.W. (ed.) Wiley Encyclopedia of Computer Science and Engineering. John Wiley & Sons, Inc., Hoboken (2008)
[4] Barnett, M., Leino, K.R.M., Schulte, W.: The Spec# Programming System: An Overview. In: Barthe, G., Burdy, L., Huisman, M., Lanet, J.-L., Muntean, T. (eds.) CASSIS 2004. LNCS, vol. 3362, pp. 49–69. Springer, Heidelberg (2005)
[5] Voas, J.M., McGraw, G.: Software Fault Injection: Inoculating Programs Against Errors. John Wiley & Sons (1998)
[6] Derezińska, A.: Advanced Mutation Operators Applicable in C# Programs. In: Sacha, K. (ed.) Software Engineering Techniques: Design for Quality. IFIP, vol. 227, pp. 283–288. Springer, Boston (2006)
[7] Jia, Y., Harman, M.: An Analysis and Survey of the Development of Mutation Testing. IEEE Transactions on Software Engineering 37(5), 649–678 (2011)
[8] Saleh, I.: Spec# Mutation Testing DataSet (2013), http://filebox.vt.edu/users/imostafa/DataSets/FormalSpecification/
[9] Wah, B.W.: Wiley Encyclopedia of Computer Science and Engineering, 1st edn. Wiley-Interscience (2009)
[10] Hoare, C.A.R.: An Axiomatic Basis for Computer Programming. Communications of the ACM 12(10), 576–580 (1969)
[11] Leino, K.R.M., Monahan, R.: Automatic Verification of Textbook Programs that Use Comprehensions. Presented at the ECOOP Workshop, Berlin, Germany (2007)
[12] Dijkstra, E.W., Feijen, W.H.J., Sterringa, J.: A Method of Programming, 1st English Edn. Addison-Wesley (1988)
[13] Tukey, J.W.: Exploratory Data Analysis, 1st edn. Addison Wesley (1977)
[14] Leino, K.R.M., Müller, P.: Using the Spec# Language, Methodology, and Tools to Write Bug-Free Programs. In: Müller, P. (ed.) LASER Summer School 2007/2008. LNCS, vol. 6029, pp. 91–139. Springer, Heidelberg (2010)

[15] DeMillo, R.A., Guindi, D.S., McCracken, W.M., Offutt, A.J., King, K.N.: An extended overview of the Mothra software testing environment. Presented at the Proceedings of the Second Workshop on Software Testing, Verification, and Analysis, pp. 142–151 (1988)

[16] Derezinska, A., Szustek, A.: Tool-Supported Advanced Mutation Approach for Verification of C# Programs, Los Alamitos, CA, USA, pp. 261–268 (2008)

[17] Derezinska, A.: Quality Assessment of Mutation Operators Dedicated for C# Programs. Presented at the Sixth International Conference on Quality Software, QSIC 2006, pp. 227–234 (2006)

[18] Jones, C.B.: Software Development: A Rigorous Approach, 1st edn. Prentice Hall (1980)

[19] Sufrin, B., Morgan, C., Sorensen, I., Hayes, I.: Notes for a Z handbook: Part 1-The mathematical language, Oxford University, Computing Laboratory, Programming Research Group (1984)

[20] Meyer, B.: Eiffel: The Language. Prentice Hall (1992)

[21] Hackett, B., Das, M., Wang, D., Yang, Z.: Modular checking for buffer overflows in the large, New York, NY, USA, pp. 232–241 (2006)

[22] Leavens, G.T., Cheon, Y., Clifton, C., Ruby, C., Cok, D.R.: How the Design of JML Accommodates both Runtime Assertion Checking and Formal Verification. Science of Computer Programming 55(1-3), 185–208 (2005)

[23] Nipkow, T., Paulson, L.C., Wenzel, M.: Isabelle/HOL: A Proof Assistant for Higher-Order Logic, 1st edn. Springer (2002)

[24] Cok, D.R., Kiniry, J.R.: ESC/Java2: Uniting eSC/Java and JML. In: Barthe, G., Burdy, L., Huisman, M., Lanet, J.-L., Muntean, T. (eds.) CASSIS 2004. LNCS, vol. 3362, pp. 108–128. Springer, Heidelberg (2005)

[25] Leavens, G.T., Leino, K.R.M., Muller, P.: Specification and verification challenges for sequential object-oriented programs. Formal Aspects of Computing 19, 159–189 (2007)

[26] Gogolla, M.: Benefits and Problems of Formal Methods. In: Llamosí, A., Strohmeier, A. (eds.) Ada-Europe 2004. LNCS, vol. 3063, pp. 1–15. Springer, Heidelberg (2004)

[27] Saleh, I., Kulczycki, G., Blake, M.B.: Formal Specification and Verification of Data-Centric Service Composition. In: IEEE International Conference on Web Services, ICWS 2010, pp. 131–138 (2010)

[28] Saleh, I., Kulczycki, G., Blake, M.B.: Demystifying Data-Centric Web Services. IEEE Internet Computing 13(5), 86–90 (2009)

[29] Saleh, I., Kulczycki, G., Blake, M.B., Wei, Y.: Formal Methods for Data-Centric Web Services: From Model to Implementation. In: IEEE International Conference on Web Services, ICWS 2013, pp. 332–339 (2013)

Compositional Static Analysis for Implicit Join Synchronization in a Transactional Setting

Thi Mai Thuong Tran[1], Martin Steffen[1], and Hoang Truong[2,*]

[1] Department of Informatics, University of Oslo, Norway
[2] University of Engineering and Technology, VNU Hanoi

Abstract. We present an effect-based static analysis to calculate upper bounds on multithreaded and nested transactions as measure for the resource consumption in an execution model supporting implicit join synchronization. The analysis is compositional and takes into account implicit join synchronizations that arise when more than one thread jointly commit a transaction. Central for a compositional and precise analysis is to capture as part of the effects a tree-representation of the future resource consumption and synchronization points (which we call joining commit trees). The analysis is formalized for a concurrent variant of Featherweight Java extended by transactional constructs. We show the soundness of the analysis.

1 Introduction

Software Transactional Memory (STM) [13,3] has recently been introduced to concurrent programming languages as an alternative for lock-based synchronization, enabling an optimistic form of synchronization for shared memory. *Nested* and *multi-threaded* transactions are advanced features of recent transactional models. Multi-threaded transactions means that inside one transaction there can be more than one thread running in parallel. *Nesting* of transactions means that a parent transaction may contain one or more child transactions which must commit before their parent. Additionally, if a transaction commits, all threads spawned inside must join via a commit. To achieve isolation, each transaction operates via reads and writes on its own local copy of the memory, called log. It is used to record these operations to allow validation or potentially rollbacks at commit time. The logs are a critical factor of memory resource consumption of STM. As each transaction operates on its own log of the variables it accesses, a crucial factor in the memory consumption is the number of thread-local transactional memories (i.e., logs) that may co-exist at the same time in parallel threads. Note that the number of logs neither corresponds to the number of transactions running in parallel (as transactions can contain more than one thread) nor to the number of parallel threads, because of the nesting of transactions. A main complication is that parallel threads do not run independently; instead, executing a commit in a transaction may lead to a form of implicit *join synchronization* with other threads inside the same transaction.

---

* This work was partly supported by the research Project QG.11.29, Vietnam National University, Hanoi.

R.M. Hierons, M.G. Merayo, and M. Bravetti (Eds.): SEFM 2013, LNCS 8137, pp. 212–228, 2013.

In this paper, we develop a type and effect system for statically approximating the resource consumption in terms of the maximum number of logs of a program. It can be more generally understood as a compositional static analysis of a concurrency model with implicit join synchronization. For the concrete formulation of the analysis, we use a variant of Featherweight Java extended with transactional constructs known as Transactional Featherweight Java (TFJ) [9]. The language features non-lexical starting and ending a transaction, concurrency, choice and sequencing. The analysis is compositional, i.e., syntax-directed. The analysis is *multi-threaded* in that, due to synchronization, it does not analyze each thread in isolation, but needs to take their interaction into account. This complicates the effect system considerably, as the synchronization is implicit in the use of commit-statements and connected to the nestedness of the transactions. To our knowledge, the issue of statically and compositionally estimating the memory resource consumption in such a setting has not been addressed.

The rest of the paper is structured as follows. Section 2 starts by illustrating the execution model and sketching the technical challenges in the design of the effect system. Section 3 introduces the syntax and operational semantics. Section 4 presents an effect system for estimating the resource consumption. The soundness of the analysis is sketched in Section 5. We conclude in Section 6 with related and future work.

2 Compositional Analysis of Implicit Join Synchronization

We start by sketching the concurrency model with nested and multi-threaded transactions. The consequences for a compositional analysis of the memory resource consumption are presented informally and by way of examples.

Example 1 (Joining commits). Consider the following (contrived) code snippet.

```
1    onacid;                                    // thread 0 (main thread)
2      onacid;
3        spawn (e₁;commit;commit);              // thread 1
4        onacid;
5          spawn (e₂;commit;commit;commit);     // thread 2
6        commit;
7        e₃
8      commit;
9      e₄;
```

The main expression of thread 0 spawns two new threads 1 and 2. The onacid-statement expresses the start of a transaction and commit the end. Hence, thread 1 starts its execution at a nesting depth of 2 and thread 2 at depth 3. See also Fig. 1a, where the values of n represent the nesting depth of open transactions at different points in the main thread. We often write in the illustrations and examples [and] for starting resp. committing a transaction. Note that e.g. thread 1 is executing *inside* the first two transactions started by its parent thread and that it uses two commits (after e_1) to close those transactions. Important is that parent and child thread(s) commit an enclosing transaction at the same time, i.e., in a form of join synchronization. We call an occurrence of a commit-statement which synchronizes in that way a *joining commit*. Fig. 1b makes the nesting of transactions more explicit and the right-hand edge of the corresponding boxes marks the joining commits. E.g., e_2 and e_3 cannot execute in parallel since e_2 is sequentialized by a joining commit before e_3 starts.   □

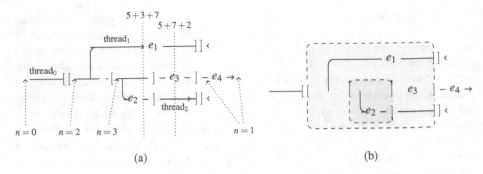

(a)   (b)

Fig. 1. Nested, multi-threaded transactions and join synchronization

Our goal is a compositional, static worst-case estimation of memory resource consumption for the sketched execution model. To achieve isolation, an important transactional property, each thread operates on a local copy of the needed memory which is written back to global memory when and if the corresponding transaction commits; that thread-local and transactional-local memory is called log. We measure the resource consumption at a given point by the *number* of logs co-existing at the same time. This ignores that different logs have different memory needs (e.g., accessing more variables transactionally). Abstracting away from this difference, we concentrate on the synchronization and nesting structure underlying the concurrency model. A more fine-grained estimation of resource consumption per log is an orthogonal issue and the corresponding refinement can be incorporated. The refinement would be based on a conservative estimation of the memory consumption per *individual* transaction, which in turn depends on the resource consumption per variable used in the transaction and potentially, dependent on the transactional model, how many times variables are accessed.

Example 2 (Resource consumption). In Example 1, assume that e_1 opens and closes three nested transactions (i.e., is of the form $[\dots[\dots[\dots]\dots]\dots]\dots)$, e_2 four, e_3 five, and e_4 six. The resource consumption after spawning e_2's thread is at most $15 = 5 + 3 + 7$ (at the left vertical line): the main thread executes inside three transactions, thread 1 inside five (3 from e_1 plus 2 "inherited" from the parent), and thread 2 inside 7. At the point when thread 0 executes e_3, i.e., after its first commit, the worst case is $14 = 5 + 7 + 2$. Note that e_2 cannot run *in parallel* with e_3 whereas e_1 can: the commit before e_3 synchronizes with the commit after e_2 which sequentializes their execution. Thus e_1 still contributes 5, e_2 contributes only 2, and the main thread of e_3 contributes 7 (i.e, 5 from e_3 and 2 from the enclosing transactions). $\qquad\qquad\Box$

To be scalable, the analysis should be *compositional*. In principle, the resource consumption of a *sequential* composition $e_1; e_2$ is approximated by the *maximum* of consumption of its constituent parts. For e_1 and e_2 running (independently) in parallel, the consumption of $e_1 \parallel e_2$ is approximated by the *sum* of the respective contributions. The challenges in our setting are:

Multi-threaded analysis: due to joining commits, threads running in parallel do not necessarily run independently and a sequential composition spawn $e_1; e_2$ does not sequentialize e_1 and e_2. They may synchronize, which introduces sequentialization, and to be precise, the analysis must be aware of which program parts can run in parallel and which cannot. Assuming independent parallelism would allow us to analyze each thread in isolation. Such a single-threaded analysis would still yield a sound over-approximation, but would be too imprecise.

Implicit synchronization: Compositional analysis is rendered intricate as the synchronization is *not* explicitly represented syntactically. In particular, there is no clean syntactic separation between sequential and parallel composition. E.g., writing $(e_1 \parallel e_2); e_3$ would make the sequential separation of $e_1 \parallel e_2$ from e_3 explicit and would make a compositional analysis straightforward. Here instead, the sequentialization constraints are entailed by joining commits and it's not explicitly represented with which other threads, if any, a particular commit should synchronize.

Thus, the model has neither independent parallelism nor full sequentialization, but synchronization is affected by the nesting structure of the multi-threaded transactions.

Example 3. Let us split the code of Example 1 after the first spawn to analyze the two parts, say e_l and e_r independently. Writing m for the effect that over-approximates the memory consumption, a rule for sequential composition could resemble the following:

$$\frac{\vdash e_l :: m_1 \qquad \vdash e_r :: m_2 \qquad m = f(m_1, m_2)}{\vdash e_l; e_r :: m}$$

In the schematic rule, $\vdash e :: m$ is read as "expression e has effect m as interface specification". For compositionality, the "interface" information captured in the effects must be rich enough such that m can be calculated from m_1 and m_2. Especially, the upper bound of the overall resource consumption, i.e., the value we are ultimately interested in, is in itself non-compositional. Consider Fig. 2, which corresponds to Fig. 1a except that we separated the contributions of e_l and e_r (by the surrounding boxes). As the execution of e_l partly occurs *before* e_r and partly *in parallel*, m_1 must distinguish the sequential and the parallel contribution of e_1, i.e., the contribution of the spawned thread. Moreover, the parallel part of m_1 is partly synchronized with e_r by joining commits, and thus the effects must contain information about the corresponding synchronization points. Ultimately, the judgments of the effect system use a six-tuple of information that allows a compositional analysis of sequential and parallel composition (plus the other language constructs). A central part of the effect system to achieve compositional analysis is a tree-representation of the future resource consumption and joining commits, which we call jc-trees.   □

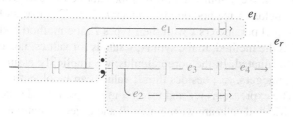

Fig. 2. Compositional analysis (sequential composition $e_l; e_r$)

Table 1. Abstract syntax

$$
\begin{aligned}
P &::= \mathbf{0} \mid P \parallel P \mid p\langle e \rangle & \text{processes/threads} \\
L &::= \text{class } C\{\vec{f}{:}\vec{T};K;\vec{M}\} & \text{class definitions} \\
K &::= C(\vec{f}:\vec{T})\{\text{this}.\vec{f} := \vec{f}\} & \text{constructors} \\
M &::= m(\vec{x}{:}\vec{T})\{e\} : T & \text{methods} \\
e &::= v \mid v.f \mid v.f := v \mid \text{if } v \text{ then } e \text{ else } e \\
&\quad \mid\ \text{let } x{:}T = e \text{ in } e \mid v.m(\vec{v}) & \text{expressions} \\
&\quad \mid\ \text{new } C(\vec{v}) \mid \text{spawn } e \mid \text{onacid} \mid \text{commit} \\
v &::= r \mid x \mid \text{null} & \text{values}
\end{aligned}
$$

3   A Transactional Calculus

Next we present the syntax and semantics of TFJ. We have chosen this calculus as the vehicle for our investigation, as it supports a quite expressive transactional concurrency model, and secondly, it allows us to present the formal semantical analysis in a concise manner. Note, however, that the core of our analysis, i.e., a compositional analysis of concurrent threads with join-synchronization does not depend on the concrete choice of language. TFJ as presented here is, with some adaptations, taken from [9]. The main adaptations, as in [10], are: we added standard constructs such as sequential composition (in the form of the let-construct) and conditionals. Besides that, we did not use evaluation-context based rules for the operational semantics, which simplifies the analysis. The underlying type system (without the effects) is standard and omitted here.

3.1   Syntax

Table 1 shows the abstract syntax of TFJ. A program consists of a number of processes/threads $p\langle e \rangle$ running in parallel, where p is the thread's identifier and e the expression being executed. The empty process is written $\mathbf{0}$. The syntactic category L captures class definitions. In absence of inheritance, a class class $C\{\vec{f}{:}\vec{T};K;\vec{M}\}$ consists of a name C, a list of fields $\vec{f}$ with corresponding type declarations $\vec{T}$ (assuming that all f_i's are different), a constructor K, and a list $\vec{M}$ of method definitions. A constructor $C(\vec{f}{:}\vec{T})\{\text{this}.\vec{f} := \vec{f}\}$ of the corresponding class C initializes the fields of instances of that class, these fields are mentioned as the formal parameters of the constructor. We assume that each class has exactly one constructor, i.e., we do not allow constructor overloading. Similarly, we assume that all methods defined in a class have a different name; likewise for fields. A method definition $m(\vec{x}{:}\vec{T})\{e\} : T$ consists of the name m of the method, the formal parameters $\vec{x}$ with their types $\vec{T}$, the method body e, and finally the return type T of the method. In the syntax, v stands for values, i.e., expressions that can no longer be evaluated. In the core calculus, we implicitly assume standard values like booleans, integers, ...; besides those, values can be object references r, variables x or null. The expressions $v.f$ and $v_1.f := v_2$ represent field access and field update respectively. Method calls are written $v.m(\vec{v})$ and object instantiation is new $C(\vec{v})$.

The next two expressions deal with the basic, sequential control structures: conditionals and sequential composition (represented by the let-construct). The language is multi-threaded: spawn e starts a new thread of activity which evaluates e in parallel with the spawning thread. Specific for TFJ are the two dual constructs onacid and commit. The expression onacid starts a new transaction and executing commit successfully termi-nates a transaction. For a thread spawned inside a transaction, we impose the following restriction: after a joining commit with its parent, the child thread is not allowed to start another transaction. This restriction is imposed to simplify the analysis later and is not a real restriction in practice as one can transform programs easily to adhere to that convention (at the expense of spawning further threads).

3.2 Semantics

The operational semantics of TFJ is given in two different levels: a local and a global one. The local semantics of Table 2 deals with the evaluation of *one expression/thread* and reducing configurations $E \vdash e$. Local transitions are thus of the form $E \vdash e \to E' \vdash e'$, where e is one expression and E a *local environment*. Note that in the chosen presenta-tion, the expression starts uniformly with a let and the redex is always the left expression of the let construct. Locally, the relevant commands only concern the current thread and consist of reading, writing, invoking a method, and creating new objects.

Definition 1 (Local environment). *A* local environment E *of type* LEnv *is a finite sequence of the form* $l_1{:}\rho_1, \dots, l_k{:}\rho_k$, *i.e., of pairs of transaction labels* l_i *and a corre-sponding log* ρ_i. *We write* $|E|$ *for the size of the local environment, i.e., the number of pairs* $l{:}\rho$ *in the local environment.*

Transactions are identified by labels l, and as transactions can be nested, a thread can execute "inside" a number of transactions. So, the E in the above definition is ordered, where e.g. l_k to the right refers to the inner-most transaction, i.e., the one most recently started and committing removes bindings from right to left. For a thread with local environment E, the number $|E|$ represents the nesting depth of the thread, i.e., how many transactions the thread has started but not yet committed. The corresponding *logs* ρ_i can be thought of as "local copies" of the heap. The log ρ_i, a sequence of mappings from references to values, is used to keep track of changes by a thread in transaction l_i.

The first four rules deal straightforwardly with the basic, sequential control flow. Unlike the first four rules, the remaining ones do access the heap. Thus, the local envi-ronment E is consulted to look up object references and then *changed* in the step. The access and update of E is given *abstractly* by corresponding access functions *read*, *write*, and *extend* (which look-up a reference, update a reference, resp. allocate a new reference on the heap). Note that also the *read*-function actually *changes* the environ-ment from E to E' in the step. The reason is that in a transaction-based implementation, read-access to a variable may be *logged*, i.e., remembered appropriately, to be able to detect conflicts and to do a roll-back if necessary. The premises assume that the class table is given implicitly where *fields*(C) looks up fields of class C and *mbody*(C,m) looks up the method m of class C. Otherwise, the rules for field look-up, field update, method calls, and object instantiation are standard.

The rules of the *global* semantics are given in Table 3. The semantics works on configurations of the form $\Gamma \vdash P$, where P is a *program* and Γ is a global environment. Besides that, we need a special configuration *error* representing an error state. Basically, a program P consists of a number of threads evaluated in parallel (cf. Table 1), where each thread corresponds to one expression, whose evaluation is described by the local rules. Now describing the behavior of a number of (labeled) threads or processes $p\langle e \rangle$, we need one E for each thread p. This means, Γ is a "sequence" (or rather a set) of $p{:}E$ bindings where p is the name of a thread and E is its corresponding local environment.

Definition 2 (Global enviroment). *A global environment Γ of type GEnv is a finite mapping, written as $p_1{:}E_1, \ldots, p_k{:}E_k$, from threads names p_i to local environments E_i (the order of bindings plays no role, and each thread name can occur at most once).*

So global steps are of the form:

$$\Gamma \vdash P \Longrightarrow \Gamma' \vdash P' \quad \text{or} \quad \Gamma \vdash P \Longrightarrow error \, . \tag{1}$$

Also the global steps make use of a number of functions accessing and changing the (this time global) environment. As before, some semantical functions are left abstract. However, their *abstract properties* relevant for proving soundness of our analysis are given later in Definition 3 after discussing the global rules. Note further, that two specific implementations of those functions (an optimistic and a pessimistic) have been given in [9]. As the functions' concrete details are irrelevant for our *static* analysis, we refer the interested reader to [9] for possible concretizations of the semantics. Rule G-PLAIN simply *lifts* a local step to the global level, using the reflect-operation, which roughly makes local updates of a thread globally visible; the premise $\Gamma \vdash p{:}E$ means $p{:}E \in \Gamma$. Rule G-SPAWN deals with starting a thread. The next three rules treat the two central commands of the calculus, those dealing with the transactions. The first one G-TRANS covers onacid, which starts a transaction. The *start* function creates a new label l in the local environment E of thread p. The two rules G-COMM and G-COMM-ERROR formalize the successful commit resp. an erronous use of the commit-statement outside any transaction. In G-COMM, l is the label of the transaction

Table 2. Semantics (local)

$E \vdash \texttt{let}\, x : T = v \,\texttt{in}\, e \rightarrow E \vdash e[v/x] \quad \text{R-RED}$

$E \vdash \texttt{let}\, x_2 : T_2 = (\texttt{let}\, x_1 : T_1 = e_1 \,\texttt{in}\, e) \,\texttt{in}\, e' \rightarrow E \vdash \texttt{let}\, x_1 : T_1 = e_1 \,\texttt{in}\, (\texttt{let}\, x_2 : T_2 = e \,\texttt{in}\, e') \quad \text{R-LET}$

$E \vdash \texttt{let}\, x : T = (\texttt{if true then}\, e_1 \,\texttt{else}\, e_2) \,\texttt{in}\, e \rightarrow E \vdash \texttt{let}\, x : T = e_1 \,\texttt{in}\, e \quad \text{R-COND}_1$

$E \vdash \texttt{let}\, x : T = (\texttt{if false then}\, e_1 \,\texttt{else}\, e_2) \,\texttt{in}\, e \rightarrow E \vdash \texttt{let}\, x : T = e_2 \,\texttt{in}\, e \quad \text{R-COND}_2$

$$\frac{read(E,r) = E',C(\vec{u}) \quad fields(C) = \vec{f}}{E \vdash \texttt{let}\, x{:}T = r.f_i \,\texttt{in}\, e \rightarrow E' \vdash \texttt{let}\, x{:}T = u_i \,\texttt{in}\, e} \;\text{R-LOOKUP}$$

$$\frac{read(E,r) = E',C(\vec{r}) \quad fields(C) = \vec{f} \quad write(r \mapsto (C(\vec{r})[f_i \mapsto r']),E') = E''}{E \vdash \texttt{let}\, x{:}T = r.f_i := r' \,\texttt{in}\, e \rightarrow E'' \vdash \texttt{let}\, x{:}T = r' \,\texttt{in}\, e} \;\text{R-UPD}$$

$$\frac{read(E,r) = E',C(\vec{u}) \quad mbody(C,m) = (\vec{x},e)}{E \vdash \texttt{let}\, x{:}T = r.m(\vec{r}) \,\texttt{in}\, e' \rightarrow E' \vdash \texttt{let}\, x : T = e[\vec{r}/\vec{x}][r/\texttt{this}] \,\texttt{in}\, e'} \;\text{R-CALL}$$

$$\frac{r\,fresh \quad E' = extend(r \mapsto C(\vec{u}),E)}{E \vdash \texttt{let}\, x{:}T = \texttt{new}\, C(\vec{u}) \,\texttt{in}\, e \rightarrow E' \vdash \texttt{let}\, x = r \,\texttt{in}\, e} \;\text{R-NEW}$$

Table 3. Semantics (global)

$$\frac{\Gamma \vdash p:E \qquad E \vdash e \to E' \vdash e' \qquad reflect(p,E',\Gamma) = \Gamma'}{\Gamma \vdash P \parallel p\langle e\rangle \Longrightarrow \Gamma' \vdash P \parallel p\langle e'\rangle} \text{ G-PLAIN}$$

$$\frac{p' \text{ fresh} \qquad spawn(p,p',\Gamma) = \Gamma'}{\Gamma \vdash P \parallel p\langle \texttt{let } x:T = \texttt{spawn } e_1 \texttt{ in } e_2\rangle \Longrightarrow \Gamma' \vdash P \parallel p\langle \texttt{let } x:T = \texttt{null in } e_2\rangle \parallel p'\langle e_1\rangle} \text{ G-SPAWN}$$

$$\frac{l \text{ fresh} \qquad start(l,p,\Gamma) = \Gamma'}{\Gamma \vdash P \parallel p\langle \texttt{let } x:T = \texttt{onacid in } e\rangle \Longrightarrow \Gamma' \vdash P \parallel p\langle \texttt{let } x:T = \texttt{null in } e\rangle} \text{ G-TRANS}$$

$$\frac{\begin{array}{c} \Gamma = \Gamma'', p:E \qquad E = E', l:\rho \qquad intranse(\Gamma,l) = \vec{p} = p_1 \dots p_k \\ commit(\vec{p},\vec{E},\Gamma) = \Gamma' \qquad p_1:E_1, p_2:E_2, \dots p_k:E_k \in \Gamma \qquad \vec{E} = E_1, E_2, \dots, E_k \end{array}}{\Gamma \vdash P \parallel \dots \parallel p_i\langle \texttt{let } x:T_i = \texttt{commit in } e_i\rangle \parallel \dots \Longrightarrow \Gamma' \vdash P \parallel \dots \parallel p_i\langle \texttt{let } x:T_i = \texttt{null in } e_i\rangle \parallel \dots} \text{ G-COMM}$$

$$\frac{\Gamma = \Gamma'', p:E \qquad E = \emptyset}{\Gamma \vdash P \parallel p\langle \texttt{let } x:T = \texttt{commit in } e\rangle \Longrightarrow error} \text{ G-COMM-ERROR}$$

to be committed and the function $intranse(\Gamma,l)$ finds the identities $p_1, \dots, p_k$ of all concurrent threads in the transaction l and which *all* join in the commit. In the erroneous case of G-COMM-ERROR, the local environment E is empty; i.e., the thread executes a commit outside of any transaction, which constitutes an error.

Definition 3. *The properties of the abstract functions are specified as follows:*

1. *The function reflect satisfies the following condition: if $reflect(p,E,\Gamma) = \Gamma'$ and $\Gamma = p_1:E_1, \dots, p_k:E_k$, then $\Gamma' = p_1:E_1', \dots, p_k:E_k'$ with $|E_i| = |E_i'|$ (for all i).*
2. *The function spawn satisfies the following condition: Assume $\Gamma = p:E, \Gamma''$ and $p' \notin \Gamma$ and $spawn(p,p',\Gamma) = \Gamma'$, then $\Gamma' = \Gamma, p':E'$ s.t. $|E| = |E'|$.*
3. *The function start satisfies the following condition: if $start(l,p_i,\Gamma) = \Gamma'$ for $\Gamma = p_1:E_1, \dots, p_i:E_i, \dots, p_k:E_k$ and for a fresh l, then $\Gamma' = p_1:E_1, \dots, p_i:E_i', \dots, p_k:E_k$, with $|E_i'| = |E_i| + 1$.*
4. *The function intranse satisfies the following condition: Assume $\Gamma = \Gamma'', p:E$ s.t. $E = E', l:\rho$ and $intranse(\Gamma,l) = \vec{p}$, then*
   (a) *$p \in \vec{p}$ and*
   (b) *for all $p_i \in \vec{p}$ we have $\Gamma = \dots, p_i : (E_i', l:\rho_i), \dots$.*
   (c) *for all threads p' with $p' \notin \vec{p}$ and $\Gamma = \dots, p':(E', l':\rho'), \dots$, we have $l' \neq l$.*
5. *The function commit satisfies the following condition: if $commit(\vec{p}, \vec{E}, \Gamma) = \Gamma'$ for $\Gamma = \Gamma''$, $p:(E, l:\rho)$ and for a $\vec{p} = intranse(\Gamma,l)$ then $\Gamma' = \dots, p_j:E_j', \dots, p_i:E_i', \dots$ where $p_i \in \vec{p}, p_j \notin \vec{p}, p_j:E_j \in \Gamma$, with $|E_j'| = |E_j|$ and $|E_i'| = |E_i| - 1$.*

4   Effect System

Next we present our analysis as an effect system. The underlying types T include names C of classes, basic types B (natural numbers, booleans, etc.) and Void. The underlying type system for judgments of the form $\Gamma \vdash e : T$ ("under type assumptions Γ, expression e has type T") is standard and therefore omitted here.

Thread-local Effects, Sequential Composition, and Joining Commits. On the local level, the judgments of the effect part are of the following form:

$$n_1 \vdash e :: n_2, h, l, \vec{t}, S , \tag{2}$$

where n_1, n_2, h, and l are natural numbers with the following interpretation. n_1 and n_2 are the pre- and post-condition for the expression e, capturing the current nesting depth: starting at a nesting depth of n_1, the depth is n_2 after termination of e. We call the numbers n_1 resp. n_2 the current balance of the thread before and after execution. Starting from the pre-condition n_1, the numbers h and l approximate the maximum resp., the minimum value of the balance *during* the execution of e. Executing e, however, may spawn new child threads and the remaining elements $\vec{t}$ and S take their contribution into account. Roughly speaking, the information S is needed to achieve compositionality wrt. sequential composition and $\vec{t}$ for compositionality wrt. parallel composition.

The S-part represents the resources of threads being spawned in e, more precisely their resource consumption *after* e. S is needed when considering e in a sequential composition with a trailing expression. E.g., in the sequential composition of Figure 2, the S of the left expression corresponds to the part of the left box which overlaps with the trailing expression on the right. Depending on the nesting depth at the point of being spawned, a thread may or may not be synchronized by a joining commit in the trailing expression. E.g., splitting the program of Figure 1a after the second spawn and before the first commit, this commit affects only the thread of e_2 but not the one of e_1. To distinguish the two situations, S must contain, for each thread, the thread's nesting depth at the point it is spawned. Thus, S is of the form $\{(p_1, c_1), (p_2, c_2), \ldots\}$, i.e., a multi-set of pairs of natural numbers. For all spawned threads, S keeps its maximal contribution to the resource consumption at the point after e, i.e., (p_i, c_i) represents that the thread i can have maximally a resource need of $p_i + c_i$, where p_i represents the contribution of the spawning thread ("parent"), i.e., the nesting depth at the point when the thread is being spawned, and c_i the additional contribution of the child threads themselves. In contrast, $\vec{t}$ is needed for compositionality wrt. parallel composition. The $\vec{t}$ is a sequence of non-negative numbers, representing the maximal, overall ("total") resource consumption during the execution of e, including the contribution of all threads (the current and the spawned ones) separated by joining commits of the main thread. We call $\vec{t}$ a joining-commit sequence, or *jc-sequence* for short. In Example 3, the right-hand expression $[\text{spawn } (e_2]]])]e_3]e_4$ has one joining commit, i.e., the jc-sequence is of length 2. Assuming that the execution of the expression starts at nesting depth 2 (as is the case at the end of the left-hand expression) the jc-sequence is $\vec{t} = 10, 7$ (where $10 = ((4+3)+3) \vee ((5+2)+2)$ and $7 = 6+1$). For uniformity, we use $\vee$ resp. $\wedge$ not only for the least upper bound resp. greatest lower bound in general, but also for the maximum, resp. the minimum of natural numbers.

The rules for expressions are shown in Table 4. The rules for variables, the null reference, for field look-up and field update, and for object instantiation are omitted (cf. [11]), as they neither affect the balance nor is any other thread involved. Note that not "counting" the resource consumption of these operations reflects the decision, as stated earlier, that we simply use the number of logs running in parallel as measure for memory consumption. The committing in rule T-COMMIT similarly keeps the maximal value constant. Considered in isolation, the commit is a joining commit, and hence $\vec{t}$ has two elements, where the resource consumption is decreased by one after the commit.

The treatment of sequential composition is more complicated, for the reasons explained in Section 2. In particular, calculating the jc-sequence $\vec{u}$ and the parallel weight S for the composed expression from the corresponding information in the premises is intricate. The following two definitions formalize the necessary calculations:

Definition 4 (Parallel weight). *Let S be a multi-set of the form $\{(p_1,c_1),\dots,(p_k,c_k)\}$ where the p_i, c_i, and l are natural numbers. The overall parallel weight of S is defined as $|S| = \sum_i(p_i + c_i)$. Furthermore we define the following functions:*

$$par(S,l) = \{(p,c) \in S \mid p \le l\} \qquad seq(S,l) = \{(p,c) \in S \mid p > l\}. \qquad (3)$$
$$\lfloor S \rfloor_l = \{(l,0),(l,0),\dots\} \qquad S \downarrow_l = par(S,l) \cup \lfloor seq(S,l) \rfloor_l$$

where for $\lfloor S \rfloor_l$, the number of tuples in S equals the number of $(l,0)$ in $\lfloor S \rfloor_l$.

To determine S in T-LET, the spawned weight S_1 of e_1 is split into two halves:

1. The part $par(S_1,l_2)$ of S_1 unaffected by a commit in e_2 and thus able to run in parallel with e_2.
2. The part $seq(S_1,l_2)$ of S_1 affected by a commit in e_2 via a join synchronization.

The parallel weight S_1 of e_1 is a multi-set of pairs (p_i, c_i), one pair for each spawned thread, where the first element p_i of the pair represents the balance of the parent thread at the time of the spawning, i.e., the nesting depth inherited from the parent thread. Whether the contribution (p_i, c_i) of a thread spawned in e_1 counts as being composed in parallel or affected by a join synchronization with e_2 depends on whether e_2 does a commit which closes a transaction *containing* the thread of (p_i, c_i). The $par(S_1,l_2)$ consists of the half of S_1 unaffected by any join synchronization. Even if $seq(S_1,l_2)$ in contrast synchronizes via joining commits in e_2, it still contributes to the resource consumption *after* e_2, because transactions may be nested, and after the joining synchronization, the rest of a spawned thread still consumes resources corresponding to the not-yet-committed parent transactions. The operation $\lfloor seq(S_1,l_2) \rfloor_{l_2}$ calculates that remaining contribution. So $\lfloor S_1 \rfloor_{l_2}$ contains the consumption *after* e_1 of threads spawned *during* e_1. In the conclusion of T-LET, that estimation is added to e_2's own contribution S_2 by multi-set union, resulting in $S_1 \downarrow_{l_2} \cup S_2$ overall. The correctness of the calculation in T-LET depends on the restriction that once a spawned thread commits a transaction inherited from its parent thread, it will not open another transaction. Note, however, that corresponds to the standard semantics of the explicit join-construct, e.g., in Java, letting the caller wait for the termination of the thread it intends to "join".

Definition 5 (Sequential composition of jc-sequences). *Let $\vec{s} = s_0,\dots,s_k$, $\vec{t} = t_0,\dots,t_m$, and $m \ge p \ge 0$. Then $\vec{s} \oplus_p \vec{t}$ is defined as: $\vec{s} \oplus_p \vec{t} = s_0,\dots,(s_k \vee t_0 \dots \vee t_p),t_{p+1},\dots,t_m$. Given a parallel weight S and a $n \ge m \ge 0$, then $\oslash_n$ is defined as $S \oslash_n \vec{t} = t_0',t_1',\dots,t_m'$ where $t_0' = t_0 + |S|$, $t_1' = t_1 + |\lfloor S \rfloor_{n-1}|$, $\dots$, $t_m' = t_m + |\lfloor S \rfloor_{n-m}|$.*

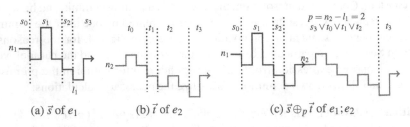

Fig. 3. Sequential composition of jc-sequences (cf. Definition 5)

The compositional calculation of the jc-sequence $\vec{u}$ (cf. Definition 5) takes care of two phenomena: Firstly, the parallel weight S_1 at the end of e_1 may increase the resource consumption of the jc-sequence $\vec{t}$. This is formalized by the $\ominus\_$ operation of Definition 5. Secondly, joining commits of e_2 may no longer be joining commits of the composed expression $\texttt{let } x = e_1 \texttt{ in } e_2$. For instance, in Example 3, the (only) joining commit of e_r (the one separating e_3 from e_4) is no longer a joining commit of $e_l; e_r$, as it cannot synchronize with anything outside the composed expression. The calculation of the composed jc-sequence from the constituent ones as $\vec{s} \oplus_p \vec{t}$ "merges" an appropriate number of elements from $\vec{t}$ (using $\vee$) depending on how many joining commits disappear in the composition. This number p is given by $n_2 - l_1$. See also the illustration in Fig. 3, where the respective joining commits are indicated by the vertical, dotted lines. So in rule T-LET, the overall $\vec{u}$ is given as $\vec{s} \oplus_p (S_1 \ominus_{n_2} \vec{t})$. The calculation of the remaining effects in T-LET is straightforward: given the balance n_1 as pre-condition, the post-condition n_2 of e_1 serves as pre-condition for the subsequent e_2, whose post-balance n_3 gives the corresponding final post-balance. The values h and l are calculated by the least upper bound, resp., the greatest lower bound of the corresponding numbers of e_1 and e_2. The treatment of h, l, and of the current balance is simple because the syntax of sequential composition reflects and separates the contributions of e_1 and e_2.

The treatment of conditionals in rule T-COND is comparatively simple, after having defined an appropriate order on the jc-sequences and the parallel weights.

Table 4. Effect system

$$\frac{}{n \vdash \texttt{onacid} :: n+1, n+1, n, [n+1], \emptyset} \text{ T-ONACID} \qquad \frac{n \geq 1}{n \vdash \texttt{commit} :: n-1, n, n-1, [n; n-1], \emptyset} \text{ T-COMMIT}$$

$$\frac{n_1 \vdash e_1 :: n_2, h_1, l_1, \vec{s}, S_1 \qquad n_2 \vdash e_2 :: n_3, h_2, l_2, \vec{t}, S_2}{h = h_1 \vee h_2 \qquad l = l_1 \wedge l_2 \qquad p = n_2 - l_1 \qquad S = S_1 \Downarrow_{l_2} \cup S_2 \qquad \vec{u} = \vec{s} \oplus_p (S_1 \ominus_{n_2} \vec{t})}{n_1 \vdash \texttt{let } x{:}T = e_1 \texttt{ in } e_2 :: n_3, h, l, \vec{u}, S} \text{ T-LET}$$

$$\frac{n \vdash e_1 :: n', h_1, l_1, \vec{s}, S_1 \qquad n \vdash e_2 :: n', h_2, l_2, \vec{t}, S_2}{n \vdash \texttt{if } v \texttt{ then } e_1 \texttt{ else } e_2 :: n', h_1 \vee h_2, l_1 \wedge l_2, \vec{s} \vee \vec{t}, S_1 \sqcup S_2} \text{ T-COND} \qquad \frac{n_1 \vdash e :: 0, h, 0, \vec{s}, S}{n_1 \vdash \texttt{spawn } e :: n_1, n_1, n_1, [n_1 + s_0], S \cup \{(n_1, h - n_1)\}} \text{ T-SPAWN}$$

$$\frac{mtype(C, m) :: n'_1 \to n'_2, h, l, \vec{t}, S \qquad n'_1 \leq n_1 \qquad n = n_1 - n'_1}{n_1 \vdash v.m(\vec{v}) :: n'_2 + n, h + n, l + n, \vec{t} + n, S + n} \text{ T-CALL}$$

Definition 6 (Order). *The order relation on jc-sequences (of equal length)* $\vec{s} \le \vec{t}$ *is defined pointwise and we write* $\vec{s} \vee \vec{t}$ *for the corresponding least upper bound. For parallel weights, the order* $S_1 \sqsubseteq S_2$ *is defined as follows. For pairs of natural numbers and in abuse of notation,* $(p_1, c_1) \sqsubseteq (p_2, c_2)$ *iff* $p_1 = p_2$ *and* $c_1 \le c_2$. *Then for* $S_1 = \{(p_1, c_1), \ldots, (p_k, c_k)\}$ *and* $S_2 = \{(p'_1, c'_1), \ldots, (p'_k, c'_k), (p'_{k+1}, c'_{k+1}), \ldots\}$, $S_1 \sqsubseteq S_2$ *if* $(p_i, c_i) \sqsubseteq (p'_i, c'_i)$, *for all* $1 \le i \le k$. *We write* $S_1 \sqcup S_2$ *for the corresponding least upper bound of* S_1 *and* S_2 *wrt.* $\sqsubseteq$.

When spawning a new thread e (cf. rule T-SPAWN), the pre-condition n_1 remains unchanged, as the effect of e as determined by the premise does not concern the current, i.e., spawning thread. Likewise, the maximal and minimal value are simply n_1, as well. The jc-sequence of total resource consumption takes into account the contribution s_0 of the spawned thread before *its* first joining commit plus the resource consumption n_1 of the current thread. Finally, the parallel weight S of the spawned expression is increased by the maximal value h of e's thread, where that contribution is split into the "inherited" part n_1 and the rest $h - n_1$. The effect of a method call $v.m(\vec{v})$ (cf. T-CALL) is given by the interface information of method m in class C appropriately increased by the difference n of the balance n_1 at the call-site and the specified pre-condition n'_1; the interface information for the method is looked up using *mtype* in the given class table (the function is standard and its definition is omitted here). The appropriate adaptation of the interface information concerning $\vec{t}$ and S is defined as follows:

Definition 7 (Shift). *Given a natural number* n, *the addition* $\vec{t} + n$ *on a jc-sequence* $\vec{t}$ *is defined point-wise. For parallel weights* $S = \{(p_1, c_1), \ldots, (p_k, c_k)\}$, $S + n$ *is defined as* $\{(p_1 + n, c_1), \ldots, (p_k + n, c_k)\}$.

Global Effects, Parallel Composition, and Joining Commit Trees. The rest of the section is concerned with formalizing the resource analysis on the global level, in essence, capturing the parallel composition of threads (cf. Table 5 below). The key is again to find an appropriate representation of the resource effects which is compositional wrt. parallel composition. At the local level, one key was to capture the synchronization point of a thread in what we called *jc-sequences*. Now that more than one thread is involved, that data-structure is generalized to *jc-trees* which are basically finitely branching, finite trees where the nodes are labeled by a transaction label and an integer. With t as jc-tree, the judgments at the global level are of the following form: $\Gamma \vdash P :: t$.

Definition 8 (Jc-tree). *Joining commit trees (or jc-trees for short) are defined as tree of type* JCtree = Node of Nat × Lab × (List of JCtree), *with typical element* t. *We write* $\vec{t}$ *for lists of jc-trees. We write also* [] *for the empty list, and* Node$(n, l, \vec{t})$ *for a jc-tree whose root carries the natural number* n *as weight and* l *as label, and with children* $\vec{t}$.

Definition 9 (Weight). *The* weight *of a jc-tree is given inductively as* $|\text{Node}(n, l, \vec{t})| = n \vee \sum_{i=1}^{|\vec{t}|} (|t_i|)$. *The initial* weight *of a join tree* t, *written* $|t|_1$, *is the weight of its leaves.*

Definition 10 (Parallel merge). *We define the following two functions* $\otimes_1$ *of type* JCtree $\times$ JCForest $\to$ JCForest *and* $\otimes_2$ *of type* JCForest^2 $\to$ JCForest *by mutual induction. In abuse of notation, we will write* $\otimes$ *for both in the following.*

$$t \otimes_1 [] = [t]$$
$$\text{Node}(n_1, l, f_1) \otimes_1 (\text{Node}(n_2, l, f_2) :: f) = \text{Node}(n_1 + n_2, l, f_1 \otimes_2 f_2) :: f$$
$$\text{Node}(n_1, l_1, f_1) \otimes_1 (\text{Node}(n_2, l_2, f_2) :: f) = \text{Node}(n_2, l_2, f_2) :: (\text{Node}(n_1, l_1, f_1) \otimes_1 f) \qquad l_1 \neq l_2$$

$$[] \otimes_2 f = f$$
$$t :: f_1 \otimes_2 f_2 = f_1 \otimes_2 (t \otimes_1 f_2)$$

Remember from Definition 1, that local environments are of the form $l_1{:}\rho_1, \ldots, l_k{:}\rho_k$. In the semantics, the transaction labelled l_k is the inner-most one.

Definition 11 (Lifting). *The function lift of type* $LEnv \times \text{Nat}^+ \to$ JCtree *is given inductively as:*

$$lift([], [n]) = \text{Node}(n, \bot, [])$$
$$lift((l{:}\rho :: E), \vec{s} :: n) = \text{Node}(n, l, [lift(E, \vec{s})]) .$$

Note that the function is undefined if $|E| \neq |\vec{s}| - 1$. It is an invariant of the semantics, that $|E| = |\vec{s}| - 1$, and hence the function is well-defined for all reachable configurations. Defining the weight (and in abuse of notation) of a jc-sequence $\vec{s}$ as the maximum of their elements, we obviously have $|\vec{s}| = |lift(E, \vec{s})|$.

Table 5. Effect system

$\dfrac{\lvert E\rvert \vdash e :: n, h, l, \vec{s}, S \quad t = lift(E, \vec{s})}{p{:}E \vdash p\langle e\rangle :: t}$ T-THREAD	$\dfrac{\Gamma_1 \vdash P_1 : t_1 \quad \Gamma_2 \vdash P_2 : t_2}{\Gamma_1, \Gamma_2 \vdash P_1 \parallel P_2 : t_1 \otimes_2 t_2}$ T-PAR

5   Correctness

This section establishes the soundness of the analysis, i.e., that the static estimation over-approximates the actual potential resource consumption for all reachable configurations. We start by defining the actual resource consumption of a program:

Definition 12 (Resource consumption). *The weight of a local environment E, written $|E|$ is defined as its length, i.e., the number of its $l{:}\rho$-bindings. The weight of a global environment Γ, written $|\Gamma|$ is defined as the sum of weights of its local environments.*

The following lemmas establish a number of facts about the operations used in the calculation of resource consumption needed later. The proofs, omitted here for lack of space, can be found in the technical report [11]. The next two lemmas show that the way the resource consumption is calculated in the let-rule is associative, which is a crucial ingredient in subject reduction.

Lemma 1 (Associativity of parallel weight). *Let S_1, S_2 be parallel weights and l be a non-negative natural number. Define the function f as $f(S_1, l, S_2) = S_1 \downarrow_l \cup S_2$. Then $f(f(S_1, l_2, S_2), l_3, S_3) = f(S_1, l_2 \wedge l_3, f(S_2, l_3, S_3))$.*

Lemma 2 (Associativity of $\oplus$ and $\ominus$). *Let $l_1 = n_1 - |s| + 1$, $l_2 = n_2 - |\vec{t}| + 1$, $p_1 = n_2 - l_1$, and $p_2 = n_3 - l_2$. Then $\vec{s} \oplus_{p_1} (S_1 \ominus_{n_2} (\vec{t} \oplus_{p_2} (S_2 \ominus_{n_3} \vec{u}))) = (\vec{s} \oplus_{p_1} (S_1 \ominus_{n_2} \vec{t})) \oplus_{p_2} ((S_2 \cup S_1 \downarrow_{l_2}) \ominus_{n_3} \vec{u})$.*

The order on trees is defined "point-wise" in that the smaller tree must be a sub-tree (respecting the labelling) of the larger one and furthermore each node of the smaller tree with weight w_1 is represented by the corresponding node with a weight $w_2 \geq w_1$.

Definition 13 (Order on trees). *We define the binary relation $\leq$ on jc trees inductively as follows: $\mathsf{Node}(n, l, \vec{s}) \leq \mathsf{Node}(m, l, \vec{t})$ if $n \leq m$ and for each tree s_i in $\vec{s}$, there exists a t_j in $\vec{t}$ such that $s_i \leq t_j$. (Note that the labels l in a jc tree are unique.)*

Lemma 3 (Lifting of ordering). *If $\vec{s} \leq \vec{t}$ (as comparison between jc-sequences), then $\mathsf{lift}(E, \vec{s}) \leq \mathsf{lift}(E, \vec{t})$ (as comparison between jc trees).*

Lemma 4 (Lifting and commit). $\mathsf{lift}(E, l{:}\rho, n :: \vec{u}) \geq \mathsf{lift}(E, \vec{u})$.

Lemma 5 (Monotonicity). *If $t_1 \leq t_1'$ and $t_2 \leq t_2'$, then $(t_1 \otimes t_2) \leq (t_1' \otimes t_2')$.*

Next we prove preservation of well-typedness under reduction, i.e., subject reduction, split into two parts, preservation under local resp. global reduction steps.

Lemma 6 (Subject reduction (local)). *If $n_1 \vdash e_1 :: n_2, h_1, l_1, \vec{s}, S_1$ and $E_1 \vdash e_1 \rightarrow E_2 \vdash e_2$, then $n_1 \vdash e_2 :: n_2, h_2, l_2, \vec{t}, S_2$ s.t. $h_2 \leq h_1$, $l_2 \geq l_1$, $\vec{t} \leq \vec{s}$, and $S_2 \sqsubseteq S_1$.*

Lemma 7 (Subject reduction). *If $\Gamma \vdash P :: t$ and $\Gamma \vdash P \Longrightarrow \Gamma' \vdash P'$ then $\Gamma' \vdash P' :: t'$ where $t' \leq t$.*

The next lemma states a basic correctness property of our analysis, namely that for well-typed configurations, the actual resource consumption $|\Gamma|$ is over-approximated via the result $|t|$ of the analysis. We prove a slightly stronger statement namely that the actual resource consumption is approximated by the initial weight $|t|_1$.

Lemma 8. *If $\Gamma \vdash P :: t$, then $|\Gamma| \leq |t|_1$.*

The final result as corollary of subject reduction and the previous lemma: the statically calculated result is an over-approximation for all reachable configurations:

Theorem 1 (Correctness). *Given an initial configuration $\Gamma_0 \vdash p_0\langle e_0 \rangle$ and $\Gamma_0 \vdash p_0\langle e_0 \rangle :: t$ (with Γ_0 as empty global context). If $\Gamma_0 \vdash p_0\langle e_0 \rangle \Longrightarrow^* \Gamma \vdash P$, then $|\Gamma| \leq |t|$.*

6 Conclusion

We have formalized a static, compositional effect-based analysis to estimate the resource bounds for a transactional model with nested and multi-threaded transactions. The analysis focuses on transactional memory systems where thread-local copies of memory resources (logs) caused by nested and multi-threaded transactions is our main concern. As usual, the challenge in achieving a sound static analysis lies in obtaining the following three goals at the same time: 1) compositionality, 2) precision, and 3) soundness. Without compositionality, the analysis is guaranteed not to scale for large programs, therefore not usable in practice. Without precision, compositionality and soundness can trivially be achieved by overly abstracting all details and ultimately rejecting all programs as potentially erroneous. Of course without soundness, it is pointless to formally analyze programs. Achieving all three goals in a satisfactory manner requires human ingenuity. In our setting the effect system can, in a *compositional* way, statically approximate the maximum number of logs that co-exist at run-time. This allows to infer the memory consumption of the transactional constructs in the program. To achieve a higher degree of precision in the approximation, it is important to take the underlying concurrency model and its synchronization into account. The main challenge is that the execution model has neither independent parallelism nor full sequentialization. To our knowledge, this is the first static analysis taking care of memory resource consumption for such a concurrency model. Abstracting away from the specifics of memory consumption and the concrete concurrent calculus, the effect system presented here can be seen as a careful, compositional account of a parallel model based on join-synchronization. It is promising to use our compositional techniques as explored here also to achieve different program analyses in a similar manner for programs based on fork/join parallelism. We expect that adapting our techniques to a model with *explicit* join synchronization, as e.g., in Java, leads to a simplification, as the synchronization is syntactically represented in the program code.

Related work. Estimating memory, or more generally, resource usage has been studied, in various other settings. To specify upper bounds for the memory usage of dynamic, recursive data types, the notion of sized types have been introduced in [8]. Their system, a type and effect system as well, certifies a time limit for functional (and single-threaded) programs, relying on annotations by the programmer specifying time limits for each individual function. Hofmann and Jost [6] use a linear type system to compute linear bounds on heap space for a first-order functional language. One significant contribution of this work is the inference mechanism through linear programming techniques. Extensions from linear to polynomial resource bounds are presented in [5] and [4]. [15] deals with a first-order, call-by-value, garbage-collected functional language. Their approach is based on program analysis and model checking and not type-based. For imperative and object-oriented languages Wei-Ngan Chin et al. [2] treat explicit memory management in a core object-oriented language. Programmers have to annotate the memory usage and size relations for methods as well as explicit de-allocation. In [7], Hofmann and Jost combine amortized analysis, linear programming and functional programming to calculate the heap space bound as a function of input for an object oriented language. In [1] the authors present an algorithm to statically compute memory consumption of a method as a non-linear function of the method's parameters. The bounds are not precise. The main difference of our work in comparison to the above related ones is in that we are dealing not only with a multi-threaded analysis —many of the cited works are restricted to sequential languages— but also the complex and implicit synchronization structure entailed by the transactional model. The work in [14], as here, provides resource estimations in a concurrent (component-based) setting. The concurrency model in that work, however, is considerably simpler, as sequential and parallel composition are *explicit* constructs in the investigated calculus. Simpler is also the treatment in [16], which presents an analysis which is which does not treat parallel composition in a compositional manner, i.e., the compositional treatment is single-threaded. As a consequence, in that work, the effects do not capture the tree-like join-synchronization as here, at the expense of compositionality for parallel composition.

Current and future work. We formalized the calculus and the type system in the Coq theorem prover (and using the OTT semantical framework [12]) and are currently working on a formalization of the correctness proof with the longer-term goal to use Coq's program extraction to obtain a formally correct implementation of the effect type system. Besides that, we plan to refine the effect system by deriving more detailed information about the logs (e.g. memory cells per log, or number of variables per log and so on) to infer memory consumption more precisely (which is an orthogonal problem, as mentioned). Furthermore, a challenging step is to automatically *infer* interface information concerning the resource consumption for method declarations.

References

1. Braberman, V., Garbervetsky, D., Yovine, S.: A static analysis for synthesizing parametric specifications of dynamic memory consumption. Journal of Object Technology 5(5) (2006)
2. Chin, W.-N., Nguyen, H.H., Qin, S.C., Rinard, M.: Memory usage verification for OO programs. In: Hankin, C., Siveroni, I. (eds.) SAS 2005. LNCS, vol. 3672, pp. 70–86. Springer, Heidelberg (2005)
3. Harris, T., Larus, J.R., Rawja, R.: Transactional Memory, 2nd edn. Morgan & Claypool (2010)
4. Hoffmann, J., Aehlig, K., Hofmann, M.: Multivariate amortized resource analysis. In: Proceedings of POPL 2011. ACM (January 2011)
5. Hoffmann, J., Hofmann, M.: Amortized resource analysis with polynomial potential. A static inference of polynomial bounds for functional programs. In: Gordon, A.D. (ed.) ESOP 2010. LNCS, vol. 6012, pp. 287–306. Springer, Heidelberg (2010)
6. Hofmann, M., Jost, S.: Static prediction of heap space usage for first-order functional programs. In: Proceedings of POPL 2003. ACM (January 2003)
7. Hofmann, M., Jost, S.: Type-based amortised heap-space analysis. In: Sestoft, P. (ed.) ESOP 2006. LNCS, vol. 3924, pp. 22–37. Springer, Heidelberg (2006)
8. Hughes, J., Pareto, L., Sabry, A.: Proving the correctness of reactive systems using sized types. In: Proceedings of POPL 1996. ACM (January 1996)
9. Jagannathan, S., Vitek, J., Welc, A., Hosking, A.: A transactional object calculus. Science of Computer Programming 57(2) (August 2005)
10. Mai Thuong Tran, T., Steffen, M.: Safe commits for Transactional Featherweight Java. In: Méry, D., Merz, S. (eds.) IFM 2010. LNCS, vol. 6396, pp. 290–304. Springer, Heidelberg (2010)
11. Mai Thuong Tran, T., Steffen, M., Truong, H.: Estimating resource bounds for software transactions. Technical report 414, University of Oslo, Dept. of Informatics (December 2011)
12. Sewell, P., Nardelli, F.Z., Owens, S., Peskine, G., Ridge, T., Sarkar, S., Strniša, R.: Ott: Effective tool support for the working semanticist. Journal of Functional Programming 20(1) (2010)

13. Shavit, N., Toitu, D.: Software transactional memory. In: 22nd POPL. ACM (January 1995)
14. Truong, H., Bezem, M.: Finding resource bounds in the presence of explicit deallocation. In: Van Hung, D., Wirsing, M. (eds.) ICTAC 2005. LNCS, vol. 3722, pp. 227–241. Springer, Heidelberg (2005)
15. Unnikrishnan, L., Stoller, S.D., Liu, Y.A.: Optimized live heap bound analysis. In: Zuck, L.D., Attie, P.C., Cortesi, A., Mukhopadhyay, S. (eds.) VMCAI 2003. LNCS, vol. 2575, pp. 70–85. Springer, Heidelberg (2003)
16. Xuan, T.V., Anh, H.T., Mai Thuong Tran, T., Steffen, M.: A type system for finding upper resource bounds of multi-threaded programs with nested transactions. In: ACM Proceedings of the 3rd ACM International Symposium on Information and Communication Technology, SoICT, ACM (2012)

{log} as a Test Case Generator for the Test Template Framework

Maximiliano Cristiá[1], Gianfranco Rossi[2], and Claudia Frydman[3]

[1] CIFASIS and UNR, Rosario, Argentina
cristia@cifasis-conicet.gov.ar
[2] Università degli studi di Parma, Parma, Italy
gianfranco.rossi@unipr.it
[3] LSIS-CIFASIS, Marseille, France
claudia.frydman@lsis.org

Abstract. {log} (pronounced 'setlog') is a Constraint Logic Programming language that embodies the fundamental forms of set designation and a number of primitive operations for set management. As such, it can find solutions of first-order logic formulas involving set-theoretic operators. The Test Template Framework (TTF) is a model-based testing method for the Z notation. In the TTF, test cases are generated from test specifications, which are predicates written in Z. In turn, the Z notation is based on first-order logic and set theory. In this paper we show how {log} can be applied as a test case generator for the TTF. According to our experiments, {log} produces promising results compared to other powerful constraint solvers supporting the Z notation, such as ProB.

1 Seeking a Test Case Generator for the TTF

Model-Based Testing (MBT) attempts to generate test cases to test a program from its specification. These techniques have been proposed for, and applied to, several formal notations such as Z [1], finite state machines and their extensions [2], B [3], algebraic specifications [4], etc. The Test Template Framework (TTF) was first proposed by Stocks and Carrington [1] as a MBT method for the Z notation. Recently, Cristiá and others provided tool support for the TTF by means of Fastest [5–7], and extended it to deal with Z constructs not included in the original presentation [8] and beyond test case generation [9, 10].

Given a Z specification, the TTF takes each Z operation and partitions its input space in a number of so-called *test specifications*. For the purpose of this paper, it does not really matter how these test specifications are generated because the problem we are approaching here starts once they are given. In this context, a test specification is a conjunction of atomic predicates written in the Z notation. That is, a test specification is a conjunction of atomic predicates involving sets as well as binary relations, functions and partial functions, sequences and other mathematical structures as defined in the Z Mathematical Toolkit (ZMT) [11]. Clearly, a test specification can also be seen as the set of elements satisfying the conjunction of atomic predicates.

R.M. Hierons, M.G. Merayo, and M. Bravetti (Eds.): SEFM 2013, LNCS 8137, pp. 229–243, 2013.
© Springer-Verlag Berlin Heidelberg 2013

According to the TTF, a *test case* is an element belonging to a test specification. In other words, a test case is a witness satisfying the predicate that characterizes a test specification. Hence, in order to find a test case for a given test specification it is necessary to find a solution for a Z formula. When Fastest was first implemented (early 2007) a rough, simple satisfiability algorithm was implemented, which proved to be reasonable effective and efficient [5, 7]. However, this algorithm tends to be slow on complex test specifications. Furthermore, given the advances in the field of tools such as SMT Solvers [12] and Constraint Solvers [13, 14] it is worth to evaluate them as test case generators for the TTF since this is a clear application for them.

In [16] we have analyzed the application of SMT Solvers for this task. Concerning the TTF and the way it works, our results with SMT Solvers were not entirely satisfactory since these tools found just a few test cases. It is important to observe that the ZMT defines some mathematical concepts in a different way with respect to SMT Solvers. For example, in the ZMT the set of functions is included in the set of partial functions, which is included in the type of binary relations, which in turn is the power set of any cross product. SMT Solvers usually do not define the concept of partial functions but only total functions, and in that case they are primitive objects (i.e. they are not defined as sets of ordered pairs). This makes it difficult to use these tools for the TTF.

In this paper we extend our analysis to two Constraint Solvers, namely ProB [17] and $\{log\}$ [18, 19]. $\{log\}$ is a Constraint Logic Programming (CLP) language that embodies the fundamental forms of set designation and a number of primitive operations for set management; and ProB is an animator and model checker, featuring constraint solving capabilities, for the B-Method but also accepting a significant subset of the Z notation. Both ProB and $\{log\}$ natively support sets and set-theoretic operations.

In order to apply these solvers to the problem of finding test cases from test specifications within the TTF it is necessary to define an encoding of (at least a significant portion of) the ZMT into the input languages of the solvers. While the embedding of the ZMT into ProB turns out to be quite natural, the embedding of the ZMT into $\{log\}$ has not been investigated before.

Thus, an original contribution of this paper is to show how $\{log\}$ can be adapted to work with concepts and operators defined in the ZMT and how the latter can be embedded into the former. Furthermore, we present the results of an empirical assessment of $\{log\}$ and ProB used as test case generators for the TTF, in which we compare the effectiveness and efficiency of both systems in finding solutions (i.e. test cases) out of a number of satisfiable test specifications. While both $\{log\}$ and ProB show good performances when compared with Fastest, it seems that the former, with the proposed extensions, can get better results than the latter as regards the specific application taken into account (i.e. it finds more test cases in less time).

The encoding of the ZMT into $\{log\}$, plus the results of the empirical assessment and those presented in [16], may have a non trivial impact on tools for notations such as VDM, B and even TLA+ and Alloy. In effect, all of these notations are based on similar set theories and, thus, can benefit from the encoding presented here since their users can use {*log*} as a satisfiability solver or a specification animator.

This paper assumes the reader is familiar with the mathematics underlying either Z or B and with general notions of formal software verification. Sections 2 and 3 introduce the TTF and {*log*}, respectively. In Section 4 we show the modifications and extensions introduced in {*log*} to make it more suitable as a test case generator for the TTF. Section 5 presents an encoding of a significant portion of the ZMT into the input language of {*log*}. The results of an empirical assessment comparing {*log*} and ProB are shown in Section 6. Finally, in Sections 7 and 8 we discuss the results shown in this paper and give our conclusions.

2   Test Cases in the TTF

In the TTF, test cases are derived from test specifications. The work presented in this paper starts once test specifications have been generated, making it unnecessary to explain the process to get them. Test specifications are sets satisfying predicates that depend on input and state variables. In the TTF, both test specifications and test cases are described in Z by means of schemata. For example, the first schema in Fig. 1 corresponds to a test specification borrowed from one of our case studies, which is a Z specification of a real satellite software. In the figure, $BYTE$ is a given type (i.e. uninterpreted sort) and $DTYPE ::= SD | HD | MD$. Observe that although mem does not participate in $TransmitSD_{24}^{SP}$, a test case generator must be able to bind to it a set of 1024 ordered pairs representing a function. The second schema in Figure 1 is a test case (generated by {*log*}) for $TransmitSD_{24}^{SP}$. Note how the TTF uses schema inclusion to link test cases with test specifications.

Although this example does not use partial functions nor sequences, these features are heavily used in Z specifications and the TTF works with them. Hence, many of the test specifications used in our empirical assessment include partial functions and sequences, and other set operators as well. Any tool that could be used as test case generator for the TTF should be able to deal with such mathematical objects. Note that the problem here is not the logic structure of the test specification (it is just a conjunction of atomic predicates), but rather the ability to manage efficiently such mathematical objects.

$TransmitSD_{24}^{SP}$ is a satisfiable test specification. However, the TTF tends to generate many unsatisfiable test specifications. Fastest implements a test specification pruning method that proved to be effective, efficient and easily extensible [6, 7]. Hence, we are more concerned in finding a better test case generator rather than a replacement for the pruning method.

3   Solving Set Formulas with {*log*}

{*log*} [18–20] is a CLP language that extends Prolog with general forms of set data structures and basic set-theoretic operations in the form of primitive

$\underline{\quad TransmitSD_{24}^{SP}}$ _____

$c, t : DTYPE \to \mathbb{N}; \; mem : 1 \mathinner{.\,.} 1024 \to BYTE; \; sdwp : \mathbb{N}$

$c \; SD = 0 \land sdwp < 3 \land 33 \mathinner{.\,.} 160 \neq \varnothing$

$33 + (t \; SD - c \; SD) * 2 \mathinner{.\,.} 33 + (t \; SD - c \; SD + 1) * 2 \neq \varnothing$

$33 \mathinner{.\,.} 160 \cap 33 + (t \; SD - c \; SD) * 2 \mathinner{.\,.} 33 + (t \; SD - c \; SD + 1) * 2 \neq \varnothing$

$\neg \; 33 \mathinner{.\,.} 160 \subseteq 33 + (t \; SD - c \; SD) * 2 \mathinner{.\,.} 33 + (t \; SD - c \; SD + 1) * 2$

$\neg \; 33 + (t \; SD - c \; SD) * 2 \mathinner{.\,.} 33 + (t \; SD - c \; SD + 1) * 2 \subseteq 33 \mathinner{.\,.} 160$

$33 + (t \; SD - c \; SD) * 2 \mathinner{.\,.} 33 + (t \; SD - c \; SD + 1) * 2 \neq 33 \mathinner{.\,.} 160$

$\underline{\quad TransmitSD_{24}^{TC}}$ _____

$TransmitSD_{24}^{SP}$

$c = \{ sd \mapsto 0, hd \mapsto 1, md \mapsto 2 \}$

$t = \{ sd \mapsto 63, hd \mapsto 0, md \mapsto 1 \}$

$sdwp = 0$

$mem = \{ 1 \mapsto G11084, 2 \mapsto G11116, \ldots \text{ and } 1022 \text{ more elements} \ldots \}$

Fig. 1. Typical test specification and test case in the TTF

constraints. Sets are primarily designated by *set terms*, that is, terms of one of the forms: {}, whose interpretation is the empty set, or $\{t_1, \ldots, t_n \mid s\}$, where s is a set term, whose interpretation is the set $\{t_1\} \cup \{t_2\} \cup \cdots \cup \{t_n\} \cup s$. The kind of sets that can be constructed in $\{log\}$ are the so-called *hereditarily finite sets*, that is finitely nested sets that are finite at each level of nesting. For example,

$$\{1,2,3\}, \; \{X,\{\{\},\{a\}\},\{\{\{b\}\}\}\}, \; \text{and} \; \{X \mid S\}$$

are all admissible set terms. Note that properties of the set constructor, namely permutativity and right absorption, allow the order and repetition of elements in the set term to be immaterial. Thus, for example, the set terms $\{1,1,2\}$, $\{2,1\}$, and $\{1,2\}$ all denote the same set composed of two elements, 1 and 2. Note that similarly to Prolog's lists, a set $\{t_1, \ldots, t_n \mid s\}$ can be partially specified, in that either some of its elements $t_1, \ldots, t_n$ or the remaining part s can contain unbound variables (hence "unknowns").

Sets can be also denoted intensionally by set formers of the form $\{ X : \mathsf{exists}([Y_1, \ldots, Y_n], G) \}$, where G is a $\{log\}$-goal (see below) and $X, Y_1, \ldots, Y_n$ are variables occurring in G. The logical meaning of the intensional definition of a set s is $\forall X (X \in s \leftrightarrow \exists X, Y_1, \ldots, Y_n(G))$. The procedural treatment of an intensional definition in $\{log\}$, however, is based on set grouping (see, e.g., [21]): collect in the set s all instances of X satisfying G for some instantiation of $Y_1, \ldots, Y_n$. Thus intensional set formers are always replaced by the corresponding extensional sets. Obviously, this limits the applicability of intensional set formers to cases in which the denoted set is finite and relatively "small".

Finally, sets can be denoted by *interval terms*, that is terms of the form $\mathsf{int}(a,b)$, where a and b are integer constants, whose interpretation is the integer interval $[a, b]$. Differently from intensional sets, however, intervals are not converted to the corresponding extensional sets; rather, constraints dealing with intervals directly work on the endpoints of the intervals.

Basic set-theoretic operations are provided in {*log*} as predefined predicates, and dealt with as constraints. For example, the predicates in and nin are used to represent membership and not membership, respectively, the predicate subset represents set inclusion (i.e., subset(r, s) holds iff $r \subseteq s$ holds), while inters represents the intersection relations (i.e., inters(r, s, t) holds iff $t = r \cap s$). Basically, a {*log*}-*constraint* is a conjunction of such atomic predicates. For example,

```
1 in R & 1 nin S & inters(R,S,T) & T = {X}
```

where R, S, T and X are variables, is an admissible {*log*}-constraint, whose interpretation states that set T is the intersection between sets R and S, R must contain 1 and S must not, and T must be a singleton set.

The original collection of set-based primitive constraints has been extended in [22] to include simple integer arithmetic constraints over Finite Domains as provided by CLP(FD) systems (cf. e.g. [15]). Thus the set of predefined predicates in {*log*} includes predicates to represent the usual comparison relations, such as $<, >, =<$, etc., whereas the set of function symbols includes integer constants and symbols to represent the standard arithmetic operations, such as $+, -, *,$ div, etc. Accordingly, a {*log*}-constraint can be formed by set predicates as well as by integer comparison predicates. For example,

```
inters(R,S,T) & size(T,N) & N =< 2
```

states that the cardinality of $R \cap S$ must be not greater than 2.

The {*log*}-interpreter contains a *constraint solver* that is able to check satisfiability of {*log*}-constraints with respect to the underlying set and integer arithmetic theories. Moreover, when a constraint c holds, the constraint solver is able to compute, one after the other, all its solutions (i.e., all viable assignments of values to variables occurring in c). In particular, automatic labeling is called at the end of the computation to force the assignment of values from their domains to all integer variables occurring in the constraint, leading to a chronological backtracking search of the solution space. For example, the constraint:

```
X in int(1,5) & Y in int(4,10) & inters({X},{Y},R) & X >= Y
```

is proved to be satisfiable and the following three solutions are computed:

```
X = 4, Y = 4, R = {4};   X = 5, Y = 5, R = {5};   X = 5, Y = 4, R = {}.
```

Possibly remaining irreducible constraints are also returned as part of the computed answer for a given constraint. For example, solving the constraint inters({1},{Y},R) will return the two following answers:

```
R = {1}, Y = 1;   R = {}, Y neq 1.
```

Clauses, goals, and programs in {*log*} are defined as usual in CLP. In particular, a {*log*}-*goal* is a formula of the form B_1 & B_2 & ... & B_k, where $B_1, \ldots, B_k$ are either user-defined atomic predicates, or atomic {*log*}-constraints, or disjunctions of either user-defined or predefined predicates, or Restricted Universal Quantifiers (RUQs). Disjunctions have the form G_1 or G_2, where G_1 and G_2 are {*log*}-goals, and are dealt with through nondeterminism: if G_1 fails then the computation backtracks, and G_2 is considered instead. RUQs are atoms of the form forall(X in s, exists($[Y_1, \ldots, Y_n], G$)), where s denotes a set and G is a $\{log\}$-goal containing $X, Y_1, \ldots, Y_n$. The logical meaning of this atom is $\forall X(X \in s \rightarrow \exists Y_1, \ldots, Y_n(G))$, that is G represents a property that all elements of s are required to satisfy. When s has a known value, the RUQ can be used to iterate over s, whereas, when s is unbound, the RUQ allows s to be nondeterministically bound to all sets satisfying the property G. For example, the goal forall(X in S,X in {1,2,3}) will bound S to all possible subsets of the set {1,2,3}. The following is an example of a $\{log\}$ program:

```
is_rel(R) :- forall(P in R, exists([X,Y], P = [X,Y])).
```

```
dom({},{}).
dom({[X,Y]/Rel},Dom) :- dom(Rel,D) & Dom = {X/D} & X nin D.
```

This program defines two predicates, is_rel and dom. is_rel(R) is true if R is a binary relation, that is a set of pairs of the form [X,Y]. dom(R,D) is true if D is the domain of the relation R. The following is a goal for the above program:

```
R = {[1,5],[2,7]} & is_rel(R) & dom(R,D)
```

and the computed solution for D is D = {1,2}. It is important to note that is_rel(R) can be used both to test and to compute R; similarly, dom(R,D) can be used both to compute D from R, and to compute R from D, or simply to test whether the relation represented by dom holds or not.

$\{log\}$ is fully implemented in Prolog and can be downloaded from [20]. It can be used both as a stand-alone interactive interpreter and as a Prolog library within any Prolog program.

4   Improving $\{log\}$ for the TTF

In order to use $\{log\}$ as a test case generator for the TTF we need to shown how (at least) a significant portion of the ZMT can be embedded into $\{log\}$'s language. This requires primarily the definition of new predicates that implement fundamental notions of the ZMT that are not directly supported by $\{log\}$.

The new predicates are defined in a $\{log\}$'s library specially developed for the TTF. They include predicates for checking whether a set is a binary relation or a partial function, for determining the range of a binary relation or the domain of a sequence, for calculating a function on an argument, and so on.

An example of one of such predicates is the predicate is_rel shown in Section 3: is_rel(R) is true if the set R is a binary relation.

As another example, the following clauses restate the usual ZMT definition of a partial function as a $\{log\}$ predicate: is_pfun(F) is true if F is set of ordered pairs where any two of them cannot have the same first component:

```
is_pfun(F) :- forall(P1 in F, forall(P2 in F, nofork(P1,P2))).
```

```
nofork([X1,Y1],[X2,Y2]) :- (X1 neq X2 or (X1 = X2 & Y1 = Y2)).
```

Note that if the the second disjunct in `nofork` is omitted then `is_pfun(F)` can only be used to test if F is a partial function or not, but it cannot be used to build a partial function. In that case, calling `is_pfun(F)` with F unbound, will return only the solution `F = {}` and nothing else. Therefore, the second disjunct in `nofork` is crucial to make {*log*} a test case generator for the TTF.

Other fundamental notions of the ZMT are implemented in a similar manner within the {*log*}-TTF library. The availability of general forms of set designation in {*log*} makes this task relatively easy. However, the procedural behavior of this straightforward approach may turn out to be quite unsatisfactory in many cases.

One of the main problems with this solution is the "generality" of the defined predicates. As a matter of fact, the same predicate can be used either to test or to compute values for its arguments, values can be either completely or partially specified and, in the case of set variables, they can be represented either as sets or as intervals. For example, dom(Rel, Dom) can be used both to compute the domain of a given relation and to compute the relation associated with a given domain This means that, for example, the goal `dom(Rel,int(1,10))` succeeds but it generates through backtracking 10! equivalent solutions—which are permutations of each other—simply because `int(1,10)` is computed as a set. Similarly, that goal but with a bigger interval, e.g. `int(1,1000)`, takes too much time even to compute the first solution. Though abstractly an interval is just a special case of a set, in practice some operations (e.g., iterating over all its elements) can be performed much more efficiently over intervals than over sets.

To overcome these weaknesses we split the definitions of many of the predicates added to support part of the ZMT into different subcases, which are selected according to the different possible instantiations of their parameters. For example, predicate `dom` has now two different subcases:

```
dom1({},{}).
dom1({[X,Y]/R},D) :- D = {X/S} & X nin S & dom1(R,S).

dom2({[A,Y]},D) :- D = int(A,A).
dom2({[A,Y]/R},D) :-
     D = int(A,B) & A < B & A1 is A + 1 & dom2(R,int(A1,B)).
```

The definition of `dom(Rel,Dom)` is modified accordingly so to allow it to select the proper subcase: `dom1` is selected when Dom is either an unbound variable or it is bound to a set; vice versa, `dom2` is selected when Dom is bound to an interval (in both cases, Rel can be either bound or unbound). With these definitions, the goal shown above, `dom(Rel,int(1,1000))`, terminates in a few milliseconds and it generates one solution only.

Moreover, cases in which the presence of unbound variables may lead to a huge number of different solutions are avoided as much as possible by making use of the *delay* mechanism offered by {*log*}. For example,

```
dsubset(S1,S2) :- delay(subset(S1,S2), nonvar(S1)).
```

defines a version of the predicate `subset` that delays execution of `subset(S1,S2)` while S1 is unbound. Thus, for example, given the goal `dsubset(S,int(1,100))` & `S = {0|R}`, where S is an unbound variable, it will be immediately proved to be unsatisfiable since {0|R} is trivially proved to be not a subset of int(1,100), whereas the same goal using subset would cause 2^{100} different solutions for S to be attempted before concluding it is unsatisfiable, leading to unacceptable execution time in practice. Note that, if at the end of the whole computation, a delayed goal is still suspended then it is anyway executed, disregarding its delaying condition.

The second main problem with the straightforward solution presented at the beginning of this section is that often intervals need to be processed even if their endpoints are not precisely known yet. For example, we would like to solve a goal such as subset(int(A1,B1),int(A2,B2)), where some of the interval endpoints A1, A2, B1, B2 are unbound variables. Unfortunately, the current version of {log} does not allow this kind of generality in interval management. As is common in constraint solvers dealing with Finite Domains (e.g., CLP(FD)), interval endpoints in {log} must be integer constants. However, differently from many other solvers, {log} allows intervals to be managed as first-class objects of the language, being intervals just a special case of sets. For example, we can compute the intersection of two intervals, or the union of two intervals, or the union of an interval and a set, and so on. The endpoints of the involved intervals, however, must be known.

To overcome these limitations, at least for those cases that are of interest for our specific application, we define new versions of the primitive constraints dealing with intervals whose endpoints can be unknown. For example, the improved version of constraint subset, called isubset, deals efficiently with the case where both of its arguments are intervals, through the following predicate:

```
intint_subset(S,T) :-
    S=int(I,J) & T=int(K,N) & I =< J & K =< N & I >= K & J =< N.
```

If some endpoints of the involved intervals are unknown, then calling isubset simply causes the proper integer constraints over the endpoints to be posted. Note that we require that in an interval int(a, b), b is always greater or equal than a. We exclude the possibility that int(a, b) with $b > a$ is interpreted as the empty set, which conversely was previously allowed in {log}. In fact, giving this possibility would cause the empty set to have an infinite number of different denotations, which may turn out to be very unpractical when interval endpoints are allowed to be unknown and solutions for them must be computed explicitly. Finally, note that the delayed version of the {log} predicates for the TTF are modified so as to use these improved versions in place of the usual set constraints (e.g., dsubset uses isubset in place of subset).

The improved versions of the set constraints have been added to {log} as user-defined predicates but they will possibly be moved to the interpreter level once a general algorithm for all these special cases is found. As a matter of fact, allowing partially specified sets and intervals with unknown endpoints to be used freely in set constraints requires non-trivial problems to be solved. For instance, even the simple equation int(A, B) = {1, Y, 5, X, 4 | R}, where X, Y, A, B, and R are unbound variables, has no obvious solution. Therefore such kind of generalizations are left for future work.

5   Embedding the ZMT into *{log}*

In this section we present an embedding of the ZMT into *{log}*, in which we extensively exploit the new features added to *{log}* introduced in the previous section. The embedding rules are given as follows:

$$\text{rule name} \frac{Z \ notation}{\{log\} \ \textsf{language}}$$

where the text above the line is some Z term and the text below the line is one or more *{log}* formulas. Some embedding rules are listed in Fig. 2. The rules not shown here can be consulted in [23]. The Z terms are syntactic entities sometimes annotated with their types. For example, in rule seq, X is any type.

$$\mathbb{Z} \frac{\mathbb{Z}}{\textsf{int}(-10^9, 10^9)} \qquad \text{basic types} \frac{[X]}{\textsf{set}(X)} \qquad \text{free types} \frac{X ::= c_1 | \ldots | c_n}{X = \{c_1, \ldots, c_n\}}$$

$$\times \frac{x \mapsto y}{[X, Y]} \qquad \text{seq} \frac{s : \text{seq}\, X}{\textsf{list}(s)} \qquad \mathbb{P} | \mathbb{F} \frac{A : (\mathbb{P} | \mathbb{F}) X}{\textsf{dsubset}(A, X)}$$

$$\leftrightarrow \frac{R : X \leftrightarrow Y}{\textsf{is\_rel}(R)} \qquad \nrightarrow \frac{f : X \nrightarrow Y}{\textsf{is\_pfun}(f)} \qquad \rightarrow \frac{f : X \rightarrow Y}{\textsf{is\_pfun}(f) \ \& \ \textsf{dom}(f, X)}$$

$$\subseteq \frac{A \subseteq B}{\textsf{dsubset}(A, B)} \qquad \nsubseteq \frac{\neg\, A \subseteq B}{\textsf{dnsubset}(A, B)} \qquad \text{apply} \frac{f : X \nrightarrow Y \quad f\, x}{\textsf{apply}(f, X, Y)}$$

$$\# \frac{A : \mathbb{F}\, X \quad \#A}{\textsf{size}(A, N)} \qquad \cap \frac{A \cap B}{\textsf{dinters}(A, B, C)} \qquad \text{dom} \frac{R : X \leftrightarrow Y \quad \text{dom}\, R}{\textsf{dom}(R, D)}$$

Fig. 2. Some typical embedding rules

The embedding rule labeled "basic types" is not really necessary. In effect, given that the elements of basic types have no structure and no properties beyond equality, declaring them in *{log}* is unnecessary because the tool will automatically generate constants as needed. Furthermore, *{log}* will deduce that X is a set if that name participates in a set expression. It should be noted that the constants declared in rule "free types" must all start with a lowercase letter because otherwise *{log}* will regard them as variables. Note that ordered pairs are embedded as Prolog lists of length two. Some rules, such as apply or size, need to introduce fresh variables. In that case, the expression, for instance $f\, x$, is replaced by the new variable. For example, $f\, x > 0$ is embedded as $\textsf{apply}(F, X, Y) \ \& \ Y > 0$. is_rel, is_pfun, dom, dinters, dsubset and apply are predicates included in the *{log}*'s-TTF library.

There are some embedding rules not shown in the figure. Lower-case variables declared in Z are embedded with a name starting with upper-case, since otherwise *{log}* takes them as constants. Given a Z arithmetic expression, each sub-expression is given a name by introducing a new variable which is later used to form the full expression. For example, $x * (y + z)$ is embedded as M is $Y + Z$ & N is $X * M$. In this way, $\{log\}$ can identify common sub-expressions improving its constraint solving capabilities.

This encoding works as long as the following hypotheses are satisfied:

Hypothesis 1. The Z specification has been type-checked and all proof obligations concerning domain checks have been discharged [24].

Hypothesis 2. All the test specifications where a partial function is applied outside its domain have been eliminated by running the pruning algorithm implemented in Fastest.

Hypothesis 3. Domain and ranges of binary relations have been normalized.

We believe these hypothesis are reasonable and easy to achieve. If they are not verified before the translation is performed, the solutions returned by $\{log\}$ may turn out to be inconsistent at the Z level. Hypothesis 3 makes it unnecessary to explicit the domain and range of binary relations because $\{log\}$ will generate a binary relation populated by any terms provided they verify the other predicates in the goal (while normalization introduces domain and ranges as predicates). For example, $R : 1 .. 10 \leftrightarrow X$ is normalized as $R : \mathbb{Z} \leftrightarrow X \wedge \operatorname{dom} R \subseteq 1 .. 10$, which is simply translated as is_rel(R) & dom(R, D) & dsubset$(D, \operatorname{int}(1, 10))$.

Besides, note that the untyped character of $\{log\}$ does not conflict with Z, at least as a test case generator for the TTF. Consider a Z specification with two basic types, X and Y, and the test specification $[A : \mathbb{P} X;\ B : \mathbb{P} Y;\ v : X;\ w : Y \mid v \in A \wedge w \in B]$. When this is translated into $\{log\}$ it becomes: dsubset(A, X) & dsubset(B, Y) & V in A & W in B. Since X and Y are unbound variables, part of a possible solution for this goal could be A = {a}, B = {a}, V = a, W = a. Although in this paper we are concerned only with the translation from Z to $\{log\}$, we want to emphasize that when a test case returned by $\{log\}$ is translated back to Z the types of the variables at the Z level must be considered. For example, the solution above must be translated as $A = \{aX\} \wedge B = \{aY\} \wedge v = aX \wedge w = aY$, where aX and aY are assumed to be constants of type X and Y, respectively, created during the translation by noting that A and B, at the Z level, have different types.

6 Empirical Assessment

In this section we empirically assess $\{log\}$ as a test case generator for the TTF. In order to evaluate its effectiveness and efficiency we compare it with ProB, which is a mainstream tool with constraint solving capabilities for the B notation (which in turn uses a mathematical toolkit similar to the ZMT).

Since Fastest was first implemented, it has been tested and validated with eleven Z specifications, some of which are formalizations of real requirements. For each of them, a number of test specifications are generated. After eliminating those that are unsatisfiable, Fastest tries to find a test case for the remaining ones. However, it fails to find test cases for 154 out of 475 satisfiable test specifications. In [16], we have chosen 68 of these test specifications for which Fastest fails to evaluate different tools as test case generators for the TTF[1]. We consider that these test specifications are representative of the problem at hand since, although they are satisfiable, Fastest was unable to solve them, meaning that they are among the most complex.

In order to evaluate *{log}* and compare it with ProB we make use of this same collection of test specifications. Each specification is translated from Z into the input languages of *{log}* by applying the encoding described in Sect. 5, and to ProB (in this case the encoding is straightforward requiring only a syntactic translation). So far, the translation is done "by hand", since we consider that implementing an automatic translator before having some evidence of what tool is the best test case generator for Fastest could have been a waste of time. At the same time, the manual translation can be as unreliable as an unverified program implementing the translation. To minimize errors in the translations, however, all the test specifications were manually verified by two different persons besides who wrote them. The Z test specifications and their corresponding translations will become test cases for the automatic translator that has been started after the assessment was completed.

These experiments were ran on the following platform: Intel Core™ i5-2410M CPU at 2.30GHz with 4 Gb of main memory, running Linux Ubuntu 12.04 (precise) of 32-bit with kernel 3.2.0-30-generic-pae. *{log}* 4.6.16 over SWI-Prolog 5.8.0 for i386 and ProB 1.3.5-beta14 over SICStus Prolog 4.2.0 (x86-linux-glibc2.7) were used during the experiments. The original Z test specifications and their translation into *{log}* and ProB can be downloaded from http://www.fceia.unr.edu.ar/~mcristia/setlog-ttf.tar.gz. The translation of each test specification is saved in a file ready to be loaded into the corresponding tool. Scripts to run the experiments are also provided. The results can be analyzed with simple **grep** commands.

We ran two experiments for each tool differing in the timeouts set to let the tools to find a solution for each test specification (otherwise they may run forever in some goals). The two timeouts are 1 second and 1 minute. Hence, both tools can return two possible answers: a) the solution for the goal; or b) some error condition like timeout or an indication that the goal cannot be solved due to some limitation of the tool.

The intention of Table 1 is to provide some measure of the complexity and size of each case study from which the 68 test specifications were taken (for more information see [7]). **R/T** means whether the Z specification was written from real requirements or not. **LOZC** stands for lines of Z code in LaTeX mark-up. Columns **State** and **Oper** represent the number of state variables and operations, respectively, defined in each specification. **Unsolved** is the number of satisfiable test specifications that Fastest failed to solve in each case study.

---

[1] We have chosen 68 test specifications out of 154 because the unchosen specifications belong to the same case study, they are all very similar to each other (in many of them only a variable ranging over an enumerated type changes its value leaving the problematic predicates the same), and similar to some of those included in the experiments.

Table 1. Complexity and size of the case studies

N	Case study	R/T	LOZC	State	Oper.	Unsolved
1	Savings accounts (3)	Toy	165	3	6	8
2	Savings accounts (1)	Toy	171	1	5	2
3	Launcher vehicle	Real	139	4	1	8
4	Plavis	Real	608	13	13	29
5	SWPDC	Real	1,238	18	17	12
6	Scheduler	Toy	240	3	10	4
7	Security class	Toy	172	4	7	4
8	Pool of sensors	Toy	46	1	1	1

Table 2 summarizes the results of this empirical assessment. As can be seen, the table is divided in two parts. The first one shows the figures for ProB, and the second those for $\{log\}$. Each part, in turn, is divided into the two experiments ran for each tool. For each experiment the number of solved goals (**Sol**) and unsolved goals (**Uns**) of each case study, are shown. The last row of the table shows the time spent by each tool in processing the 68 goals for each experiment.

As can be seen, these experiments show that $\{log\}$ outperforms ProB in the number of solved goals and in the time spent in doing that. In the 1 second experiment, $\{log\}$ solves 52 goals in 29 seconds while ProB solves 40 in 1 minute, that is a 30% increase in effectiveness and a 50% increase in efficiency. Despite of what Table 2 may suggest, $\{log\}$ does not solve all the goals that ProB does. Indeed, in case studies 4 and 5 both tools discover the same number of test cases but each tool solves goals that the other does not. Combining all the goals solved by both tools, in the 1 minute experiment we get a total of 58 goals solved. This suggests that combining both tools can be beneficial for Fastest and that there

Table 2. Summary of the empirical results

N	ProB				$\{log\}$			
	1 s		1 m		1 s		1 m	
	Sol	Uns	Sol	Uns	Sol	Uns	Sol	Uns
1	7	1	7	1	8		8	
2	1	1	1	1	2		2	
3	8		8		8		8	
4	17	12	17	12	17	12	17	12
5		12	10	2	10	2	10	2
6	2	2	2	2	2	2	4	
7	4		4		4		4	
8	1		1		1		1	
Totals	40	28	50	18	52	16	54	14
Time	1 m 0 s		19 m 40 s		0 m 29 s		13 m 43 s	

are more improvements to add to {*log*}. Note that the tools differ the most in the 1 second experiments, where {*log*} solves 52 goals and ProB 40. This might suggest that {*log*} implements rules that initially narrow the search space better than ProB. The fact that sets in ProB are implemented as Prolog's lists whereas in {*log*} they are first-class objects, might also have a non-negligible impact.

7 Discussion

According to [17], in ProB "sets are represented by Prolog lists" and "any global set of the B machine, ..., will be mapped to a finite domain within SICStus Prolog's CLP(FD) constraint solver". Conversely, {*log*} is based on a well-developed theory of sets and deals with sets and set constraints as first-class entities of the language. Moreover, in order to get better efficiency it combines general set constraint solving with efficient constraint solving over Finite Domains. This combination allows {*log*} to offer various advantages compared to CLP(FD). On the one hand, the presence of very general and flexible set abstractions in {*log*} provides a convenient framework to model problems that are naturally expressed in terms of sets, whereas CLP(FD) may require quite unnatural mappings to integers and sets of integers. On the other hand, the deep combination of the two models, i.e. that of hereditarily finite sets and that of Finite Domains, allows domains in {*log*} to be constructed and manipulated as other sets through general set constraints, rather than having to be completely specified in advance as usual in FD constraint programming. The improvement added to {*log*} for the TTF, which allows intervals to have endpoints with unknown values (see Section 4) is another step ahead with respect to CLP(FD).

The results shown in this paper might indicate that treating sets as first-class objects of a CLP language would be the right choice to further enlarge the class of goals that can be solved in a reasonable time. All this, in turn, might be an indication that sets present fundamental differences with respect to other data structures—such as functions, lists, arrays, etc.—requiring specific theories and algorithms to solve the satisfiability problem of set theory. The results shown in [16] would also indicate that set processing would require a theory such as the one underlying {*log*}, and not those underlying SMT solvers. The previous analysis might partially conflict with [25, 26], since in these papers the authors are able to discharge a number of proof obligations generated in B specifications by encoding its mathematical model in some SMT solvers. However, although dual problems, satisfiability is not exactly the same than proof.

Yet another indication reinforcing the previous analysis is the fact that we have observed that {*log*} might not solve some goals because binary relations, partial functions and lists are not treated as first-class entities. For instance, if a goal requires some partial functions to have different cardinalities, but there is no constraint over their elements, {*log*} may iterate over sets of, say, size one trying with different elements, but not different sizes. If there is a large number of elements it would make {*log*} to run for a long time before finding the solution—if it ever terminates. According to the ZMT, lists and (total and partial) functions are all binary relations. Adding specific constraint solving capabilities for binary relations including concepts such as domain and range could make {*log*} to be more effective in dealing with all of them. So far, as shown in sections 4 and 5, binary relations are treated as sets of ordered pairs, i.e. not as first-class objects.

8   Conclusions

We have shown how {*log*} has been improved to use it as a test case generator for the TTF. An empirical assessment suggests that {*log*} would perform better than ProB, in finding more test cases in less time. After these experiments we can say that {*log*} should be considered as a good constraint solver candidate for Fastest and, probably, for other tools of model-based notations such as Z, B, TLA+, Alloy and VDM, given that they are based on similar set theories.

In the near future we plan to write the translator between Z and {*log*} in order to automatize test case generation in Fastest. Also, we will investigate whether or not binary relations (and thus partial functions, sequences, etc.) should be promoted to first-class objects of the CLP language embodied by {*log*}, so it improves once again its constraint solving capabilities.

Acknowledgments. This work has been partially supported by the GNCS project "Specifiche insiemistiche eseguibili e loro verifica formale", and by AN-PCyT PICT 2011-1002.

References

1. Stocks, P., Carrington, D.: A Framework for Specification-Based Testing. IEEE Trans. on Software Engineering 22(11), 777–793 (1996)
2. Grieskamp, W., Gurevich, Y., Schulte, W., Veanes, M.: Generating finite state machines from abstract state machines. In: ISSTA 2002: Proc. 2002 ACM SIGSOFT Int'l Symp. on Software Testing and Analysis, pp. 112–122. ACM (2002)
3. Legeard, B., Peureux, F., Utting, M.: A Comparison of the BTT and TTF Test-Generation Methods. In: Bert, D., Bowen, J.P., Henson, M.C., Robinson, K. (eds.) ZB 2002. LNCS, vol. 2272, p. 309. Springer, Heidelberg (2002)
4. Bernot, G., Gaudel, M.C., Marre, B.: Software testing based on formal specifications: a theory and a tool. Softw. Eng. J. 6(6), 387–405 (1991)
5. Cristiá, M., Monetti, P.R.: Implementing and Applying the Stocks-Carrington Framework for Model-Based Testing. In: Breitman, K., Cavalcanti, A. (eds.) ICFEM 2009. LNCS, vol. 5885, pp. 167–185. Springer, Heidelberg (2009)
6. Cristiá, M., Albertengo, P., Rodríguez Monetti, P.: Pruning testing trees in the Test Template Framework by detecting mathematical contradictions. In: Fiadeiro, J.L., Gnesi, S. (eds.) SEFM, pp. 268–277. IEEE Computer Society (2010)
7. Cristiá, M., Albertengo, P., Frydman, C., Plüss, B., Monetti, P.R.: Tool support for the Test Template Framework. Software Testing, Verification and Reliability, n/a–n/a (2012), http://dx.doi.org/10.1002/stvr.1477
8. Cristiá, M., Frydman, C.S.: Extending the Test Template Framework to deal with axiomatic descriptions, quantifiers and set comprehensions. In: [27], pp. 280–293

9. Cristiá, M., Plüss, B.: Generating natural language descriptions of Z test cases. In: Kelleher, J.D., Namee, B.M., van der Sluis, I., Belz, A., Gatt, A., Koller, A. (eds.) INLG, pp. 173–177. The Association for Computer Linguistics (2010)
10. Cristia, M., Hollmann, D., Albertengo, P., Frydman, C., Monetti, P.R.: A language for test case refinement in the Test Template Framework. In: Qin, S., Qiu, Z. (eds.) ICFEM 2011. LNCS, vol. 6991, pp. 601–616. Springer, Heidelberg (2011)
11. Saaltink, M.: The Z/EVES mathematical toolkit version 2.2 for Z/EVES version 1.5. Technical report, ORA Canada (1997)
12. Nieuwenhuis, R., Oliveras, A., Tinelli, C.: Solving SAT and SAT modulo theories: From an abstract Davis–Putnam–Logemann–Loveland procedure to DPLL(T). J. ACM 53, 937–977 (2006)
13. Apt, K.R., Fages, F., Rossi, F., Szeredi, P., Váncza, J. (eds.): CSCLP 2003. LNCS (LNAI), vol. 3010. Springer, Heidelberg (2004)
14. Stuckey, P.J., Becket, R., Fischer, J.: Philosophy of the minizinc challenge. Constraints 15(3), 307–316 (2010)
15. Schulte, C., Carlsson, M.: Finite Domain Constraint Programming Systems. In: Rossi, F., van Beek, P., Walsh, T. (eds.) Handbook of Constraint Programming, pp. 493–524. Elsevier (2006)
16. Cristiá, M., Frydman, C.: Applying SMT solvers to the Test Template Framework. In: Petrenko, A.K., Schlingloff, H. (eds.) Proc. 7th Workshop on Model-Based Testing, Tallinn, Estonia, March 25. Electronic Proc. in Theoretical Computer Science, vol. 80, pp. 28–42. Open Publishing Association (2012)
17. Leuschel, M., Butler, M.: ProB: A model checker for B. In: Araki, K., Gnesi, S., Mandrioli, D. (eds.) FME 2003. LNCS, vol. 2805, pp. 855–874 Springer, Heidelberg (2003)
18. Dovier, A., Omodeo, E.G., Pontelli, E., Rossi, G.: A language for programming in logic with finite sets. J. Log. Program. 28(1), 1–44 (1996)
19. Dovier, A., Piazza, C., Pontelli, E., Rossi, G.: Sets and constraint logic programming. ACM Trans. Program. Lang. Syst. 22(5), 861–931 (2000)
20. Rossi, G.: {log}, http://people.math.unipr.it/gianfranco.rossi/ setlog.Home.html (last access)
21. Dovier, A., Pontelli, E., Rossi, G.: Intensional sets in *CLP*. In: Palamidessi, C. (ed.) ICLP 2003. LNCS, vol. 2916, pp. 284–299. Springer, Heidelberg (2003)
22. Palù, A.D., Dovier, A., Pontelli, E., Rossi, G.: Integrating finite domain constraints and clp with sets. In: PPDP, pp. 219–229. ACM (2003)
23. Cristiá, M., Rossi, G.: Translation of TTF test specifications into {log}, http://www.fceia.unr.edu.ar/~mcristia/publicaciones/ encoding-ttf-setlog.pdf (last access: December 2012)
24. Saaltink, M.: The Z/EVES System. In: Till, D., Bowen, J.P., Hinchey, M.G. (eds.) ZUM 1997. LNCS, vol. 1212, pp. 72–85. Springer, Heidelberg (1997)
25. Déharbe, D., Fontaine, P., Guyot, Y., Voisin, L.: SMT solvers for Rodin. In: [27], pp. 194–207
26. Mentré, D., Marché, C., Filliâtre, J.C., Asuka, M.: Discharging proof obligations from Atelier B using multiple automated provers. In: [27], pp. 238–251
27. Derrick, J., Fitzgerald, J., Gnesi, S., Khurshid, S., Leuschel, M., Reeves, S., Riccobene, E. (eds.): ABZ 2012. LNCS, vol. 7316. Springer, Heidelberg (2012)

Zero Overhead Runtime Monitoring*

Daniel Wonisch, Alexander Schremmer, and Heike Wehrheim

University of Paderborn
Germany
{alexander.schremmer,heike.wehrheim}@upb.de

Abstract. Runtime monitoring aims at ensuring program safety by monitoring the program's behaviour during execution and taking appropriate action before a program violates some property. Runtime monitoring is in particular important when an exhaustive formal verification fails. While the approach allows for a safe execution of programs, it may impose a significant runtime overhead.

In this paper, we propose a novel technique combining verification and monitoring which incurs no overhead during runtime at all. The technique proceeds by using the inconclusive result of a verification run as the basis for transforming the program into one where all potential points of failure are replaced by HALT statements. The new program is safe by construction, behaviourally equivalent to the original program (except for unsafe behaviour), and has the same performance characteristics.

1 Introduction

Runtime verification aims at checking the adherence of software to specific properties during the actual execution of the program. It is in particular applied when an exhaustive formal verification (e.g. via model checking) cannot be performed due to the complexity of the software. Runtime monitoring is a specific form of runtime verification which uses monitoring concepts to observe the program behaviour, either by directly inlining monitors into the program [13,15,16] or by using tools or specific hardware for observation. Different languages for specifying the properties to be monitored [1] as well as synthesis techniques for monitor generation [2] exist. While ensuring safe program execution, monitoring can incur a significant runtime overhead. Therefore, a number of approaches [12,8] aim at *residual* monitor generation where the results of prior (typically static) analysis' are used to make the monitor (and thus the monitoring overhead) smaller. These techniques can however not completely remove all monitoring code in the general case.

In this paper, we propose a technique which can completely dispense with monitoring even though an exhaustive formal verification might have failed due to the programs complexity. Like e.g. [12] the technique builds on a prior analysis, here in the form of an overapproximating predicate analysis as carried out by

---

* This work was partially supported by the German Research Foundation (DFG) within the Collaborative Research Centre "On-The-Fly Computing" (SFB 901).

R.M. Hierons, M.G. Merayo, and M. Bravetti (Eds.): SEFM 2013, LNCS 8137, pp. 244–258, 2013.

the tool CPACHECKER [7]. Our interest is in trace properties specified by finite automata (also called path or protocol properties), i.e. requirements on the allowed sequences of events. Events are first of all method calls, but could also be arbitrary other statements. The predicate analysis of CPACHECKER times out once the available memory is exceeded. In this case, the analysis will end with an *inconclusive* result [5] showing potential points of failure (PPFs, terminology from [12]; error states in CPACHECKER terminology) where the property might be violated. Instead of using this result for residual monitor generation, we use it to transform the original program into a new one which needs no tracking of monitor state transitions at all anymore. More precisely, we take the abstract reachability tree (ART) as generated by the predicate analysis and transform it into a program by taking it as the control flow graph of the new program. The only change we make are at nodes representing PPFs: here, we will replace the original statement (which appears on the edge of the ART) by a HALT statement[1]. The resulting new program is then safe by construction (the program stops before it fails). At the same time, the new program will execute exactly the same safe traces as the old one since the HALT statements will only be reached in the unsafe case. We have thus achieved the same effect as common runtime monitoring techniques.

Apart from the prior predicate analysis the only overhead coming with our technique is in the *size* of the transformed program. It usually is larger than the original program (in terms of lines of code), which can have an effect on the compilation time and the size of the memory used for storing the program. However, its runtime performance (ignoring cache effects) is the same (or even better) than that of the original program: on safe paths the original and the transformed program will execute exactly the same sequence of statements, on unsafe paths the transformed program halts as soon as running into the failure becomes unavoidable. Hence, original and transformed program are behaviourally equivalent except for unsafe paths.

The paper is structured as follows. The next section gives background information about programs and the construction of the ART. Section 3 describes how the ART is transformed into a new program and what kind of properties this transformation guarantees. Section 4 shows the results of an experimental evaluation. The last section concludes and discusses related work.

2 Background

For the presentation in this paper, we consider programs to be written in a simple imperative programming language with assignments, assume operations, gotos and function calls as only possible statements, and boolean and integer variables only. The programs considered in Section 4 reporting on experimental results are however not restricted this way: they are written in C, or more specifically given in CIL. Assume operations together with gotos can be used to express

---

[1] Alternatively, we could throw an exception, write a log, print an error message or insert user-specified code here.

if-then-else statements and loops. For readability, we will directly write if-then-else and while or for statements in our examples. Figure 1 shows our running example of an (intentionally simple) program which is calling some lock and unlock functions. The objective is to guarantee that this programs adheres to common locking idioms (which it does), i.e., in particular no unlock can occur before a lock. For this simple program, we can of course automatically verify this property. In general, this might however not always be possible, thus some kind of runtime monitoring ensuring safe execution might come into play.

```
1:    boolean initialized = false;
2:    int lastLock = 0;
3:    init();
4:    lock();
5:    initialized = true;
6:    for (int i = 1; i < n; i++) {
7:        if (! initialized)
8:            init();
9:        if (i - lastLock == 2) {
10:           lock();
11:           lastLock = i;
12:       } else {
13:           unlock();
14:   }}
```

Fig. 2. Property Automaton. Disallows two lock() or unlock() in a row.

Fig. 1. Example program LOCKS

Formally, a *program* $P = (A, l_0)$ is represented as a *control-flow automaton* (CFA) A together with a start location l_0. A CFA $A = (L, G)$ consists of a set of (program) locations L and a set of edges $G \subseteq L \times Ops \times L$ that describe possible transitions from one program location to another by executing certain operations Ops. A *concrete data state* $c : X \to \mathbb{Z} \cup \{true, false\}$ of a program P is a mapping from the set of variables X of the program to integer or boolean values. The set of all concrete data states in a program P is denoted by $\mathscr{C}$. A set of concrete data states can be described by a first-order predicate logic formula φ over the program variables (which we make use of during predicate analysis). We write $[\![\varphi]\!] := \{c \in \mathscr{C} \mid c \models \varphi\}$ for the set of concrete data states represented by some formula φ. Furthermore, we write $\gamma(c)$ for the representation of a concrete data state as formula (i.e. $[\![\gamma(c)]\!] = \{c\}$). Note that we assume the program to be started in some arbitrary data state c_0.

A tuple (l, c) of a location and a concrete data state of a program is called *concrete state*. The *concrete semantics* of an operation $op \in Ops$ is defined in terms of the *strongest postcondition operator* $SP_{op}(\cdot)$. Intuitively, the strongest postcondition operator $SP_{op}(\varphi)$ of a formula φ wrt. to an operation op is the strongest formula ψ which represents all states which can be reached by op from a state satisfying φ. Formally, we have $SP_{x:=expr}(\varphi) = \exists \hat{x} : \varphi_{[x \mapsto \hat{x}]} \wedge (x = expr_{[x \mapsto \hat{x}]})$ for an assignment operation $x := expr$, $SP_{assume(p)}(\varphi) = \varphi \wedge p$ for an assume operation $assume(p)$ ($assume(\cdot)$ omitted in figures, only condition stated) and $SP_{f()}(\varphi) = \varphi$ for a function call $f()$. Thus, we assume function calls to not change the data state of a program. This assumption is, however, not mandatory; our monitoring approach can as well be applied on top of a proper interprocedural analysis. In addition, we introduce the operation HALT which may not appear in the input program and behaves like a skip operation (i.e. does nothing) but allows us to distinguish an explicit program halt from an endless loop.

We write $(l, c) \xrightarrow{g} (l', c')$ for concrete states (l, c), (l', c') and edge $g := (l, op, l')$, if $c' \in [\![SP_{op}(\gamma(c))]\!]$. We write $(l, c) \to (l', c')$ if there is an edge $g = (l, op, l')$ such that $(l, c) \xrightarrow{g} (l', c')$. The feasible $paths$ of a program $P = (A, l_0)$ with CFA $A = (L, G)$ are the sequences of concrete states and operations the program can pass through:

$$paths(P) := \{c_0\, op_0 \cdots c_{n-1}\, op_{n-1}\, c_n \mid \exists l_0, \ldots, l_n \in L, \exists g_0, \ldots, g_{n-1} \in G :$$
$$(l_0, c_0) \xrightarrow{g_0} \cdots \xrightarrow{g_{n-1}} (l_n, c_n) \wedge \forall 0 \le i < n : g_i = (l_i, op_i, l_{i+1})\}$$

Let $trace(\pi)$ be the trace given by a path $\pi = c_0\, op_0 \cdots c_{n-1}\, op_{n-1}\, c_n$:

$$trace(\pi) := op_0 \cdots op_{n-1}$$

We are ultimately interested in guaranteeing that the program obeys some *safety properties*. Safety properties are given in terms of protocol automata which describe the allowed sequences of operations.

Definition 1. *A protocol or property automaton $A_{prop} = (\Sigma, S, s_0, s_{err}, \delta)$ consists of an alphabet Σ, a finite set of states S with initial state s_0 and error state s_{err}, and transition relation $\delta \subseteq S \times \Sigma \times S$. The transition relation is deterministic. The error state has outgoing transitions $(s_{err}, op, s_{err}) \in \delta$ for all $op \in \Sigma$. The alphabet Σ may contain every operation except for HALT.*

The language $L(A_{prop})$ of a protocol automaton is the set of traces $op_1 \ldots op_n$ such that $\delta^*(s_0, op_1 \ldots op_n) \neq s_{err}$.

The property automaton in Figure 2 describes all valid locking patterns: first, a call of $init()$ needs to be performed and then $lock()$ and $unlock()$ have to occur in turns. The operations occuring in property automata are usually function calls, however, these can also be any syntactic program statement that is expressible as a BLAST automaton [4].

The property automaton only speaks about part of the program operations, namely those in Σ. A comparison of program and protocol automaton traces thus needs to project the traces of the program onto the alphabet of the automaton (projection written as $\upharpoonright$). Hence, program P *satisfies* the safety property of protocol automaton A_{prop}, $P \models A_{prop}$, if $\{trace(\pi) \mid \pi \in paths(P)\} \upharpoonright \Sigma \subseteq L(A_{prop})$. The subset of paths of a program P satisfying the safety property is written $correctpaths(P) := \{\pi \mid \pi \in paths(P) \wedge trace(\pi) \upharpoonright \Sigma \in L(A_{prop})\}$.

Our technique proceeds by first of all trying to *verify* whether the program satisfies the safety property. To this end, we use predicate analysis (as supplied by CPACHECKER [7]). If we succeed, the program is safe and can safely be executed. If verification fails (due to the complexity of the program or time/memory limits), we nevertheless use the information the verifier has obtained about the program so far. This information is available in the form of an *abstract reachability tree* (ART).

For the verification CPACHECKER builds the product of the property automaton and an abstraction of the concrete state space as an ART. More precisely, the concrete data states are abstracted by quantifier-free first order predicate logic formulas over the variables of the program. We let PS denote the set of all such formulas. We only sketch the algorithm behind ART construction, for details see for instance [7]. What is important for us, is its form. The nodes of the ART take the form (l, s, φ) describing the location l the program is in, the current state s of the property automaton and a predicate formula φ as an abstraction of the data state. Nodes with property automaton state s_{err} are called *error nodes*. Edges between nodes are labelled with operations of the program, namely the operation which brings us from one node to the next.

Definition 2. *An* abstract reachability tree $T = (N, G, C)$ *consists of a set of nodes* $N \subseteq L \times S \times PS$, *a set of edges* $G \subseteq N \times Ops \times N$ *and a covering* $C : N \to N$.

The covering is used to stop exploration of the abstract state space at a particular node once we find that the node is covered by an already existing one: if $C(l, s, \varphi) = (l', s', \varphi')$ then $l = l'$, $s = s'$ and $\llbracket \varphi \rrbracket \subseteq \llbracket \varphi' \rrbracket$. The ART is constructed by starting with the initial state $(l_0, s_0, true)$. The successor of an already constructed node n is constructed by searching for successor nodes in the CFA, computing the abstract post operation on the predicate formula of n and determining the successor property automaton state. After generation of a new ART node, the algorithm checks whether the new ART node is covered by an existing one and generates an entry in the covering if necessary. One result of this process is that loops are unrolled such that within ART nodes program locations are only associated to a single state of the property automaton: if a program when reaching location l can potentially be in more than one state of the (concurrently running) protocol automaton, these will become separate nodes in the ART.

The verification follows a CEGAR (counter example guided abstraction refinement) approach. It starts with an empty set of predicates, i.e. at the beginning values of the program variables are not considered at all during ART construction. When the thus constructed ART contains an error node (a potential point of failure, PPF) and the user-supplied time/memory limits are not yet exceeded, it is validated whether this error node is also reachable in the concrete program. If not (spurious counterexample), new predicates are added and construction of a more precise ART is initiated. This is known as *abstraction refinement* (or short: refinement). The procedure either ends with a *conclusive* result (an error is definitely found or absence of errors definitely shown) or might stop somewhere in between with an *inconclusive* result due to a timeout or memory overflow. We thus also speak of conclusive or inconclusive ARTs.

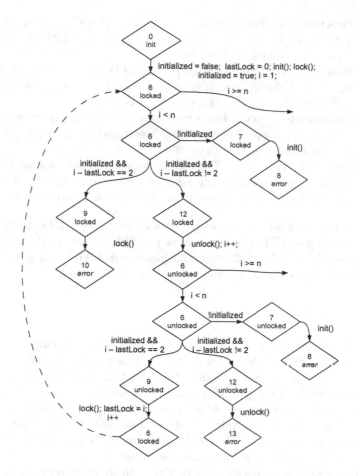

Fig. 3. An ART for program LOCKS using no predicates

Figure 3 shows the ART of program LOCKS as constructed by CPACHECKER with an empty set of predicates. The nodes thus so far only consist of program locations and property automaton states. Note that instead of a truely distinct location identifier, the nodes bear line numbers instead. We sometimes write more than one operation on an edge to make the ART more compact. The dotted line depicts the covering. The states labelled *error* are PPFs: they might not be reachable in the concrete program, but if they are, the property is violated.

The constructed ART (N, G_{art}, C) satisfies some healthiness conditions which we need further on for the correctness of our transformation (and which are guaranteed by CPACHECKER).

Soundness. If $((l, s, \varphi), op, (l', s', \varphi')) \in G_{art}$, then for all $c \in \llbracket \varphi \rrbracket$ with $(l, c) \overset{(l, op, l')}{\rightarrow}$ (l', c') we have $c' \in \llbracket \varphi' \rrbracket$. Furthermore, if $op \in \Sigma$, then $(s, op, s') \in \delta_{A_{prop}}$, and $s = s'$ else.

Well-constructedness. For every $((l, \cdot, \cdot), op, (l', \cdot, \cdot)) \in G_{art}$, we have an edge (l, op, l') in the CFG. For $P = (A, l_0)$ and root of the ART (l_0, s_0, φ_0), we have $l = l_0$, $s = s_0$ and $[\![\varphi_0]\!] = \mathscr{C}$.

Completeness. If (l, op, l') is an edge in the CFG of the program, then for all $(l, s, \varphi) \in N \setminus \text{dom}(C)$ with $\varphi \not\equiv false$ and $s \neq s_{err}$, we have some $(l', \cdot, \cdot) \in N$ such that $((l, s, \varphi), op, (l', \cdot, \cdot)) \in G_{art}$.

Error path contains exactly one error node. For every error node $n := (l, s_{err}, \cdot) \in N$ there is neither a successor node n' with $(n, \cdot, n') \in G_{art}$ nor a covering node n' with $C(n) = n'$.

Determinism. For every $n \in N$, there is only one successor node in G_{art} except when nodes have outgoing assume edges (i.e., edges labelled with a condition). In this case, also more than one successor node of n is allowed.

All these properties hold for conclusive and inconclusive ARTs. If the verifier gives us a conclusive ART, the program is provably safe or contains a definite error which needs to be fixed. If we get an inconclusive ART, safety needs to be guaranteed by other means, for example runtime monitoring.

3   Program Transformation

The objective of runtime monitoring is to guarantee safe execution of the program although it might possibly contain errors. This can for instance be achieved by weaving a monitor into the program. Here, we take a different approach. For generating a version of the program which does not run into errors, we transform the program into a new one which is error-free and – except for the unsafe behaviour – behaviourally equivalent to the original one. The basis for the transformation is an inconclusive ART, and by using the ART as a control flow graph of a program, we transform it into a new program.

The transformation begins by constructing – in its most basic form – a goto program from the ART. Later optimisations bring this into a more readable form, but here we just formally define transformation into goto programs by giving the new program again in the form of a control flow automaton and an initial location. The idea is quite simple: every node in the ART becomes a location in the new program, and the operations executed when going from one node to the next are those on the edges in the ART. Furthermore, edges to error nodes in the ART are translated as a HALT operation and a loop is inserted from the CFA node corresponding to the error node to itself. In the programs this is written as HALT: goto HALT.

Definition 3. *Let $T = (N, G, C)$ be an abstract reachability tree. The transformed program, program_of(T), is a program $P' = ((L', G'), l'_0)$ with $L' = N \setminus \text{dom}(C)$, $l'_0 = root(T) = (l_0, s_0, true)$ and edges defined as*

$$(l_1, op, l_2) \in G' \ if \ \begin{cases} (l_1, op, l_2) \in G & if \ l_2 \notin D \wedge state(l_2) \neq s_{err} \\ (l_1, \cdot, l_2) \in G \wedge op = HALT & if \ l_2 \notin D \wedge state(l_2) = s_{err} \\ (l_1, op, l_3) \in G \wedge (l_3, l_2) \in C & else \end{cases}$$

where state(l) := s for l = (·, s, ·) and D := dom(C). Additionally, we add an edge (l, HALT, l) to G' for every l = (·, s_err, ·) ∈ N.

This is well defined because $dom(G) \cap dom(C) = \emptyset$, $C(N) \cap dom(C) = \emptyset$, the ART is deterministic, and an error node cannot be covered by another node (see the property ERROR PATH CONTAINS EXACTLY ONE ERROR NODE). This representation can be easily brought back into a programming language notation using gotos, and with some effort into a program without gotos and proper loops instead (assuming the resulting loop structure is reducible). The left of Figure 4 shows the program which is the result of the transformation of the ART of the last section. The ART had four error nodes and thus we get four HALT statements here. Note that we have - like in the original program - used loops and if-then-else statements instead of gotos and assume operations to improve readability.

```
1:   boolean initialized = false;          1:   boolean initialized = false;
2:   int lastLock = 0;                      2:   int lastLock = 0;
3:   init();                                3:   init();
4:   lock();                                4:   lock();
5:   initialized = true;                    5:   initialized = true;
6:   for (int i = 1; i < n; i++) {          6:   for (int i = 1; i < n; i++) {
7:     if (! initialized)                   7:
8:       HALT0: goto HALT0;                  8:
9:     if (i - lastLock == 2) {             9:     if (i - lastLock == 2) {
10:      HALT1: goto HALT1;                 10:       HALT1: goto HALT1;
11:    } else {                             11:    } else {
12:      unlock();                          12:      unlock();
13:      i++;                               13:      i++;
14:      if (i >= n)                        14:      if (i >= n)
15:        break;                           15:        break;
16:                                         16:
17:      if (! initialized)                 17:
18:        HALT2: goto HALT2;               18:
19:      if (i - lastLock == 2) {           19:      if (i - lastLock == 2) {
20:        lock();                          20:        lock();
21:        lastLock = i;                    21:        lastLock = i;
22:      } else {                           22:      } else {
23:        HALT3: goto HALT3;               23:        HALT3: goto HALT3;
24: }}}                                     24: }}}
```

Fig. 4. Transformed programs for $r_{max} = 0$ and $r_{max} = 1$

Due to the fact that the edges in the ART and thus the statements in the new program are exactly those of the original program assuming that there are no error nodes on this path, we obtain a new program which is equivalent to the original one for these paths: it possesses the same error-free paths. For P, we can use our definition $correctpaths(\cdot)$ to represent the set of error-free paths. But for P', we need to restrict this set to those paths that do not end in a state that formely violated the property to make the set of error-free paths comparable. Therefore we define a modified set $correctpaths'(P) := \{\pi \mid \pi \in correctpaths(P) \land \pi$ does not end in HALT$\}$, in which ending in HALT means that the last operation in the path is HALT.

Theorem 1. *Let P be a program. Let $ART = (N, G_{art}, C)$ be an abstract reachablity tree for P. Let $P' = program\_of(ART)$. Then $correctpaths(P) = correctpaths'(P')$.*

Proof. Let $P = ((L, G), l_0)$ and $P' = ((L', G'), l_0')$

"$\subseteq$" Let $c_0\, op_0 \ldots c_{n-1}\, op_{n-1}\, c_n \in correctpaths(P)$. By definition there are then $l_0, \ldots, l_n \in L$, $op_0, \ldots, op_{n-1} \in Ops$ such that $(l_0, c_0) \overset{op_0}{\to} \ldots \overset{op_{n-1}}{\to} (l_n, c_n)$. We show by induction over n that there are $l_0', \ldots, l_n' \in L'$ such that $(l_0', c_0) \overset{op_0}{\to} \ldots \overset{op_{n-1}}{\to} (l_n', c_n)$. and $op_i \neq HALT$ for all $0 \leq i \leq n-1$.
Induction basis: For $n = 0$, let $(l, s, \varphi) \in N$ be the abstract element corresponding to l_0'. As the ART is well-constructed, we have $l = l_0$ and $[\![\varphi]\!] = \mathscr{C}$. Thus, $c_0 \in [\![\varphi]\!]$.
Induction hypothesis: For every program path $(l_0, c_0) \overset{op_0}{\to} \ldots \overset{op_{n'-1}}{\to} (l_{n'}, c_{n'})$ of fixed length $n' := n$ in $correctpaths(P)$, there is a program path $(l_0', c_0) \overset{op_0}{\to} \ldots \overset{op_{n'-1}}{\to} (l_{n'}', c_{n'})$ in $correctpaths'(P')$. Furthermore, we have $c_{n'} \in [\![\varphi]\!]$, $l = l_{n'}$ if $(l, s, \varphi) \in N$ is the ART node that $l_{n'}'$ represents.
Induction step: By induction hypothesis we find $l_0', \ldots, l_{n-1}' \in L'$ such that $(l_0', c_0) \overset{op_0}{\to} \ldots \overset{op_{n-2}}{\to} (l_{n-1}', c_{n-1})$. Let $n_1 := (l, s, \varphi) \in N$ be the ART node corresponding to l_{n-1}'. Again by induction hypothesis we have $l_{n-1} = l$ and $c_{n-1} \in [\![\varphi]\!]$. By definition of program paths we have $g := (l_{n-1}, op_{n-1}, l_n) \in G$. Thus, by completeness of the ART and since $\varphi \not\equiv false$ ($[\![\varphi]\!] \neq \emptyset$ since $c_{n-1} \in [\![\varphi]\!]$) and l_{n-1} is not a error node (otherwise this path would not have been in $correctpaths(P)$), we have some $n_2 := (l', s', \varphi') \in N$ such that $(n_1, op_{n-1}, n_2) \in G_{art}$ and $l' = l_n$. If $n_2 \notin dom(C)$ we have $n_2 \in N'$, $(n_1, op_{n-1}, n_2) \in G'$, and thus $(l_{n-1}', op, l_n') \in N'$, where $l_n' \in L'$ is the node corresponding to n_2. Otherwise, if $n_2 \in dom(C)$ we have some $n_3 := C(n_2)$, $n_3 \notin dom(C)$, and $(n_1, op_{n-1}, n_3) \in G'$. By soundness of the abstractions in the ART we furthermore have $c_n \in [\![\varphi']\!]$ and $c_n \in [\![\varphi'']\!]$ for $n_3 = (l', s', \varphi'')$.

"$\supseteq$" Let $c_0\, op_0 \ldots c_{n-1}\, op_{n-1}\, c_n \in correctpaths'(P')$. By definition there are then $l_0', \ldots, l_n' \in L'$, $op_0, \ldots, op_{n-1} \in Ops$ such that $(l_0', c_0') \overset{op_0}{\to} \ldots \overset{op_{n-1}}{\to} (l_n', c_n')$, $op_i \neq HALT$. Let $(l_i, s_i, \varphi_i) \in N$ be the abstract element corresponding to l_i' ($i \in \{0, \ldots, n\}$). We show by induction over n that $(l_0, c_0) \overset{op_0}{\to} \ldots \overset{op_{n-1}}{\to} (l_n, c_n)$ is a path of P with $\wedge_{i \in [0..n]} c_i = c_i'$.
Induction basis: For $n = 0$, let $(l, s, \varphi) \in N$ be the abstract element corresponding to l_0'. As the ART is well-constructed, we have $l = l_0$ and $c_0' \in [\![\varphi]\!]$. For the initial node φ is true and thus $c_0 := c_0'$ is a valid initial state of P.
Induction hypothesis: For every feasible program path $(l_0', c_0') \overset{op_0}{\to} \ldots \overset{op_{n'-1}}{\to} (l_{n'}', c_{n'}')$ of fixed length $n' := n$ in P' with $(l_i, s_i, \varphi_i) \in N$ and $\wedge_{i \in [0..n']} c_i = c_i'$ denoting the abstract element corresponding to l_i' ($i \in \{0, \ldots, n'\}$) we have $(l_0, c_0) \overset{op_0}{\to} \ldots \overset{op_{n'-1}}{\to} (l_{n'}, c_{n'})$ in P.

Induction step: By induction hypothesis we find $l_0, \ldots, l_{n-1} \in L$ such that $(l_0, c_0) \overset{op_0}{\rightarrow} \ldots \overset{op_{n-2}}{\rightarrow} (l_{n-1}, c_{n-1})$ is a path in P. Let $n_1 := (l_{n-1}, s_{n-1}, \varphi_{n-1}) \in N$ and $n_2 := (l_n, s_n, \varphi_n) \in N$ be the ART nodes corresponding to l'_{n-1} and l'_n, respectively. Since the *ART* is well-constructed and n_1, n_2 cannot be error nodes (otherwise the path would not be in $correctpaths'(P')$), we have $(l_{n-1}, op_{n-1}, l_n) \in G$. Thus $(l_{n-1}, c_{n-1}) \overset{op_{n-1}}{\rightarrow} (l_n, c_n)$ in P with $c'_{n-1} = c_{n-1} \wedge c'_n = c_n$ follows (op_{n-1} executed on some concrete state c_{n-1} will always yield the same successor state c_n). □

Furthermore, we perform an optimisation that does not affect the correctness of the transformation. We omit all edges $((\cdot, \cdot, \cdot), \cdot, (\cdot, \cdot, false)) \in G_{art}$ in the ART leading to nodes labelled false as these represent steps the program will never execute. If after this removal there is just one outgoing edge from a node and this edge is labelled with an assume operation, we delete this assume. Additionally, it is possible to prune all paths which only lead to error nodes.

The run time of the program stays the same or even decreases. This is the case when the optimisation removes assume operations on edges (because the ART shows that this condition always holds at the particular node).

Our transformation indeed ensures safety: the transformed program satisfies the safety property of the automaton, even in cases where the original program was not safe.

Theorem 2. *Let P be a program. Let $P' = ((L, G), l_0) := program\_of(T)$, where $T = (N_T, G_T, C_T)$ is an ART for P wrt. A_{prop}. Then $P' \models A_{prop}$.*

Proof. We need to show that $paths(P') = correctpaths(P')$. As $correctpaths(P')$ is always a subset of $paths(P')$ by definition, we only need to show $paths(P') \subseteq correctpaths(P')$. Let $\pi := c_0 \, op_0 \, \ldots \, op_{n-1} \, c_n \in paths(P')$. By definition, there exist the locations $l_0, \ldots, l_n \in L$ and the edges $g_0, \ldots, g_{n-1} \in G$ with $(l_0, c_0) \overset{g_0}{\rightarrow} \ldots \overset{g_{n-1}}{\rightarrow} (l_n, c_n) \wedge \forall 0 \leq i < n : g_i = (l_i, op_i, l_{i+1})$. Assume $\pi \notin correctpaths(P')$. Then $trace(\pi) \upharpoonright \Sigma \notin L(A_{prop})$, therefore there must be a smallest index i with $\delta^*(s_0, (op_0, \ldots, op_i) \upharpoonright \Sigma) = s_{err}$ and $op_i \neq HALT$ because HALT may not be in the alphabet of the property automaton A_{prop}. But s_i must be equal to s_{err} because of the soundness of the ART. Thus by construction of the transformation, we find the operation $op_i = HALT$ in the program which is a contradiction. We conclude that $\pi \notin paths(P')$. □

In general, we might have more than one inconclusive ART available for the transformation. One parameter that determines how far the analysis proceeds is the limit of performed refinements r_{max}. By setting this parameter to a low value, the analysis time can be reduced. Conversely, setting it to ∞ leads to an analysis that is most precise but may not terminate. Thus, the analysis that proceeds the transformation is tunable.

The ART shown in the last section was constructed with $r_{max} = 0$ (giving us no predicates). Figure 5 shows an ART for program LOCKS generated with $r_{max} = 1$. As $r_{max} = 0$ means that no refinements happen at all, the generated

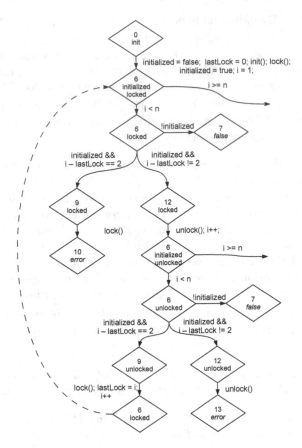

Fig. 5. ART generated with $r_{max} = 1$

ART of the last section does not contain any predicates and none of the four error nodes could be ruled out. In the ART of the more precise analysis for $r_{max} = 1$, one can see that two error nodes could be pruned and the preceeding node was set to the predicate **false** instead. This means that the particular path is infeasible. Subsequent iterations of the CEGAR algorithm of CPACHECKER would rule out more error nodes until CPACHECKER would manage to prove the whole program safe. This would finally lead to a smaller state space, i.e. ART, and therefore to a smaller transformed program. The corresponding program for this ART can be seen in the right of Figure 4: we only have two halt statements left because the verifier has already shown that the other two PPFs (error nodes) are not reachable.

In summary, we have thus obtained a technique which – alike runtime monitoring – guarantees safe execution of a possibly unsafe program. It does so although the prior verification has not shown safety, and without adding and tracking monitor variables in the code.

4 Experimental Results

As the transformation usually increases program size, we evaluated how much larger the particular program gets after transformation. We implemented our technique in the program-analysis tool CPACHECKER [7]. We chose the Adjustable-Block Encoding (ABE) [3] predicate analysis. All experiments were performed on a 64 bit Ubuntu 12.10 machine with 6 GB RAM, an Intel i7-2620M at 2.7 GHz CPU, and OpenJDK 7u9 (JVM 23.2-b09). The analysis time does not include the startup time of the JVM and CPACHECKER itself (around 1-2 s). The amount of operations in the program can be estimated by looking at the lines of code (LOC) because our transformation to C code inserts a newline at least for every statement and curly brace.

Besides the basic approach described so far, our implementation contains a further optimization to keep the size of the transformed program small. Instead of performing a single predicate analysis and ART generation only, we perform two passes: the first pass generates the product construction of the CFA and the property automaton yielding ART T_1, and the second pass performs a normal predicate analysis yielding ART T_2. In other words, T_1 is the result of performing the predicate analysis with an empty set of predicates. As a last step, we traverse T_1 and remove every (error) node $(l, s_{err}, true)$ ($true$ represents the empty predicate) such that no (l, s_{err}, φ) appears in T_2 for any φ. T_1 is then subject to the generation of the new program. The correctness of this step is based on the fact that if the predicate analysis proved that the combination of location and protocol error state is not reachable at all, we can deduce that it must also be unreachable in T_1, because T_1 and T_2 are both overapproximating the program behaviour.

Table 1 shows the benchmark results[2] for different kinds of programs and different monitor automata. Refinements were disabled, i.e., we used $r_{max} = 0$ and all ARTs were inconclusive. The *analysis* step includes the protocol automaton analysis. This step together with the *transformation* step is run to generate the C representation of the ART. On the right side of the table, the lines of code (LOC) of the generated program as well as the remaining potential points of failure are shown.

Except for the lock example from above, the programs in Table 1 were taken from the benchmark set of the Software Verification competition 2012[3] as to apply our technique on standard benchmark C programs. The token ring benchmark was initially a SystemC program passing tokens between different simulated threads that was amended with a scheduler. The ssl_server (originally named s3_srvr) benchmark is an excerpt from the OpenSSL project mimicking a server-side SSL connection handler. For the ssl_server program, we derived different protocol automata of varying complexity. The protocol automaton in

---

[2] All benchmark files necessary to reproduce the results are available in the public repository of CPACHECKER under https://svn.sosy-lab.org/software/cpachecker/branches/runtime_verification/.

[3] See http://sv-comp.sosy-lab.org/.

case of the token ring benchmark simply checks whether every task is started at most once by the scheduler at the same time. The token ring benchmarks are already complex enough to blast the resource limitations of our workstation at five parallel processes and $r_{max} = \infty$ therefore requiring runtime verification.

Table 1. Benchmark results for different programs and properties, with $r_{max} = 0$

Program name	Analysis			Transformation		
(Monitor name)	LOC	Time	Mem.	Time	LOC	PPFs
lock2.c	32	0.037s	88MB	0.004s	81	4
token_ring.02.cil.c	596	0.795s	88MB	0.041s	4023	5
token_ring.03.cil.c	724	1.789s	166MB	0.205s	13967	27
token_ring.04.cil.c	846	4.328s	322MB	0.322s	43830	98
s3_srvr.cil.c (mon1)	861	0.963s	112MB	0.062s	5129	1
s3_srvr.cil.c (mon2)	861	0.837s	112MB	0.030s	4284	1
s3_srvr.cil.c (mon3)	861	0.815s	112MB	0.039s	4284	1
s3_srvr.cil.c (mon4)	861	0.848s	112MB	0.040s	4284	1
s3_srvr.cil.c (mon5)	861	1.199s	158MB	0.076s	7658	2
s3_srvr.cil.c (mon6)	861	1.520s	158MB	0.134s	9332	3

The analysis excels with a fast analysis time while recognizing a varying amount of PPFs in the code and inserting HALT statements at those. As explained before, this does not mean that additional checks are introduced in the code. Instead, these HALT statements are woven into the code at places that might fail with regard to the protocol automaton.

One might wonder whether the code size growth increases the execution time of the benchmarks because of cache or compiler optimization effects. All relevant programs that were collected by the Software Verification Competition branch on nondeterministic integer values and are not meant to be compiled and executed (in fact, attempts to remove the nondeterministic code lead to programs that do not terminate at all). For this reason, it was hard for us to derive execution times for the above benchmarks. Yet we can conclude from performed benchmarks of our locks example that the execution time is reduced by 25%. We assume that the inherent loop unrolling (compare Figure 1 and Figure 4) contributed to this speedup.

5   Conclusion

In this paper, we have proposed a new overhead-free technique for runtime monitoring which can avoid tracking monitor state variables. It proceeds by using information obtained from inconclusive verification runs as a basis for a program transformation. The resulting program is guaranteed to be safe and behaviourally equivalent to the original program up to the unsafe traces.

Related Work. While runtime monitoring [13,15,16] first focused on properties to be shown on the assembler level of programs and then quickly evolved to high-level languages, newer works revolve around typestate properties [17] and the generation of residual monitors.

Much work focuses on verifying protocol-like properties of programs. This starts as early as the eighties with the work on *typestate analysis*. Typestate is a concept which enhances types with information about their state and the operations executable in particular states. Recent approaches have enhanced typestate analysis with ideas of predicate abstraction and abstraction refinement [11,10], however not employing monitoring in case of inconclusive analysis results. Type-state properties are more powerful than the protocol properties because the former may express properties of single objects instead of the whole program. Other works use an inconclusive typestate analysis to generate residual monitors to be used in runtime verification [12,8]. This can be seen as a form of partial evaluation of the monitoring code. *Monitor-oriented programming* (MOP) [9,16] allows runtime monitoring of type-state properties for annotated code. The annotations can be performed in formal languages and are woven into the code in the case of inline monitoring. However, there is to the best of our knowledge no technique that allows to perform runtime monitoring of typestate properties without inserting monitoring code when the underlying analysis used in the particular *residual monitor generation* algorithm (e.g. [8]) is inconclusive. Moreover, as these algorithms are based on data flow analysis, they do not exhibit the full precision of our abstract reachability tree approach: we perform a path-sensitive analysis that ensures that every location of the transformed program has only one monitor state.

The idea of using the abstract reachability tree of a program obtained by a predicate analysis is also the idea underlying conditional model checking [5]. While the transformation of an ART into a program is generally envisaged (for the purpose of benchmark generation), the approach focuses on generating conditions for use in further verification runs. Generation of programs from parts of an ART, namely certain counterexamples, is also the basis of the work on *path invariants* [6] which presents an effective way of abstraction refinement.

A technique for avoiding the introduction of additional program variables for encoding the monitor state is presented in [14]. Instead of using a monitor state variable, they directly employ member fields of the objects being monitored. The relation between monitor state and object state has however to be defined manually. Moreover, while they can avoid monitor variables, they still need to insert code for checking conditions on the objects states according to the monitor.

Future Work. In the future, we plan to work on extending the range of properties that our transformation can handle. For example, we think that null-pointer dereferences, despite being a property that talks about single objects, can be checked for with our approach by applying a code transformation before starting the analysis.

References

1. Barringer, H., Rydeheard, D.E., Havelund, K.: Rule Systems for Run-time Monitoring: from Eagle to RuleR. J. Log. Comput. 20(3), 675–706 (2010)
2. Bauer, A., Leucker, M., Schallhart, C.: Runtime Verification for LTL and TLTL. ACM Trans. Softw. Eng. Methodol. 20(4), 14 (2011)
3. Beyer, D., Keremoglu, M., Wendler, P.: Predicate Abstraction with Adjustable-Block Encoding. In: FMCAD 2010, pp. 189–197 (2010)
4. Beyer, D., Chlipala, A.J., Henzinger, T.A., Jhala, R., Majumdar, R.: The BLAST query language for software verification. In: Giacobazzi, R. (ed.) SAS 2004. LNCS, vol. 3148, pp. 2–18. Springer, Heidelberg (2004)
5. Beyer, D., Henzinger, T.A., Keremoglu, M.E., Wendler, P.: Conditional model checking: a technique to pass information between verifiers. In: Tracz, W., Robillard, M.P., Bultan, T. (eds.) SIGSOFT FSE, p. 57. ACM (2012)
6. Beyer, D., Henzinger, T.A., Majumdar, R., Rybalchenko, A.: Path invariants. In: Ferrante, J., McKinley, K.S. (eds.) PLDI, pp. 300–309. ACM (2007)
7. Beyer, D., Keremoglu, M.E.: CPACHECKER: A tool for configurable software verification. In: Gopalakrishnan, G., Qadeer, S. (eds.) CAV 2011. LNCS, vol. 6806, pp. 184–190. Springer, Heidelberg (2011)
8. Bodden, E., Lam, P., Hendren, L.: Clara: A framework for partially evaluating finite-state runtime monitors ahead of time. In: Barringer, H., et al. (eds.) RV 2010. LNCS, vol. 6418, pp. 183–197. Springer, Heidelberg (2010)
9. Chen, F., D'Amorim, M., Roşu, G.: A formal monitoring-based framework for software development and analysis. In: Davies, J., Schulte, W., Barnett, M. (eds.) ICFEM 2004. LNCS, vol. 3308, pp. 357–372. Springer, Heidelberg (2004)
10. Das, M., Lerner, S., Seigle, M.: ESP: Path-Sensitive Program Verification in Polynomial Time. In: PLDI, pp. 57–68 (2002)
11. Dhurjati, D., Das, M., Yang, Y.: Path-sensitive dataflow analysis with iterative refinement. In: Yi, K. (ed.) SAS 2006. LNCS, vol. 4134, pp. 425–442. Springer, Heidelberg (2006)
12. Dwyer, M.B., Purandare, R.: Residual dynamic typestate analysis exploiting static analysis: results to reformulate and reduce the cost of dynamic analysis. In: Automated Software Engineering (ASE), pp. 124–133. ACM (2007)
13. Erlingsson, Ú., Schneider, F.B.: IRM Enforcement of Java Stack Inspection. In: IEEE Symposium on Security and Privacy, pp. 246–255 (2000)
14. Hallé, S., Tremblay-Lessard, R.: A case for "Piggyback" runtime monitoring. In: Margaria, T., Steffen, B. (eds.) ISoLA 2012, Part I. LNCS, vol. 7609, pp. 295–311. Springer, Heidelberg (2012)
15. Kim, M., Viswanathan, M., Kannan, S., Lee, I., Sokolsky, O.: Java-MaC: A Run-Time Assurance Approach for Java Programs. Formal Methods in System Design 24(2), 129–155 (2004)
16. Meredith, P.O., Jin, D., Griffith, D., Chen, F., Rosu, G.: An overview of the MOP runtime verification framework. STTT 14(3), 249–289 (2012)
17. Strom, R.E., Yemini, S.: Typestate: A programming language concept for enhancing software reliability. IEEE Trans. Software Eng. 12(1), 157–171 (1986)

Run-Time Verification of Coboxes

Frank S. de Boer[1,2], Stijn de Gouw[1,2], and Peter Y. H. Wong[3]

[1] CWI, Amsterdam, The Netherlands
[2] Leiden University, The Netherlands
[3] SDL Fredhopper, Amsterdam, The Netherlands

Abstract. Run-time verification is one of the most useful techniques for detecting faults. In this paper we show how to model the observable behavior of concurrently running object groups (coboxes) in SAGA (Software trace Analysis using Grammars and Attributes) which is a run-time checker that provides a smooth integration of the specification and the efficient run-time checking of both data- and protocol-oriented properties of message sequences. We illustrate the effectiveness of our method by an industrial case study from the eCommerce software company Fredhopper.

1 Introduction

In [15] Java is extended with a concurrency model based on the notion of concurrently running object groups, so-called coboxes, which provide a powerful generalization of the concept of active objects. Coboxes can be dynamically created and objects within a cobox have only direct access to the fields of the other objects belonging to the same cobox. Since one of the main requirements of the design of coboxes is a smooth integration with object-oriented languages like Java, coboxes themselves do not have an identity, e.g., all communication between coboxes refer to the objects within coboxes. Communication between coboxes is based on asynchronous method calls with standard objects as targets. An asynchronous method call spawns a local thread within the cobox to which the targeted object belongs. Such a thread consists of the usual stack of internal method calls. Coboxes support multiple local threads which are executed in an interleaved manner. The local threads of a cobox are scheduled cooperatively, along the lines of the Creol modeling language described in [11]. This means, that at most one thread can be active in a cobox at a time, and that the active thread has to give up its control explicitly to allow other threads of the same cobox to become active.

ABS (Abstract Behavioral Specification language) is a novel language based on coboxes for modeling and analysis of complex distributed systems. It is a fully executable language with code generators for Java, Maude and Scala. In [10] a formal semantics of ABS was introduced based on asynchronous messages between coboxes. However, as of yet, no formal method for specifying and run-time verifying traces of such asynchronous messages has been developed. The main contribution of this paper is tool support for the efficient run-time verification

R.M. Hierons, M.G. Merayo, and M. Bravetti (Eds.): SEFM 2013, LNCS 8137, pp. 259–273, 2013.
© Springer-Verlag Berlin Heidelberg 2013

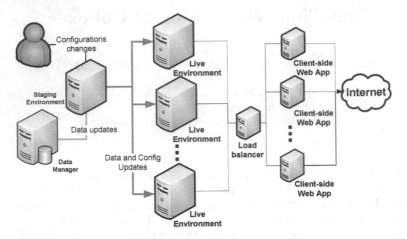

Fig. 1. An example FAS deployment

of asynchronous message passing between coboxes, independent from any backend. This latter requirement is important because in general the analysis of a particular backend is complicated by low-level implementation details. Further, it allows to generalize the analysis to all (including future) backends.

Run-time verification is one of the most useful techniques for detecting faults, and can be applied during any program execution context, including debugging, testing, and production [4]. We show how to use attribute grammars extended with assertions to specify and verify (at run-time) properties of the messages sent between coboxes. To this end, we first improve the efficiency of the run-time verification tool SAGA [6], which smoothly integrates both data- and protocol-oriented properties of message sequences. Both time and space complexity of SAGA is linear in the size of the message sequence. Further we extend it to support design-by-contract for coboxes. We illustrate the effectiveness of our method by an industrial case study from the eCommerce software company Fredhopper.

2   Case Study

The Fredhopper Access Server (FAS) is a distributed concurrent object-oriented system that provides search and merchandising services to eCommerce companies. Briefly, FAS provides to its clients structured search capabilities within the client's data. Each FAS installation is deployed to a customer according to the FAS deployment architecture (See Figure 1).

FAS consists of a set of live environments and a single staging environment. A live environment processes queries from client web applications via web services. FAS aims at providing a constant query capacity to client-side web applications. A staging environment is responsible for receiving data updates in XML format, indexing the XML, and distributing the resulting indices across all live environments according to the *Replication Protocol*. The Replication Protocol is

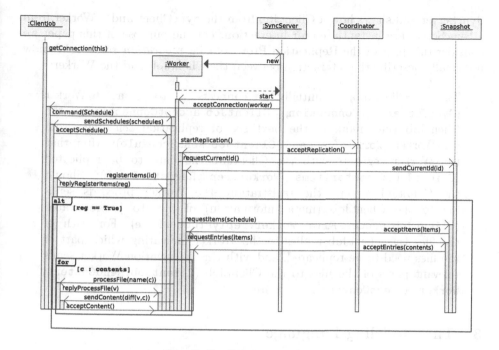

Fig. 2. Replication interaction

implemented by the *Replication System*. The Replication System consists of a *SyncServer* at the staging environment and one *SyncClient* for each live environment. The SyncServer determines the *schedule* of replication, as well as its content, while SyncClient receives data and configuration updates according to the schedule.

Replication Protocol

The SyncServer communicates to SyncClients by creating *Worker* objects. Workers serve as the interface to the server-side of the Replication Protocol. On the other hand, SyncClients schedule and create *ClientJob* objects to handle communications to the client-side of the Replication Protocol. When transferring data between the staging and the live environments, it is important that the data remains *immutable*. To ensure immutability without interfering with the read-/write access of the staging environment's underlying file system, the SyncServer creates a *Snapshot* object that encapsulates a snapshot of the necessary part of the staging environment's file system, and periodically *refreshes* it against the file system. This ensures that data remains immutable until it is deemed safe to modify it. The SyncServer uses a *Coordinator* object to determine the safe state in which the Snapshot can be refreshed. Figure 2 shows a UML sequence diagram concerning parts of the replication protocol with the interaction between a SyncClient, a ClientJob, a Worker, a SyncServer, a Coordinator and a Snapshot. The figure assumes that SyncClient has already established connection with a

SyncServer and shows how a ClientJob from the SyncClient and a Worker from a SyncServer are instantiated for interaction. For the purpose of this paper we consider this part of the Replication Protocol as a *replication session*. We now informally describe the interaction between the ClientJob and the Worker:

The ClientJob initially connects to a Worker (`SyncServer.getConnection`, `ClientJob.acceptConnection`); the ClientJob then requests the next set of replication schedules from the Worker (`Worker.command`, `ClientJob.sendSchedule`); After that the Worker registers with the ClientJob the data to be replicated (`ClientJob.registerItems`, `Worker.replyRegisterItems`); Should the ClientJob accept the registration, the Worker proceeds sending to the ClientJob (meta information) of files to be replicated (`ClientJob.processFile`, `Worker.replyProcessFile`). For each of the files the ClientJob replies to the Worker indicating which part of the files need to be replicated, and with this information Worker sends relevant parts of the files to the ClientJob (`ClientJob.sendContent`, `Worker.acceptContent`).

3   The Modeling Language

We formally describe coboxes by means of a modeling language which is based on the *Abstract Behavioral Specification* language [10]. Throughout the paper we refer to our own modeling language by ACOG (pure Actor-based Concurrent Object Groups). ACOG is designed with a layered architecture, at the base are functional abstractions around a standard notion of parametric algebraic data types (ADTs). Next we have an OO-imperative layer similar to (but much simpler than) JAVA. ACOG generalizes the concurrency model of Creol [11] from single concurrent objects to concurrent object groups (coboxes). As in [15] coboxes encapsulate synchronous, multi-threaded, shared state computation on a single processor. In contrast to thread-based concurrency, task scheduling is *cooperative*, i.e., switching between tasks of the same object happens only at specific scheduling points during the execution, which are explicit in the source code and can be syntactically identified. This allows writing concurrent programs in a much less error-prone way than in a thread-based model and makes ACOG models suitable for static analysis. In our dialect, unlike in [15], coboxes communicate only via pure asynchronous messages, and as such form an actor-based model as initially introduced by [1] and further developed in [16].

The following fragment of ClientJobImpl illustrates cobox creation and asynchronous communications.

```
class ClientJobImpl(SyncServer server, SyncClient client, Schedule s)
implements ClientJob {
  Set<Schedule> schedules = EmptySet;
  Unit executeJob() { server!getConnection(this); }
  Unit acceptConnection(Worker w) { .. }
```

```
  Unit sendSchedules(Set<Schedule> ss) { .. }
  Unit scheduleJobs() { .. }}

class SyncServerImpl(Coordinator coord) implements SyncServer {
  Unit getConnection(ClientJob job) {
    Bool shutdown = this.isShutdownRequested();
    if (shutdown) {
      job!acceptConnection(null);
    } else {
      Worker w = new cog WorkerImpl(job, this, coord);
      job!acceptConnection(w); }}}
```

The following shows the implementation of ClientJobImpl after connecting with
a Worker.

```
class ClientJobImpl(SyncServer server, SyncClient client, Schedule s)
implements ClientJob {
  Set<Schedule> schedules = EmptySet;
  Unit sendSchedules(Set<Schedule> ss) { schedules = ss; }
  Unit acceptConnection(Worker w) {
    if (w != null) {
      w!command(Schedule(s));
      await schedules != EmptySet;
      this.scheduleJobs();}}..}

class WorkerImpl(ClientJob job, SyncServer server) implements Worker {
  Unit command(Command c) { .. job!sendSchedules(schedules); }}
```

The method acceptConnection invokes method command on the worker and
suspends using the statement **await** schedules != EmptySet to wait for the
next set of schedules to arrive. The next set of schedules is set by invoking the
method sendSchedules on the ClientJob.

4   Behavioral Interfaces for Coboxes

In this section we introduce *attribute grammars* extended with assertions to
specify and verify properties of the traces generated between coboxes. As such,
extended attribute grammars provide a new formalism for contracts in general,
and coboxes in particular. In contrast to classes or interfaces, coboxes are runtime entities which do not have a single fixed interface[1]. Below we first discuss
how we can still refer statically, in the program text, to these run-time entities
by means of so-called communication views.

---

[1] We consider interfaces here to be a list of all signatures of the methods supported
by some object in the cobox.

4.1   Communication Views

To be able to refer to coboxes in syntactical constructs (such as specifications), we introduce the following (optional) annotation of cobox instantiations:

$$S ::= y = \text{new cog [Name] } C(\bar{e})$$

The semantics of the language remain unchanged. Note that the same cobox name can be shared among several coboxes (i.e. is in general not unique) since different cobox creation statements can specify the same cobox name.

Coboxes do not have a fixed interface, as the methods which can be invoked on an object in a cobox (and consequently appear in traces) are not fixed statically. In particular, during execution objects of any type can be added to a cobox, which clearly affects the possible traces of the cobox. Additionally, for practical reasons it is often convenient to focus on a particular subset of methods, leaving out methods irrelevant for specification purposes. This is especially useful for incomplete specifications. To solve both these problems, we introduce *communication views*. A communication view can be thought of as an interface for a named cobox. Figure 3 shows an example communication view associated with all coboxes named WorkerGroup. Formally a communication view is a

```
view WorkerView grammar Worker.g specifies WorkerGroup {
  send Coordinator.startReplication(Worker w) st,
  send ClientJob.registerItems(Worker w, Int id) pr,
  receive Worker.sendCurrendId(Int id) id,
  receive Worker.replyRegisterItems(Bool reg) ar,
  receive Worker.acceptItems(Set<Item> items) is,
  receive Worker.acceptEntries(Set<Map<String, Content>> contents) es
}
```

Fig. 3. Communication View

partial mapping from messages to abstract event names. A communication view thus simply introduces names tailored for specification purposes (see the next subsection about grammars for more details on how this event name is used). Partiality allows the user to select only those asynchronous methods relevant for specification purposes. Any method not listed in the view will be irrelevant in the specification of WorkerGroups.

Note that in this asynchronous setting we can distinguish three different events: sending a message (at the call-site), receiving the message in the queue (at the callee-site), and scheduling the message for execution (i.e. the point in time when the corresponding method starts executing). By the asynchronous nature of the ABS, we cannot detect in the ABS itself when a message has been put into the queue. Therefore we restrict to the other two events. Since we implement the run-time checker independently from any back-end (see also Section 5), we are forced to use the ABS itself for the detection of the observable events.

The **send** keyword identifies calls from objects in the WorkerGroup to methods of objects in another cobox (in other words: methods required by an object in the WorkerGroup). Conversely, the keyword **receive** identifies the scheduling of calls from another cobox to an object in a WorkerGroup. It is possible that methods listed in the view actually can never be called in practice (and therefore won't appear in the local trace of a cobox). In the above view, this happens if in a WorkerGroup there is no object of the class **Worker**.

4.2 Grammars

In this subsection we describe how properties of the set of allowed traces of a cobox can be specified in a convenient, high-level and declarative manner. We illustrate our approach by partially specifying the behavior depicted by the UML sequence diagram in Figure 2. Informally the property we focus on is:

> The Worker first notifies the Coordinator its intention to commence a replication session, the Worker would then receive the last transaction id identifying the version of the data to be replicated, the Worker sends this id to the ClientJob to see if the client is required to update its data up to the specified version. The Worker then expects an answer. Only if the answer is positive can the Worker retrieve replication items from the snapshot, moreover, the number of files sets to be replicated to the ClientJob must correspond to the number of replication items retrieved.

Grammars provide a convenient way to define the protocol behavior of the allowed traces. The terminals of the grammar are the message names given in a communication view. The formalization of the above property uses the communication view depicted in Figure 3. The productions of the grammar underlying the attribute grammar in Figure 4 specify the legal orderings of these messages named in the view. For example, the productions

$$S ::= \epsilon \mid st\ T$$
$$T ::= \epsilon \mid id\ U$$

specify that the message 'id' is preceded by the message 'st'.

While grammars provide a convenient way to specify the *protocol structure* of the valid traces, they do not take data such as parameters and return values of method calls and returns into account. Thus the question arises how to specify the *data-flow* of valid traces. To that end, we extend the grammar with attributes and assertions over these attributes. Each terminal symbol has *built-in* attributes consisting of the parameter names for referring to the object identities of the actual parameters, and **callee** for referencing the identity of the callee. Non-terminals have *user-defined* attributes to define data properties of sequences of terminals. In each production, the value of the attributes of the non-terminals appearing on the right-hand side of the production is defined.[2] For example, in the following production, the attribute 'w' for the non-terminal 'T' is defined.

---

[2] In the literature, such attributes are called inherited attributes.

$$S ::= \epsilon \mid st \ T \ (T.\mathtt{w} = st.\mathtt{w};)$$

Attribute definitions are surrounded by '(' and ')'. However the attributes themselves do not alter the language generated by the attribute grammar, they only *define* properties of data-flow of the trace. We extend the attribute grammar with assertions to specify properties of attributes. For example, the assertion in the second production of

$$T ::= \epsilon \mid id \ U \ (U.\mathtt{w} = T.\mathtt{w}; \ U.\mathtt{i} = id.\mathtt{id};)$$
$$U ::= \epsilon \mid pr \ \{\mathbf{assert} \ U.\mathtt{w} == pr.\mathtt{w} \ \&\& \ U.\mathtt{i} == pr.\mathtt{id};\} \ V$$

expresses that the 'id' passed as a parameter to the method 'registerItems' (represented in the grammar by the terminal $pr.\mathtt{id};$) must be the same as the one previously passed into 'sendCurrentId' (terminal $id.\mathtt{id}$). Assertions are surrounded by '{' and '}' to distinguish them visually from attribute definitions.

The full attribute grammar Figure 4 formalizes the informal property stated in the beginning of this subsection. The grammar specifies that for each Worker object, in its own object cobox, the Coordinator must be notified of the start of the replication by invoking its method `startReplication` (*st*). Only then can the Worker receive (from an unspecified cobox) the identifier of the current version of the data to be replicated (*id*). Next the Worker invokes the method `registerItems` on the corresponding ClientJob about this version of the data (*pr*). The grammar here asserts that the identifier is indeed the same as that received via the method call `sendCurrendId`. The Worker then expects to receive a method call `replyRegisterItems` indicating if the replication should proceed, the Worker then can recieve method call `acceptItems` for the data items to be replicated. The grammar here asserts that this can only happen if the previous call indicated the replication should proceed. The Worker then can receive method call `acceptEntries` for the set of Directories, each identified by a data item. Since each data item refers to a directory, the grammar here asserts the number of items is the same as the number of directories.

$$
\begin{array}{ll}
S & ::= \epsilon \mid st \ T \ (T.\mathtt{w} = st.\mathtt{w};) \\
T & ::= \epsilon \mid id \ U \ (U.\mathtt{w} = T.\mathtt{w}; \ U.\mathtt{i} = id.\mathtt{id};) \\
U & ::= \epsilon \mid pr \ \{\mathbf{assert} \ U.\mathtt{w} == pr.\mathtt{w} \ \&\& \ U.\mathtt{i} == pr.\mathtt{id};\} \ V \\
V & ::= \epsilon \mid ar \ W \ (W.\mathtt{b} = ar.\mathtt{reg};) \\
W & ::= \epsilon \mid is \ \{\mathbf{assert} \ W.\mathtt{b};\} \ X \ (X.\mathtt{s} = \mathtt{size}(is.\mathtt{items});) \\
X & ::= \epsilon \mid es \ \{\mathbf{assert} \ X.\mathtt{s} == \mathtt{size}(es.\mathtt{contents});\}
\end{array}
$$

Fig. 4. Attribute Grammars

To further illustrate the above concepts, we consider an additional behavioral interface for the WorkerGroup cobox. To allow users to make changes to the replication schedules during the run-time of FAS, every ClientJob would request the next set of replication schedules and send them to SyncClient for scheduling. Here is an informal description of the property, where Figure 5 presents the

```
view ScheduleView grammar Schedule.g specifies WorkerGroup {
  receive Worker.command(Command c) cm,
  send ClientJob.sendSchedules(Set<Schedule> ss) sn,
  send SyncServer.requestListSchedules(Worker w) lt,
  send SyncServer.requestSchedule(Worker w, String name) gt,
  send Coordinator.requestStartReplication(Worker w) st
}
```

Fig. 5. Communication View for Scheduling

$$
\begin{aligned}
S &::= \epsilon \mid cm\ T\ (T.\texttt{c} = cm.\texttt{c};) \\
T &::= \epsilon \mid gt\ \{\textbf{assert } T.\texttt{c} \mathrel{!=} \texttt{ListSchedule} \texttt{ \&\&} \\
  &\qquad\quad gt.\texttt{n} == \texttt{name}(T.\texttt{c});\}\ U\ (U.\texttt{c} = T.\texttt{c};) \\
  &\quad\ \mid lt\ \{\textbf{assert } T.\texttt{c} == \texttt{ListSchedule};\}\ U\ (U.\texttt{c} = T.\texttt{c};) \\
U &::= \epsilon \mid sn\ \{\textbf{assert } sn.\texttt{ss} \mathrel{!=} \texttt{EmptySet};\}\ V\ (V.\texttt{c} = U.\texttt{c};) \\
V &::= \epsilon \mid st\ \{\textbf{assert } V.\texttt{c} \mathrel{!=} \texttt{ListSchedule};\}
\end{aligned}
$$

Fig. 6. Attribute Grammar for Scheduling

communication view capturing the relevant messages and Figure 6 presents the grammar that formalizes the property:

A ClientJob may request for either all replication schedules or a single schedule. The ClientJob does this by sending a command to the Worker (cm). If the command is of the value `ListSchedule`, the Worker is to acquire all schedules from the SyncServer (lt) and return them to the ClientJob (sn). Otherwise, the Worker is to acquire only the specified schedule (gt) and return it to the ClientJob (sn). If the ClientJob asks for all schedules, it must not proceed further with the replication session and terminate (st).

In summary, communication views provide an interface of a named cobox. The behavior of such an interface is specified by means of an attribute grammar extended with assertions. This grammar represents the legal traces of the named cobox as words of the language generated by the grammar, which gives rise to a natural notion of the satisfaction relation between programs and specifications. Properties of the control-flow and data-flow are integrated in a single formalism: the grammar productions specify the valid orderings of the messages (the control-flow of the valid traces), whereas assertions specify the data-flow.

5 Implementation

The input of SAGA consists of three ingredients: a communication view, an attribute grammar extended with assertions and an ABS model. The output is an ordinary ABS model which behaves the same as the input program, except that it throws an assertion failure when the current execution violates the specification. Since the resulting ABS model is an ordinary ABS model, all analysis tools [18] (including a debugging environment with visualization and a state-of-the-art cost analyzer) and back-ends which exist for the ABS can be used on it directly. Because of the intrinsic complexity of developing efficient and user-friendly parser generators, we require that the implementation of the parser-generator should be decoupled from the rest of the implementation of SAGA. This has lead to a component-based design (Figure 7) consisting of a parser-generator component and source-code weaving component. We discuss these components, and the second requirement on performance of the generated parser, in more detail below.

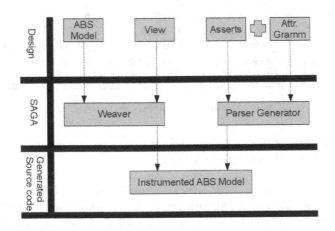

Fig. 7. SAGA tool architecture

Component for parsing deterministic attribute grammars with inherited attributes. This parser-generator component processes only the attribute grammar and generates a parser for it, with ABS as the target language. Parsers for attribute grammars in general take a stream of terminals as input, and output a parse tree according to the grammar productions (where non-terminal nodes are annotated with their attribute values). In our case, the attribute grammars also contain assertions, and the generated parser additionally checks that all assertions in the grammar are true.

Due to the power of general context-free grammars (even without attributes), they can be quite expensive to parse. By combining results of [17] and Lee [12] we can deduce the time complexity of parsing n tokens lays between $O(n^2)$ and $O(n^{2.38})$. However, in our case, whenever a new message (asynchronous call) is added to the trace, all parse trees of all prefixes have been computed previously. The question arises how efficient the new parse trees can be computed by exploiting the parse trees of the prefixes. Unfortunately, for general context-free grammars, this cannot be done in constant time. For if this was possible in constant time, parsing the full trace results in a parser which works in linear time (n terminals which all take a constant amount of time), which is lower than the theoretical quadratic lower-bound. We therefore restrict our attention to deterministic regular attribute grammars with only inherited attributes. All grammars used in the case study have this form and parsing the new trace in such grammars can be done in constant time, since they can be translated to a finite automaton with conditions (assertions) and attribute updates as actions to execute on transitions. Parsing the new message consists of taking a single step in this automaton. Moreover for such grammars, the space complexity is also very low: it is not necessary to store the entire trace, only the attribute values of the previous trace must be stored.

Source-code weaving component. The weaving component processes the communication view and the given ABS model, and outputs a new ABS model in which each call to a method appearing in the view is transformed. The transformation inserts code which checks whether the method call which is about to be executed is allowed by the attribute grammar, and if this is not the case, prevents unsafe behavior by throwing an assertion failure. In contrast to receive events, the transformation for send events is invasive, in the sense that it cannot be done only locally in the body of those methods actually appearing in the view, but instead it has to be done at all call-sites (in client code). To see this, suppose that the transformation *was* done locally, say in the beginning of the method body. Due to concurrency and scheduling policies, other methods which were called at a later time could have been scheduled earlier. In such a scenario, these other methods are checked earlier than the order in which they are actually called by a client.

The transformation is done in two steps. First, all calls to methods that occur in a communication view are isolated using pattern matching in the meta-program. We created a Rascal ABS grammar for that purpose. Second, all call-statements are preceded by code which checks that the current object is part of a named cobox (note that this check really has to be done at run-time due to the dynamic nature of coboxes). If this is the case, the trace is updated by taking a step in the finite automaton where additionally the assertion is checked. If there is no transition for the message from the current state, we throw an assertion error. Intuitively such an error corresponds to a protocol violation.

6 Experience Report

In order to understand the Fredhopper Access Server (FAS), a system with over 150,000 lines of Java code, suitable abstractions are crucial. We developed an ACOG model which describes the behavior of the replication system, a crucial (and one of the most complex) component in the FAS. We then specified and checked this behavior by means of attribute grammars with SAGA.

Table 1 shows metrics for the Java implementation and the ACOG model of the Replication System (without the attribute grammar). The figures in the table illustrate the expressive power of the modeling language: the ACOG model is half the size of the Java implementation. Additionally the ACOG model includes model-level information such as deployment components and simulation

Table 1. Metrics of Java and ACOG of the Replication System

Metrics	Java	ACOG
Nr. of lines of code	6400	3300
Nr. of classes	44	40
Nr. of interfaces	2	43
Nr. of functions	N/A	80
Nr. of data types	N/A	17

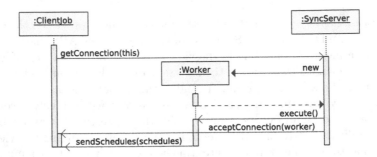

Fig. 8. Protocol violation

of external inputs in the ACOG model, which the Java implementation lacks. The ACOG model includes also scheduling information, as well as models of file systems and data bases, while the Java implementation leverages libraries and its API. This accounts for >1,000 lines of ACOG code.

We detected a crucial protocol violation while running SAGA over the ACOG model of the Replication System (see Figure 8). The sequence of messages depicted by the UML sequence diagram violates the grammar Scheduler.g shown in Figure 6. Specifically, the cobox for the Worker object sends the method call SyncServer.requestListSchedules before receiving the method call Worker.command. The following shows part of the implementation of WorkerImpl that is responsible for this violation.

```
class WorkerImpl(ClientJob job, SyncServer server, Coordinator coord)
implements Worker {
  Maybe<Command> cmd = Just(ListSchedule);
  Unit execute() {
    if (cmd == Just(ListSchedule)) {
      server!requestListSchedules(this);
    } else {
      server!requestSchedule(this, name(cmd))); }}
  Unit command(Command c) { this.cmd == Just(cmd); }}
```

The reason for the violation is that when the cobox receives the method call Worker.execute the above implementation does not wait receiving the method call Worker.command before sending the method call

`SyncServer.requestListSchedules`. The reason this is possible is because the instance field cmd is initialized incorrectly with the value `Just(ListSchedule)` that would allow the conditional statement inside the method `execute` to invoke the method `SyncServer.requestListSchedules`. The following shows the correct version of this part of the implementation.

```
class WorkerImpl(ClientJob job, SyncServer server, Coordinator coord)
implements Worker {
  Maybe<Command> cmd = Nothing;
  Unit execute() {
    this.coord = coord;
    await cmd != Nothing;
    if (cmd == Just(ListSchedule)) {
      server!requestListSchedules(this);
    } else {
      server!requestSchedule(this, name(cmd))); }}
  Unit command(Command c) { this.cmd == Just(cmd); }}
```

In the correct implementation, the field cmd is initialized with the value Nothing and an **await** statement is used to ensure cmd is set by receiving the method call `Worker.command()` before proceeding further.

7   Conclusion

We showed using an industrial case study how both protocol-oriented properties and data-oriented properties of message sequences sent between coboxes can be specified conveniently in a single formalism of attribute grammars extended with assertions. Moreover we developed and discussed the corresponding tool support provided by SAGA. SAGA can be obtained from http://www.cwi.nl/~cdegouw.

Related Work. In [9] a survey is presented of behavioral interface specification languages and their use in static analysis of correctness of object-oriented programs. In particular, there exists an extensive literature on the static analysis of systems of concurrent objects. For example, in [8] a proof system for partial correctness reasoning about concurrent objects is established based on traces and class invariants. We present the first specification language for the analysis of concurrent *groups* of objects (coboxes), and implemented an efficient run-time checker. This paper builds on the previous work [6], which integrates (in a single formalism) both data- and protocol-oriented properties of message sequences of single-threaded Java programs. Here we extend this work to a concurrent modeling language, which requires a very different tool architecture, and add support for incremental parsing of message sequences with a linear space- and time-complexity. There exist many interesting approaches to run-time verification, e.g., monitoring message sequences, but all of these approaches only work in the context of Java and its low-level concurrency model based on multithreading.

For example, Martin et al. [13] introduce the Program Query Language (PQL) for detecting errors in sequences of communication events. PQL was updated last in 2006 and does not support user-defined properties of data. Allan et al. [2] develop an extension of AspectJ with a trace-based language feature called Tracematches that enables the programmer to trigger the execution of extra code by specifying a regular pattern of events in a computation trace. The underlying pattern matching involves a binding of values to free variables. Nobakht et al. [14] monitors calls and returns using the Java Debugger Architecture. Their specification language is equivalent in expressive power to regular expressions. Because the grammar for the specifications is fixed, the user can not specify a convenient structure themselves, and data is not considered. Chen et al. [3] present Java-MOP, a run-time monitoring tool based on aspect-oriented programming which uses context-free grammars to describe properties of the control flow of traces. However JavaMOP does not integrate data-oriented properties for use in design-by-contract a la JML. General data-oriented properties can only be specified by the injection of Java **assert**-statements using AspectJ, essentially bypassing JavaMOP. Moreover even this manual injection can only be used to specify a data-property of the single last message sent/received, not for data properties of the full history. As such, JavaMOP provides no direct and high-level support for data-oriented properties. LARVA is developed by Colombo et al. [5]. The specification language has an imperative flavour: users define a finite state machine to define the allowed traces (i.e. one has to manually 'implement' a parser for the regular expression). Data properties are supported in a limited manner, by enriching the state machine with conditions on method parameters or return values (not on sequences of them).

DeLine and Fähndrich [7] propose a statically checkable typestate system for object-oriented programs. Typestate specifications of protocols correspond to finite state machines, data and assertions are not considered in their approach.

Future Work. For practical reasons, good error reporting is essential. Note however that since error reporting, for example in case of assertion failures, prints to the screen (and consequently relies on low-level I/O details), it is not back-end independent. Using the ABS foreign language interface, it is possible to execute native Java or Maude code which implements the error reporting. As a relatively simple first step, we could for instance use SDEdit, a sequence diagram editor already used in the ABS, to visualize traces violating the grammars. Since traces tend to be large, finding relevant abstractions of the trace is crucial here.

Currently SAGA supports deterministic regular grammars with just inherited attributes. Such grammars can be incrementally parsed. This immediately suggest another future line of work: is there a larger class of grammars which can be parsed incrementally?

As the final direction of future work we would like to investigate ways to control the complexity of extensions of the modeling language including futures and promises (in the Cobox concurrency model).

References

1. Agha, G.: Actors: A model of concurrent computation in distributed systems. MIT Press, Cambridge (1990)
2. Allan, C., Avgustinov, P., Christensen, A.S., Hendren, L., Kuzins, S., Lhoták, O., de Moor, O., Sereni, D., Sittampalam, G., Tibble, J.: Adding trace matching with free variables to aspectj. SIGPLAN Not. 40(10), 345–364 (2005)
3. Chen, F., Roşu, G.: MOP: an efficient and generic runtime verification framework. SIGPLAN Not. 42(10), 569–588 (2007)
4. Clarke, L.A., Rosenblum, D.S.: A historical perspective on runtime assertion checking in software development. ACM SIGSOFT Software Engineering Notes 31(3), 25–37 (2006)
5. Colombo, C., Pace, G.J., Schneider, G.: Larva — safer monitoring of real-time java programs (tool paper). In: SEFM 2005, pp. 33–37 (2009)
6. de Boer, F.S., de Gouw, S., Johnsen, E.B., Wong, P.Y.H.: Run-time checking of data- and protocol-oriented properties of java programs: An industrial case study. In: SAC (to appear, 2013)
7. DeLine, R., Fähndrich, M.: Typestates for Objects. In: Odersky, M. (ed.) ECOOP 2004. LNCS, vol. 3086, pp. 465–490. Springer, Heidelberg (2004)
8. Din, C.C., Dovland, J., Johnsen, E.B., Owe, O.: Observable behavior of distributed systems: Component reasoning for concurrent objects. J. Log. Algebr. Program. 81(3), 227–256 (2012)
9. Hatcliff, J., Leavens, G.T., Leino, K.R.M., Müller, P., Parkinson, M.: Behavioral interface specification languages. ACM Comput. Surv. 44(3), 16:1–16:58 (2012)
10. Johnsen, E.B., Hähnle, R., Schäfer, J., Schlatte, R., Steffen, M.: ABS: A core language for abstract behavioral specification. In: Aichernig, B.K., de Boer, F.S., Bonsangue, M.M. (eds.) FMCO 2010. LNCS, vol. 6957, pp. 142–164. Springer, Heidelberg (2011)
11. Johnsen, E.B., Owe, O.: An asynchronous communication model for distributed concurrent objects. SSM 6(1), 35–58 (2007)
12. Lee, L.: Fast context-free grammar parsing requires fast boolean matrix multiplication. J. ACM 49(1), 1–15 (2002)
13. Martin, M., Livshits, B., Lam, M.S.: Finding application errors and security flaws using pql: a program query language. SIGPLAN Not. 40(10), 365–383 (2005)
14. Nobakht, B., Bonsangue, M.M., de Boer, F.S., de Gouw, S.: Monitoring method call sequences using annotations. In: Barbosa, L.S., Lumpe, M. (eds.) FACS 2010. LNCS, vol. 6921, pp. 53–70. Springer, Heidelberg (2012)
15. Schäfer, J., Poetzsch-Heffter, A.: JCoBox: Generalizing active objects to concurrent components. In: D'Hondt, T. (ed.) ECOOP 2010. LNCS, vol. 6183, pp. 275–299. Springer, Heidelberg (2010)
16. Sirjani, M., Movaghar, A., Shali, A., de Boer, F.S.: Modeling and verification of reactive systems using Rebeca. Fundam. Inform. 63(4), 385–410 (2004)
17. Valiant, L.G.: General context-free recognition in less than cubic time. J. Comput. Syst. Sci. 10(2), 308–315 (1975)
18. Wong, P.Y.H., Albert, E., Muschevici, R., Proença, J., Schäfer, J., Schlatte, R.: The ABS tool suite: modelling, executing and analysing distributed adaptable object-oriented systems. STTT 14(5), 567–588 (2012)

Automated Mediator Synthesis: Combining Behavioural and Ontological Reasoning

Amel Bennaceur[1], Chris Chilton[2], Malte Isberner[3], and Bengt Jonsson[4]

[1] ARLES, Inria Paris - Rocquencourt, France
[2] Department of Computer Science, University of Oxford, UK
[3] Technical University of Dortmund, Germany
[4] Department of Information Technology, Uppsala University, Sweden

Abstract. Software systems are increasingly composed of independently developed heterogeneous components. To ensure interoperability, mediators are needed that coordinate actions and translate exchanged messages between the components. We present a technique for automated synthesis of mediators, by means of a quotient operator, that is based on behavioural models of the components and an ontological model of the data domain. By not requiring a specification of the composed system, the method supports both off-line and run-time synthesis. The obtained mediator is the most general component that ensures freedom of both communication mismatches and deadlock in the composition. Validation of the approach is given by implementation of a prototype tool, while applicability is illustrated on heterogeneous holiday booking components.

Keywords: mediator synthesis, quotient, ontology, deadlock-freeness.

1 Introduction

Modern software-intensive systems are increasingly composed of numerous independently developed and network-connected software components. These components often exhibit heterogeneous behaviour, which prevents them from interacting with one another according to a particular protocol. To circumvent this problem, *mediators* (or mediating adapters [YS97, CMS+09]) can be designed, which are intermediary software entities that allow heterogeneous software components to interact seamlessly, by coordinating their behaviours and translating the messages that they exchange. Due to the vast number of potential interaction patterns, it is not feasible to design a generic mediator that will allow an arbitrary collection of components to communicate. Instead, one approach towards facilitating communication involves the automated synthesis of a mediator, based on the behaviours of the components needing to interact.

Automatic mediator synthesis presupposes formal models of the participating components, each specifying the allowed sequences of interactions. Models can be directly specified by component developers, or can be automatically inferred (given their interfaces) by black-box inference [MHS+12]. Existing

R.M. Hierons, M.G. Merayo, and M. Bravetti (Eds.): SEFM 2013, LNCS 8137, pp. 274–288, 2013.

approaches for mediator synthesis also need specifications representing the composed behaviour of the components. For instance, synthesis of protocol converters in [CL90, PdAHSV02] requires a specification of the service delivered by the composed system; similarly, in synthesising mediators for composed web services, an explicit specification of the relationships between the data parameters in different interface primitives is needed [BPT10]. Providing such specifications is an obstacle to automated synthesis, especially at run-time.

In this paper, we propose a rigorous methodology for the automated synthesis of mediators, based on models of the components and of the data domain, which does not require an explicit specification of the intended composition, making the techniques suitable for both off-line and run-time synthesis. Components may have incompatible behaviours and utilise different interaction vocabularies. To bridge this heterogeneity barrier, we rely on a domain ontology, which shows the relationships between data concepts of the interaction vocabularies. The domain ontology is generic to the application area of the components, and so no extra information need be supplied at synthesis time.

Our synthesis method is structured into two phases. First, the domain ontology is used to derive a correspondence between actions of different components, together with ordering constraints that must be respected between them. In the second phase, we synthesise a mediator using a quotient operator, by utilising the behavioural models of the participating components and the ordering constraints derived from the ontology. Our quotient operator extends existing definitions [BR08], in that it is sensitive to progress properties. Thus, mediators generated by our methodology are free from communication mismatches, ensure progress towards the goals of individual components, and respect the data constraints implicitly given by the domain ontology.

Outline. Section 2 introduces our component modelling formalism, along with the notions of parallel composition, refinement and quotient, which are essential for our synthesis methodology. Ontologies are presented in Section 3, where their role in modelling the semantics of component actions is explained. Section 4 describes the methodology for automatically synthesising mediators free of communication mismatches and premature deadlock, while Section 5 describes our prototype implementation and discusses its applicability. Section 6 examines related work, while Section 7 concludes and suggests future work.

2   Primer on the Compositional Specification Theory

In this section, we introduce the necessary parts of our compositional specification theory for modelling components [CCJK12]. The behaviour of a component specifies the sequences of allowed interactions between the component and its environment, which can be represented by a labelled transition system (LTS). The labels are partitioned into input and output actions, although internal actions can also be accommodated. In a state, the component is willing to receive (from the environment) any enabled input, and may emit any enabled output. If the environment supplies an input that is not enabled, an *inconsistency* arises, which can be understood as either underspecification, or an undesired situation corresponding to run-time error or bad behaviour.

To model deadlock and termination, a state can be designated as *quiescent*. The intuition is that a component must not block (i.e., must eventually emit an output if no input appears) in a non-quiescent state. The modelling formalism itself does not distinguish between undesirable deadlock and termination.

Our methodology is equally applicable to deterministic and non-deterministic models, using the theory in [CCJK12]. Some definitions can be simplified in the deterministic case, and for simplicity we will use these in this paper. Our specification theory can then be seen as interface automata extended with the capability to model deadlock and termination [dAH01].

Definition 1 (Behavioural model). *A behavioural model of a component $\mathcal{P}$ is a tuple $\langle A_{\mathcal{P}}^I, A_{\mathcal{P}}^O, S_{\mathcal{P}}, s_{\mathcal{P}}^0, \delta_{\mathcal{P}}, Q_{\mathcal{P}} \rangle$, where $A_{\mathcal{P}}^I$ and $A_{\mathcal{P}}^O$ are disjoint sets referred to as the inputs and outputs (the union of which we denote by $A_{\mathcal{P}}$), $S_{\mathcal{P}}$ is a finite set of states with $s_{\mathcal{P}}^0 \in S_{\mathcal{P}}$ being the designated initial state, $\delta_{\mathcal{P}} : S_{\mathcal{P}} \times A_{\mathcal{P}} \rightharpoonup S_{\mathcal{P}} is the partial transition function, and $Q_{\mathcal{P}} \subseteq S_{\mathcal{P}}$ are the quiescent states.*

We will not be fussy in distinguishing components from their models, and will often refer to "the component A" for "the behavioural model of A".

In a behavioural model of a component, we distinguish undesirable deadlocks from termination by introducing a designated ✓ action treated as an input. The convention is that ✓ can only be received when the component has successfully terminated.

Refinement of components is defined using the alternating simulation for interface automata extended to cope with quiescence. It guarantees safe-substitutivity of components and preservation of deadlock-freeness.

Definition 2 (Refinement). *Let $\mathcal{P}$ and $\mathcal{Q}$ be components. Then $\mathcal{Q}$ is a refinement of $\mathcal{P}$, written $\mathcal{Q} \sqsubseteq \mathcal{P}$, if $A_{\mathcal{P}}^I \subseteq A_{\mathcal{Q}}^I$ and $A_{\mathcal{Q}}^O \subseteq A_{\mathcal{P}}^O$, and there is a relation $\sqsubseteq \subseteq S_{\mathcal{Q}} \times S_{\mathcal{P}}$, called an alternating simulation, such that whenever $s_{\mathcal{Q}} \sqsubseteq s_{\mathcal{P}}$:*

- *if $i \in A_{\mathcal{P}}^I$ is enabled in $s_{\mathcal{P}}$, then i is enabled in $s_{\mathcal{Q}}$ and $\delta_{\mathcal{Q}}(s_{\mathcal{Q}}, i) \sqsubseteq \delta_{\mathcal{P}}(s_{\mathcal{P}}, i)$,*
- *if $o \in A_{\mathcal{Q}}^O$ is enabled in $s_{\mathcal{Q}}$, then o is enabled in $s_{\mathcal{P}}$ and $\delta_{\mathcal{Q}}(s_{\mathcal{Q}}, o) \sqsubseteq \delta_{\mathcal{P}}(s_{\mathcal{P}}, o)$,*
- *if $s_{\mathcal{Q}} \in Q_{\mathcal{Q}}$, then $s_{\mathcal{P}} \in Q_{\mathcal{P}}$,*

and such that $s_{\mathcal{Q}}^0 \sqsubseteq s_{\mathcal{P}}^0$.

The *parallel composition* of two components represents the combined effect of them running asynchronously, and synchronizing on actions that are common to their sets of inputs and outputs. To preserve the effect that a single output from a component can be received by multiple components in its environment, we must define the parallel composition to repeatedly broadcast an output: this means that an input a and output a combine to form an output a. As each output must be under the control of at most one component, the parallel composition is only defined when the composed components have disjoint sets of outputs. To obtain a modular definition of parallel composition, we first define a generic *product* of two transition functions.

Definition 3 (Product). *Let* $\mathcal{P}$ *and* $\mathcal{Q}$ *be components. The product of the transitions functions* $\delta_{\mathcal{P}}$ *of* $\mathcal{P}$ *and* $\delta_{\mathcal{Q}}$ *of* $\mathcal{Q}$ *is the partial function* $\delta_{\mathcal{P} \otimes \mathcal{Q}} : (S_{\mathcal{P}} \times S_{\mathcal{Q}}) \times (\mathcal{A}_{\mathcal{P}} \cup \mathcal{A}_{\mathcal{Q}}) \rightharpoonup (S_{\mathcal{P}} \times S_{\mathcal{Q}})$, *where* $\delta_{\mathcal{P} \otimes \mathcal{Q}}(\langle s_{\mathcal{P}}, s_{\mathcal{Q}} \rangle, a)$ *is defined as:*

- $\langle \delta_{\mathcal{P}}(s_{\mathcal{P}}, a), \delta_{\mathcal{Q}}(s_{\mathcal{Q}}, a) \rangle$ *when* $a \in \mathcal{A}_{\mathcal{P}} \cap \mathcal{A}_{\mathcal{Q}}$, *and both* $\delta_{\mathcal{P}}(s_{\mathcal{P}}, a)$ *and* $\delta_{\mathcal{Q}}(s_{\mathcal{Q}}, a)$ *are defined,*
- $\langle \delta_{\mathcal{P}}(s_{\mathcal{P}}, a), s_{\mathcal{Q}} \rangle$ *when* $a \in \mathcal{A}_{\mathcal{P}} \setminus \mathcal{A}_{\mathcal{Q}}$ *and* $\delta_{\mathcal{P}}(s_{\mathcal{P}}, a)$ *is defined,*
- *symmetrically,* $\langle s_{\mathcal{P}}, \delta_{\mathcal{Q}}(s_{\mathcal{Q}}, a) \rangle$ *when* $a \in \mathcal{A}_{\mathcal{Q}} \setminus \mathcal{A}_{\mathcal{P}}$ *and* $\delta_{\mathcal{Q}}(s_{\mathcal{Q}}, a)$ *is defined,*

and $\delta_{\mathcal{P} \otimes \mathcal{Q}}(\langle s_{\mathcal{P}}, s_{\mathcal{Q}} \rangle, a)$ *is undefined otherwise.* □

A pair of states $\langle s_{\mathcal{P}}, s_{\mathcal{Q}} \rangle \in (S_{\mathcal{P}} \times S_{\mathcal{Q}})$ of $\mathcal{P}$ and $\mathcal{Q}$ is said to be *incompatible* if for some output action $a \in \mathcal{A}_{\mathcal{P}}^O \cup \mathcal{A}_{\mathcal{Q}}^O$, either $\delta_{\mathcal{P}}(s_{\mathcal{P}}, a)$ or $\delta_{\mathcal{Q}}(s_{\mathcal{Q}}, a)$ is defined, but $\delta_{\mathcal{P} \otimes \mathcal{Q}}(\langle s_{\mathcal{P}}, s_{\mathcal{Q}} \rangle, a)$ is undefined. Intuitively, in an incompatible pair of states, one component can perform an output that is not enabled as an input in the other component, thus creating a communication mismatch. A pair of states $\langle s_{\mathcal{P}}, s_{\mathcal{Q}} \rangle \in (S_{\mathcal{P}} \times S_{\mathcal{Q}})$ is said to be *potentially incompatible* if there is a (possibly empty) sequence of outputs $a_1 \cdots a_n$ in $\mathcal{A}_{\mathcal{P}}^O \cup \mathcal{A}_{\mathcal{Q}}^O$ that leads to an incompatible pair of states (i.e., $\delta_{\mathcal{P} \otimes \mathcal{Q}}(\ldots (\delta_{\mathcal{P} \otimes \mathcal{Q}}(\delta_{\mathcal{P} \otimes \mathcal{Q}}(\langle s_{\mathcal{P}}, s_{\mathcal{Q}} \rangle, a_1), a_2) \ldots), a_n)$ is incompatible).

We use the product operation in the definition of parallel composition.

Definition 4 (Parallel composition). *Let* $\mathcal{P}$ *and* $\mathcal{Q}$ *be components such that* $\mathcal{A}_{\mathcal{P}}^O \cap \mathcal{A}_{\mathcal{Q}}^O = \emptyset$. *If* $\langle s_{\mathcal{Q}}^0, s_{\mathcal{P}}^0 \rangle$ *is not potentially incompatible, then the* parallel composition *of* $\mathcal{P}$ *and* $\mathcal{Q}$ *exists and is defined as the component* $\mathcal{P} \parallel \mathcal{Q} = \langle (\mathcal{A}_{\mathcal{P}}^I \cup \mathcal{A}_{\mathcal{Q}}^I) \setminus (\mathcal{A}_{\mathcal{P}}^O \cup \mathcal{A}_{\mathcal{Q}}^O), \mathcal{A}_{\mathcal{P}}^O \cup \mathcal{A}_{\mathcal{Q}}^O, S_{\mathcal{P}} \times S_{\mathcal{Q}}, (s_{\mathcal{P}}^0, s_{\mathcal{Q}}^0), \delta_{\mathcal{P} \parallel \mathcal{Q}}, Q_{\mathcal{P}} \times Q_{\mathcal{Q}} \rangle$, *where:* $\delta_{\mathcal{P} \parallel \mathcal{Q}}(\langle s_{\mathcal{P}}, s_{\mathcal{Q}} \rangle, a) = \delta_{\mathcal{P} \otimes \mathcal{Q}}(\langle s_{\mathcal{P}}, s_{\mathcal{Q}} \rangle, a)$ *whenever* $\delta_{\mathcal{P} \otimes \mathcal{Q}}(\langle s_{\mathcal{P}}, s_{\mathcal{Q}} \rangle, a)$ *is defined and not potentially incompatible, otherwise* $\delta_{\mathcal{P} \parallel \mathcal{Q}}(\langle s_{\mathcal{P}}, s_{\mathcal{Q}} \rangle, a)$ *is undefined.*

Intuitively, the transition function of $\mathcal{P} \parallel \mathcal{Q}$ is undefined for inputs that lead to potentially incompatible pairs of states. If the environment supplies such an input, then $\mathcal{P} \parallel \mathcal{Q}$ can potentially reach an incompatible pair of states, and such a situation is regarded as inconsistent. The component $\mathcal{P} \parallel \mathcal{Q}$ is quiescent if both $\mathcal{P}$ and $\mathcal{Q}$ are quiescent.

Travel Agency Example. To illustrate our synthesis methodology, we consider a simple yet challenging example of a componentised and heterogeneous travel agency system, initially presented in [BBG+11]. The first component, called *USClient*, is a client-side software entity that allows customers to search for a holiday package, which consists of a hotel, a flight, and a car, and to purchase one if they so desire. The second component, called *EUService*, is a server-side service that provides operations for selecting the constituent parts of a holiday package (i.e., a hotel, a flight, and a car) separately.

The behaviour of the *USClient* and *EUService* components is represented by the models in Figures 1 and 2. Component models are represented pictorially by enclosing the transition system within a box corresponding to the interface. Labelled arrows pointing at the interface correspond to inputs, whereas arrows emanating from the interface correspond to outputs. Quiescent states are represented by squares, and other states by circles.

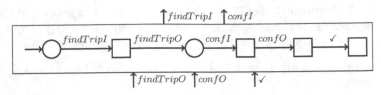

Fig. 1. Model of *USClient*

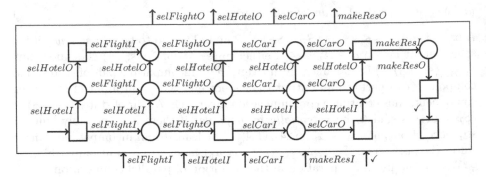

Fig. 2. Model of *EUService*

USClient sends *findTripI*, which is a request for a travel package that includes the travel preference of the customer (i.e., destination, departure and return dates). Then, *USClient* receives *findTripO*, which is a response including a trip proposition. *USClient* confirms the reservation by sending the *confI* request and receiving the acknowledgement within the *confO* response.

EUService receives the *selHotelI*, *selFlightI*, or *selCarI* requests for finding a hotel, flight, or a car respectively given some customer preferences, which consists of a destination, departure and return dates. It then replies with one of the corresponding responses *selHotelO*, *selFlightO*, or *selCarO*, which include propositions for a hotel, flight, and car respectively. While requests for a hotel and a flight can be performed in any order, the request for a car can only be performed once the flight has been selected. Once all parts of a trip are validated, the *EUService* expects to receive a *makeResI* request for completing the reservation, and sends the corresponding response *makeResO*.

The ✓ action, which may occur precisely at the end of the transaction, indicates that each component terminates only at the end of the transaction.

The two components have a functional discrepancy that prevents them from directly interacting to secure a holiday, even though, at a high-level of abstraction, *EUService* provides the functionality required by *USClient*. It is our intention to automatically synthesise a mediator allowing the two components to successfully interoperate. The synthesis approach is based on the behavioural models of each component, together with an ontology that represents knowledge about the domain in which the components belong.

Quotient. The final operation that we consider is that of quotient, which can be regarded as the adjoint (roughly "inverse") of parallel composition. Given a specification for a system $\mathcal{R}$, together with a component $\mathcal{P}$ implementing part of $\mathcal{R}$, the quotient, denoted $\mathcal{R}/\mathcal{P}$, yields the *weakest* specification for the remaining part of $\mathcal{R}$ to be implemented. Thus, $\mathcal{R}/\mathcal{P}$ is the weakest component such that $\mathcal{P} \parallel (\mathcal{R}/\mathcal{P}) \sqsubseteq \mathcal{R}$. It is sufficient to understand quotient in this way without examining the formal definition below. Consequently, the remainder of this section may be skipped without losing the ability to understand our synthesis methodology.

Here, we define the quotient $\mathcal{R}/\mathcal{P}$ under the assumptions that $A_{\mathcal{P}} \subseteq A_{\mathcal{R}}$, reflecting that $\mathcal{P}$ is a sub-component of $\mathcal{R}$, and $A_{\mathcal{P}}^O \subseteq A_{\mathcal{R}}^O$, which is implied by $\mathcal{P} \parallel (\mathcal{R}/\mathcal{P}) \sqsubseteq \mathcal{R}$. We postulate that $A_{\mathcal{R}/\mathcal{P}}^O = A_{\mathcal{R}}^O \setminus A_{\mathcal{P}}^O$ and $A_{\mathcal{R}/\mathcal{P}}^I = A_{\mathcal{P}}^O \cup A_{\mathcal{R}}^I$, which allows $\mathcal{R}/\mathcal{P}$ to monitor all the actions of $\mathcal{P}$ and $\mathcal{R}$.

Definition 5 (Quotient). *Let $\mathcal{P}$ and $\mathcal{R}$ be components such that $A_{\mathcal{P}}^O \subseteq A_{\mathcal{R}}^O$ and $A_{\mathcal{P}} \subseteq A_{\mathcal{R}}$. The quotient of $\mathcal{P}$ from $\mathcal{R}$ is the component $\mathcal{R}/\mathcal{P} = \langle A_{\mathcal{P}}^O \cup A_{\mathcal{R}}^I, A_{\mathcal{R}}^O \setminus A_{\mathcal{P}}^O, S_{\mathcal{R}/\mathcal{P}}, (s_{\mathcal{P}}^0, s_{\mathcal{R}}^0), \delta_{\mathcal{R}/\mathcal{P}}, Q_{\mathcal{R}/\mathcal{P}} \rangle$, defined only when $(s_{\mathcal{P}}^0, s_{\mathcal{R}}^0) \in S_{\mathcal{R}/\mathcal{P}}$, where:*

- $S_{\mathcal{R}/\mathcal{P}}$ *is the largest subset of $(S_{\mathcal{P}} \times S_{\mathcal{R}})$ such that*
  - *if $\langle s_{\mathcal{P}}, s_{\mathcal{R}} \rangle \in S_{\mathcal{R}/\mathcal{P}}$ and either $a \in A_{\mathcal{P}}^O$ is enabled in $s_{\mathcal{P}}$, or $a \in A_{\mathcal{P}}^I \cap A_{\mathcal{R}}^I$ is enabled in $s_{\mathcal{R}}$, then $\delta_{\mathcal{P} \otimes \mathcal{R}}(\langle s_{\mathcal{P}}, s_{\mathcal{R}} \rangle, a)$ is defined and $\delta_{\mathcal{P} \otimes \mathcal{R}}(\langle s_{\mathcal{P}}, s_{\mathcal{R}} \rangle, a) \in S_{\mathcal{R}/\mathcal{P}}$*
  - *if $\langle s_{\mathcal{P}}, s_{\mathcal{R}} \rangle \in S_{\mathcal{R}/\mathcal{P}}$ and $s_{\mathcal{P}} \in Q_{\mathcal{P}}$ and $s_{\mathcal{R}} \notin Q_{\mathcal{R}}$, then there is some $a \in A_{\mathcal{R}/\mathcal{P}}^O$ such that $\delta_{\mathcal{P} \otimes \mathcal{R}}(\langle s_{\mathcal{P}}, s_{\mathcal{R}} \rangle, a) \in S_{\mathcal{R}/\mathcal{P}}$*
- $\delta_{\mathcal{R}/\mathcal{P}}(\langle s_{\mathcal{P}}, s_{\mathcal{R}} \rangle, a) = \delta_{\mathcal{P} \otimes \mathcal{R}}(\langle s_{\mathcal{P}}, s_{\mathcal{R}} \rangle, a)$ *whenever $\langle s_{\mathcal{P}}, s_{\mathcal{R}} \rangle \in S_{\mathcal{R}/\mathcal{P}}$ and $\delta_{\mathcal{P} \otimes \mathcal{R}}(\langle s_{\mathcal{P}}, s_{\mathcal{R}} \rangle, a) \in S_{\mathcal{R}/\mathcal{P}}$, otherwise $\delta_{\mathcal{R}/\mathcal{P}}(\langle s_{\mathcal{P}}, s_{\mathcal{R}} \rangle, a)$ is undefined*
- $Q_{\mathcal{R}/\mathcal{P}} = S_{\mathcal{R}/\mathcal{P}} \cap ((S_{\mathcal{P}} \times Q_{\mathcal{R}}) \cup (S_{\mathcal{P}} \setminus Q_{\mathcal{P}}) \times S_{\mathcal{R}})$.

Intuitively, the quotient can be constructed in a manner similar to the parallel composition of $\mathcal{P}$ and $\mathcal{R}$, but avoiding situations where: $\mathcal{P}$ can produce an output not matched by $\mathcal{R}$; $\mathcal{R}$ can accept an input in $A_{\mathcal{R}}^I \cap A_{\mathcal{P}}^I$ that $\mathcal{P}$ cannot accept; and $\mathcal{P}$ is quiescent, $\mathcal{R}$ is not, and $\mathcal{R}/\mathcal{P}$ cannot enforce an output action.

Theorem 1. *Let $\mathcal{P}$ and $\mathcal{R}$ be components such that $A_{\mathcal{P}}^O \subseteq A_{\mathcal{R}}^O$ and $A_{\mathcal{P}} \subseteq A_{\mathcal{R}}$. If there exists a component $\mathcal{Q}$ with inputs $A_{\mathcal{R}/\mathcal{P}}^I$ and outputs $A_{\mathcal{R}/\mathcal{P}}^O$, such that $\mathcal{P} \parallel \mathcal{Q} \sqsubseteq \mathcal{R}$, then $\mathcal{R}/\mathcal{P}$ is defined, $\mathcal{P} \parallel (\mathcal{R}/\mathcal{P}) \sqsubseteq \mathcal{R}$ and $\mathcal{Q} \sqsubseteq (\mathcal{R}/\mathcal{P})$.*

3   Ontological Modelling and Reasoning

An ontology is *"a specification of a representational vocabulary for a shared domain of discourse"* [Gru93]. The goal of an ontology is to model and reason about domain knowledge. OWL DL[1] (Web Ontology Language), which is the W3C standard language to model ontologies, is based on a description logic (DL), which specifies the vocabulary of a domain using concepts, attributes of each concept, and relationships between these concepts.

---

[1] http://www.w3.org/TR/owl2-overview/

We provide an overview of the syntax and semantics of the basic DL constructs in Figure 3 and refer the interested reader to [BCM+03] for further details. Each concept is given a definition as a set of logical axioms, which can either be atomic or defined using different operators such as disjunction, conjunction, and quantifiers. The attributes of a concept are defined using an object property, which associates the concept with a built-in data type.

For example, consider an extract of the travel agency ontology depicted in Figure 4. The Flight concept is characterised by attributes hasDepartureDate and hasReturnDate of the built-in type DateTime, and hasFlightID of type String.

We describe the aggregation of concepts using the W3C recommendation for part-whole relations[2] (hasPart), where different concepts are composed together to build a whole. A concept E is an aggregation of concepts C and D, written $E = C \oplus D$, providing both C and D are parts of E, i.e., $E = \exists \mathsf{hasPart}.C \sqcap \exists \mathsf{hasPart}.D$. For example, the Trip concept is defined as the aggregation of the Flight, Hotel, and Car concepts, meaning that each trip instance $t \in$ Trip encompasses a Flight instance ($\exists f \in$ Flight $\land (t, f) \in$ hasPart), as well as Hotel and Car instances. The rationale is that the mediator is able to generate a concept by concatenating the attributes of all its parts (while avoiding duplication of attributes). Dually, the mediator can create several concepts by distributing the attributes of the aggregated concept across its different parts. This corresponds to the merging and splitting of messages.

	DL Syntax	DL Semantics
Conjunction	$C \sqcap D$	$(C \sqcap D)^{\mathcal{I}} = C^{\mathcal{I}} \cap D^{\mathcal{I}}$
Disjunction	$C \sqcup D$	$(C \sqcup D)^{\mathcal{I}} = C^{\mathcal{I}} \cup D^{\mathcal{I}}$
Universal quantifier	$\forall R.C$	$(\forall R.C)^{\mathcal{I}} = \{x \in \Delta^{\mathcal{I}} \mid \forall y.(x, y) \in R^{\mathcal{I}} \Rightarrow y \in C^{\mathcal{I}}\}$
Existential quantifier	$\exists R.C$	$(\exists R.C)^{\mathcal{I}} = \{x \in \Delta^{\mathcal{I}} \mid \exists y.(x, y) \in R^{\mathcal{I}} \land y \in C^{\mathcal{I}}\}$
Aggregation	$C \oplus D$	$(C \oplus D)^{\mathcal{I}} = \{x \in \Delta^{\mathcal{I}} \mid \exists y.(x, y) \in \mathsf{hasPart}^{\mathcal{I}} \land y \in C^{\mathcal{I}}$
		$\land \exists z.(x, z) \in \mathsf{hasPart}^{\mathcal{I}} \land z \in D^{\mathcal{I}}\}$

An interpretation $\mathcal{I}$ consists of a non-empty set $\Delta^{\mathcal{I}}$ (the domain of the interpretation) and an interpretation function, which assigns to every atomic concept A a set $A^{\mathcal{I}} \subseteq \Delta^{\mathcal{I}}$ and to every atomic object property R a binary relation $R^{\mathcal{I}} \subseteq \Delta^{\mathcal{I}} \times \Delta^{\mathcal{I}}$. C and D are concepts and R is an object property.

Fig. 3. Overview of DL operators

DL is used to support automatic reasoning about concepts and their relationships, in order to infer new relations that may not have been recognised by the ontology designers. Traditionally, the basic reasoning mechanism is *subsumption*. Intuitively, if a concept C is subsumed by a concept D, written $C \leqslant_O D$, then any instance of C also belongs to D. In addition, all the relationships in which D instances can be involved are applicable to C instances, i.e., all properties of D are also properties of C. Subsumption is a partial order relation, i.e., it is reflexive, antisymmetric, and transitive. As a result, the ontology can be represented as a hierarchy of concepts, which can be automatically inferred by

---

[2] http://www.w3.org/2001/sw/BestPractices/OEP/SimplePartWhole/

ontology reasoners based on the axioms defining the ontological concepts. Subsumption allows for the replacement of inequivalent messages, provided all of the necessary data is conveyed. For instance, a mediator can generate a concept out of a more specific concept, since the latter includes all the necessary attributes of the former (cf subtyping in object-oriented systems).

Ontologies are used to represent the semantics of actions in components, by making explicit the meaning of the interaction primitives. Each action of a component refers to a concept in the ontology, which has an object property hasData specifying the semantics of the data embedded in the action sent or received by the component. For example, the input action $selFlightI \in \mathcal{A}_{EUService}^{I}$ is associated with the TravelPreferences concept (i.e., $selFlightI = \exists$hasData.TravelPreferences). The output action $selFlightO \in \mathcal{A}_{EUService}^{O}$ is associated with the Flight concept, that is $selFlightO = \exists$hasData.Flight. The idea here is that *EUService* allows the selection of a flight by receiving a request message that contains the attributes of the TravelPreferences concept, that is, a destination along with departure and return dates. Once the request has been processed, *EUService* returns a response that includes the flight information, which consists of a hotel identifier, and check in and check out dates. The output action $findTripI \in \mathcal{A}_{USClient}^{O}$ is also associated with the TravelPreferences concept, that is $findTripI = \exists$hasData.TravelPreferences. The input action $findTripO \in \mathcal{A}_{USClient}^{I}$ is associated with the Trip concept, that is $findTripO = \exists$hasData.Trip. *USClient* sends a request message that includes the travel preference of the customer, and receives a response with a trip, i.e., a holiday package consisting of a flight, hotel, and car.

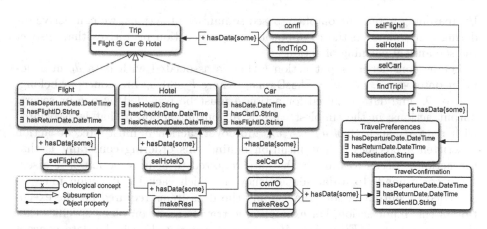

Fig. 4. The travel agency ontology

4   Automated Mediator Synthesis

In this section, we describe our synthesis methodology for generating mediators that allow components to successfully communicate with one another. Given components $\mathcal{P}$ and $\mathcal{Q}$, a component $\mathcal{M}$ is said to be a mediator if:

G1. $\mathcal{P} \parallel \mathcal{M} \parallel \mathcal{Q}$ is defined, which implies that the composition will never exhibit any communication mismatches;

G2. $\mathcal{P} \parallel \mathcal{M} \parallel \mathcal{Q}$ is guaranteed to progress until both $\mathcal{P}$ and $\mathcal{Q}$ have reached a successfully terminating state; and

G3. $\mathcal{P} \parallel \mathcal{M} \parallel \mathcal{Q}$ must satisfy constraints on correspondences between actions, and on data flow, that are implicitly imposed by the ontology.

Our methodology finds the most general mediator $\mathcal{M}$ satisfying the above requirements, meaning that it is least refined with respect to the refinement $\sqsubseteq$ of Definition 2. Due to the arbitrariness of the components needing to communicate (especially if they are functionally different), existence of a mediator is not guaranteed. This correlates with the fact that quotient is a partial operator. As part of our automated synthesis methodology, the following steps are performed:

1. Using the ontology, we first derive temporal constraints on the occurrences of actions in $\mathcal{P}$ and $\mathcal{Q}$ in order to respect the data flow on actions. These constraints are represented by a component $\mathcal{B}$ that *observes* the executions of $\mathcal{P} \parallel \mathcal{M} \parallel \mathcal{Q}$ and generates an inconsistency when a constraint is violated.

2. After, we perform a quotient operation that automatically synthesises a mediator $\mathcal{M}$ such that $\mathcal{P} \parallel \mathcal{M} \parallel \mathcal{Q}$ satisfies requirements G1 and G2, along with the ordering constraints represented by the observer $\mathcal{B}$ (G3).

In the following two subsections, we explain these steps in more detail.

4.1   Inferring Ordering Constraints from Ontologies

By reasoning about the ontology-based semantics of actions, we can derive ordering constraints on the components' communication primitives that respect the semantical meaning of actions.

Let us consider an input action b that is associated with data d_b in a domain ontology $\mathcal{O}$, i.e., $b = \exists\mathsf{hasData}.d_b$ where b and d_b are concepts belonging to $\mathcal{O}$. The data required for action b must be provided by one or several output actions; in the simplest case by an output action a that is associated with data d_a such that $d_a \leqslant_{\mathcal{O}} d_b$. Moreover, action a must precede action b, written a precedes b. The intuition behind this ordering constraint is that the action a needs to provide the data required to achieve action b; it essentially corresponds to a data-dependency in which each input action must be preceded by output actions that supply the data items required for the execution of this input action. For example, the travel agency ontology specifies that the input action $selFlightI \in \mathcal{A}^I_{EUService}$ is associated with the data concept TravelPreference. Since the only output action associated with this data concept is $findTripI \in \mathcal{A}^I_{USClient}$, and TravelPreference $\leqslant_{\mathcal{O}}$ TravelPreference due to reflexivity of subsumption, we derive the ordering constraint $findTripI$ precedes $selFlightI$.

In the general case, a collection of input actions $\{b_1, \ldots, b_m\}$, which are associated with data concepts $\{d_{b_1}, \ldots, d_{b_m}\}$ respectively, must be preceded by some collection of output actions $\{a_1, \ldots, a_n\}$, which are associated with data

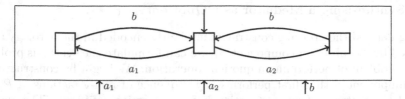

Fig. 5. Component $Seq(\{a_1, a_2\}, b)$ enforcing a_1 precedes b **or** a_2 precedes b

concepts $\{d_{a_1}, \ldots, d_{a_n}\}$ such that $d_{a_1} \oplus \cdots \oplus d_{a_n} \leqslant_{\mathcal{O}} d_{b_1} \oplus \cdots \oplus d_{b_m}$. If there are several such collections of output actions, it suffices that $\{b_1, \ldots, b_m\}$ is preceded by one of them. Clearly, we can restrict our consideration to minimal such collections of output actions. For example, the input action $findTripO \in \mathcal{A}^I_{USClient}$ must be preceded by the collection of output actions $\{selFlightO, selHotelO, selCarO\} \subseteq \mathcal{A}^O_{EUService}$, since it is the only minimal collection, whose aggregated data is subsumed by the data of $findTripO$, i.e., Flight$\oplus$Hotel$\oplus$Car $\leqslant_{\mathcal{O}}$ Trip.

In order to extract such relations, we verify among possible combinations of input/output actions of both components those verifying the data flow conditions. Even though computing all possible preceding relations is NP-complete, we rely on efficient search algorithms, which are based on constraint programming, to make the computation effective in real-world settings [Con12a, pp. 49-57].

For each minimal disjunction of precedes relationships inferred from the ontology, we construct an observation component that has as interface the collection of primitives that appear in the relationship. For instance, the disjunction a_1 precedes b **or** a_2 precedes b is represented by a component whose behaviour forces either a_1 or a_2 to precede b, denoted by $Seq(\{a_1, a_2\}, b)$. Its behavior is shown in Figure 5. Note that all the actions are treated as inputs and all states are quiescent since the component is only observing the actions. If the mediator or a component violates a constraint, the corresponding observer will generate an inconsistency. The component $\mathcal{B}$ respecting the combined effect of all the ontological constraints is then defined as the parallel composition of the representations of the individual relationships. Note that this is always defined.

Considering the travel agency example, by reasoning about the semantics of the actions of $USClient$ and $EUService$ using the ontology depicted in Figure 4, we infer that $findTripI$ precedes $selFlightI$, $findTripI$ precedes $selHotelI$, $findTripI$ precedes $selCarI$, $selFlightO$ precedes $findTripO$, $selHotelO$ precedes $findTripO$, $selCarO$ precedes $findTripO$, $confI$ precedes $makeResI$, and $makeResO$ precedes $confO$, which leads to the following observer component:

$$\mathcal{B} = (\; Seq(findTripI, selFlightI) \;\|\; Seq(findTripI, selHotelI)$$
$$\|\; Seq(findTripI, selCarI) \quad\|\; Seq(selFlightO, findTripO)$$
$$\|\; Seq(selHotelO, findTripO) \;\|\; Seq(selCarO, findTripO)$$
$$\|\; Seq(confI, makeResI) \quad\;\|\; Seq(makeResO, confO)).$$

4.2   Synthesising a Mediator as a Quotient

Having derived the ordering constraints implicitly encoded in the ontology (represented by the observer component $\mathcal{B}$), we can formulate the synthesis problem as the problem of performing a quotient operation. We begin by constructing a *goal* component $\mathcal{G}$ that first performs any sequence of non-$\checkmark$ actions of $\mathcal{P}$ and $\mathcal{Q}$, and thereafter perform a $\checkmark$ action before becoming quiescent. The goal $\mathcal{G}$, which can automatically be generated from the syntax of $\mathcal{P}$ and $\mathcal{Q}$, is shown in Figure 6. The synthesis problem involves finding a most general mediator $\mathcal{M}$

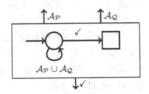

Fig. 6. Component representing the goal $\mathcal{G}$

such that $\mathcal{P} \parallel \mathcal{M} \parallel \mathcal{Q} \parallel \mathcal{B} \sqsubseteq \mathcal{G}$. Note that the process $\mathcal{G}$ has all actions of $\mathcal{P}$ and $\mathcal{Q}$ as outputs. This means that each input action of either $\mathcal{P}$ or $\mathcal{Q}$ must be an output action of $\mathcal{M}$, implying that $\mathcal{P} \parallel \mathcal{M} \parallel \mathcal{Q}$ has no input actions (i.e., is a closed system). If such a mediator $\mathcal{M}$ exists, it is equal to the quotient $\mathcal{G}/(\mathcal{P} \parallel \mathcal{Q} \parallel \mathcal{B})$, for which it can be shown that requirements G1–G3 hold:

G1 is guaranteed by the fact that $\mathcal{M}$ being defined implies that $\mathcal{P} \parallel \mathcal{M} \parallel \mathcal{Q} \parallel \mathcal{B}$ is defined. Hence $\mathcal{P} \parallel \mathcal{M} \parallel \mathcal{Q}$ cannot enter an incompatible state.

G2 is satisfied since $\mathcal{G}$ can only become quiescent after having seen $\checkmark$, which means that $\mathcal{P} \parallel \mathcal{M} \parallel \mathcal{Q} \parallel \mathcal{B}$ can only become quiescent after having seen $\checkmark$. Consequently, $\mathcal{P} \parallel \mathcal{M} \parallel \mathcal{Q}$ can only deadlock when all components have terminated successfully.

G3 is satisfied for the following reason. The data flow constraints are satisfied since $\mathcal{B}$ will generate an inconsistency whenever the sequence of actions does not satisfy them. This implies $\mathcal{P} \parallel \mathcal{M} \parallel \mathcal{Q}$ will never produce any action that violates the constraints on occurrences of actions expressed by $\mathcal{B}$.

Remark. Our methodology has considered the case where $\mathcal{P} \parallel \mathcal{M} \parallel \mathcal{Q}$ is modeled as a closed system. In the case where $\mathcal{P} \parallel \mathcal{M} \parallel \mathcal{Q}$ is an open system and we have a model $\mathcal{E}$ of its environment, we can use the same technique by finding a mediator $\mathcal{M}$ such that $\mathcal{P} \parallel \mathcal{M} \parallel \mathcal{Q} \parallel \mathcal{B} \parallel \mathcal{E} \sqsubseteq \mathcal{G}$, where we assume that $\mathcal{E}$ is just another component.

Travel Agency Example. The mediator for the packaged holiday example is shown in Figure 7. Its inputs are the outputs of *EUService* $\parallel$ *USClient* and its outputs are the inputs of *EUService* $\parallel$ *USClient*. The main idea is that the mediator first intercepts the output produced by *USClient* from the *findTripI* action, transforms it into the equivalent actions for *EUService* (*selHotelI*, *selFlightI* and *selCarI*), and then sends them to *EUService* (also respecting the constraint

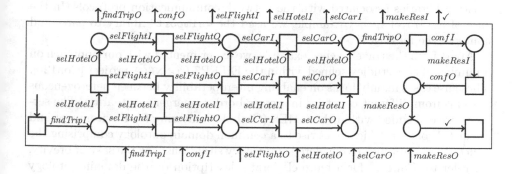

Fig. 7. The mediator for the travel agency example

that *selFlightO* must be sent before *selCarI*). Upon reception of the corresponding responses *selHotelO*, *selFlightO* and *selCarO* from *EUService*, the mediator forwards the expected output action *findTripO* to *USClient*. The process then evolves in a similar manner for confirmation of the reservation.

5   Implementation

We implemented the synthesis approach defined in this paper as a prototype tool available at `http://www.rocq.inria.fr/arles/software/onto-quotient/`. The Pellet reasoner[3] is used to build the hierarchy of concepts in the ontology and extract all the subsumption relations. The problem of inferring ordering constraints is formalised as a constraint satisfaction problem, which we solve efficiently using the Choco[4] constraint solver. In a second step, we generate the behavioural model of the observer $\mathcal{B}$ based on the generated ordering constraints, compute the goal specification as shown in Fig. 6, and calculate the quotient. It should be noted that even though $\mathcal{B}$ and $\mathcal{G}$ are always of a similar shape (since they are automatically generated), the implementation allows for arbitrary behavioural models to be used as observer and goal specifications.

In order to enable the components to interoperate, the synthesised behavioural model of the mediator needs to be concretised and deployed into a concrete artefact so as to realise the specified translations and coordination. This artefact is called *emergent middleware* [BBG+11]. The emergent middleware concretises the mediator model by incorporating information about underlying network layers. In particular, the emergent middleware: (i) intercepts the input messages, (ii) parses them so as to abstract from the communication details and represent them in terms of actions as expected by the mediator, (iii) performs the necessary data transformations, and (iv) uses the transformed data to construct an output message in the format expected by the interacting component. This is performed using specific parsers and composers, which are generated based on

---

[3] `http://clarkparsia.com/pellet/`
[4] `http://choco.emn.fr/`

existing libraries associated with the network communication protocols. In the case of the travel agency example, we used the `wsimport`[5] library to parse and compose the messages.

Apart from the travel agency example, we experimented with our approach on a number of case studies defined within the EU FP7 CONNECT project [Con12b]. These use cases mainly focus on enabling interoperability between heterogeneous systems from different countries in a cross-border emergency situation. The services are embedded within the GMES (Global Monitoring for Environment and Security) context, which gives rise to a common domain ontology comprising the concepts relevant in the considered emergency situations. For the sake of brevity, we refer to [Con12b] for a more elaborate description on the domain ontology and the systems involved.

In all the considered examples, we were able to generate a mediator automatically by means of quotient. The quotient could be computed virtually without any delay, even though in our prototype implementation we merely focused on functionality. We are thus confident that our approach will scale well even when applied to more complex case studies, which we are planning to evaluate as future work.

6   Related Work

Pioneering work on mediator synthesis involves the use of formal methods for protocol conversion, given behavioural models of the participating components. Existing approaches for the synthesis of protocol converters require a specification of the service delivered by the composed system. Lam [Lam88] assumes a declarative specification of a common protocol to which both protocols can be abstracted, which presupposes an intuitive understanding of the protocols to be mediated. Calvert and Lam [CL90] propose a quotient operation for mediating communication protocols, which is related to, but different from, our quotient operation. They require a global specification of the composed system, which makes it difficult to apply automated mediator synthesis at run-time. A quotient operation for deterministic interface automata has been presented by Bhaduri and Ramesh [BR08]. Our quotient extends this definition by considering also quiescence (deadlock) properties.

To improve the automation of mediator synthesis, Yellin and Strom [YS97] define an algorithm to generate mediators automatically assuming that there exist one-to-one correspondences between their actions, which have to be provided by the developer. Bertoli *et al.* [BPT10] also assume the correspondence to be given and use a planning-based algorithm to generate the mediator. Bersani *et al.* [BCF+10] define an approach based on SMT-based model checking but assume that the protocols have the same alphabet. Finally, Inverardi and Tivoli [IT13] adopt a compositional approach where the mediator is generated based on pre-defined patterns of translations, which have to be given by the developer. Common to all the aforementioned methods is the assumption of *a priori* knowledge about the components to be mediated and hence the

---

[5] http://docs.oracle.com/javase/6/docs/technotes/tools/share/wsimport.html

correspondence between their actions must be provided beforehand by developers using their intuitive understanding of the application domain.

The emergence of the Semantic Web has led to the use of ontologies in system integration as a means of interpreting the meaning of data or associated services as they are dynamically encountered in the World-Wide Web. The Web Service Execution Environment (WSMX) [CM05] provides a framework to mediate interactions between heterogeneous Web Services by inspecting their individual protocols and performing the necessary translation using predefined mediation patterns. However, the composition of these patterns is not considered, and there is no guarantee of deadlock-freeness. Vaculín *et al.* [VNS09] synthesise mediators between a client and a service specified as OWL-S processes by generating all the traces of the client protocol and finding the appropriate mapping for each trace by simulating the service protocol.

In this paper, we define an approach that extends and improves existing work on mediator synthesis by using ontologies to reason about the domain and automatically infer the correspondence between the actions of the components involved. This removes the need for a declarative specification of the global system or the assumption that the components share the same alphabet.

7 Discussion and Evaluation

We have devised a methodology for synthesising mediators to support the interoperability of components. Unlike existing techniques, we make use of an ontology that relates the functional behaviour of the components, meaning that the components do not have to share similar communication alphabets. The synthesis technique is automated in the sense that the user does not need to specify what the mediator should do, as this can be inferred using behavioural and ontological reasoning. The synthesis is performed by means of a quotient operation, which has received renewed interest in the literature recently. The synthesised mediators are free of communication mismatches, and by consideration of quiescence are guaranteed not to deadlock prematurely or inopportunely.

As a matter of simplicity, we have shunned away from components exhibiting non-determinism and hidden transitions, although our theory can support these by using the definitions of parallel composition and quotient in [CCJK12]. Future work includes incremental re-synthesis of mediators so as to respond efficiently to changes in the individual components or in the ontology.

Acknowledgements. This work is carried out as part of the European FP7 ICT FET Connect project (http://connect-forever.eu/). The last author was supported in part by the UPMARC centre of excellence.

References

[BBG+11]   Blair, G.S., Bennaceur, A., Georgantas, N., Grace, P., Issarny, V., Nundloll, V., Paolucci, M.: The role of ontologies in emergent middleware: Supporting interoperability in complex distributed systems. In: Kon, F., Kermarrec, A.-M. (eds.) Middleware 2011. LNCS, vol. 7049, pp. 410–430. Springer, Heidelberg (2011)

[BCF+10]   Bersani, M.M., Cavallaro, L., Frigeri, A., Pradella, M., Rossi, M.: SMT-based verification of ltl specification with integer constraints and its application to runtime checking of service substitutability. In: Proc. SEFM, pp. 244–254. IEEE (2010)

[BCM+03]   Baader, F., Calvanese, D., McGuinness, D., Nardi, D., Schneider, P.: The Description Logic Handbook. Cambridge University Press (2003)

[BPT10]   Bertoli, P., Pistore, M., Traverso, P.: Automated composition of web services via planning in asynchronous domains. Artificial Intelligence 174(3-4), 316–361 (2010)

[BR08]   Bhaduri, P., Ramesh, S.: Interface synthesis and protocol conversion. Form. Asp. Comput. 20(2), 205–224 (2008)

[CCJK12]   Chen, T., Chilton, C., Jonsson, B., Kwiatkowska, M.: A compositional specification theory for component behaviours. In: Seidl, H. (ed.) ESOP 2012. LNCS, vol. 7211, pp. 148–168. Springer, Heidelberg (2012)

[CL90]   Calvert, K.L., Lam, S.S.: Formal methods for protocol conversion. IEEE Journal on Selected Areas in Communications 8(1), 127–142 (1990)

[CM05]   Cimpian, E., Mocan, A.: WSMX process mediation based on choreographies. In: Bussler, C.J., Haller, A. (eds.) BPM 2005 Workshops. LNCS, vol. 3812, pp. 130–143. Springer, Heidelberg (2006)

[CMS+09]   Cámara, J., Martín, J., Salaün, G., Cubo, J., Ouederni, M., Canal, C., Pimentel, E.: ITACA: An integrated toolbox for the automatic composition and adaptation of web services. In: ICSE, pp. 627–630 (2009)

[Con12a]   CONNECT Consortium. Deliverable D3.4: Dynamic Connector Synthesis: Principles, Methods, Tools and Assessment. FET IP CONNECT EU project (2012), http://hal.inria.fr/hal-00805618

[Con12b]   CONNECT Consortium. Deliverable D6.4: Assessment report: Experimenting with CONNECT in Systems of Systems, and Mobile Environments. FET IP CONNECT EU project (2012), http://hal.inria.fr/hal-00793920

[dAH01]   de Alfaro, L., Henzinger, T.A.: Interface automata. SIGSOFT Softw. Eng. Notes 26(5), 109–120 (2001)

[Gru93]   Gruber, T.R.: A translation approach to portable ontology specifications. Knowledge Acquisition 5(2), 199–220 (1993)

[IT13]   Inverardi, P., Tivoli, M.: Automatic synthesis of modular connectors via composition of protocol mediation patterns. In: ICSE (to appear, 2013)

[Lam88]   Lam, S.: Protocol conversion. IEEE Transaction Software Engineering 14(3), 353–362 (1988)

[MHS+12]   Merten, M., Howar, F., Steffen, B., Pellicione, P., Tivoli, M.: Automated inference of models for black box systems based on interface descriptions. In: Margaria, T., Steffen, B. (eds.) ISoLA 2012, Part I. LNCS, vol. 7609, pp. 79–96. Springer, Heidelberg (2012)

[PdAHSV02] Passerone, R., de Alfaro, L., Henzinger, T.A., Sangiovanni-Vincentelli, A.L.: Convertibility verification and converter synthesis: two faces of the same coin. In: Proc. IEEE/ACM Int. Conf. on Computer-aided Design, pp. 132–139. ACM (2002)

[VNS09]   Vaculín, R., Neruda, R., Sycara, K.P.: The process mediation framework for semantic web services. International Journal of Agent-Oriented Software Engineering, IJAOSE 3(1), 27–58 (2009)

[YS97]   Yellin, D.M., Strom, R.E.: Protocol specifications and component adaptors. ACM Trans. Program. Lang. Syst. 19(2), 292–333 (1997)

Program Transformation Based on Symbolic Execution and Deduction*

Ran Ji, Reiner Hähnle, and Richard Bubel

Department of Computer Science
Technische Universität Darmstadt, Germany
{ran,haehnle,bubel}@cs.tu-darmstadt.de

Abstract. We present a program transformation framework based on symbolic execution and deduction. Its virtues are: (i) behavior preservation of the transformed program is guaranteed by a sound program logic, and (ii) automated first-order solvers are used for simplification and optimization. Transformation consists of two phases: first the source program is symbolically executed by sequent calculus rules in a program logic. This involves a precise analysis of variable dependencies, aliasing, and elimination of infeasible execution paths. In the second phase, the target program is synthesized by a leaves-to-root traversal of the symbolic execution tree by backward application of (extended) sequent calculus rules. We prove soundness by a suitable notion of bisimulation and we discuss one possible approach to automated program optimization.

1 Introduction

State-of-the-art program verification systems can show the correctness of complex software written in industrial programming languages [1]. The main reason why functional verification is not used routinely is that considerable expertise is required to come up with formal specifications [2], invariants, and proof hints. Nevertheless, modern software verification systems are an impressive achievement: they contain a fully formal semantics of industrial programming languages and, due to automated first-order reasoning and highly developed heuristics, in fact a high degree of automation is achieved: more than 99,9% of the proof steps are typically completely automatic. Given the right annotations and contracts, often 100% automation is possible. This paper is about leveraging the enormous potential of verification tools that at the moment goes unused.

The central observation is that everything making functional verification hard, is in fact not needed if one is mainly interested in simplifying and optimizing a program rather than proving it correct. First, there is no need for complex formal specifications: the property that two programs are bisimilar on observable locations is easy to express schematically. Second, complex invariants are only required to prove non-trivial postconditions. If the preservation of behavior becomes the only property to be proven, then simple, schematic invariants will do.

---

* This work has been partially supported by the IST program of the European Commission, Future and Emerging Technologies under the IST-231620 HATS project.

R.M. Hierons, M.G. Merayo, and M. Bravetti (Eds.): SEFM 2013, LNCS 8137, pp. 289–304, 2013.
© Springer-Verlag Berlin Heidelberg 2013

Hence, complex formulas are absent, which does away with the need for difficult quantifier instantiations.

On the other hand, standard verification tools are not set up to relate a source and a target program, which is what is needed for program simplification and optimization. The main contribution of this paper is to adapt the program logic of a state-of-the-art program verifier [3] to the task of sound program transformation and to show that fully automatic program simplification and optimization with guaranteed soundness is possible as a consequence.

This paper extends previous work [4], where the idea of program specialization via a verification tool was presented for the first time. We remodeled the ad-hoc semantics of the earlier paper in terms of standard bisimulation theory [5]. While this greatly improves the presentation, more importantly, it enables the new optimization described in Sect. 5.

Aiming at a concise presentation, we employ the small OO imperative programming language PL. It contains essential features of OO languages, but abstracts away from technicalities that complicate the presentation. Sect. 2 introduces PL and Sect. 3 defines a program logic for it with semantics and a calculus. These are adapted to the requirements of program transformation in Sect. 4. In Sect. 5 we harvest from our effort and add a non-trivial optimization strategy. We close with related work (Sect. 6) and future work (Sect. 7).

2   Programming Language

PL supports classes, objects, attributes, method polymorphism (but not method overloading). Unsupported features are generic types, exceptions, multi-threading, floating points, and garbage collection. The types of PL are the types derived from class declarations, the type int of mathematical integers ($\mathbb{Z}$), and the standard Boolean type boolean.

A PL program p is a non-empty set of class declarations, where each class defines a class type. PL contains at least two class types Object and Null. The class hierarchy (without Null) forms a tree with class Object as root. The type Null is a singleton with null as its only element and may be used in place of any class type. It is the smallest class type.

A class $Cl := (cname, scname_{opt}, fld, mtd)$ consists of (i) a classname $cname$ unique in p, (ii) the name of its superclass $scname$ (optional, only omitted for $cname = $ Object), (iii) a list of field declarations fld and method declarations mtd. The syntax coincides with that of Java. The only features lacking from Java are constructors and initialization blocks. We use some conventions: if not stated otherwise, any sequence of statements is viewed as if it were the body of a static, void method declared in a class Default with no fields.

Any complex statement can be easily decomposed into a sequence of simpler statements without changing the meaning of a program, e.g., y = z ++; can be decomposed into int t = z; z = z + 1; y = t;, where t is a *fresh* variable, not used anywhere else. As we shall see later, a suitable notion of simplicity is essential, for example, to compute variable dependencies and simplify symbolic states. This is built into our semantics and calculus, so we need a precise definition of *simple statements*. Statements in the syntactic category *spStmnt* have at most one source of side effect each. This can be a non-terminating expression (such as a null pointer access), a method call, or an assignment to a location.

$spStmnt ::= spLvarDecl \mid locVar'='spExp';' \mid locVar'='spAtr';'$
$\qquad\qquad \mid spAtr'='spExp';'$
$spLvarDecl ::= Type\ \texttt{IDENT}';'$
$spExp ::= (locVar.)_{opt}spMthdCall \mid spOpExp \mid litVar$
$spMthdCall ::= \texttt{mthdName}'('litVar_{opt}(','litVar)^{*}')'$
$spOpExp ::= !litVar \mid -litVar \mid litVar\ binOpr\ litVar$
$litVar ::= litval \mid locVar \qquad\qquad litval ::= \mathbb{Z} \mid \texttt{TRUE} \mid \texttt{FALSE} \mid \texttt{null}$
$binOpr ::= < \mid <= \mid >= \mid > \mid == \mid \& \mid | \mid * \mid / \mid \% \mid + \mid -$
$locVar ::= \texttt{IDENT} \qquad\qquad spAtr ::= locVar.\texttt{IDENT}$

3 Program Logic and Sequent Calculus

Symbolic execution was introduced independently by King [6] and others in the early 1970s. The main idea is to take symbolic values (terms) instead of concrete ones for the initial values of input variables, fields, etc., for program execution. The interpreter then performs algebraic computations on terms instead of computing concrete results. In this paper, following [7], symbolic execution is done by applying *sequent calculus* rules of a program logic. Sequent calculi are often used to verify a program against a specification [7], but here we focus on symbolic execution, which we embed into a program logic for the purpose of being able to argue the correctness of program transformations and optimizations.

3.1 Program Logic

Our program logic is *dynamic logic (DL)* [8]. The target program occurs in unencoded form as a first-class citizen inside the logic's connectives. Sorted first-order dynamic logic is sorted first-order logic that is syntactically closed wrt program correctness modalities $[\cdot]\cdot$ (box) and $\langle\cdot\rangle\cdot$ (diamond). The first argument is a program and the second a dynamic logic formula. Let p denote a program and ϕ a dynamic logic formula then $[p]\phi$ and $\langle p\rangle\phi$ are DL-formulas. Informally, the former expresses that if p is executed and terminates *then* in all reached final states ϕ holds; the latter means that if p is executed then it terminates *and* in at least one of the reached final states ϕ holds.

We consider only deterministic programs, hence, a program p executed in a given state s *either* terminates and reaches exactly *one* final state *or* it does not terminate and there are no reachable final states. The box modality expresses *partial correctness* of a program, while the diamond modality coincides with *total correctness*. A dynamic logic based on PL-programs is called PL-DL. The signature of the program logic depends on a *context* PL-*program* C.

Definition 1 (PL-Signature Σ_C). *A signature* $\Sigma_C = (\mathsf{Srt}, \preceq, \mathsf{Pred}, \mathsf{Func}, \mathsf{LgV})$ *consists of: (i) a set of names* Srt *called* sorts *containing at least one sort for each primitive type and one for each class* Cl *declared in* C: $\mathsf{Srt} \supseteq \{\mathsf{int}, \mathsf{boolean}\} \cup \{Cl \mid for\ all\ classes\ Cl\ declared\ in\ C\}$; *(ii) a partial subtyping order* $\preceq$: $\mathsf{Srt} \times \mathsf{Srt}$ *that models the subtype hierarchy of* C *faithfully; (iii) infinite sets of predicate symbols* $\mathsf{Pred} := \{p : T_1 \times \ldots \times T_n \mid T_i \in \mathsf{Srt}, n \in \mathbb{N}\}$ *and function symbols* $\mathsf{Func} := \{f : T_1 \times \ldots \times T_n \to T \mid T_i, T \in \mathsf{Srt}, n \in \mathbb{N}\}$. *We call* $\alpha(p) = T_1 \times \ldots \times T_n$ *and* $\alpha(f) = T_1 \times \ldots \times T_n \to T$ *the signature of the predicate/function symbol.* $\mathsf{Func} := \mathsf{Func}_r \cup \mathsf{PV} \cup \mathsf{Attr}$ *is further divided into disjoint subsets:*

- *the* rigid *function symbols* Func_r, *which do not depend on the current state of program execution;*
- *the* program variables $\mathsf{PV} = \{\mathtt{i}, \mathtt{j}, \ldots\}$, *which are non-rigid constants;*
- *the* attribute *function symbols* Attr, *such that for each attribute* $\mathtt{a}$ *of type* T *declared in class* Cl *an attribute function* $\mathtt{a}@Cl : Cl \to T \in \mathsf{Attr}$ *exists. We omit the* $@C$ *from attribute names if no ambiguity arises.*

(iv) a set of logical variables $\mathsf{LgV} := \{x : T \mid T \in \mathsf{Srt}\}$.

Π_{Σ_C} denotes the set of all executable PL programs (i.e., sequences of statements) with locations over signature Σ_C. In the remaining paper, we use the notion of a program to refer to a sequence of executable PL-statements. If we want to include class, interface or method declarations, we either include them explicitly or make a reference to the context program C.

Terms t and formulas ϕ are defined as usual, thus omitted here for brevity. We use *updates* u to describe state changes by means of an explicit substitution. An *elementary update* $\mathtt{i} := t$ or $t.\mathtt{a} := t$ is a pair of location and term. They are of *single static assignment (SSA)* form, with the same meaning as simple assignments. Elementary updates are composed to *parallel updates* $u_1 \| u_2$ and work like simultaneous assignments. Updates u are defined by the grammar $u ::= \mathtt{i} := t \mid t.\mathtt{a} := t \mid u \| u \mid \{u\}u$ (where $\mathtt{a} \in \mathsf{Attr}$) together with the usual well-typedness conditions. Updates applied on terms or formulas, written $\{u\}t$ resp. $\{u\}\phi$, are again terms or formulas. Updates applied on terms or formulas, written $\{u\}t$ resp. $\{u\}\phi$, are again terms or formulas. Terms, formulas and updates are evaluated with respect to a PL-DL Kripke structure:

Definition 2 (Kripke structure). *A PL-DL Kripke structure* $\mathcal{K}_{\Sigma_{PL}} = (\mathcal{D}, I, S)$ *consists of (i) a set of elements* $\mathcal{D}$ *called* domain, *(ii) an interpretation* I *with*

- $I(T) = \mathcal{D}_T$, $T \in \mathsf{Srt}$ *assigning each sort its non-empty domain* $\mathcal{D}_T$. *It adheres to the restrictions imposed by the subtype order* $\preceq$; $\mathtt{Null}$ *is always interpreted as a singleton set and subtype of all class types;*
- $I(f) : \mathcal{D}_{T_1} \times \ldots \times \mathcal{D}_{T_n} \to \mathcal{D}_T$ *for each rigid function symbol* $f : T_1 \times \ldots \times T_n \to T \in \mathsf{Func}_r$;
- $I(p) \subseteq \mathcal{D}_{T_1} \times \ldots \times \mathcal{D}_{T_n}$ *for each predicate symbol* $p : T_1 \times \ldots \times T_n \in \mathsf{Pred}$;

and (iii) a set of states S *assigning meaning to non-rigid function symbols: let* $s \in S$ *then* $s(\mathtt{a}@Cl) : \mathcal{D}_{Cl} \to \mathcal{D}_T$, $\mathtt{a}@Cl : Cl \to T \in \mathsf{Attr}$ *and* $s(\mathtt{i}) : \mathcal{D}_T$, $\mathtt{i} \in \mathsf{PV}$. *The pair* $D = (\mathcal{D}, I)$ *is called a first-order structure.*

$$val_{D,s,\beta}(\mathtt{x} := t)(s) = s[\mathtt{x} \leftarrow t]$$
$$val_{D,s,\beta}(o.\mathtt{a} := t)(s) = s[(\mathtt{a})(val_{D,s,\beta}(o)) \leftarrow t]$$
$$val_{D,s,\beta}(u_1 \| u_2)(s) = val_{D,s,\beta}(u_2)(val_{D,s,\beta}(u_1)(s))$$
$$val_{D,s,\beta}(\{u_1\}u_2)(s) = val_{D,s',\beta}(u_2)(s'), \text{ where } s' = val_{D,s,\beta}(u_1)(s)$$
$$val_{D,s}(\mathtt{x} = e) = \{s'[\mathtt{x} \leftarrow d] \mid (s', d) \in val_{D,s}(e)\}, \ \mathtt{x} \in \mathsf{PV}$$
$$val_{D,s}(o.\mathtt{a} = e) = \{s''[\mathtt{a}(d_o) \leftarrow d_e] \mid (s', d_o) \in val_{D,s}(o) \wedge (s'', d_e) \in val_{D,s'}(e)\}$$
$$val_{D,s}(\mathtt{p_1}; \mathtt{p_2}) = \bigcup_{s' \in val_{D,s}(\mathtt{p_1})} val_{D,s'}(\mathtt{p_2})$$

$$val_{D,s}(\mathtt{if}(e)\ \{\mathtt{p}\}\ \mathtt{else}\ \{\mathtt{q}\}) = \begin{cases} val_{D,s',\beta}(\mathtt{p}), & (s', \mathit{True}) \in val_{D,s}(e) \\ val_{D,s',\beta}(\mathtt{q}), & (s', \mathit{False}) \in val_{D,s}(e) \\ \emptyset, & \text{otherwise} \end{cases}$$

$$val_{D,s}(\mathtt{while}(e)\{\mathtt{p}\}) = \begin{cases} \bigcup_{s_1 \in S_1} val_{D,s_1}(\mathtt{while}(e)\{\mathtt{p}\}) \text{ where } S_1 = val_{D,s'}(\mathtt{p}), \\ \qquad \text{if } (s', \mathit{True}) \in val_{D,s}(e) \\ \{s'\}, \text{ if } (s', \mathit{False}) \in val_{D,s}(e) \\ \emptyset, \text{ otherwise} \end{cases}$$

Fig. 1. Definition of PL-DL semantic evaluation function (excerpt)

A *variable assignment* $\beta : \mathsf{LgV} \to \mathcal{D}_T$ maps a logical variable $x : T$ to its domain $\mathcal{D}_T$. A term, formula or update is evaluated relative to a given first-order structure $D = (\mathcal{D}, I)$, a state $s \in S$ and a variable assignment β, while programs and expressions are evaluated relative to a D and $s \in S$. The evaluation function *val* is defined recursively. It evaluates (i) every term $t : T$ to a value $val_{D,s,\beta}(t) \in \mathcal{D}_T$; (ii) every formula ϕ to a truth value $val_{D,s,\beta}(\phi) \in \{tt, ff\}$; (iii) every update u to a state transformer $val_{D,s,\beta}(u) \in S \to S$, (iv) every statement st to a set of states $val_{D,s}(st) \subseteq 2^S$; and (v) every expression $e : T$ to a set of pairs of state and value $val_{D,s}(e) \subseteq 2^{S \times T}$. As PL is deterministic, all sets of states or state-value pairs have at most one element.

Fig. 1 shows an excerpt of the semantic definition of updates and programs, more definitions are in our technical report [9]. The expression $s[\mathtt{x} \leftarrow \mathtt{v}]$ denotes a state coincides with s except at $\mathtt{x}$ which is mapped to the evaluation of $\mathtt{v}$.

Example 1 (Update semantics). We illustrate the semantics of updates of Fig. 1. Evaluating $\{\mathtt{i} := \mathtt{j} + 1\}\mathtt{i} \geq \mathtt{j}$ in a state s is identical to evaluating the formula $\mathtt{i} \geq \mathtt{j}$ in a state s' which coincides with s except for the value of $\mathtt{i}$ which is evaluated to the value of $val_{D,s,\beta}(\mathtt{j} + 1)$. Evaluation of the parallel update $\mathtt{i} := \mathtt{j} \| \mathtt{j} := \mathtt{i}$ in a state s leads to the successor state s' identical to s except that the values of $\mathtt{i}$ and $\mathtt{j}$ are swapped. The parallel update $\mathtt{i} := 3 \| \mathtt{i} := 4$ has a *conflict* as $\mathtt{i}$ is assigned different values. In such a case the last occurring assignment $\mathtt{i} := 4$ overrides all previous ones of the same location. Evaluation of $\{\mathtt{i} := \mathtt{j}\}\{\mathtt{j} := \mathtt{i}\}\phi$ in a state s results in evaluating ϕ in a state, where $\mathtt{i}$ has the value of $\mathtt{j}$, and $\mathtt{j}$ remains unchanged.

Remark. $\{\mathtt{i} := \mathtt{j}\}\{\mathtt{j} := \mathtt{i}\}\phi$ is the sequential application of updates $\mathtt{i} := \mathtt{j}$ and $\mathtt{j} := \mathtt{i}$ on the formula ϕ. To ease the presentation, we overload the concept of update and also call $\{\mathtt{i} := \mathtt{j}\}\{\mathtt{j} := \mathtt{i}\}$ as an update. In the following context, if not stated otherwise, we use the upper-case letter $\mathcal{U}$ to denote this kind of "misused" update, compared to the real update that is denoted by a lower-case letter u. An update $\mathcal{U}$ could be the form of $\{u\}$ and $\{u_1\} \ldots \{u_n\}$.

$$\text{emptyBox } \frac{\Gamma \Rightarrow \mathcal{U}\phi, \Delta}{\Gamma \Rightarrow \mathcal{U}[]\phi, \Delta} \qquad \text{assignment } \frac{\Gamma \Rightarrow \mathcal{U}\{x := litVar\}[\omega]\phi, \Delta}{\Gamma \Rightarrow \mathcal{U}[x = litVar; \omega]\phi, \Delta}$$

$$\text{assignAddition } \frac{\Gamma \Rightarrow \mathcal{U}\{x := litVar_1 + litVar_2\}[\omega]\phi, \Delta}{\Gamma \Rightarrow \mathcal{U}[x = litVar_1 + litVar_2; \omega]\phi, \Delta}$$

$$\text{ifElse } \frac{\Gamma, \mathcal{U}b = \text{TRUE} \Rightarrow \mathcal{U}[p; \omega]\phi, \Delta \qquad \Gamma, \mathcal{U}\neg b = \text{TRUE} \Rightarrow \mathcal{U}[q; \omega]\phi, \Delta}{\Gamma \Rightarrow \mathcal{U}[\text{if } (b) \ \{p\} \ \text{else} \ \{q\} \ \omega]\phi, \Delta}$$

$$\text{loopInvariant } \frac{\begin{array}{ll} \Gamma \Rightarrow \mathcal{U}inv, \Delta & (\text{init}) \\ \Gamma, \mathcal{U}\mathcal{V}_{mod}(b = \text{TRUE} \wedge inv) \Rightarrow \mathcal{U}\mathcal{V}_{mod}[p]inv, \Delta & (\text{preserves}) \\ \Gamma, \mathcal{U}\mathcal{V}_{mod}(b = \text{FALSE} \wedge inv) \Rightarrow \mathcal{U}\mathcal{V}_{mod}[\omega]\phi, \Delta & (\text{use case}) \end{array}}{\Gamma \Rightarrow \mathcal{U}[\text{while } (b) \ \{p\} \ \omega]\phi, \Delta}$$

Fig. 2. Selected sequent calculus rules (for more detail see [9,3])

3.2 Sequent Calculus

We define a sequent calculus for PL-DL. Symbolic execution of a PL-program is performed by application of sequent calculus rules. Soundness of the rules ensures validity of provable PL-DL formulas in a program verification setting [3].

A *sequent* is a pair of sets of formulas $\Gamma = \{\phi_1, \ldots, \phi_n\}$ (antecedent) and $\Delta = \{\psi_1, \ldots, \psi_m\}$ (succedent) of the form $\Gamma \Rightarrow \Delta$. Its semantics is defined by the formula $\bigwedge_{\phi \in \Gamma} \phi \to \bigvee_{\psi \in \Delta} \psi$. A *sequent calculus rule* has one conclusion and zero or more premises. It is applied to a sequent s by matching its conclusion against s. The instantiated premises are then added as children of s. Our PL-DL sequent calculus behaves as a symbolic interpreter for PL. A *sequent* for PL-DL is always of the form $\Gamma \Rightarrow \mathcal{U}[p]\phi, \Delta$. During symbolic execution performed by the sequent rules (see Fig. 2) the antecedents Γ accumulate path conditions and contain possible preconditions. The updates $\mathcal{U}$ record the current symbolic value at each point during program execution and the ϕ's represent postconditions. Symbolic execution of a program p works as follows:

1. Select an open proof goal with a $[\cdot]$ modality. If no $[\cdot]$ exists on any branch, then symbolic execution is completed. Focus on the first active statement (possibly empty) of the program in the modality.
2. If it is a complex statement, apply rules to decompose it into simple statements and goto 1., otherwise continue.
3. Apply the sequent calculus rule corresponding to the active statement.
4. Simplify the resulting updates and apply first-order simplification to the premises. This might result in some closed branches. It is possible to detect and eliminate infeasible paths in this way. Goto 1.

Example 2. We look at typical proof goals that arise during symbolic execution:

1. $\Gamma, i > j \Rightarrow \mathcal{U}[\text{if } (i>j) \ \{p\} \ \text{else} \ \{q\} \ \omega]\phi$: Applying rule ifElse and simplification eliminates the else branch and symb. exec. continues with p ω.
2. $\Gamma \Rightarrow \{i := c \| \ldots\}[j = i; \ \omega]\phi$ where c is a constant: It is sound to replace the statement j = i with j = c and continue with symbolic execution. This is known as *constant propagation*. More techniques for *partial evaluation* can be integrated into symbolic execution [10].

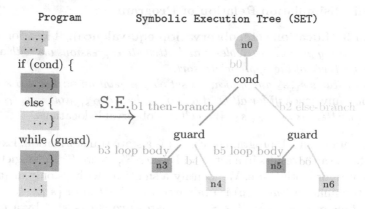

Fig. 3. Symbolic execution tree with loop invariant applied

3. $\Gamma \Rightarrow \{\text{o1.a} := \text{v1}\| \ldots\}[\text{o2.a} = \text{v2}; \ \omega]\phi$: After executing $\text{o2.a} = \text{v2}$, the *alias* is analyzed as follows: (i) if $\text{o2} = \text{null}$ is true the program does not terminate; (ii) else, if $\text{o2} = \text{o1}$ holds, the value of o1.a in the update is overriden and the new update is $\{\text{o1.a} := \text{v2}\| \ldots \|\text{o2.a} := \text{v2}\}$; (iii) else the new update is $\{\text{o1.a} := \text{v1}\| \ldots \|\text{o2.a} := \text{v2}\}$. Neither of (i)–(iii) might be provable and symbolic execution split into these three cases when encountering a possibly aliased object access.

The result of symbolic execution for a PL program p following the sequent calculus rules is a *symbolic execution tree (SET)*, as illustrated in Fig. 3. Complete symbolic execution trees are finite acyclic trees whose root is labeled with $\Gamma \Rightarrow [\text{p}]\phi, \Delta$ and no leaf has a $[\cdot]$ modality. W.l.o.g. we can assume that each inner node i is annotated by a sequent $\Gamma_i \Rightarrow \mathcal{U}_i[\text{p}_i]\phi_i, \Delta_i$, where p_i is the program to be executed. Every child node is generated by rule application from its parent. A *branching node* represents a statement whose execution causes branching, e.g., conditional, object access, loops etc. We call a *sequential block* a maximal program fragment in an SET that is symbolically executed without branching. For instance, there are 7 sequential blocks in the SET on the right of Fig. 3.

4   Sequent Calculus for Program Transformation

The structure of a symbolic execution tree makes it possible to synthesize a program by bottom-up traversal. The idea is to apply the sequent calculus rules reversely and generate the program step-by-step. This requires to extend the sequent calculus rules with means for program synthesis. Obviously, the synthesized program should behave exactly as the original one, at least for the *observable locations*. To this end we introduce the notion of *weak bisimulation* for PL programs and show its soundness for program transformation (see [9]).

4.1   Weak Bisimulation Relation of Program

Definition 3 (Location sets, observation equivalence). *A location set Loc is a set containing program variables* x *and attribute expressions* o.a *with* a $\in$ Attr *and o being a term of the appropriate sort.*

Given two states s_1, s_2 and a location set obs. A relation $\approx$: $Loc \times S \times S$ is an observation equivalence iff for all D, β and ol $\in$ obs, $val_{D,s_1,\beta}(ol) = val_{D,s_2,\beta}(ol)$ holds. It is written as $s_1 \approx_{obs} s_2$. We call obs observable locations.

The semantics of a PL program p (Fig. 1) is a state transformation. Executing p from a start state s results in a set of end states S', where S' is a singleton $\{s'\}$ if p terminates, or $\emptyset$ otherwise. We identify a singleton with its only member, so in case of termination, $val_{D,s}(p)$ is evaluated to s' instead of $\{s'\}$.

A *transition relation* $\longrightarrow$: $\Pi \times S \times S$ relates two states s, s' by a program p iff p starts in state s and terminates in state s', written $s \xrightarrow{p} s'$. We have: $s \xrightarrow{p} s'$, where $s' = val_{D,s}(p)$. If p does not terminate, we write $s \xrightarrow{p}$.

Since a complex statement can be decomposed into a set of simple statements, which is done during symbolic execution, we can assume that a program p consists of simple statements. Execution of p leads to a sequence of state transitions: $s \xrightarrow{p} s' \equiv s_0 \xrightarrow{sSt_0} s_1 \xrightarrow{sSt_1} \ldots \xrightarrow{sSt_{n-1}} s_n \xrightarrow{sSt_n} s_{n+1}$, where $s = s_0$, $s' = s_{n+1}$, s_i a *program state* and sSt_i a simple statement $(0 \leq i \leq n)$. A program state has the same semantics as the *state* defined in a Kripke structure, so we use both notations without distinction.

Some simple statements reassign values (write) to a location ol in the observable locations that affects the evaluation of ol in the final state. We distinguish these simple statements from those that do not affect the observable locations.

Definition 4 (Observable and internal statement/transition). *Consider states s, s', a simple statement* sSt, *a transition relation* $\longrightarrow$, *where* $s \xrightarrow{sSt} s'$, *and the observable locations obs; we call* sSt *an observable statement and* $\longrightarrow$ *an observable transition, iff for all D, β, there exists ol $\in$ obs, and $val_{D,s',\beta}(ol) \neq val_{D,s,\beta}(ol)$. We write* $\xrightarrow{sSt}_{obs}$. *Otherwise,* sSt *is called an* internal statement *and* $\longrightarrow$ *an internal transition, written* $\longrightarrow_{int}$.

In this definition, observable/internal transitions are *minimal* transitions that relate two states with a simple statement. We indicate the simple statement sSt in the notion of the observable transition $\xrightarrow{sSt}_{obs}$, since sSt reflects the changes of the observable locations. In contrast, an internal statement does not appear in the notion of the internal transition.

Example 3. Given observable locations set $obs=\{x, y\}$, the simple statement "x = 1 + z;" is observable, because x's value is reassigned (could be the same value). The statement "z = x + y;" is internal, since the evaluation of x, y are not changed, even though the value of each variable is read by z.

Remark. An observable transition may change the set of observable locations. Assume an observable transition $s \xrightarrow{sSt}_{obs} s'$ changes the evaluation of some location $ol \in obs$ in state s'. To continue with the execution of program p' from state s', the set of observable locations obs' in state s' should also contain the locations ol' that *read* the value of ol in some statement in p', because the change to ol can lead to a change of ol' at some later point in p'.

Example 4. Consider $obs=\{x, y\}$ and program fragment "$z = x + y; x = 1 + z;$". $z = x + y;$ becomes observable because the value of z is changed and it will be used later in the observable statement $x = 1 + z;$. The observable location set obs' should also contain z after the execution of $z = x + y;$.

Definition 5 (Weak transition). *The transition relation $\Longrightarrow_{int}$ is the reflexive and transitive closure of $\longrightarrow_{int}$: $s \Longrightarrow_{int} s'$ holds iff for states $s_0,\ldots,s_n$, $n \geq 0$, we have $s = s_0$, $s' = s_n$ and $s_0 \longrightarrow_{int} s_1 \longrightarrow_{int} \cdots \longrightarrow_{int} s_n$. In the case of $n = 0$, $s \Longrightarrow_{int} s$ holds. The transition relation $\overset{sSt}{\Longrightarrow}_{obs}$ is the composition of the relations $\Longrightarrow_{int}$, $\overset{sSt}{\longrightarrow}_{obs}$ and $\Longrightarrow_{int}$: $s \overset{sSt}{\Longrightarrow}_{obs} s'$ holds iff there are states s_1 and s_2 such that $s \Longrightarrow_{int} s_1 \overset{sSt}{\longrightarrow}_{obs} s_2 \Longrightarrow_{int} s'$. The weak transition $\overset{sSt}{\Longrightarrow}_{obs}$ represents either $\overset{sSt}{\Longrightarrow}_{obs}$, if sSt observable or $\Longrightarrow_{int}$ otherwise. In other words, a weak transition is a sequence of minimal transitions that contains at most one observable transition.*

Definition 6 (Weak bisimulation for states). *Given two programs p_1, p_2 and observable locations obs, obs', let sSt_1 be a simple statement and s_1, s_1' two program states of p_1, and sSt_2 is a simple statement and s_2, s_2' are two program states of p_2. A relation $\approx$ is a weak bisimulation for states iff $s_1 \approx_{obs} s_2$ implies:*

- *if $s_1 \overset{\widehat{sSt_1}}{\Longrightarrow}_{obs} s_1'$, then $s_2 \overset{\widehat{sSt_2}}{\Longrightarrow}_{obs} s_2'$ and $s_1' \approx_{obs'} s_2'$*
- *if $s_2 \overset{\widehat{sSt_2}}{\Longrightarrow}_{obs} s_2'$, then $s_1 \overset{\widehat{sSt_1}}{\Longrightarrow}_{obs} s_1'$ and $s_2' \approx_{obs'} s_1'$*

where $val_{D,s_1}(sSt_1) \approx_{obs'} val_{D,s_2}(sSt_2)$.

Definition 7 (Weak bisimulation for programs). *Let p_1, p_2 be two programs, obs, obs' observable locations, and $\approx$ a weak bisimulation relation for states. $\approx$ is a weak bisimulation for programs, written $p_1 \approx_{obs} p_2$, if for the sequence of state transitions:*

$$s_1 \overset{p_1}{\longrightarrow} s_1' \equiv s_1^0 \overset{sSt_1^0}{\longrightarrow} s_1^1 \overset{sSt_1^1}{\longrightarrow} \ldots \overset{sSt_1^{n-1}}{\longrightarrow} s_1^n \overset{sSt_1^n}{\longrightarrow} s_1^{n+1}, \text{ with } s_1 = s_1^0, s_1' = s_1^{n+1},$$

$$s_2 \overset{p_2}{\longrightarrow} s_2' \equiv s_2^0 \overset{sSt_2^0}{\longrightarrow} s_2^1 \overset{sSt_2^1}{\longrightarrow} \ldots \overset{sSt_2^{m-1}}{\longrightarrow} s_2^m \overset{sSt_2^m}{\longrightarrow} s_2^{m+1}, \text{ with } s_2 = s_2^0, s_2' = s_2^{m+1},$$

we have (i) $s_2' \approx_{obs} s_1'$; (ii) for each state s_1^i there exists a state s_2^j such that $s_1^i \approx_{obs'} s_2^j$; (iii) for each state s_2^j there exists a state s_1^i such that $s_2^j \approx_{obs'} s_1^i$, where $0 \leq i \leq n$ and $0 \leq j \leq m$.

The above definition requires a weak transition that relates two states with at most one observable transition. This definition reflects the *structural* properties of a program and can be characterized as a *small-step semantics* [11]. The lemma Def. 7 to a *big-step semantics* [12].

Lemma 1. *Let p, q be programs and obs the set of observable locations. If $p \approx_{obs} q$ then for any first-order structure D and state s, $val_{D,s}(p) \approx_{obs} val_{D,s}(q)$ holds.*

4.2 The Weak Bisimulation Modality

We introduce a weak bisimulation modality which allows us to relate two programs that behave indistinguishably on the observable locations.

Definition 8 (Weak bisimulation modality—syntax). *The bisimulation modality* $[\, p \,\lozenge\, q \,]@(obs, use)$ *is a modal operator providing compartments for programs* p, q *and location sets obs and use. We extend our definition of formulas: Let* ϕ *be a PL-DL formula and* p, q *two PL programs and* obs, use *two location sets such that* $pv(\phi) \subseteq obs$ *where* $pv(\phi)$ *is the set of all program variables occurring in* ϕ, *then* $[\, p \,\lozenge\, q \,]@(obs, use)\phi$ *is also a PL-DL formula.*

The intuition behind the location set $usedVar(s, p, obs)$ defined below is to capture precisely those locations whose value influences the final value of an observable location $l \in obs$ after executing a program p. We approximate the set later by the set of all program variables in p that are used before being redefined.

Definition 9 (Used program variable). *A variable* $v \in PV$ *is called* used *by a program* p *w.r.t. a location set obs, if there exists an* $l \in obs$ *such that*
$$D, s \models \forall v_l. \exists v_0. (((\langle p \rangle l = v_l) \rightarrow (\{v := v_0\}\langle p \rangle l \neq v_l))$$

The set $usedVar(s, p, obs)$ *is defined as the smallest set containing all heap locations and all used program variables of* p *w.r.t. obs.*

The formula defining a used variable v of a program p encodes that there is an interference with a location contained in obs. E.g., variable z in Ex. 4 is a used variable. We formalize the semantics of the weak bisimulation modality:

Definition 10 (Weak bisimulation modality—semantics). *Given* p, q *programs,* D, s, β, *and obs, use as above;* $val_{D,s,\beta}([\, p \,\lozenge\, q \,]@(obs, use)\phi) = tt$ *iff*

1. $val_{D,s,\beta}([p]\phi) = tt$
2. $use \supseteq usedVar(s, q, obs)$
3. *for all* $s' \approx_{obs \cup use} s$ *we have* $val_{D,s}(p) \approx_{obs \cup use} val_{D,s'}(q)$

4.3 Sequent Calculus Rules for the Bisimulation Modality

The sequent calculus rules for the bisimulation modality are of the form:
$$\Gamma_1 \Rightarrow \mathcal{U}_1[\, p_1 \,\lozenge\, q_1 \,]@(obs_1, use_1)\phi_1, \Delta_1$$
$$\ldots$$
$$\text{ruleName} \quad \frac{\Gamma_n \Rightarrow \mathcal{U}_n[\, p_n \,\lozenge\, q_n \,]@(obs_n, use_n)\phi_n, \Delta_n}{\Gamma \Rightarrow \mathcal{U}[\, p \,\lozenge\, q \,]@(obs, use)\phi, \Delta}$$

Fig. 4 shows some extended sequent calculus rules, more are available in [9]. Unlike standard sequent calculus rules that are executed from root to leaves, sequent rule application for the bisimulation modality consists of two phases: In the first phase, the source program p is evaluated as usual. In addition, the observable location sets obs_i are propagated, since they contain the locations observable by p_i and ϕ_i that will be used in the second phase. Typically, obs

$$\text{emptyBox} \ \frac{\Gamma \Rightarrow \mathcal{U}@(obs, \_)\phi, \Delta}{\Gamma \Rightarrow \mathcal{U}[\ \texttt{nop} \ \lozenge \ \texttt{nop}\ ]@(obs, obs)\phi, \Delta}$$

$$\text{assignment} \ \frac{\Gamma \Rightarrow \mathcal{U}\{\texttt{l} := \texttt{r}\}[\ \omega \ \lozenge \ \overline{\omega}\ ]@(obs, use)\phi, \Delta}{\left(\begin{array}{ll} \Gamma \Rightarrow \mathcal{U}[\ l = r; \omega \ \lozenge \ l \doteq r; \overline{\omega}\ ]@(obs, use - \{l\} \cup \{r\})\phi, \Delta & \text{if } l \in use \\ \Gamma \Rightarrow \mathcal{U}[\ l = r; \omega \ \lozenge \ \overline{\omega}\ ]@(obs, use)\phi, \Delta & \text{otherwise} \end{array} \right)}$$

$$\text{ifElse} \ \frac{\begin{array}{c} \Gamma, \mathcal{U}b \Rightarrow \mathcal{U}[\ p; \omega \ \lozenge \ \overline{p; \omega}\ ]@(obs, use_{p;\omega})\phi, \Delta \\ \Gamma, \mathcal{U}\neg b \Rightarrow \mathcal{U}[\ q; \omega \ \lozenge \ \overline{q; \omega}\ ]@(obs, use_{q;\omega})\phi, \Delta \end{array}}{\begin{array}{c} \Gamma \Rightarrow \mathcal{U}[\ \texttt{if } (b) \ \{p\} \ \texttt{else} \ \{q\}; \omega \ \lozenge \\ \texttt{if } (b) \ \{\overline{p;\omega}\} \ \texttt{else} \ \{\overline{q;\omega}\}\ ]@(obs, use_{p;\omega} \cup use_{q;\omega} \cup \{b\})\phi, \Delta \end{array}}$$

(with b boolean variable.)

$$\text{loopInvariant} \ \frac{\begin{array}{c} \Gamma \Rightarrow \mathcal{U}inv, \Delta \\ \Gamma, \mathcal{U}\mathcal{V}_{mod}(\texttt{b} = \textbf{TRUE} \wedge inv) \Rightarrow \mathcal{U}\mathcal{V}_{mod} \\ [\ p \ \lozenge \ \overline{p}\ ]@(obs \cup use_1 \cup \{b\}, use_2)inv, \Delta \\ \Gamma, \mathcal{U}\mathcal{V}_{mod}(\texttt{b} = \textbf{FALSE} \wedge inv) \Rightarrow \mathcal{U}\mathcal{V}_{mod}[\ \omega \ \lozenge \ \overline{\omega}\ ]@(obs, use_1)\phi, \Delta \end{array}}{\Gamma \Rightarrow \mathcal{U}[\ \texttt{while(b)}\{p\} \, \omega \ \lozenge \ \texttt{while(b)}\{\overline{p}\} \, \overline{\omega}\ ]@(obs, use_1 \cup use_2 \cup \{b\})\phi, \Delta}$$

Fig. 4. A collection of sequent calculus rules for program transformation

contains the return variables of a method and the locations used in the continuation of the program, e.g., program variables used after a loop must be reflected in the observable locations of the loop body. The result of this phase is a symbolic execution tree as illustrated in Fig. 3. In the second phase, we synthesize the target program q and used variable set use from q_i and use_i by applying the rules in a leaves-to-root manner. One starts with a leaf node and apply the emptyBox rule, then stepwise generates the program within its sequential block, e.g., b3,..., b6 in Fig. 3. These are combined by rules corresponding to statements that contain a sequential block, such as loopInvariant (containing b3 and b4). One continues with the sequential block containing the compound statements, e.g., b2, until the root is reached. Note that the order of processing the sequential blocks matters, for instance, the program for the sequential block b4 must be generated before that for b3, because the observable locations in node n3 depend on the used variable set of b4 according to the loopInvariant rule.

Lemma 2. *The extended sequent calculus rules are sound. (For the proof see [9])*

5 Optimization

Sect. 4.2 introduced an approach to program simplification based on the extended sequent calculus rules. The generated program consists only of simple statements and is optimized to a certain degree, because the used variable set avoids generating unnecessary statements. Updates reflect the state of program execution. In particular, the update in a sequential block records the evaluation of the locations in that sequential block, it can be used for further optimization.

5.1   Update Simplification

Within a sequential block, after application of sequent rules (e.g., assignment), we often obtain an update $\mathcal{U}$ of the form $\{u_1\}\ldots\{u_n\}$. It can be simplified into a single update $\{u\}$, namely the *normal form* (NF) of update.

Definition 11 (Normal form of update). *An update is in* normal form, *denoted by* $\mathcal{U}^{nf}$, *if it has the shape* $\{u_1\|\ldots\|u_n\}$, $n \geq 0$, *where each* u_i *is an elementary update and there is no conflict between* u_i *and* u_j *for any* $i \neq j$.

The normal form of an update $\mathcal{U} = \{u_1\}\ldots\{u_n\}$ can be achieved by applying a sequence of *update simplification* steps. Soundness of these rules and that they achieve normal form are proven in [13]. The update rules are reproduced in [9].

Like elementary updates, updates in normal form are in SSA. It is easy to maintain normal form of updates in a sequential block when applying the extended sequent calculus rules of Fig. 4. This can be used for further optimization of the synthesized program. Take the assignment rule, for example: after each forward rule application, we do an update simplification step to maintain the normal form of the update for that sequential block; when a statement is synthesized by applying the rule backwards, we use the *update* instead of the executed assignment statement, to obtain the value of the location to be assigned; then we generate the assignment statement with that value.

Example 5. Consider the program "i = j + 1; j = i; i = j + 1;". After executing the first two statements and simplification, we obtain the normal form update $\mathcal{U}_2^{nf} = \{i := j + 1\|j := j + 1\}$. Doing the same with the third statement results in $\mathcal{U}_3^{nf} = \{j := j + 1\|i := j + 2\}$, which implies that in the final state i has value $j + 2$ and j has value $j + 1$.

Let i be the only observable location, for which a program is now synthesized bottom-up, starting with the third statement. The rules in Fig. 4 would allow to generate the statement i = j + 1;. But, reading the value of location i from $\mathcal{U}_3^{nf}$ as sketched above, the statement i = j + 2; is generated. This reflects the current value of j along the sequential block and saves an assignment.

A first attempt to formalize our ideas is the following assignment rule:

$$\frac{\Gamma \Longrightarrow \mathcal{U}_1^{nf}[\,\omega \,\lozenge\, \overline{\omega}\,]@(obs, use)\phi, \Delta}{\begin{pmatrix}\Gamma \Longrightarrow \mathcal{U}^{nf}[\,l = r; \omega \,\lozenge\, l = r_1; \overline{\omega}\,]@(obs, use - \{l\} \cup \{r\})\phi, \Delta & \text{if } l \in use \\ \Gamma \Longrightarrow \mathcal{U}^{nf}[\,l = r; \omega \,\lozenge\, \overline{\omega}\,]@(obs, use)\phi, \Delta & \text{otherwise}\end{pmatrix}}$$

with $\mathcal{U}_1^{nf} = \{\ldots\|1 := r_1\}$ being the normal form of $\mathcal{U}^{nf}\{1 := r\}$

However, this rule is not sound. If we continue Ex. 5 with synthesizing the first two assignments, we obtain j = j + 1; i = j + 2; by using the new rule, which is clearly incorrect, because i has final value $j + 3$ instead of $j + 2$. The problem is that the values of locations in the normal form update are independently synthesized from each other and do not reflect how one statement is affected by the execution of previous statements in sequential execution.

To ensure correct usage of updates in program generation, we introduce the concept of a *sequentialized normal form* (SNF) of an update.

Definition 12 (Elementary update independence). *An elementary update* $l_1 := exp_1$ *is independent from another elementary update* $l_2 := exp_2$ *if* l_1 *does not occur in* exp_2 *and* l_2 *does not occur in* exp_1.

Definition 13 (Sequentialized Normal Form update). *An update is in sequentialized normal form, denoted by* $\mathcal{U}^{snf}$, *if it has the shape of a sequence of two parallel updates* $\{u_1^a\|\dots\|u_m^a\}\{u_1\|\dots\|u_n\}$, $m \geq 0, n \geq 0$.
 $\{u_1\|\dots\|u_n\}$ *is the* core *update, denoted by* $\mathcal{U}^{snf_c}$, *where each* u_i *is an elementary update of the form* $l_i := exp_i$, *and all* u_i, u_j $(i \neq j)$ *are independent and have no conflict.*
 $\{u_1^a\|\dots\|u_m^a\}$ *is the* auxiliary *update, denoted by* $\mathcal{U}^{snf_a}$, *where (i) each* u_i^a *is of the form* $l^k := l$ $(k \geq 0)$; *(ii)* l *is a program variable; (iii)* l^k *is a fresh program variable not occurring anywhere else in* $\mathcal{U}^{snf_a}$ *and not occurring in the location set of the core update* $l^k \notin \{l_i|0 \leq i \leq n\}$; *(iv) there is no conflict between* u_i^a *and* u_j^a *for all* $i \neq j$.

Any normal form update whose elementary updates are independent is also SNF update that has only a core part.

Example 6 (SNF update).

- $\{i^0 := i\|i^1 := i\}\{i := i^0 \mid 1\|j := i^1\}$ is in sequentialized normal form (SNF).
- $\{i^0 := j\|i^1 := i\}\{i := i^0+1\|j := i^1\}$ and $\{i^0 := i+1\|i^1 := i\}\{i := i^0+1\|j := i^1\}$ are not in SNF: $i^0 := j$ has different base variables on the left and right, while $i^0 := i+1$ has a complex term on the right, both contradicting (i).

To compute the SNF of an update, we need two more rules:

- *(associativity)* $\{u_1\}\{u_2\}\{u_3\} \rightsquigarrow \{u_1\}(\{u_2\}\{u_3\})$
- *(introducing auxiliary)* $\{u\} \rightsquigarrow \{\mathbf{x}^0 := \mathbf{x}\}(\{\mathbf{x} := \mathbf{x}^0\}\{u\})$, where $\mathbf{x}^0 \notin pv$

Lemma 3. *The associativity rule and introducing auxiliary rule are sound.*

We can maintain the SNF of an update on a sequential block as follows: after executing a program statement, apply the associativity rule and compute the core update; if the newly added elementary update $l := r$ is not independent from some update in the core, then apply introduce auxiliary rule to introduce $\{l^0 := l\}$, then compute the new auxiliary update and core update.

5.2 Extended Sequent Calculus Rules Involving Updates

With the help of the SNF of an update, the assignment rule becomes:

$$\Gamma \Longrightarrow \mathcal{U}_1^{snf}[\,\omega\,\lozenge\,\overline{\omega}\,]@(obs, use)\phi, \Delta$$

$$\left(\begin{array}{l}\Gamma \Longrightarrow \mathcal{U}^{snf}[\,l = r; \omega\,\lozenge\,l = r_1; \overline{\omega}\,]@(obs, use - \{l\} \cup \{r\})\phi, \Delta \quad \text{if } l \in use \\ \Gamma \Longrightarrow \mathcal{U}^{snf}[\,l = r; \omega\,\lozenge\,\overline{\omega}\,]@(obs, use)\phi, \Delta \qquad\qquad\qquad \text{otherwise}\end{array}\right)$$

where $\mathcal{U}_1^{snf} = \mathcal{U}_1^{snf_a}\{\dots\|\mathbf{1} := \mathbf{r}_1\}$ is the SNF of $\mathcal{U}^{snf}\{\mathbf{1} := \mathbf{r}\}$).

Whenever the core update is empty, the auxAssignment rule

$$\frac{\Gamma \Longrightarrow \mathcal{U}_1^{snf_a}[\, \omega \,\, \emptyset \,\, \overline{\omega}\,]@(obs, use)\phi, \Delta}{\left(\begin{array}{ll} \Gamma \Longrightarrow \mathcal{U}^{snf_a}[\, \omega \,\, \emptyset \,\, \mathtt{T}_l\,\, l^0 = l; \overline{\omega}\,]@(obs, use - \{l^0\} \cup \{l\})\phi, \Delta & \text{if } l^0 \in use \\ \Gamma \Longrightarrow \mathcal{U}^{snf_a}[\, \omega \,\, \emptyset \,\, \overline{\omega}\,]@(obs, use)\phi, \Delta & \text{otherwise} \end{array} \right)}$$

where $\mathcal{U}^{snf_a} = \{u\}$ and $\mathcal{U}_1^{snf_a} = \{u \| l^0 := l\}$ being the auxiliary update

is used. I.e., the auxiliary assignments are always generated at the start of a sequential block. Most other rules are obtained by replacing $\mathcal{U}$ with $\mathcal{U}^{snf}$, see [9].

Example 7. We demonstrate that the program from Ex. 5 is now handled correctly. After executing the first two statements and simplifying the update, we get the normal form update $\mathcal{U}_2^{nf} = \{\mathtt{i} := \mathtt{j} + 1 \| \mathtt{j} := \mathtt{j} + 1\}$. Here a dependency issue occurs, so we introduce the auxiliary update $\{\mathtt{j}^0 := \mathtt{j}\}$ and simplify to the sequentialized normal form update $\mathcal{U}_2^{snf} = \{\mathtt{j}^0 := \mathtt{j}\}\{\mathtt{i} := \mathtt{j}^0 + 1 \| \mathtt{j} := \mathtt{j}^0 + 1\}$. Continuing with the third statement and performing update simplification results in the SNF update $\mathcal{U}_3^{snf} = \{\mathtt{j}^0 := \mathtt{j}\}\{\mathtt{j} := \mathtt{j}^0 + 1 \| \mathtt{i} := \mathtt{j}^0 + 2\}$. By applying the rules above, we synthesize the program int $\mathtt{j}^0 = \mathtt{j}; \mathtt{i} = \mathtt{j}^0 + 2$;, which still saves one assignment and is sound.

Remark. The program is first synthesized within a sequential block and then constructed. The SNF updates used in the above rules belong to the current sequential block. An execution path may contain several sequential blocks. We keep the SNF update for each sequential block without simplifying them further into a bigger SNF update for the entire execution path. E.g. in Fig. 3, the execution path from node n0 to n4 involves 3 sequential blocks b0, b1 and b4. When we synthesize the program in b4, more precisely, we should write $\mathcal{U}_0^{snf}\mathcal{U}_2^{snf}\mathcal{U}_4^{snf}$ to represent the update used in the rules. However, we just care about the SNF update of the b4 when generating the program for b4, so in the above rules, $\mathcal{U}^{snf}$ refers to $\mathcal{U}_4^{snf}$ and the other SNF updates are omitted.

Lemma 4. *The extended sequent calculus rules involving updates are sound.*

6   Related Work

JSpec [14] is a state-of-the-art program specializer for Java. It uses an *offline* partial evaluation technique that depends on *binding time analysis*. Our work is based on symbolic execution to derive information on-the-fly, similar to *online* partial evaluation [15], however, we do not generate the program during symbolic execution, but synthesize it in the second phase. In principle, our first phase can obtain as much information as online partial evaluation, and the second phase can generate a more precise optimized program. A major advantage of our approach is that the generated program is guaranteed to be correct. There is work on proving the correctness of a partial evaluator by [16], but they need to encode the correctness properties into a logic programming language.

Verifying Compiler [17] project aims at the development of a compiler that verifies the program during compilation. On contrast, our work might be called *Compiling Verifier*, since the optimized program is generated on the basis of a verification system. Recently, compiler verification became possible [18], however, it aims at verifying a full compiler with fixed rules, which is very expensive, while our approach works at a specific target program and is fully automatic.

The product program technique [19] can be used to verify that two closely related programs preserve behavior, but the programs must be given and loop invariants must be supplied. This has been applied for loop vectorization [20], where specific heuristics do away with the need for invariants and target program is synthesized. The main differences to our work are that we aim at general programs and we use a different synthesis principle.

7   Conclusions and Future Work

We presented a sound framework for program transformation and optimization. It employs symbolic execution, deduction and bisimulation to achieve a precise analysis of variable dependencies and aliasing, and yields an optimized program that has the same behavior as the original program with respect to the observable locations. We presented also an improved and sound approach to obtain a more optimized program by involving updates into the program generation.

The language PL in this paper is a subset of Java, but our technique is valid in general. We intend to extend our approaches to full Java. Observable locations need not be restricted to return variables as in here, but, for example, could be publicly observable variables in an information flow setting. We plan to apply our approaches to language-based security. Finally, the bisimulation modality is not restricted to the same source and target programming language, so we plan to generate Java bytecode from Java source code which will result in a deductive Java compiler that guarantees sound and optimizing compilation.

References

1. Alkassar, E., Hillebrand, M.A., Paul, W.J., Petrova, E.: Automated verification of a small hypervisor. In: Leavens, G.T., O'Hearn, P., Rajamani, S.K. (eds.) VSTTE 2010. LNCS, vol. 6217, pp. 40–54. Springer, Heidelberg (2010)
2. Baumann, C., Beckert, B., Blasum, H., Bormer, T.: Lessons learned from microkernel verification – specification is the new bottleneck. In: SSV. EPTCS, vol. 102, pp. 18–32 (2012)
3. Beckert, B., Hähnle, R., Schmitt, P.H. (eds.): Verification of Object-Oriented Software. LNCS (LNAI), vol. 4334. Springer, Heidelberg (2007)
4. Bubel, R., Hähnle, R., Ji, R.: Program specialization via a software verification tool. In: Aichernig, B.K., de Boer, F.S., Bonsangue, M.M. (eds.) FMCO 2010. LNCS, vol. 6957, pp. 80–101. Springer, Heidelberg (2011)
5. Sangiorgi, D.: Introduction to Bisimulation and Coinduction (2011)
6. King, J.C.: Symbolic execution and program testing. Communications of the ACM 19(7), 385–394 (1976)

7. Ahrendt, W., Baar, T., Beckert, B., Bubel, R., Giese, M., Hähnle, R., Menzel, W., Mostowski, W., Roth, A., Schlager, S., Schmitt, P.H.: The KeY tool: integrating object oriented design and formal verification. SoSyM 4(1), 32–54 (2005)

8. Harel, D., Kozen, D., Tiuryn, J.: Dynamic Logic. MIT Press (2000)

9. Ji, R., Hähnle, R., Bubel, R.: Program transformation based on symbolic execution and deduction, technical report (2013)

10. Bubel, R., Hähnle, R., Ji, R.: Interleaving symbolic execution and partial evaluation. In: de Boer, F.S., Bonsangue, M.M., Hallerstede, S., Leuschel, M. (eds.) FMCO 2009. LNCS, vol. 6286, pp. 125–146. Springer, Heidelberg (2010)

11. Plotkin, G.D.: A structural approach to operational semantics. J. Log. Algebr. Program. 60-61, 17–139 (2004)

12. Kahn, G.: Natural semantics. In: Brandenburg, F.J., Wirsing, M., Vidal-Naquet, G. (eds.) STACS 1987. LNCS, vol. 247, pp. 22–39. Springer, Heidelberg (1987)

13. Rümmer, P.: Sequential, parallel, and quantified updates of first-order structures. In: Hermann, M., Voronkov, A. (eds.) LPAR 2006. LNCS (LNAI), vol. 4246, pp. 422–436. Springer, Heidelberg (2006)

14. Schultz, U.P., Lawall, J.L., Consel, C.: Automatic program specialization for Java. ACM-TPLS 25(4), 452–499 (2003)

15. Ruf, E.S.: Topics in online partial evaluation. PhD thesis, Stanford University, Stanford, CA, USA, UMI Order No. GAX93-26550 (1993)

16. Hatcliff, J., Danvy, O.: A computational formalization for partial evaluation. Mathematical Structures in Computer Science 7(5), 507–541 (1997)

17. Hoare, T.: The verifying compiler: A grand challenge for computing research. J. ACM 50, 63–69 (2003)

18. Leroy, X.: Formal verification of a realistic compiler. CACM 52(7), 107–115 (2009)

19. Barthe, G., Crespo, J.M., Kunz, C.: Relational verification using product programs. In: Butler, M., Schulte, W. (eds.) FM 2011. LNCS, vol. 6664, pp. 200–214. Springer, Heidelberg (2011)

20. Barthe, G., Crespo, J.M., Gulwani, S., Kunz, C., Marron, M.: From relational verification to SIMD loop synthesis. In: PPOPP, pp. 123–134. ACM (2013)

Constraint Specification and Test Generation for OSEK/VDX-Based Operating Systems*

Yunja Choi

School of Computer Science and Engineering, Kyungpook National University, Korea
yuchoi76@knu.ac.kr

Abstract. This work suggests a method for systematically constructing an environment model for automotive operating systems compliant
with the OSEK/VDX international standard by introducing a constraint
specification language, OSEK_CSL, and defining its underlying formal
models. OSEK_CSL is designed for specifying constraints of OSEK/VDX
using a pre-defined set of constraint types identified from the
OSEK/VDX standard. Each constraint specified in OSEK_CSL is interpreted as a context-free language and is converted into push-down
automata using NuSMV, which allows automated test sequence generation using LTL model checking. This approach supports selective applications of constraints and thus is able to control the "degree" of test
sequences with respect to test purposes. An application of the suggested
approach demonstrates its effectiveness in identifying safety problems.

1 Introduction

An automotive operating system is typical safety-critical software and therefore
requires extensive analysis using formal methods. However, existing formal approaches in this domain [6,7] have either been seen difficult to use or do not
scale in practice. Instead, conformance testing [12] has been a de facto verification method in industry; for example, in order to get a certificate for an
operating system compliant with the OSEK/VDX international standard [1],
a system must pass a test suite distributed by a certification agency. A major
problem with conformance testing is that the tests are designed for checking
functionalities, not for checking safety, and do not aim at comprehensive verification. Our previous work [4] revealed some potential safety problems in an
OSEK/VDX-based operating system using model checking, which would have
slipped through with conformance testing.

Though a comprehensive but cost-effective verification approach is hard to
find, we may be able to control the degree of comprehensiveness by modular-
izing systems and selectively applying verification techniques so that we can
achieve comprehensiveness to an anticipated degree with moderate cost. This
work aims at automated test sequence generation that allows comprehensive

* This work was supported by the National Research Foundation of Korea Grant
funded by the Korean Government (NRF-2012R1A1A4A01011788).

R.M. Hierons, M.G. Merayo, and M. Bravetti (Eds.): SEFM 2013, LNCS 8137, pp. 305–319, 2013.

checking of possible interactions between an automotive operating system and its application tasks. This is achieved by (1) introducing a constraint specification language, $OSEK\_CSL$, designed for specifying constraints identified from the OSEK/VDX standard, (2) defining its underlying formalism in pushdown automata whose formal models are modularly defined in the input language of the symbolic model checker NuSMV [13], and (3) generating test sequences using LTL model checking.

OSEK_CSL is devised to make the specification of operational environments modular and systematic; it is a simple and intuitive constraint specification language consisting of only four basic building blocks, each of which can be independently specified and imposed on a system model. Each constraint specified in OSEK_CSL is systematically translated into NuSMV and combined with a generic task model. The task model is pre-defined as a NuSMV module representing the abstract behavior of a generic task as required in the standard. It is an abstract task model since it includes only the basic requirements from the OSEK/VDX standard without any implementation details. We have standardized the mapping between each constraint and a NuSMV module so that any number of constraints can be added by engineers and their corresponding NuSMV modules can be instantiated automatically.

Test sequence generation is automated through LTL model checking on the NuSMV model using trap properties designed to cover all transitions for each constraint/task module. Our approach enables us to control the degree of test sequences from "perfect" to "erroneous" and "false", depending on the number of constraints imposed for LTL model checking. In this way, the generated test sequences include correct inputs as well as undesirable or unexpected inputs, as required by safety analysis.

Our approach is applied to Trampoline [2], an open source operating system based on OSEK/VDX, and identified two assertion violations and a segmentation fault error that had been missed by existing approaches, including conformation testing and model checking.

The remainder of this paper is organized as follows: Section 2 briefly sketches the background of this work and the overall approach. Section 3 introduces our OSEK_CSL language. Section 4 explains the NuSMV module for a representative OSEK_CSL constraint type and the test sequence generation approach using LTL model checking. An application result using the suggested approach is presented in Section 5, followed by a discussion on related work (Section 6) and the conclusion (Section 7).

2   Background and Approach

OSEK/VDX is a joint project of the automotive industry, which aims at establishing an industry standard for an open-ended architecture for distributed control units in vehicles. The standard has been adopted by major automobile manufacturers as well as by the AUTOSAR open source architecture defined by a consortium of over 50 automotive manufacturers worldwide.

Conformance testing is a standard verification method for the certification of OSEK/VDX-based operating systems. However, conformance test suites are typically insufficient for identifying safety problems. As OSEK/VDX explicitly specifies more than 26 basic APIs, thorough conformance testing would require at least $26 \times 2 \times 3$ test cases, even if we assume two arguments per API and even if only boundary values for the arguments were chosen. The possible number of execution sequences for these $26 \times 2 \times 3$ test cases would rise to 156 factorials, a large number to be tested in practice.

Our previous works tried to address this issue using property-based code slicing and test generation [4,14]. The idea was to perform focused verification by slicing the operating system kernel with respect to the given safety properties. Those approaches have proven increased verification efficiency and effectiveness in identifying safety issues. Nevertheless, model checking still costs a lot (e.g., 30 Gbytes of memory were consumed during verification of one safety property) and requires some knowledge of the underlying technique. Property-based slicing and test generation were cheaper and easier to apply in practice compared to a similar approach using model checking, but comprehensiveness was not achieved. Both cases over-approximated the system environment by allowing non-deterministic API calls from tasks and by informally imposing constraints on the environment model or during the scenario generation process.

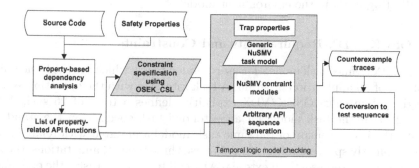

Fig. 1. Overall approach

Figure 1 illustrates an overview of our improved approach. First, we optionally identify API functions related to given safety properties through a dependency analysis using a static code analyzer, as explained in [14]. This process is not mandatory, but helpful in reducing the test input space. Once the list of (property-related) API functions has been determined, users need to specify the desired system constraints using OSEK_CSL and choose which of those constraints will be actually imposed during test sequence generation. OSEK_CSL consists of four basic constructs, each representing a constraint type. We have defined an NuSMV module for each construct as a pushdown automaton. A generic task model for OSEK/VDX-compliant operating systems is also predefined as an NuSMV module. Finally, a set of trap properties is specified in LTL by asserting that not every state or transition is reachable in each NuSMV module.

Temporal logic model checking is performed to verify whether the given trap properties are satisfied by the model, defined as a conjunction of the generic task model, the set of constraint modules, and arbitrary API sequences. If a trap property is refuted, the corresponding counterexample sequence is converted into a test sequence.

Since the first part of the approach was already explained in [14] and the approach is independent of whether property-based extraction of API functions is used or not (entire API functions can be used as they are), this paper focuses on constraint specification using OSEK_CSL, constraint modeling in NuSMV, and test sequence generation using temporal logic model checking.

3   Constraint Specification Language

A typical and straightforward environment of an operating system is an arbitrary call sequence of API functions provided by the operating system, which apparently simulates an actual environment, but includes too many impossible or undesirable interactions and results in a large number of false alarms when verification is performed. Analyzing counterexamples and identifying false alarms is a time-consuming process. To reduce such inefficiency, this work suggests a systematic method for formalizing constraints from the OSEK/VDX standard and reflecting them in the environment model.

3.1   OSEK/VDX Requirements and Constraints

OSEK/VDX defines task models for user-defined tasks, which are the basic building blocks of an application program. A task interacts with the operating system through system calls. OSEK/VDX explicitly defines a total of 26 such APIs. Figure 2 (a) is the task model for an extended task specified in the standard. Figure 2 (b) is our version of the same task model annotated with related APIs and an explicitly specified initial state. We use three types of annotations; the one finishing with '?' represents an external API call from other tasks, the one finishing with '!' is an internal API call, and the one surrounded by <> is an internal event caused by system scheduling. For example, the transition from *running* to *suspended* is triggered by the internal API call to either *TerminateTask* or *ChainTask*, but the transitions between *ready* and *running* are caused by priority-based task scheduling.

The OSEK/VDX standard explicitly/implicitly specifies constraints among the APIs, some of which are listed in Table 1. Analyzing those constraints reveals that they can be categorized into four types.

1. A system call f_1 shall be followed by f_2 (though not necessarily directly).
2. The number of calls to f is limited by n.
3. A system call f shall not be called in between two system calls f_1 and f_2.
4. No system call shall be made after a call to f.

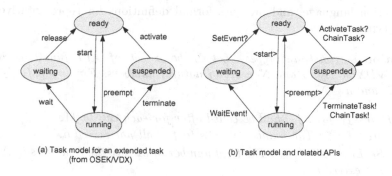

(a) Task model for an extended task
(from OSEK/VDX)

(b) Task model and related APIs

Fig. 2. Task model and related APIs

For example, if *GetResource* is called, the matching system call *ReleaseResource* must be called afterwards, and *WaitEvent* shall not be called in between them.

The types of constraints can also be classified by scope since some constrain global behavior and others constrain local behavior; *GetResource* and *ReleaseResource* are in the local scope because once a task calls the *GetResource* system call, *ReleaseResource* needs to be called in the same task. On the other hand, *WaitEvent* and *SetEvent* are in the global scope. The task that calls *SetEvent* should be different from the task that calls *WaitEvent* for the same event, but they need to be called in pairs. *TerminateTask* and *ChainTask* are the examples that cannot be followed by any system calls in the same task.

3.2 Constraint Specification Language OSEK_CSL

To formally specify such constraints, we define a simple constraint specification language called OSEK_CSL (Constraint Specification Language for OSEK/VDX). OSEK_CSL consists of four basic constraint types, which can be defined with context-free grammars and their corresponding pushdown automata. This section introduces each basic constraint type, defines the constraint

Table 1. Constraints from the OSEK/VDX standard

	Constraints
C1	Ending a task without a call to TerminateTask or ChainTask is strictly forbidden and causes undefined behavior.
C2	TerminateTask, ChainTask, Schedule, WaitEvent shall not be called while a resource is occupied.
C3	A task calling WaitEvent shall go to the waiting state and shall not be activated again before SetEvent is called by other tasks.
C4	OSEK strictly forbids nested access to the same resource.
C5	A task shall not terminate without releasing resources.

specification language, and provides formal definitions for representative constraint types.

Definition 1 *(constraint types) Let Σ be a set of API functions in the OSEK/VDX standard and N a set of natural numbers. For any $f, f_1, f_2 \in \Sigma$, $A' \subseteq \Sigma$, and $n \in N$,*

1. *$InPairs(f_1, f_2)$: f_2 shall be called after for each call to $f1$.*
2. *$Limited(f, n)$: The number of calls to f shall not exceed n.*
   - *$SetLimited(A', n)$: The total number of calls to the functions in A' shall not exceed n.*
3. *$NotInBetween(f, f_1, f_2)$: A call to f shall not be allowed in between calls to f_1 and f_2.*
4. *$MustEndWith(f)$: f shall be called eventually and no calls shall be allowed afterwards.*

Each constraint type can be defined as a context-free language or a regular language over Σ. For example, $Limited(f, n)$ and $SetLimited(A', n)$ are regular languages that can be formalized using finite automata. $InPairs$, on the other hand, requires a little more thought since it cannot be expressed in regular language, as we need to keep track of the number of calls to a specific system call. In fact, the derivation rule for $InPairs(a, b)$ can be defined as follows:

$$S \rightarrow aSb \mid abS \mid Sab \mid xS \mid \lambda, \ x \notin \{a, b\}.$$

For $NotInBetween(c, a, b)$, where $InPairs(a, b)$ is true, the derivation rules $S \rightarrow aSb$ and $S \rightarrow xS$ are refined:

$$S \rightarrow aS'b \mid abS \mid Sab \mid xS \mid \lambda, \ x \notin \{a, b\}$$
$$S' \rightarrow yS' \mid S, \ y \notin C(a, b) \cup \{a, b\},$$

where $C(a, b) = \bigcup \{c \mid NotInBetween(c, a, b)\}$.

Internal formal specification of these constraints can be standardized as shown in Figure 3. Figure 3 (a) is a pushdown automaton for $InPairs(a, b) \wedge NotInBetween(c, a, b)$; s_0 is the initial state and the final state. It ignores letters other than a, moves to state s_1, pushing 0 to the stack once it receives a. In s_1, it ignores letters other than a, b, and c. It moves to s_2, pushing 1 into the stack, if it receives a. It pushes 1 for each input a, pops for each input b, does not change for each input other than a, b, c, and moves to s_0 if the input is b and the stack top is 0. Receiving input c when it is in state s_1 or s_2 results in moving to s_3, which is an error state.

Figure 3 (b) shows the formal representation of $InPairs(a, b) \wedge NotInBetween(c, a, b) \wedge Limited(a, n)$, limiting the size of the stack and checking whether the stack is full or not during the language process.

$SetLimited(A', n)$ allows us to specify the limit of the calls to a set of APIs. For example, $SetLimited(\{f_1, f_2\}, 10)$ specifies that the number of calls to f_1

plus the number of calls to f_2 shall not exceed 10, which can be categorized as a regular language. The rule for $MustEndWith(f)$ is also simple:

$$S \rightarrow xS \mid f, \text{where } x \in \Sigma - \{f\}$$

These constraints are classified into global constraint types and local constraint types. A global constraint type must hold in a global scope, i.e., among tasks, and a local constraint type must hold within a task. According to the OSEK/VDX standard, *Limited* and *SetLimited* are global, while *NotInBetween* and *MustEndWith* are local. *InPairs* can be both. For example, *InPairs(WaitEvent, SetEvent)* has global scope, but *InPairs(GetResource, ReleaseResource)* has local scope. To distinguish global *InPairs* from local ones, we add *GInPairs* to the four basic constraint types in *OSEK_CSL*.

An environment of an OSEK/VDX-based operating system is defined using *OSEK_CSL* based on these four constraint types.

Definition 2 *(Environment Model) The language induced by OSEK_CSL is the intersection of an arbitrary number of languages defined by the basic constraint types. Formally, let L_i be a language defined by one of the constraint types, and suppose there are n such languages. Then,*

$$L(OSEK\_CSL) = \bigcap_{i \in \{1..n\}} L_i.$$

This defines an environment of an OSEK/VDX-based operating system.

4   Formal Specification Using NuSMV

Since there can be a number of constraints, we need to compute their intersections in order to identify a language accepted by all specified constraints.

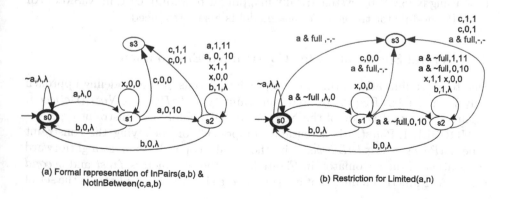

(a) Formal representation of InPairs(a,b) &
    NotInBetween(c,a,b)

(b) Restriction for Limited(a,n)

Fig. 3. Formal representation of constraint types

```
1 MODULE InPairs(first, second, alphabet, exclusiveSet, task)
2  VAR
3    state : {s0, s1, s2, s3};
4    mystack : STACK(first, second, alphabet, task.state, state);
5
6  ASSIGN
7    init(state):= s0;          /* initial state */
8    init(mystack.top):=0;      /* initial value of the stack top */
9    ...
10   next(state):=              /* defines the transition relation */
11     case task.state = running & !terminationRequested :
12       case state = s0  :
13             case next(alphabet)=first & mystack.top= 0      : s1;
14                  TRUE                                        : state;
15           esac;
16         state = s1  :
17             case  next(alphabet)=first & mystack[mystack.top]=0  : s2;
18                   next(alphabet)=second & mystack[mystack.top]=0  : s0;
19                   next(alphabet) in exclusiveSet                 : s3;
20                   TRUE                                           : state;
21           esac;
22       ...
23     esac;
```

Fig. 4. NuSMV MODULE for InPairs constraint type

We perform the computation using the model checker NuSMV under the assumption that the maximum number of system calls is bounded. This assumption is necessary since NuSMV is based on a finite state machine which cannot handle stacks of indefinite size as in constraint automata. Despite the limitation, NuSMV was chosen because of its modular structure, its simple but sufficient expression for specifying state machines, and most importantly, its powerful model checking capability for test sequence generation.

This section describes our method for modeling the representative constraint type using NuSMV by systematically mapping it to a MODULE in NuSMV. An NuSMV module for the generic task model is also introduced.

4.1 Formal Specification for Constrained Environments

Due to space limitations, this section provides details of the modeling approach only for the most frequently used constraint type *InPairs* ∧ *NotInBetween*. Figure 4 shows a fraction of the NuSMV MODULE for the constraint type.

MODULE InPairs(..) is a reusable component for specifying the constraint type *InPairs* ∧ *NotInBetween* in the local scope. It is a straightforward translation of the automaton in Figure 3 (a); the parameters *first* and *second* are for API function names that are supposed to be in pairs, *alphabet* is the set of

API names, *task* is the name of the task that is the scope of the constraint, and *exclusiveSet* is the set of API calls that are not supposed to be called in between *first* and *second*. The *exclusiveSet* is identified from the *NotInBetween* constraints. If there are no *NotInBetween* constraints related to *first* and *second*, then the *exclusiveSet* is empty and $InPairs \land NotInBetween = InPairs$. As in Figure 3 (a), there are four states s_0, s_1, s_2, and s_3, where s_0 is the initial state. The transitions between states are defined in the *ASSIGN* construct (line 6) using the *next* keyword. All the transitions are only possible when the task is in the *running* state. The model checks this condition by $task.state = running$ (line 11). The transition rules defined in *case..esac* are a direct translation of the pushdown automata in Figure 3 (a).

Whenever a new constraint of the $InPairs \land NotInBetween$ type is required, the module is instantiated in the NuSMV main module. For example, if there are two tasks with the same type of local constraints, we declare two constraints as follows:

$$constraint\_1 : InPairs(f_1, f_2, alphabet, exclusiveSet, task\_1);$$
$$constraint\_2 : InPairs(f'_1, f'_2, alphabet, exclusiveSet', task\_2);$$

The NuSMV module for the *InPairs* constraint type in the global scope differs little from that in the local scope, since the only difference between them is whether the stack of the pushdown automata is maintained locally or globally. Therefore, the same local module can be reused for global constraints of the same type. The signature for the global constraint type *GInPairs* is defined as

$$MODULE\ GInPairs(first, second, alphabet, exclusiveSet),$$

where its body is the same as that of *InPairs* except that line 11 of Figure 4 is removed. The task information is not passed to the global module since it is independent of tasks.

4.2 Formal Specification for Generic User Tasks

A Basic NuSMV Model for a User Task. A user task is modeled according to the task model shown in Figure 2 (b). Since it is a general task model, the same formal specification is used independent of the constraint types. The following shows the basic form of the NuSMV MODULE for the task model.

```
1 MODULE Task(alphabet, id, priority)
2   VAR
3     state : {suspended, ready, waiting, running};
4
5   ASSIGN
6     next(state):=
7       case
8         state = suspended  & (next(alphabet) = ActivateTask
9                              | next(alphabet) = ChainTask )   : ready;
10        state = ready   /* & if scheduled next */             : running;
```

```
11        state = running & (next(alphabet) = TerminateTask |
12                           next(alphabet) = ChainTask    )   : suspended;
13        state = running & next(alphabet) = WaitEvent          : waiting;
14        state = waiting & next(alphabet) = SetEvent           : ready;
15        TRUE                                                  : state;
16      esac;
   ...
```

However, this basic form is not enough to model task behavior, and it needs to be elaborated more to address the OSEK/VDX requirements. The following lists some of the requirements that have a direct impact on the task model;

1. A task transits to the *running* state from the *ready* state only if it is scheduled by the operating system (line 10). Priority-based FIFO scheduling is required in OSEK/VDX.
2. Only one task shall run at a given time. Line 10 should be constrained more to ensure this.
3. Task priority can be dynamically changed based on the PCP (Priority Ceiling Protocol). Since task scheduling is priority-based, the change of task priority needs to be specified.
4. PCP requires resource management. Therefore, we cannot correctly model task behavior without specifying resource management.

In order to address these requirements, the basic task model is refined by adding more abstract components and references to those components to the task model. For example, the signature of the task model changes to

```
MODULE Task(alphabet, id, priority, res1, res2, readyP, SomeoneIsRunning,
            conState),
```

where $res1$ and $res2$ are names of resources, $readyP$ is the name of the variable that keeps track of the highest number among the priorities of the tasks in the *ready* state, *SomeoneIsRunning* is a global flag indicating whether there is a running task, and *conState* is the state of the local constraint of the task. In order words, each task has references to resources, information on whether its constraints are currently satisfied or not, and some basic information about other tasks.

Handling Priority-based FIFO Scheduling. The generic task model keeps track of the state of each task and selects the task with the highest priority among all tasks in the ready state, instead of explicitly modeling a priority-based FIFO queue. This requires a simple change in line 10 of the basic task model:

```
10: state = ready & !SomeoneIsRunning :
        case priority >= readyP       : running;
             TRUE                     : state;
        esac;
```

It checks whether the state is ready and there is no task running currently. If this is true, it checks again whether the priority of the task is greater than or equal to all the priorities of the tasks in the ready state. The task moves to the running state only when all those conditions are satisfied.

Handling Priority Ceiling Protocol. The priority of a task is statically pre-defined for each task and cannot be changed throughout the whole execution life cycle, except for the case when it allocates a resource with higher priority than the task. This is called Priority Ceiling Protocol (PCP) and is designed to prevent the problem of priority inversion. The PCP is incorporated into the task model by defining transition rules for changing the priority of a task, depending on whether it allocates or releases resources. The following reflects the change of the basic task module when the system includes two resources:

```
next(priority):=
case state = running & next(alphabet)=GetResource :
   case (res1.owner=0 & (res1.priority > priority)) : res1.priority;
        (res2.owner=0 & (res2.priority > priority)) : res2.priority;
        TRUE                                         : priority;
   esac;
...
```

This model does not explicitly specify which resource is requested by which task, but models it as allocating whichever resource is available. It is originally required to specify the resource type when asking for resource allocation in the form 'GetResource(res1)', but our alphabet consists of API names without parameters for the sake of simplicity. For the input alphabet *GetResource*, it checks and allocates the first available resource. For *ReleaseResource*, it releases the last allocated resource first, as specified in the OSEK/VDX requirements.

4.3   Test Generation via LTL Model Checking

Given the generic task model and a set of constraints on the sequence of input alphabets, our goal is to generate task sequences w.r.t the API call sequence that executes all paths leading to either final states or error states of tasks and constraints. We define three types of trap properties for checking reachability:

Definition 3 *(trap   properties)   Suppose   there   are n number   of constraints   specified   in   OSEK_CSL   and m tasks.   Let $CS^i = \{cs_0^i, cs_1^i, cs_2^i, cs_3^i\}, i = 1..n$, be a set of states in the ith constraint and $S^j = \{suspended^j, ready^j, running^j, waiting^j\}, j = 1..m$, a set of states in the jth task. Then,*

1. *A trap property for checking whether there is a path from a kth state to a final state in the ith constraint/task:*

$$tp_{ik}^{cr} \stackrel{def}{=} G(CS^i.state = cs_k^i \rightarrow \; ! \; F(CS^i.state = cs_0^i)) \; /\!\!*for\;constraints*\!/$$

$$tp_{ik}^{tr} \stackrel{def}{=} G(S^i.state = s_k^i \rightarrow \; ! \; F(S^i.state = suspended^i)) \; /\!\!*for\;tasks*\!/,$$

where $cs_k^i \in CS^i$, $s_k^i \in \{ready^i, running^i, waiting^i\}$.

2. *A trap property for checking whether an ith task can be activated at least twice:*

$$tp_i^{ta} \overset{\text{def}}{=} G((task_i.state \neq suspended^i \ \& \ X(task_i.state = suspended^i)) \rightarrow$$
$$! \ F(task_i.state = ready^i))$$

3. *A set of trap properties for checking whether each element of the alphabet is exercised as an input at least once:*

$$tp_\Sigma \overset{\text{def}}{=} \{G \ ! \ (SomeoneIsRunning \ \& \ alphabet = a) \mid a \in \Sigma\}$$

Trap properties are specified in LTL (Linear Time temporal Logic), where the temporal connectives G, X and F mean "Globally", "neXt states" and "sometime in Future state", respectively. For example, tp_{ij}^{cr} means that "for all execution paths if the ith constraint is in state cs_j^i, there is no path from the state leading to the final state cs_0^i. tp_i^{ta} means that it is globally true that if the ith task is not in the *suspended* state and will transit to the *suspended* state in the next state, then there will be no path where the task reaches the *ready* state in the future. In other words, the property says that a task is not activated again once it is terminated. The set of system trap properties is the union of all three types of trap properties:

$$tp = \{tp_{ij}^{cr}, tp_{pq}^{tr}, tp_p^{ta} \mid i = 1..n, j = 0..3, p = 1..m, q = 1..3\} \cup tp_\Sigma.$$

Though we generate trap properties for all system constraints, the degree of constraints to be imposed on the model can vary. We define the *Degree of constraints (DoC)* as m/n, where n is the total number of constraints specified in OSEK_CSL and m is the number of actual constraints imposed on the NuSMV model. We say the environment model is perfect if $DoC = 1$, erroneous if $0 < DoC < 1$, and false if $DoC = 0$. We impose various degrees of constraints for counterexample generation because safety verification requires not only perfect test sequences, but also erroneous test sequences with illegal input values.

The set of trap properties is verified using the model checker NuSMV. NuSMV generates a counterexample trace if the properties are verified as false. The conversion from a counterexample trace to a test program is straightforward since the trace shows a step-by-step change of API calls for each task as shown in Table 2.

Table 2. A fraction of a counterexample trace for tp_{11}^{cr}

steps		1	2	3	4	5	6
$task_1$	state	ready	running	running	running	running	waiting
	API calls		GetResource	ReleaseResource	GetResource	WaitEvent	
$task_2$	state	running	waiting	waiting	waiting	waiting	waiting
	API calls	WaitEvent					

Table 3. Comparison of branch coverage

	$schedule_r$	$schedule_d$	$schedule_w$	$schedule_s$	$event_w$	$tasks_s$	$events_s$
Formal	100%(3/3)	60%(3/5)	66.67%(2/3)	100%(1/1)	75%(3/4)	100%(4/4)	80%(4/5)
Informal	100%(3/3)	80%(4/5)	66.67%(2/3)	100%(1/1)	75%(3/4)	100%(4/4)	80%(4/5)

5   Experiments

A total of 30 counterexamples were generated for an OSEK/VDX model with two tasks, two local constraints, and one global constraint, using the suggested approach. It took 10 minutes 43 seconds for the whole counterexample generation, performing 44 iterations and searching $3.4e + 10$ states for each LTL model checking process on average. The test sequences are used to test the OSEK/VDX-based open source operating system Trampoline [2], which was also used as a case example in our previous work using property-based code slicing and simulation-based scenario generation [14].

Table 3 shows the branch coverage of some of the Trampoline source functions identified by using property-based code slicing, comparing the coverage result using OSEK_CSL-based test sequence generation (Formal) and the result of using a random scenario generator (Informal)[1]. A total of 24 test sequences (after removing duplicated sequences) of an average length of 6 was used for the *Formal* case, while one test sequence of length 32 was used for the *Informal* case since it was the sequence that showed the best coverage from our previous work. Though we did not aim at high code coverage, Table 3 shows that the suggested approach achieves branch coverage similar to that of the best result using a random scenario generator.

The more interesting and important result is that the approach using *OSEK_CSL* actually found safety problems that were missed throughout existing model checking and testing approaches. These include two assertion violations and one segmentation fault error. For example,

```
TASK(t1){                      TASK(t2){
  WaitEvent(e1);                 ReleaseResource(r1);
}                                WaitEvent(e1);   }
```

is a test constructed from the counterexample trace generated from $G \ ! \ (SomeoneIsRunning \ \& \ alphabet = ReleaseResource)$. This is an example of erroneous test sequences that do not obey constraints, since *ReleaseResource* is called without calling *GetResrouce* first. Running this test results in the following situation:

```
trampoline: ../os/tpl\_os\_kernel.c:522: tpl\_put\_preempted\_proc:
Assertion 'tpl\_fifo\_rw[prio].size < tpl\_ready\_list[prio].size'
failed. ./doit: line 2: 25016 Aborted (core dumped) ./trampoline
```

---

[1] Abbreviated function names are used to save space.

These problems could not be identified by conformance testing or existing model-based test generation approaches because they are based on the "correct" model of OSEK/VDX and do not necessarily test illegal task behaviors.

6 Related Work

Specification-based test generation is a well-known technique. From the early 1990s, there have been numerous approaches that use formal languages to specify requirements and generate test cases [10]. Among them, references [3,9,16] are the closest to our work in that they also try to provide a solution for efficient verification of OSEK/VDX-based operating systems. [3] uses Z and SPIN for specifying test requirements and generating test sequences for OSEK/VDX. References [9] and [16] model OSEK/VDX requirements in Promela and generate test sequences by model checking trap properties using SPIN. All those works model OSEK/VDX functional requirements, but do not explicitly consider system constraints. Our work focuses on constraint specification in order to generate a more efficient interaction environment and provides modular specification methods for constraints.

Our work is also closely related to automated environment generation for software verification in general [5,15]; Tkachuk et al. [15] developed the Bandera Environment Generator, which automates the generation of environments from user-specified assumptions for Java programs. The specification is limited to regular expressions.

There have been more traditional approaches for verifying automotive software using formal methods [8,11], formally specifying OSEK/VDX requirements in CSP and performing formal verification using model checking or theorem proving. Using such formal specification languages requires experts in formal methods, who are usually not available in practice. Our approach provides an intuitive specification language with underlying formal specification so that constraints can be easily specified, transformed, and checked.

7 Conclusion

This work presents a systematic and modular method for specifying constraints for OSEK/VDX-based operating systems. Constraint specification plays an important role in constructing the correct environment of a system, enabling us to generate effective test sequences. We have analyzed types of constraints in OSEK/VDX, categorized them into four basic types, and defined an NuSMV module for each constraint type so that any constraint of a given type can be automatically instantiated. These constraints can be selectively imposed on the generic task model, generating varying degrees of test sequences. Comprehensiveness can be controlled through trap properties.

The suggested approach is extensible; though we have identified four constraint types in OSEK/VDX, there can be more. We believe that incorporating additional constraint types will not affect the existing definitions and the underlying formalism.

We note that NuSMV is an effective tool suitable for our purposes, but cannot handle infinite systems directly without abstractions. Future work will include more investigation on formal verification tools for infinite systems aimed at possible replacement of NuSMV and more extensive experiments with various measures.

References

1. OSEK/VDX operating system specification 2.2.3
2. Trampoline – opensource RTOS project, http://trampoline.rts-software.org
3. Chen, J., Aoki, T.: Conformance testing for OSEK/VDX operating system using model checking. In: 18th Asia-Pacific Software Engineering Conference (2011)
4. Choi, Y.: Safety analysis of the Trampoline OS using model checking: An experience report. In: Proceedings of 22nd IEEE International Symposium on Software Reliability Engineering (2011)
5. de la Riva, C., Tuya, J.: Automatic generation of assumptions for modular verification of software specifications. Journal of Systems and Software (2006)
6. In der Riden, T., Kanpp, S.: An approach to the pervasive formal specification and verification of an automotive system. In: Proceedings of the International Workshop on Formal Methods in Industrial Critical Systems (2005)
7. Lettnin, D., et al.: Semiformal verification of temporal properties in automotive hardware dependent software. In: Proceedings of Design, Automation, and Test in Europe Conference and Exhibition (April 2009)
8. Shi, J., et al.: ORIENTAIS: Formal verified OSEK/VDX real-time operating system. In: IEEE 17th International Conference on Engineering of Complex Computer Systems (2012)
9. Fang, L., et al.: Formal model-based test for AUTOSAR multicore RTOS. In: Proceeding of the IEEE 5th International Conference on Software Testing, Verification and Validation, pp. 251–259 (2012)
10. Hierons, R.M., et al.: Using formal specifications to support testing. ACM Computing Surveys (2009)
11. Zhao, Y., et al.: Modeling and verifying the code-level OSEK/VDX operating system with CSP. In: 5th International Symposium on Theoretical Aspects of Software Engineering, pp. 142–149 (2011)
12. John, D.: OSEK/VDX conformance testing - MODISTARC. In: Proceedings of OSEK/VDX Open Systems in Automotive Networks (1998)
13. NuSMV: A New Symbolic Model Checking, http://nusmv.irst.itc.it/
14. Park, M., Byun, T., Choi, Y.: Property-based code slicing for efficient verification of osek/vdx operating systems. In: First International Workshop on Formal Techniques for Safety-Critical Systems (2012)
15. Tkachuk, O., Dwyer, M.B., Pasareanu, C.S.: Automated environment generation for software model checking. In: 18th IEEE International Conference on Automated Software Engineering, pp. 116–129 (October 2003)
16. Yatake, K., Aoki, T.: Automatic generation of model checking scripts based on environment modeling. In: van de Pol, J., Weber, M. (eds.) SPIN 2010. LNCS, vol. 6349, pp. 58–75. Springer, Heidelberg (2010)

Author Index